Growing Plants

FOR

Hawaiian Lei

85 Plants for Gardens, Conservation, and Business

College of Tropical Agriculture and Human Resources
University of Hawai'i at Mānoa

Dedication
To the many teachers and mentors whose knowledge and devotion to Hawai'i's plants and culture inspired and informed the people who created this book—it is our privilege to be able to pass this knowledge on to others who will care for Hawai'i.

Printed by Prolong Press Ltd, Hong Kong

For information write:
Publications and Information Office
College of Tropical Agriculture and Human Resources
University of Hawai'i at Mānoa
3050 Maile Way Rm 119
Honolulu, Hawai'i 96822
USA
Phone 808-956-7036, Facsimile 808-956-5966
E-mail <ctahrpub@hawaii.edu>
Web <www.ctahr.hawaii.edu>

ISBN: 1-929325-13-4

Contents

Authors and Contributors vii

Preface ix

Acknowledgments xi

Section 1: 85 Plants to Grow for Lei Material

Explanation of the headings 1

Native and Canoe Plants

'A'ali'i 6
'Ākia 8
Hala 10
Hinahina 12
'Ilima 14
Kauna'oa 16
Kou 18
Kukui 20
Kulu'ī 22
Kupukupu / sword fern 24
Ma'o 26
Maile 28
Māmane 30
Moa 32
'Ōhi'a lehua 34
Pa'iniu 36
Pala'ā 38
Palapalai 40
Pōhinahina 42
Pūkiawe 44
Ti 46
'Ūlei 48
Wiliwili 50

Introduced Perennials

Agapanthus 52
Akulikuli-lei 54
Asparagus fern 56
Aster 58
Baby's breath 60
Bleeding heart 62
Blue jade vine 64
Bougainvillea 66
Carnation 68
Cigar flower 70
Crown flower 72
Cup-and-saucer plant 74
Dracaena tricolor 76
Dusty miller 78
Feverfew 80
Gardenia 82
Ginger (white and yellow) 84
Hoya 86
Hydrangea 88
Ixora 90
Joyweed 92
Kalanchoe 94
Kīkānia 96
Lantern *'ilima* and royal *'ilima* 98
Laua'e 100
Maunaloa 102
'Ohai ali'i 104
Orchid: Cymbidium 106
Orchid: Dendrobium 108
Orchid: Epidendrum 110
Orchid: Vanda 112
Pakalana 114
Panax 116
Pentas 118
Pīkake 120
Pincushion protea 122
Plumeria 124
Pohutukawa (New Zealand maori) ... 126
Pua kenikeni 128
Rose 130

Introduced Perennials (cont.)

Shinobu 132

Shrimp plant (white and yellow) 134

Spanish moss 136

Statice 138

Stephanotis 140

Tree heliotrope 142

Tuberose 144

Violet 146

Introduced Annuals

Ageratum 148

Alyssum 150

Celosia 152

Chrysanthemum 154

Cornflower 156

Dianthus 158

Globe amaranth 160

Marguerite daisy 162

Marigold 164

Pansy 166

Salvia 168

Strawflower 170

Torenia 172

Zinnia 174

Section 2: Growing Plants for *Lei* Helps to Preserve Hawai'i's Natural and Cultural Heritage 177

Part 1. A historical perspective on *lei* and native plant communities 178

Part 2. Hawai'i's many native organisms and their relationship to human culture before 1778 180

Hawai'i's first natives 181

Effects of time, habitat diversity, and isolation on Hawai'i's native species 183

Evolution's legacy: unique plant communities rich with native species 185

The "natural" universe of the early Hawaiian people 185

Hawaiian practices and ethics that affected natural resources 191

Hawaiians' alterations of native plant communities

Limitations on gathering in ancient Hawai'i

Gathering ethics and beliefs

Gathering protocols and specialization

Gathering boundaries

Part 3. Introduced organisms and cultural change since 1778 194

Changes in nature: introduced species 194

Polynesian introductions

Post-Cook introductions

Effects of introduced plants and animals on native ecosystems

Changes in human culture that affect Hawai'i's native ecosystems 197

Changes in land use

Changes in population density

Changes in gathering practices

"Modern" changes in attitude

Hawaiians believed that one must work for the privilege of taking

Hawaiians considered themselves *kahu* (caregivers) to native ecosystems

Part 4. Hawai'i's natural and cultural future 200

How to preserve our native ecosystems 200

Grow what you need, instead of gathering from nature, and substitute introduced plants for native plants

Support efforts to preserve our native ecosystems

E nihi ka hele . . . Go carefully, giving thought to what is *pono* (right)

How to gain a fuller appreciation of Hawaiian culture 202
    Hawaiians loved to grow things, and they loved the things they grew
    Cultivating *lei* plants brings these sources of inspiration closer to us
    We function as *kahu* to native ecosystems
Native species conservation for the future of Hawaiian culture 203
Native Hawaiian species conservation for humanity 204

Section 3. Best Production Practices for Lei Material Plants 207

General horticulture 207
    Potting media
    Soil
    Irrigation
    Roots
Propagation techniques for lei plants 209
    Propagating from seeds
        Collecting seeds, cleaning seeds, growing from seeds, seed treatments, seeds
        that do not require treatment, sowing seeds, transplanting seedlings, storing seeds
    Propagating from cuttings
    Propagating by air layering
    Propagating from divisions
    Suggested media formulations
    Fertilizers and propagation media
Suggested fertilizer programs for lei material production 216
    Fertilizers for plants grown in the ground
    Plants in containers
    Fertilizer basics
Pruning plants grown for lei material production 218
    Pruning strategies
    When to prune
    Pruning tools
    Pruning plants in the wild
Control of plant pests and diseases 222
    Monitor the crop and keep a log
    Start clean and stay clean
    Know the crop and its pests
    Take action in a timely manner
    Tips on avoiding plant diseases
    Tips on controlling weeds
    Tips on managing insects
Safe and effective use of pesticides 225
Postharvest handling of lei materials 226

Section 4: The Business of Lei Plant and Materials Production 227

Deciding if the lei materials production business is right for you 227
Matching your vision to reality 228
Starting out 229
Making your business plan a roadmap to success 229
The important questions to ask 230
    Finding people who will purchase your lei materials

How Hawaii plant materials go to market

The market for lei drives the demand for raw materials

The demand for lei and lei materials

Potential markets 234

Wholesale florists

Retail florists

Hula hālau

Direct to the final consumer

A final word about marketing to your potential customers

Making your first sale 238

Business cards and Rolodex® cards

Fax and answering machines

Web site and e-mail

Professional invoices

Samples

Production records and schedules

Flexibility

Costing and pricing your production 239

Know your cost types 240

Cash or variable or out-of-pocket costs

Fixed or overhead costs

Depreciation

Losses

More on costs

Understanding how to calculate cost of production: two examples 240

Example 1. Cost of production for an annual plant

Example 2. Cost of production for a perennial plant

Getting your finances in order 246

Pricing your plants and materials—a basic understanding 248

About banks and other lending institutions 249

Get your banker excited about you and your business

Develop "pro formas" for your business

Conquer loan-rejection dejection

Developing your business team and keeping it together 250

Navigating to success 251

Appendix—Buying or building? 252

Buying an existing business

Building a new business from scratch

Selected Bibliography 255

Plant Name Index 259

Authors and Contributors

James Hollyer
College of Tropical Agriculture and Human Resources (CTAHR), University of Hawai'i at Mānoa (UHM)

Luisa Castro
CTAHR

Dale Evans
CTAHR

Richard Criley
CTAHR

Edwin Mersino
CTAHR

Margaret Parks
CTAHR

Eileen Herring
UHM Library

Puanani Anderson-Fung
Department of Botany and Ecology, Evolution, and Conservation Biology Program, UHM; 'Ahahui Mālama i ka Lōkahi (Native Hawaiians for the Conservation of Native Ecosystems)

Greg Koob
Kalaikanu LLC

Ken Leonhardt
CTAHR

Bill Char
Native Books & Beautiful Things

Glenn Teves
CTAHR

Linda Cox
CTAHR

Kathleen Fetters
Amy B. H. Greenwell Ethnobotanical Garden, Bishop Museum

Laurie Shimizu Ide
Lei book writer

Kepā Maly
Kumu Pono Associates, Hilo

Kerin Lilleeng-Rosenberger
National Tropical Botanical Garden

Desmond Ogata
CTAHR

Dick Tsuda
CTAHR

Maile Sakamoto
Hawaii Department of Land and Natural Resources

Richard Nakagawa
Hawaii Department of Land and Natural Resources

Kelvin Sewake
CTAHR

Jamie Lucido
CTAHR

James Tavares
CTAHR

Priscilla Millen
Leeward Community College

Dave Manu Bird
Leeward Community College

David Hensley
CTAHR

Heidi Bornhorst
Foster Botanical Garden

Beatrice Krauss
Ethnobotanist

Marshall Johnson
CTAHR

John Obata
Native plant propagator

Roxanne Adams
Winston Morton
Office of Hawaiian Affairs

Susan Matsushima
Alluvion Inc.

Deborah Ward
CTAHR

Carol Chun
Lei maker

John Halloran
CTAHR

Ginny Meade
CTAHR

Janice Uchida
CTAHR

Scot Mitamura
Foster Botanical Garden

Ken Rohrbach
CTAHR

Clark Hashimoto
CTAHR

Marian Leong
Lyon Arboretum Association

Philip Thomas
Hawaiian Ecosystems at Risk

Sam Gon III
The Nature Conservancy of Hawaii

Pamela Shingaki
CTAHR

Irmalee Pomroy
Lei maker

Marie McDonald
Lei book writer

Graphics and layout design by
Miles Hakoda
with assistance from Glenn Coloma
CTAHR

Authors' and contributors' affiliations are those at the time of their participation and may not be current.

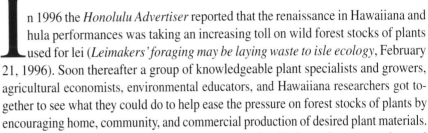

Preface

Some popular books about lei and lei making.

I n 1996 the *Honolulu Advertiser* reported that the renaissance in Hawaiiana and hula performances was taking an increasing toll on wild forest stocks of plants used for lei (*Leimakers' foraging may be laying waste to isle ecology*, February 21, 1996). Soon thereafter a group of knowledgeable plant specialists and growers, agricultural economists, environmental educators, and Hawaiiana researchers got together to see what they could do to help ease the pressure on forest stocks of plants by encouraging home, community, and commercial production of desired plant materials.

Over several years the group collected and refined information on growing and preparing plant materials for lei. A list of plants desirable for their flowers or foliage was developed (plants with seeds used in lei were generally not considered). Photographs were taken of the plants in the landscape to show what they might look like in a garden if someone chose to grow them. Also, the part of the plant harvested for lei was illustrated in a close-up photo. Finally, a photo was taken of a lei containing the plant material.

Our book is not about lei or lei making—quite a few good books on the subject are already available (a few of their covers are shown at left). Our purpose is to provide the best available information on how to grow a plant and harvest its flowers or foliage for use in a lei. This information is compiled in the first section, which describes 85 plants useful for lei, divided into three groups: (1) plants either native to Hawaii or "canoe" plants introduced by ancient settlers from Polynesia, (2) perennial plants introduced since the arrival of Captain Cook in the Hawaiian Islands, and (3) introduced annual plants. Before going on to read about individual plant species, be sure to read the introductory explanations of the categories of plant information.

Since the lei is one of the most widely known and cherished gifts the world has received from the Hawaiian people, we thought that an appreciation of its cultural significance would be of value. Thus this book's second section explores the role of lei and the traditions surrounding gathering lei materials in ancient Hawaii. As the text makes clear, the ancient Hawaiians had their own conservation ethic and concept of sustainable agriculture, and a revival of their ideas today could help preserve the islands' threatened native ecosystems.

The third section of our book briefly surveys some horticultural practices basic to plant production. It is not a complete treatment of the subjects it covers, but it provides some of the essentials on soils and plant media, propagation, fertilizers, pruning, and control of plant pests and diseases.

Finally, this book's fourth section gives some guidance to those who might be inspired to produce lei plant stock or lei materials as a business enterprise. While backyard production and communal gardens can help meet some of the needs for lei materials and prevent further degradation of natural plant resources, we anticipate that an even greater contribution can be made by entrepreneur-growers who carefully prepare to meet a particular market demand. The section provides an overview of starting a horticultural business and points the reader to additional business tools and resources.

We have tried to provide the most accurate information based on the scientific and practical sources available to us. But as you set out to grow lei materials, whether for personal use or for sale, you will have to do some experimentation. Soil and climate conditions can vary considerably over short distances in the Hawaiian Islands, and plants have varying degrees of flexibility in their adaptation to different growth conditions. And for the entrepreneur, economic viability can shift with the weather! Therefore, consider the information we present here as a starting point, and remember that in agriculture success is never guaranteed. A wise man has said that an essential key to growing plants is the grower's shadow—that's what you provide when you spend time in the garden, shadehouse, or field to observe and learn to understand the nature of plant growth and the best strategies for successful crop management. Farmers and other people in business for themselves usually know this principle well and become "lifelong learners" when it comes to their businesses and professions.

We hope you find this book an inspiration to engage in growing plants for lei. You will be helping conserve Hawai'i's native ecosystems and promote the state's "green industry" economy, and you will participate in spreading aloha through the beautiful Hawaiian tradition of the lei.

James Hollyer

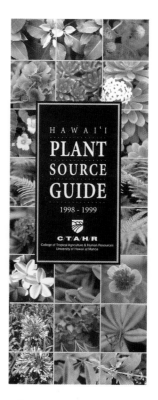

CTAHR's Hawai'i Plant Source Guide *cross-lists 98 Hawai'i nurseries and 140 plants considered desirable for house-plants, landscapes, and lei materials.*

Editor's note:

Throughout this book we have tried to use the correct spelling of Hawaiian words and names, including their pronunciation guides, the *'okina* (glottal mark) and *kahakō* (macron). In general, we treat Hawaiian words other than proper nouns as foreign language words by italicizing them; an exception is the word "lei," which is italicized only in Section 2. But even when "lei" is treated as an English word and not italicized, we follow the Hawaiian language convention of using it as both singular and plural. Readers should also note that some of the Hawaiian chants, sayings, and songs quoted in this book are printed as found in the original sources and may not conform to current orthographic standards.

Acknowledgments

One person could never prepare a book of this magnitude. The quality of the content and its presentation is a testament to the truth of the African saying, "None of us is as smart as all of us." The authors' and contributors' broad and often overlapping knowledge helped us ensure that we are providing the best information that we have as a collective. While all of the contributors provided valuable content, a special *mahalo* is due a core group who gave much to this book's production.

Of particular note during a long process has been extraordinary patience in research, rewrites, and re-checks by Luisa Castro and Margaret Parks and in editing by Dale Evans. Authors and contributors Richard Criley, Ed Mersino, Eileen Herring, Greg Koob, Puanani Anderson-Fung, Ken Leonhardt, Linda Cox, and Bill Char have all been more than generous with their time, expertise, and attention to help make sure we have the best information possible. Finally, Miles Hakoda's graphic design talent always makes us look good, and this book is no exception.

Some special comments and credits for the various sections of this book are in order. Although many of those listed as authors and contributors provided information compiled in the treatments of the 85 plants covered in this book, most of them did not see the final product, and responsibility for any errors or omissions in the content rests with James Hollyer. Margaret Parks's thesis groundwork helped formulate this book; she met with *kumu hula* to develop the 1998 CTAHR M.S. thesis, *Evaluating Two Options for Increasing the Availability of Lei Plant Materials for Use by Halau Hula: An Application of Conjoint Analysis*. The text on plant propagation in Section 3 was adapted from guidelines for propagating native Hawaiian plants written by Kerin Lilleeng-Rosenberger, former nursery manager at the National Tropical Botanical Gardens, Kaua'i; it was reviewed and expanded upon by Richard Criley, professor of horticulture and teacher of the UH-CTAHR course on advanced plant propagation, and Paul Murakami. Section 4 on business practices was written primarily by James Hollyer and Linda Cox, with review by CTAHR colleagues Ken Leonhardt, Ed Mersino, Glenn Teves, and Richard Criley. Finally, Section 2, written by Puanani Anderson-Fung and Kepā Maly, received helpful review during its development by UH professors Isabella Abbott, John Charlot, and the late Charles Lamoureux.

We are grateful to those who allowed us to take photographs of plants and lei materials on their properties: Raymond Wong, Maryanne Chun, Mike Conway, Nani Mau Gardens, Mānoa Community Garden, City and County of Honolulu Lei Day Exhibit, Foster Botanical Garden, Lyon Arboretum staff and volunteers, Leilani Nursery, Sharon's Plants LTD, and Hui Hana Hawaii. Special thanks to Clyde T. Imada, Bishop Museum Department of Natural Sciences/Botany, for the use of his photographs, which embellish Section 2. The Hawaiian Heritage Program generously shared their maps showing losses of native vegetation. CTAHR colleagues Jody Moore helped with proofreading, and Donna Shaver and Kristie Tsuda provided project support.

This book was made possible by a grant from the United States Department of Agriculture (no. 99-34172-8490) and funds from the Office of Hawaiian Affairs.

Thanks to everyone who helped create this resource for people who want to live in a more sustainable Hawai'i!

Section 1

85 Plants to Grow for Lei Material

The 85 plants described in this book are divided into three groups. Within each group they are listed alphabetically by the most generally used common English or Hawaiian name. The first group consists of 23 perennial plants that are either native to Hawaii (were here before humans arrived) or have become naturalized since their introduction by early Polynesian colonizers. The second and third groups consist of 48 perennial and 14 annual plants that have been introduced since the arrival of European colonizers in 1778. Some plants in these two groups have become naturalized, while others survive only with human assistance.

The descriptions of plants has been standardized to the extent possible. If a heading does not apply to a particular plant, it is omitted. For example, "germination time" is omitted for plants propagated by vegetative means such as cuttings.

Explanation of the headings

Other common names: The most frequently used English, Hawaiian, and "local" names of the plant are given.

Scientific name: This name, also called the plant's botanical name, consists of two basic parts: the genus name, followed by the species name. A *genus* is a group of closely related plants; a *species* is a group of plants so closely resembling one another that they suggest a common parentage. Sometimes the species name is followed by a variety name. Usually, the scientific name is followed by an abbreviation of the authority, the name (or the full name if a short one) of the person that described the plant (e.g., *Genus species* L., where the "L." signifies the botanist Carolus Linnaeus). Plants are given their scientific names under a system regulated by the International Code of Botanical Nomenclature. In this book, we omit authorities.

Scientific names are usually based on Latin and are italicized. Scientific names change when an earlier published name is discovered or when research leads botanists to reclassify plants into different groups. The scientific names used in this publication are based on two sources: the *Manual of the Flowering Plants of Hawaii* by Wagner et al. for the native and naturalized plants, and the Bishop Museum's unpublished revision-in-progress of *In Gardens of Hawaii* for the ferns and the nonnaturalized plants.

Family: A botanical family is a group of related plants that usually contains more than one genus. Some families are quite large—the Orchidaceae, for example, has over 600 genera and over 25,000 species.

Natural setting/location: This is the geographic region where the plant is thought to have originated. *Endemic* means the plant originally grew only in the area specified. *Indigenous* means the plant is naturally found both in the region mentioned and in other areas. *Introduced* means the plant was brought to the region by humans.

Current status in the wild in Hawai'i: If the plant occurs in the wild in Hawai'i, the range of its distribution, when known by the authors, is described. This information is not meant to encourage harvesting of the plant from the wild.

Cultivars: A cultivar is a named variety of a cultivated plant that has distinguishing horticultural characteristics. Cultivar names are given by the person that bred or selected the variety and are often descriptive or honorific.

Growing your own

Handling cautions: A few plants are potentially dangerous to people who handle the plant, its flowers, or certain other parts. People working with these plants should be prepared for these dangers.

Propagation

Form: This lists the plant parts and methods most commonly used in propagating the plant.

Preplanting treatment: First, processes necessary to prepare the plant material before planting are described. The instructions do not include common-sense steps, such as "Remove the seeds from the pod before planting them," or "Remove basal (bottom) leaves from the cuttings before sticking them into the medium."

Second, any recommended treatment of the planting material is described. If use of a rooting compound for cuttings is recommended, a formulation strength is given according to the following table:

	Amount of active ingredient	
Description	**percent**	**ppm**
mild	0.1	1000
medium	0.3	3000
strong	> 0.5	> 5000

Planting depth: If seeds are used, the depth they should be planted below the surface of the growth medium is given. When cuttings are used, this heading suggests how deeply the end of the cutting should be inserted into the medium (usually, the entire cutting should not be placed below the surface of the medium). It is important to maintain the orientation of the cutting—the basal part of the cutting should be inserted.

Germination time: The length of time it usually takes for the seedling to emerge from the surface of the medium is estimated.

Rooting time: The length of time it usually takes for a cutting to develop enough roots to be transplanted is estimated.

Preferred production conditions

General soil characteristics: Any known special soil requirements for the plant are given. In general, plants do best in a freely draining soil or potting medium. The material should hold moisture but should also have adequate aeration so that water drains away relatively quickly and does not saturate the root zone for prolonged periods.

Soil pH: The optimum soil pH for the plant is given when known. The pH is a soil chemical property describing whether the soil is acidic ("low" pH), neutral (pH 7), or alkaline ("high" pH). The pH scale is logarithmic, meaning that a soil with pH 5 is 10 times more acidic than pH 6, while pH 4 is 100 times more acidic than pH 6. Most plants grow best at soil pH of about 6.0–6.5, but some plants tolerate lower or higher pH to varying degrees. Below pH 5.5 or above pH 7, it is possible that certain plant nutrients will be chemically restricted in their availability to the plant, and also that certain elements in the soil may become toxic to the plant. Most general books on gardening contain a discussion of soil pH and how to modify it for best plant growth.

Light: The level of light under which the plants grow best is described.

Water: Water requirements are hard to define because they vary with the environment, the type of soil, the plant growth stage, and the characteristics of the plant. Although "drought tolerant" and "keep dry" may seem to mean the same thing, there is a difference between them. A "drought tolerant" plant tolerates dry periods, but dry soil may not be its preferred state; "keep dry" means the plant is sensitive to excessive or prolonged soil wetness.

Temperature: The range of temperatures in which the plant grows best is estimated. The plant may survive above or below that range, but it may not thrive.

Soil temperature: For some annual plants often grown in containers, a soil temperature is given that is the optimum temperature for seed germination and seedling development. Most seeds will germinate over a wide temperature range, but the percentage of germination will decrease as temperature conditions differ from the optimim range given.

Elevation: The optimum range of elevations for the plant's growth is estimated.

Salt tolerance: The ability of the plant to grow where there are high levels of salt in the soil or wind is noted; these conditions are usually found near the ocean.

Wind resistance: The plant's ability to withstand relatively strong or persistent winds is described.

Management

Fertilizer needs: The plant's general requirement for nutrients is characterized as light, medium, or heavy, and any special nutrient needs or sensitivites are mentioned. For more on this subject, see Section 3.

Recommended spacing: A minimum distance between plants in the landscape or production planting is suggested.

Adaptation to growing in containers: Most plants grow better in the ground with an unrestricted root system than in a container. However, many plants can grow adequately for a particular purpose in containers. If this is the case for producing lei material from a plant, the appropriate type and minimum size of container for it is suggested.

Pruning: The frequency, type, and degree of pruning needed are described.

Special cultural hints: Unusual conditions, practices, situations, and limitations affecting optimum growth and production are described.

Suggested companion plantings: Other plants that might be appropriate for growing with the plant are listed.

Plant characteristics

Height: This is the range of the plant's height when fully grown under average conditions.

Spread: This is the range of the plant's leaf canopy diameter when fully grown under average conditions.

Growth rate: This is the general rate of growth of the developing plant under average conditions.

Growth habit: This describes the form of the plant (tree, shrub, vine, etc.).

Flowers

(Information is provided if this plant part is used.)

Size: The range in diameter of the flower.

Color: The range of colors that can be expected in the flower.

Shape: The general form or appearance of the flower.

Fragrance: The scent, if any, that the flower has.

Flowers in first year: If the plant usually flowers in the first year, it is noted.

Flowering period: The season or month in which flowering typically occurs.

Time to flowering: The age at which a plant typically can be expected to begin flowering.

Inducing and maintaining flowering: When known, methods are described to force the plants to flower or to encourage continued flowering.

Foliage

(Information is provided if this plant part is used.)

Texture: The "grain" of the leaf, or how it feels to the touch.

(And other information categories as appropriate; see *Flowers* above.)

Fruits

(Information is provided if this plant part is used. Information categories are included as appropriate; see *Flowers* above.)

Pests

Common diseases: The most common plant diseases found on the plant in Hawai‘i are listed. A disease, in general, is a condition or organism that disturbs a plant's normal functions.

Other pests: The most common insect pests and other pest organisms that may adversely affect the plant in Hawai‘i are listed. Many insects found on plants are harmless members of the natural ecological community, and some are even beneficial in that they help control harmful pests. The organisms listed are ones that may need to be controlled if they seriously affect the growth of the plant or the quality of the material harvested from it.

Harvesting considerations

What is harvested: The part(s) of the plant harvested for lei use are listed.

Harvesting techniques: This describes how the harvested part should be removed and how much of the plant can be removed without damaging the plant.

Best time of day to harvest: The time of day to pick the plant material is suggested. For example, some flowers are in different stages of opening at different times of day.

Best way to transport from picking area: This suggests a container to carry the plant material with minimial damage.

Avoid contact with these products: Storing some plant materials with other materials can lead to damage from emitted gases; things to avoid are listed.

Notes on lei making

Best for which type of lei: This describes the type of lei for which the plant is best suited (neck, head, wrist, ankle, horse lei, etc.).

Vase life: This gives a general indication of the longevity of the plant material at room temperature and in water. This differs from storage life, which is usually at cooler temperatures to slow the respiration rate, which is particularly important for flowers to prolong their longevity.

Cleaning of plant materials: If it is necessary to clean the plant material, a method is suggested.

Storing raw lei materials: This suggests appropriate storage containers (e.g., *pu'olo*, a ti leaf container or package), the length of time the lei material can be stored, whether it should be refrigerated, and a suggested storage temperature.

Preparing for use in lei: Methods of making the plant material ready to be used in a lei are described.

Storing a completed lei before wearing: The best methods of keeping the lei fresh once it has been made are suggested.

Preserving a lei for long-term storage or display: This indicates whether or not the lei can be saved for a long period of time, and how to preserve it.

References and further reading

Selected sources of additional information are given, although the list is not intended to be exhaustive. Assistance in locating the U.S. mainland publications and trade journals mentioned can be obtained from librarians. Most of the recent publications of the University of Hawai'i College of Tropical Agriculture and Human Resources (CTAHR) can be downloaded from the college's Web site at <www. ctahr.hawaii.edu/ freepubs>. CTAHR publications more than 10 years old are usually out of print but can be found in the Hawai'i state and University of Hawai'i library systems.

ʻaʻaliʻi

OTHER COMMON NAMES: ʻaʻaliʻi kū makani, ʻaʻaliʻi kū ma kua, kūmakani, hop bush, hopseed bush

SCIENTIFIC NAME: *Dodonaea viscosa*

FAMILY: Sapindaceae (soapberry family)

NATURAL SETTING/LOCATION: indigenous, pantropical species, found on all the main Hawaiian Islands except Kahoʻolawe; grows in a wide

range of habitats from dunes at sea level up through leeward and dry forests and to the highest peaks

CURRENT STATUS IN THE WILD IN HAWAIʻI: common

CULTIVARS: female cultivars such as ʻPurpureaʼ and ʻSaratogaʼ have been selected for good fruit color

Growing your own

PROPAGATION

FORM: seeds; semi-hardwood cuttings or air layering for selected color forms

PREPLANTING TREATMENT: step on seed capsule to release small, round, black seeds, or use heavy gloves and rub capsules vigorously between hands; put seeds in water that has been brought to a boil and removed from heat, soak for about 24 hours; if seeds start to swell, sow immediately; discard floating, nonviable seeds; use strong rooting hormone on cuttings

PLANTING DEPTH: sow seeds ¼" deep in medium; insert base of cutting 1–2" into medium

GERMINATION TIME: 2–4 weeks

CUTTING ROOTING TIME: 1½–3 months

PREFERRED PRODUCTION CONDITIONS

GENERAL SOIL CHARACTERISTICS: well drained is best; tolerant of dry conditions

SOIL PH: 5.5–6.5

LIGHT: full sun

WATER: moderately drought tolerant

TEMPERATURE: tolerates dry heat; temperature 32–90°F

ELEVATION: 10–7700'

SALT TOLERANCE: good (moderate at higher elevations)

WIND RESISTANCE: good

MANAGEMENT

FERTILIZER NEEDS: medium

RECOMMENDED SPACING: 6–8' apart

ADAPTATION TO GROWING IN CONTAINERS: yes, 2-gallon tubs or larger

PRUNING: responds well to pruning; do not cut back into old wood; prune

after fruiting period to shape or keep short; can be shaped into a small tree or maintained as a shrub, hedge, or espalier (on a trellis)

SPECIAL CULTURAL HINTS: male and female plants are separate, although bisexual plants can also be found; males produce no seed capsules; if a certain "variety" (i.e., leaf size, capsule color, etc.) is desired, it is probably best to grow from cuttings or air layering; although drought tolerant, it will shed leaves during extreme drought conditions

SUGGESTED COMPANION PLANTINGS: low native shrubs from dry to moist habitats, such as ferns, ʻilima, ʻākia, kupukupu, pōhinahina, ilieʻe, ʻūlei, kuluʻī

'a'ali'i

Plant characteristics

HEIGHT: 6–24'

SPREAD: 6–15'

GROWTH RATE: moderate to fast

GROWTH HABIT: spreading shrub to small tree

SEED CAPSULES

(flowers are insignificant)

SIZE: ¼–⅝"

COLOR: ranges from white/tan to pink and deep burgundy

SHAPE: 2–5 winged

TIME TO FRUITING: fruits produced in 2nd year after outplanting

FOLIAGE

TEXTURE: leathery, shiny

COLOR: native forms have green foliage, cultivars have bronzy green to purplish-red foliage

SHAPE: spatula shaped with blunt or pointed tips

FRAGRANCE: none

PESTS

COMMON DISEASES: mycoplasma-dodonaea yellow disease (virus-like), nematodes, powdery mildew, root rot

OTHER PESTS: ants, aphids, caterpillars, mealybugs, scales, slugs, spider mites

Harvesting considerations

WHAT IS HARVESTED: fruit (winged papery capsules) and leaves

HARVESTING TECHNIQUES: cut plant tips only

BEST TIME OF DAY TO HARVEST: early morning

BEST WAY TO TRANSPORT FROM PICKING AREA: cloth bag or cardboard box

Notes on lei making

BEST FOR WHICH TYPE OF LEI: neck, head, wrist, ankle, horse

CLEANING OF PLANT MATERIALS: cold water soak

STORING RAW LEI MATERIALS: store in cardboard box and refrigerate at 40°F for up to 14 days

PREPARING FOR USE IN LEI: clip off wrinkled, limp, or poor quality areas before adding to lei

STORING A COMPLETED LEI BEFORE WEARING: soak in water for 5 minutes, drip dry, wrap in 3 sheets of damp newspaper, place in cardboard box or ti leaf *pu'olo* (package), and refrigerate

PRESERVING A LEI FOR LONG-TERM STORAGE OR DISPLAY: air-dry; capsules keep their color if kept out of the sun

References and further reading

Bornhorst, Heidi L. 1996. *Growing Native Hawaiian Plants: A How-to Guide for the Gardener.* Honolulu: Bess Press.

Culliney, John L., and Bruce P. Koebele. 1999. *A Native Hawaiian Garden: How to Grow and Care for Island Plants.* Honolulu: University of Hawai'i Press.

Metcalf, L.J. 1995. *The Propagation of New Zealand Native Plants.* Auckland, New Zealand: Godwit Press.

Nagata, Kenneth M. 1992. *How to Plant a Native Hawaiian Garden.* Honolulu: State of Hawai'i, Office of Environmental Quality Control.

Rauch, Fred D., Heidi L. Bornhorst, Rhonda Stibbe, and David Hensley. 1997. *'A'ali'i.* University of Hawai'i, CTAHR, OF-20.

Stone, Charles P., and Linda W. Pratt. 1994. *Hawai'i's Plants and Animals: Biological Sketches of Hawaii Volcanoes National Park.* Honolulu: Hawaii Natural History Association and University of Hawai'i Press.

Wagner, Warren L., Derral R. Herbst, and S.H. Sohmer. 1990. *Manual of the Flowering Plants of Hawai'i.* 2 vols. Bishop Museum Special Publication 83. Honolulu: University of Hawai'i Press and Bishop Museum Press.

'ākia

OTHER COMMON NAMES: *kauhi*, Moloka'i osmanthus

SCIENTIFIC NAME: *Wikstroemia uva-ursi*

FAMILY: Thymelaeaceae ('ākia family)

NATURAL SETTING/LOCATION: endemic to Hawaiian Islands; rare to scattered on clay flats, *a'ā* lava, dry low

elevations on Kaua'i, O'ahu, Moloka'i, and Maui

CURRENT STATUS IN THE WILD IN HAWAI'I: uncommon to rare in the wild; most commonly used in landscaping

CULTIVARS: prostrate and upright forms are available

Growing your own

HANDLING CAUTIONS: 'ākia bark and fruits may be poisonous; sap burns skin and eyes

PROPAGATION

FORM: seeds; semi-hardwood tip cuttings; air layering

PREPLANTING TREATMENT: remove seeds from pulp, soak in water for 24 hours, discard nonviable floating seeds, and start in full sun with 1–2 seeds per container; select semi-mature tip cuttings and treat with medium rooting hormone

PLANTING DEPTH: sow seed ¼–½" deep in medium; insert base of cutting 1–2" into medium

GERMINATION TIME: 1–12 months

CUTTING ROOTING TIME: 7–8 weeks under periodic mist

PREFERRED PRODUCTION CONDITIONS

GENERAL SOIL CHARACTERISTICS: well drained

SOIL PH: 6.5

LIGHT: full sun

WATER: keep dry

TEMPERATURE: 65–90°F

ELEVATION: 10–1500'

SALT TOLERANCE: good

WIND RESISTANCE: good

MANAGEMENT

FERTILIZER NEEDS: medium

RECOMMENDED SPACING: a minimum of 12" apart in rows such that a person can reach middle of plants

ADAPTATION TO GROWING IN CONTAINERS: yes, from 6" pots to large display pots and planter boxes

PRUNING: can be kept shaped but drastic pruning may cause dieback; light heading back may be necessary

SPECIAL CULTURAL HINTS: avoid water-logged soils; once established, keep on the dry side; not all plants produce fruits; propagate ripe fruits (red ones); plants from seed vary in growth form

SUGGESTED COMPANION PLANTINGS: low native shrubs from dry to moist habitats such as ferns, 'ilima, 'a'ali'i, kupukupu, pōhinahina, ilie'e, ulei, kului

‘ākia

Plant characteristics

HEIGHT: 2–5'

SPREAD: 2–5'

GROWTH RATE: slow to establish

GROWTH HABIT: dense, spreading or sprawling shrub

FLOWERS

SIZE: to ½"

COLOR: yellow-green

SHAPE: tubular, four-part

FRAGRANCE: yes, resembling honeysuckle

FLOWERS IN FIRST YEAR: no; plants from cuttings will flower faster than seedlings (2–3 years)

FLOWERING PERIOD: year-round

TIME TO FLOWERING: 12–18 months to flowering and 2–3 years to harvestable size

INDUCING AND MAINTAINING FLOWERING: not known; flowering can occur year-round without special treatment and if not under stress

FOLIAGE

TEXTURE: waxy

COLOR: pale green; selected forms are dense with blue-green foliage

SHAPE: small, oval, short-stemmed

FRAGRANCE: none

PESTS

COMMON DISEASES: root rot, root-knot nematode

OTHER PESTS: scales, snails, slugs

The lei shown also contains ‘a‘ali‘i, pūkiawe, ‘ūlei, palapalai, and ‘ōhi‘a lehua.

Harvesting considerations

WHAT IS HARVESTED: branch tips, flowers, fruit

HARVESTING TECHNIQUES: pull and twist or cut

BEST TIME OF DAY TO HARVEST: early morning

BEST WAY TO TRANSPORT FROM PICKING AREA: cloth bag

Notes on lei making

BEST FOR WHICH TYPE OF LEI: neck, head, wrist, ankle

CLEANING OF PLANT MATERIALS: cold water soak

STORING RAW LEI MATERIALS: place branch tips and flowers in water for 5 minutes before storing in ti leaf *pu‘olo* (package) or cardboard box for up to 7 days; place fruit in plastic container and store for up to 14 days; refrigerate at 40°F

PREPARING FOR USE IN LEI: clip off wrinkled, limp, or poor quality areas before adding to lei; if sewing fruit, clip all stems; flowers and fruits can be used together or separately

STORING A COMPLETED LEI BEFORE WEARING: soak lei, drip dry and refrigerate; lei can be stored in ti leaf *pu‘olo* or cardboard box; fruit can be stored in plastic container

PRESERVING A LEI FOR LONG-TERM STORAGE OR DISPLAY: cannot be preserved

References and further reading

Bornhorst, Heidi L. 1996. *Growing Native Hawaiian Plants: A How-to Guide for the Gardener*. Honolulu: Bess Press.

Culliney, John L., and Bruce P. Koebele. 1999. *A Native Hawaiian Garden: How to Grow and Care for Island Plants*. Honolulu: University of Hawai‘i Press.

Rauch, Fred D., and David Hensley. 1997. ‘*Ākia*. University of Hawai‘i, CTAHR, OF-12.

Stone, Charles P., and Linda W. Pratt. 1994. *Hawai‘i's Plants and Animals: Biological Sketches of Hawaii Volcanoes National Park*. Honolulu: Hawaii Natural History Association and University of Hawai‘i Press.

Wagner, Warren L., Derral R. Herbst, and S.H. Sohmer. 1990. *Manual of the Flowering Plants of Hawai‘i*. 2 vols. Bishop Museum Special Publication 83. Honolulu: University of Hawai‘i Press and Bishop Museum Press.

hala

OTHER COMMON NAMES: pandanus, *pū hala*, screw pine, walking fences

SCIENTIFIC NAME: *Pandanus tectorius*

FAMILY: Pandanaceae (screw pine family)

NATURAL SETTING/LOCATION: indigenous to the Hawaiian Islands; found in the lower forest areas and along the wetter shorelines on all main islands except Kahoʻolawe; also

native throughout Polynesia and Oceania

CURRENT STATUS IN THE WILD IN HAWAIʻI: common

CULTIVARS: mostly variegated forms used in landscaping; smooth leaf variety recommended for ease of harvesting

Growing your own

HANDLING CAUTIONS: most green forms have sharp, saw-toothed leaves

PROPAGATION

FORM: seeds; cuttings (large stem cuttings may be used)

PREPLANTING TREATMENT: separate the fruit segments, soak seeds in water for 24 hours; no rooting hormone needed for cuttings

PLANTING DEPTH: sow seeds on surface; plant base of cutting vertically 3–4" into medium or place cutting into medium at a nearly horizontal angle, leaving the top exposed

GERMINATION TIME: 3–5 months

CUTTING ROOTING TIME: 3 months

PREFERRED PRODUCTION CONDITIONS

GENERAL SOIL CHARACTERISTICS: well drained best; tolerant of a wide range of soils including coral sands

SOIL PH: 6.5–7.0

LIGHT: full sun

WATER: drought tolerant but thrives in areas where groundwater is present

TEMPERATURE: 60–90°F

ELEVATION: 10–2000'

SALT TOLERANCE: good

WIND RESISTANCE: good

MANAGEMENT

FERTILIZER NEEDS: heavy

RECOMMENDED SPACING: 20–30' apart in landscape, 4–5' apart if managed for foliage

ADAPTATION TO GROWING IN CONTAINERS: yes, will grow in just about any container, but quickly develops into a large plant

PRUNING: head back (cut back) to keep within picking height; remove yellow and brown leaves

SPECIAL CULTURAL HINTS: male and female flowers are produced on different trees (dioecious); male trees have drooping clusters of very fragrant male flowers called *hinano*; female trees have compact greenish heads of female flowers that mature into the pineapple-shaped composite fruit

SUGGESTED COMPANION PLANTINGS: ʻ*ulei*, ʻ*ākia*, ʻ*ilima*, *maʻo*, *loulu*, *naupaka kahakai*, ʻ*ohiʻa lehua*, ferns

hala

Plant characteristics

HEIGHT: to 30'

SPREAD: to 20' (wide-branched)

GROWTH RATE: moderate

GROWTH HABIT: open, round-headed tree with stilt-like props

FLOWERS

SIZE: male inflorescence 1' long surrounded by narrow bracts, female flower insignificant

COLOR: white

SHAPE: male flower spikes oblong, female spherical

FRAGRANCE: yes, male flowers

FLOWERS IN FIRST YEAR: no

FLOWERING PERIOD: male trees flower about every 60 days, female trees flower about 1–3 times per year

TIME TO FLOWERING: ~7 years from seed, 1 year from cutting

FOLIAGE

TEXTURE: leathery, tough, with saw-toothed edges

COLOR: dark green to variegated yellow and green

SHAPE: sword-shaped leaves up to 6' long, prickles on margins and midrib

FRUIT

SIZE: fruit ~8", fruitlets 1–2" long

COLOR: green to yellow, orange, red

SHAPE: fruitlets wedge-shaped

FRAGRANCE: woodsy

PESTS

COMMON DISEASES: none

OTHER PESTS: ants, mealybugs, mosquitoes, rats, scales, whiteflies

Harvesting considerations

WHAT IS HARVESTED: fruits, leaves, male flowers

HARVESTING TECHNIQUES: pull leaves, do not cut; cut fruits; wear gloves

BEST TIME OF DAY TO HARVEST: early morning

BEST WAY TO TRANSPORT FROM PICKING AREA: cloth bag

Notes on lei making

BEST FOR WHICH TYPE OF LEI: neck, head, wrist, ankle, horse

VASE LIFE: 1 month for leaves, 3 weeks for fruits, 4 days for flowers

CLEANING OF PLANT MATERIALS: spray flowers and leaves with water; soak fruits in lemon (or lime) water for 5 minutes

STORING RAW LEI MATERIALS: flowers and fruits can be refrigerated at 40°F for up to 7 days, leaves for up to 30 days

PREPARING FOR USE IN LEI: clip flowers and leaves before sewing; break fruitlets from fruit, pierce, and sew

STORING A COMPLETED LEI BEFORE WEARING: mist flowers and leaves with water and store in paper box; place fruits in sealed plastic container or bag without misting; refrigerate

PRESERVING A LEI FOR LONG-TERM STORAGE OR DISPLAY: air-dry

References and further reading

Bornhorst, Heidi L. 1996. *Growing Native Hawaiian Plants: A How-to Guide for the Gardener*. Honolulu: Bess Press.

Degener, Otto. 1945. *Plants of Hawaii National Park Illustrative of Plants and Customs of the South Seas*. Ann Arbor, Michigan: Edwards Brothers, Inc.

Hensley, David, Rhonda Stibbe, and Fred D. Rauch. 1997. *Hala*. University of Hawai‘i, CTAHR, OF-17.

Ide, Laurie S. 1998. *Hawaiian Lei Making: Step-by-Step Guide*. Honolulu: Mutual Publishing.

Little, Elbert L. Jr., and Roger G. Skolmen. 1989. *Common Forest Trees of Hawai‘i (Native and Introduced)*. Agriculture Handbook no. 679. Washington, D.C.: U.S. Department of Agriculture, Forest Service.

Nagata, Kenneth M. 1992. *How to Plant a Native Hawaiian Garden*. Honolulu: State of Hawai‘i, Office of Environmental Quality Control.

Rauch, Fred D. 1996. *Tropical Landscape Plants*. 3rd ed. Battle Ground, Washington: Hawaii Floriculture.

Stone, Charles P., and Linda W. Pratt. 1994. *Hawai‘i's Plants and Animals: Biological Sketches of Hawaii Volcanoes National Park*. Honolulu: Hawaii Natural History Association and University of Hawai‘i Press.

hinahina

OTHER COMMON NAMES: beach heliotrope, *hinahina kūkahakai*

SCIENTIFIC NAME: *Heliotropium anomalum* var. *argenteum*

FAMILY: Boraginaceae (borage family)

NATURAL SETTING/LOCATION: shoreline areas; *H. anomalum* is widely distributed throughout Polynesia;

H. anomalum var. *argenteum* is endemic, occurs in sandy coastal sites on Niʻihau, Kauaʻi, Oʻahu, and Molokaʻi but is apparently rare on Maui and Hawaiʻi

CURRENT STATUS IN THE WILD IN HAWAIʻI: scattered to locally common

Growing your own

PROPAGATION

FORM: seeds; tip or hard stem cuttings 2–3" long

PREPLANTING TREATMENT: no seed treatment needed; no rooting hormone needed for cuttings, but misting helps

PLANTING DEPTH: sow seeds on surface of medium; insert base of cutting 1–2" into medium

GERMINATION TIME: 1–3 months

CUTTING ROOTING TIME: 2–4 weeks

PREFERRED PRODUCTION CONDITIONS

GENERAL SOIL CHARACTERISTICS: sandy, porous

SOIL PH: 6.0–7.5

LIGHT: sunny location

WATER: moderate to light

TEMPERATURE: 60–90°F

ELEVATION: 10–900'

SALT TOLERANCE: good

WIND RESISTANCE: good

MANAGEMENT

FERTILIZER NEEDS: light

RECOMMENDED SPACING: 3–5' on center

ADAPTATION TO GROWING IN CONTAINERS: yes, 6–8" plastic pots

PRUNING: will improve appearance, but not required for production purposes.

SPECIAL CULTURAL HINTS: keep on well lit, dry side; too much shade or water makes plant leggy and not as silvery; root rot usually results from overwatering and waterlogged soil

SUGGESTED COMPANION PLANTINGS: native coastal plants such as *ʻilima, maʻo, naupaka kahakai, nehe, pōhinahina, ʻākia, hala*

hinahina

Plant characteristics

HEIGHT: 6–18"

SPREAD: 3–5'

GROWTH RATE: moderate

GROWTH HABIT: low, mat-like

FOLIAGE

TEXTURE: silky and soft with flat-lying hairs

COLOR: gray green to silver

SHAPE: semi-succulent, sword-shaped; wider near the tip than the base

FRAGRANCE: mild

PESTS

COMMON DISEASES: root rot, nematodes

OTHER PESTS: ants, aphids, mealybugs, thrips

The bottom lei shown also contains ti.

Harvesting considerations

WHAT IS HARVESTED: leaves, flowers

HARVESTING TECHNIQUES: pick carefully or cut

BEST TIME OF DAY TO HARVEST: any time

BEST WAY TO TRANSPORT FROM PICKING AREA: brown paper bag

AVOID CONTACT WITH THESE PRODUCTS: smoke, car exhaust, ripening fruits, wilting flowers

Notes on lei making

BEST FOR WHICH TYPE OF LEI: neck, head, wrist, ankle, horse

CLEANING OF PLANT MATERIALS: cold water dip

STORING RAW LEI MATERIALS: wrap in dry newspaper, place in a sealed plastic container, and refrigerate at 40°F for up to 14 days

PREPARING FOR USE IN LEI: clip off wrinkled, limp, or poor quality areas before adding to lei

STORING A COMPLETED LEI BEFORE WEARING: wrap lei in dry newspaper, place in a sealed plastic container, and refrigerate

PRESERVING A LEI FOR LONG-TERM STORAGE OR DISPLAY: air-dry

References and further reading

Bornhorst, Heidi L. 1996. *Growing Native Hawaiian Plants: A How-to Guide for the Gardener*. Honolulu: Bess Press.

Crivellone, C.F. 1991. Hinahina for Use as a Landscape Ground-cover. In: *1989 Hawaii Nursery Research*. University of Hawai'i, CTAHR Research Extension Series 126, p. 13–14.

Nagata, Kenneth M. 1992. *How to Plant a Native Hawaiian Garden*. Honolulu: State of Hawai'i, Office of Environmental Quality Control.

Wagner, Warren L., Derral R. Herbst, and S.H. Sohmer. 1990. *Manual of the Flowering Plants of Hawai'i*. 2 vols. Bishop Museum Special Publication 83. Honolulu: University of Hawai'i Press and Bishop Museum Press.

ʻilima

OTHER COMMON NAMES: *ʻilima papa*

SCIENTIFIC NAME: *Sida fallax*

FAMILY: Malvaceae (mallow family)

NATURAL SETTING/LOCATION: indigenous to Hawaiian Islands and widespread throughout Pacific islands to China; found in coastal areas, arid lava fields, and dry to mesic (medium-wet) forests; the official flower of the City and County of Honolulu

CURRENT STATUS IN THE WILD IN HAWAIʻI: common

CULTIVARS: *ʻilima-lei; ʻilima-ku-kula; ʻilima-ku-kahakai (ʻilima papa); ʻilima-koli-kukui*

Growing your own

PROPAGATION

FORM: seeds; cuttings

PREPLANTING TREATMENT: soak seeds in water that has been brought to a boil and removed from heat, let sit for about 8–24 hours; use medium rooting hormone on cuttings

PLANTING DEPTH: sow seeds ¼" deep in medium; insert base of cuttings 1–2" into medium

GERMINATION TIME: 1–3 months

CUTTING ROOTING TIME: 1–3 months

PREFERRED PRODUCTION CONDITIONS

GENERAL SOIL CHARACTERISTICS: well drained

SOIL PH: to 7.5

LIGHT: sunny location

WATER: dry (beach form) to moderate (upland form)

TEMPERATURE: 60–90°F

ELEVATION: 10–2000'

SALT TOLERANCE: good (moderate for higher elevations)

WIND RESISTANCE: good

MANAGEMENT

FERTILIZER NEEDS: light

RECOMMENDED SPACING: 2–4' apart, depending on growth form

ADAPTATION TO GROWING IN CONTAINERS: yes, 1-gallon pots or large planters

PRUNING: head back (cut back) to maintain size and shape and induce more flowering branches, but not too severely; prune dead wood

SPECIAL CULTURAL HINTS: requires good drainage, high sunlight, and minimal fertilization, especially with N; plants grown from seed will have leaf, flower, and habit variations; many variations naturally occur, therefore care should be taken to select the correct type to meet specific needs

SUGGESTED COMPANION PLANTINGS: *ʻākia, hinahina, pōhinahina, maʻo*

'ilima

Plant characteristics

HEIGHT: 6"–7'

SPREAD: depends on type; upright 3–6'

GROWTH RATE: fast

GROWTH HABIT: many plant and flower forms; shrub shapes vary from low growing and sprawling to erect, dense to sparse

FLOWERS

SIZE: ¼–¾"

COLOR: yellow-orange, reddish brown

SHAPE: round, cup-shaped; rotate, petals broadly obovate

FRAGRANCE: none

FLOWERS IN FIRST YEAR: yes

FLOWERING PERIOD: year-round

TIME TO FLOWERING: 3–4 months

INDUCING AND MAINTAINING FLOWERING: remove spent flowers

PESTS

COMMON DISEASES: root rot, leaf spot (rust fungus), lesion and reniform nematodes, damping off of seedlings

OTHER PESTS: ants, aphids, scales, slugs, snails (in wet areas), thrips, whiteflies

Harvesting considerations

WHAT IS HARVESTED: flowers

HARVESTING TECHNIQUE: pull carefully to avoid bruising

BEST TIME OF DAY TO HARVEST: early morning

BEST WAY TO TRANSPORT FROM PICKING AREA: cardboard box

AVOID CONTACT WITH THESE PRODUCTS: smoke, car exhaust, ripening fruits, wilting flowers

The lei shown also contains ti.

Notes on lei making

BEST FOR WHICH TYPE OF LEI: neck, head, wrist, ankle

CLEANING OF PLANT MATERIALS: no water

STORING RAW LEI MATERIALS: wrap in dry tissue paper, place in cardboard box, and refrigerate at 40°F for up to 2 days; no water

PREPARING FOR USE IN LEI: take calyx (green, leafy base) off, then sew; if using calyx and flowers, remove lower leaves, leaving 4 or 5 with flower buds

STORING A COMPLETED LEI BEFORE WEARING: wrap lei in dry tissue paper, place in cardboard box, and refrigerate; no water

PRESERVING A LEI FOR LONG-TERM STORAGE OR DISPLAY: air-dry

References and further reading

Bornhorst, Heidi L. 1996. *Growing Native Hawaiian Plants: A How-to Guide for the Gardener.* Honolulu: Bess Press.

Ide, Laurie S. 1998. *Hawaiian Lei Making: Step-by-Step Guide.* Honolulu: Mutual Publishing.

Nagata, Kenneth M. 1992. *How to Plant a Native Hawaiian Garden.* Honolulu: State of Hawai'i, Office of Environmental Quality Control.

Rauch, Fred D., Heidi L. Bornhorst, and David L. Hensley. 1997. *Ilima.* University of Hawai'i, CTAHR, OF-15.

Wagner, Warren L., Derral R. Herbst, and S.H. Sohmer. 1990. *Manual of the Flowering Plants of Hawai'i.* 2 vols. Bishop Museum Special Publication 83. Honolulu: University of Hawai'i Press and Bishop Museum Press.

kauna'oa

OTHER COMMON NAMES: *kauna'oa, kauna'oa kahakai, kauna'oa lei* (endemic); *kauna'oa-pehu* (indigenous); western field dodder (introduced); dodder

SCIENTIFIC NAME:
Cuscuta sandwichiana (endemic); *Cassytha filiformis* (indigenous); *Cuscuta campestris* (introduced)

FAMILY: Cuscutaceae (dodder family) (*Cuscuta*); Lauraceae (laurel family) (*Cassytha*)

NATURAL SETTING/LOCATION: *kauna'oa kahakai* is found in coastal areas on all the main Hawaiian Islands; *kauna'oa-pehu* is found in lowlands

CURRENT STATUS IN THE WILD IN HAWAI'I: scattered to locally common

Growing your own

HANDLING CAUTIONS: may irritate eyes

PROPAGATION

FORM: seeds; stem segments placed on plants will attach to and parasitize them

PREPLANTING TREATMENT: remove seeds from pulp and rinse

PLANTING DEPTH: surface-sow seeds

CUTTING ROOTING TIME: plant is rootless

PREFERRED PRODUCTION CONDITIONS

GENERAL SOIL CHARACTERISTICS: sandy or rocky soil, cinders, or tree bark of host plant

LIGHT: full sun

WATER: keep moist

TEMPERATURE: heat tolerant, 75–90°F

ELEVATION: 10–300'

SALT TOLERANCE: good

WIND RESISTANCE: good

MANAGEMENT

FERTILIZER NEEDS: fertilize host plant; spray parasite with weak foliar formulation

ADAPTATION TO GROWING IN CONTAINERS: can parasitize a container-grown host

PRUNING: break off unwanted growth

SPECIAL CULTURAL HINTS: needs host plant; may kill host plant if left unchecked

SUGGESTED COMPANION PLANTINGS: grows on many native and introduced plants; legumes are good hosts; *C. sandwichiana* may prefer woody shrubs or trees with bushy growth habit, such as *noni*

kauna'oa

Plant characteristics

HEIGHT: will layer upon itself up to 4" thick

SPREAD: unlimited

GROWTH RATE: rapid

GROWTH HABIT: parasitic vine

FOLIAGE

TEXTURE: filamentous stems (no leaves)

COLOR: stems slender, yellow to orange, lack chlorophyl

SHAPE: stringy

FRAGRANCE: none

PESTS

COMMON DISEASES: none known; can transmit viruses to host plants

OTHER PESTS: none known

The lei shown also contains *maile*.

Harvesting considerations

WHAT IS HARVESTED: vines

HARVESTING TECHNIQUES: cut

BEST TIME OF DAY TO HARVEST: any time

BEST WAY TO TRANSPORT FROM PICKING AREA: brown paper bag

AVOID CONTACT WITH THESE PRODUCTS: smoke, car exhaust, ripening fruits, wilting flowers

Notes on lei making

BEST FOR WHICH TYPE OF LEI: neck, head, wrist, ankle, horse

CLEANING OF PLANT MATERIALS: cold water soak, drip dry

STORING RAW LEI MATERIALS: wrap in dry newspaper, store in plastic container, and refrigerate at 40°F for up to 10 days for *Cassytha filiformis* and 2 days for *Cuscuta sandwichiana*; no water

PREPARING FOR USE IN LEI: remove other plant material that it was growing on; *Cuscuta sandwichiana* tends to be more woody so harder to work with than *Cassytha filiformis*

STORING A COMPLETED LEI BEFORE WEARING: wrap lei in dry newspaper, store in plastic container, and refrigerate. no water

PRESERVING A LEI FOR LONG-TERM STORAGE OR DISPLAY: air-dry

References and further reading

Ide, Laurie S. 1998. *Hawaiian Lei Making: Step-by-Step Guide*. Honolulu: Mutual Publishing.

McDonald, Marie A. 1989. *Ka Lei: the Leis of Hawaii*. Honolulu: Ku Pa'a Inc., and Press Pacifica.

Neal, Marie C. 1965. *In Gardens of Hawaii*. Bernice P. Bishop Museum Special Publication 50. Honolulu: Bishop Museum Press.

Wagner, Warren L., Derral R. Herbst, and S.H. Sohmer. 1990. *Manual of the Flowering Plants of Hawai'i*. 2 vols. Bishop Museum Special Publication 83. Honolulu: University of Hawai'i Press and Bishop Museum Press.

Wolswinkel, P. 1989. Cuscuta. In: *CRC Handbook of Flowering*. vol. 6, A.H. Halevy (ed.), p. 270–274. Boca Raton, Florida: CRC Press.

kou

OTHER COMMON NAMES: cordia

SCIENTIFIC NAME: *Cordia subcordata*

FAMILY: Boraginaceae (borage family)

NATURAL SETTING/LOCATION: Polynesian introduction, native of Malaysia; found on Kaua'i, O'ahu, Maui, and Hawai'i

CURRENT STATUS IN THE WILD IN HAWAI'I: naturalized in a few dry coastal areas; commonly used in landscaping

Growing your own

PROPAGATION

FORM: seeds (almost always seed-propagated); cuttings

PREPLANTING TREATMENT: soak fruits in water for 48 hours; use medium rooting hormone on cuttings

PLANTING DEPTH: sow seeds on surface to ½" deep; plant base of cutting 1–2" into medium

GERMINATION TIME: 20–50 days, ready to plant in the garden in 8 months

PREFERRED PRODUCTION CONDITIONS

GENERAL SOIL CHARACTERISTICS: well drained

SOIL PH: 6.0–7.5

LIGHT: full sun

WATER: drought tolerant, tolerates semi-moist conditions

TEMPERATURE: 60–90°F

ELEVATION: 10–2000'

SALT TOLERANCE: good

WIND RESISTANCE: good

MANAGEMENT

FERTILIZER NEEDS: heavy

RECOMMENDED SPACING: 10–15' apart minimum

ADAPTATION TO GROWING IN CONTAINERS: not recommended

PRUNING: prune to reduce size and induce lower branches

SPECIAL CULTURAL HINTS: its hardwood is highly valued; may hybridize with geiger tree (*Cordia sebestana*), producing intermediate fruits, foliage, and flowers

SUGGESTED COMPANION PLANTINGS: low-growing plants such as ferns, *kupukupu, 'ilima, 'ākia, naupaka kahakai, hinahina*, and *hala*

kou

Plant characteristics

HEIGHT: 15–25'

SPREAD: 6–20'

GROWTH RATE: fast

GROWTH HABIT: small, erect, evergreen tree

FLOWERS

SIZE: 1–2" in diameter

COLOR: apricot-orange

SHAPE: funnel-shaped

FRAGRANCE: none

FLOWERS IN FIRST YEAR: no

FLOWERING PERIOD: year-round

TIME TO FLOWERING: 2–3 years

INDUCING AND MAINTAINING FLOWERING: flowers throughout the period of vegetative growth

PESTS

COMMON DISEASES: none serious

OTHER PESTS: *kou* was once very common along the shorelines of Hawai'i; it became very rare in the late 1800s due to the impact of introduced pests such as the *kou* leafworm (*Ethmia nigroapicella*); isolated trees can be seriously defoliated by this caterpillar, especially along windy coastal areas; seed-attacking weevils can also be a problem

Harvesting considerations

WHAT IS HARVESTED: flowers

HARVESTING TECHNIQUES: pick flowers that have fallen to the ground

BEST TIME OF DAY TO HARVEST: morning, when flowers have freshly fallen

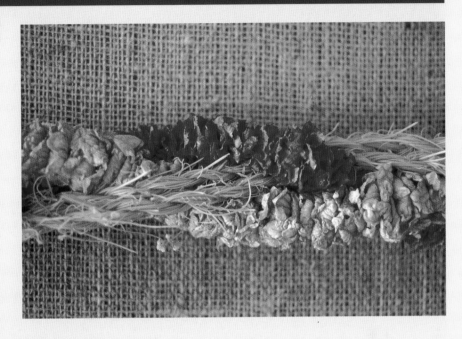

The lei shown also contains *kauna'oa*.

BEST WAY TO TRANSPORT FROM PICKING AREA: brown paper bag or cooler

AVOID CONTACT WITH THESE PRODUCTS: smoke, car exhaust, ripening fruits, and wilting flowers

Notes on lei making

BEST FOR WHICH TYPE OF LEI: neck, head, wrist, ankle

CLEANING OF PLANT MATERIALS: no water

STORING RAW LEI MATERIALS: place in cardboard container and refrigerate at 40°F for up to 2 days; no water

PREPARING FOR USE IN LEI: choose flowers that are fully open

STORING A COMPLETED LEI BEFORE WEARING: wrap lei in tissue paper, place in cardboard container, and refrigerate; no water

PRESERVING A LEI FOR LONG-TERM STORAGE OR DISPLAY: air-dry

References and further reading

Borchert, Rolf. 1986. "Cordia." In: *CRC Handbook of Flowering*. vol. V, edited by A. H. Halevy, p. 76–83. Boca Raton, Florida: CRC Press.

Education and Plant Science Departments. 1996. *Ten Native Hawaiian Trees for Urban Landscapes*. Lawai, Hawai'i: National Tropical Botanical Garden.

McDonald, Marie A. 1989. *Ka Lei: the Leis of Hawaii*. Honolulu: Ku Pa'a Inc., and Press Pacifica.

Wagner, Warren L., Derral R. Herbst, and S.H. Sohmer. 1990. *Manual of the Flowering Plants of Hawai'i*. 2 vols. Bishop Museum Special Publication 83. Honolulu: University of Hawai'i Press and Bishop Museum Press.

kukui

OTHER COMMON NAMES: candlenut tree (the official state tree of Hawai'i and flower of Moloka'i)

SCIENTIFIC NAME: *Aleurites moluccana*

FAMILY: Euphorbiaceae (spurge family)

NATURAL SETTING/LOCATION: native to Malaysia; Polynesian introduction, widespread on all main Hawaiian Islands except Kaho'olawe

CURRENT STATUS IN THE WILD IN HAWAI'I: common in mesic (medium-wet) valleys

CULTIVARS: many plant types, varying in seed and leaf type and shape and tree size

Growing your own

HANDLING CAUTIONS: sap may cause irritation

PROPAGATION

FORM: seeds; volunteer seedlings can easily be transplanted

PREPLANTING TREATMENT: scarify seed (scratch seedcoat with file), soak in water for 24 hours

PLANTING DEPTH: sow 1" deep in medium

GERMINATION TIME: 1 month

PREFERRED PRODUCTION CONDITIONS

GENERAL SOIL CHARACTERISTICS: well drained

SOIL PH: 5.0–7.5

LIGHT: semi-shady to full sun

WATER: keep moist

TEMPERATURE: 50–90°F

ELEVATION: 10–2000'

SALT TOLERANCE: good (moderate at higher elevations)

WIND RESISTANCE: moderate

MANAGEMENT

FERTILIZER NEEDS: heavy

RECOMMENDED SPACING: 25–30' apart

ADAPTATION TO GROWING IN CONTAINERS: not recommended

PRUNING: prune to reduce size; tree will naturally shed lower branches while growing, most likely in response to shading

SPECIAL CULTURAL HINTS: allow plenty of space between plants; extra maintenance required during season when abundant fruits drop

SUGGESTED COMPANION PLANTINGS: plant shade-loving species underneath (*palapalai* and *maile*)

kukui

Plant characteristics

HEIGHT: 30–60'

SPREAD: to 25'

GROWTH RATE: moderate to fast

GROWTH HABIT: tree with round canopy

FLOWERS

SIZE: clusters to 10"

COLOR: white

SHAPE: tubular in clusters

FRAGRANCE: none

FLOWERS IN FIRST YEAR: no

FLOWERING PERIOD: seasonal to year-round

TIME TO FLOWERING: 3–4 years

FOLIAGE

TEXTURE: smooth on top, fuzzy on bottom, and covered with whitish down

COLOR: pale green to green

SHAPE: variable, broadly pointed to narrow, maple-leaf shaped

FRAGRANCE: none

PESTS

COMMON DISEASES: fungal leaf spots and root-knot nematodes

OTHER PESTS: ants, mealybugs, scales

Harvesting considerations

WHAT IS HARVESTED: flowers and leaves with 1–2" stem (seeds also are used in lei, but this is not covered here)

HARVESTING TECHNIQUES: cut

BEST TIME OF DAY TO HARVEST: early morning

BEST WAY TO TRANSPORT FROM PICKING AREA: plastic bag or container

Notes on lei making

BEST FOR WHICH TYPE OF LEI: neck, head, wrist, ankle, horse

VASE LIFE: 3 days for flowers, 7 days for leaves

CLEANING OF PLANT MATERIALS: cold water soak

STORING RAW LEI MATERIALS: place leaves on a damp paper towel and store in a plastic container; pick partially open flowers, soak in water for 5 minutes, wrap in paper towels, and place in sealed plastic container; refrigerate at 40°F, 7–14 days

PREPARING FOR USE IN LEI: choose small leaves and buds

STORING A COMPLETED LEI BEFORE WEARING: soak lei in water, drip dry, wrap in damp newspaper, place in cardboard or plastic container, and refrigerate

PRESERVING A LEI FOR LONG-TERM STORAGE OR DISPLAY: air-dry

References and further reading

Degener, O. 1973. *Plants of Hawaii National Parks Illustrative of Plants and Customs of the South Seas.* Ann Arbor, Michigan: Braun-Brumfield, Inc.

Ide, Laurie S. 1998. *Hawaiian Lei Making: Step-by-Step Guide.* Honolulu: Mutual Publishing.

Little, Elbert L., Jr., and Roger G. Skolmen. 1989. *Common Forest Trees of Hawai'i (Native and Introduced).* Agriculture Handbook No. 679. Washington, D.C.: U.S. Department of Agriculture, Forest Service.

Nagata, Kenneth M. 1992. *How to Plant a Native Hawaiian Garden.* Honolulu: State of Hawai'i, Office of Environmental Quality Control.

Neal, Marie C. 1965. *In Gardens of Hawaii,* Bernice P. Bishop Museum Special Publication 50. Honolulu: Bishop Museum Press.

Rauch, Fred D. 1996. *Tropical Landscape Plants.* 3rd ed. Battle Ground, Washington: Hawaii Floriculture.

Scott, Susan, and Craig Thomas. 2000. *Poisonous Plants of Paradise: First Aid and Medical Treatment for Injuries from Hawai'i's Plants.* Honolulu: University of Hawai'i Press.

kuluʻi

OTHER COMMON NAMES: none

SCIENTIFIC NAME: *Nototrichium sandwicense*

FAMILY: Amaranthaceae (amaranth family)

NATURAL SETTING/LOCATION: endemic to Hawaiian Islands; found in dry forest and lava fields on all main islands; rare on Oʻahu

CURRENT STATUS IN THE WILD IN HAWAIʻI: scattered to sometimes common

CULTIVARS: there is typically only one cultivar found in nurseries, but over 20 varieties have been described

Growing your own

PROPAGATION

FORM: seeds; cuttings 4–6" long are generally easier and faster than seeds

PREPLANTING TREATMENT: treat cutting with medium rooting hormone

PLANTING DEPTH: sow seeds on surface or slightly (¼") below; plant base of cutting 1–2" deep in medium (perlite and vermiculite)

GERMINATION TIME: 1–3 months

CUTTING ROOTING TIME: 2–4 weeks, 2–3 weeks with rooting hormone under mist

PREFERRED PRODUCTION CONDITIONS

GENERAL SOIL CHARACTERISTICS: well drained, rocky

SOIL PH: 6.5–7.0

LIGHT: from shade to sunny location (depends on biotype)

WATER: keep dry, tolerates moisture

TEMPERATURE: 50–90°F

ELEVATION: 10–2500' or more

SALT TOLERANCE: moderate to poor

WIND RESISTANCE: good

MANAGEMENT

FERTILIZER NEEDS: medium

RECOMMENDED SPACING: 5–6' apart

ADAPTATION TO GROWING IN CONTAINERS: yes, plastic pots or large planters

PRUNING: older plants may become straggly, therefore prune to manage size and shape and stimulate vigorous new shoots

SPECIAL CULTURAL HINTS: additional careful fertilizing will create larger leaves and longer petioles

SUGGESTED COMPANION PLANTINGS: ʻākia, maʻo

kuluʻi

Plant characteristics

HEIGHT: 3–15'

SPREAD: 5–10'

GROWTH RATE: moderate

GROWTH HABIT: spreading, multi-stemmed shrub to small tree

FLOWERS

SIZE: spikes ½–3" long (to 5"), ⅛–¼" diameter

COLOR: white

SHAPE: spikes with many flowers

FRAGRANCE: none

FLOWERS IN FIRST YEAR: no

FLOWERING PERIOD: summer

TIME TO FLOWERING: 2 years

FOLIAGE

TEXTURE: densely hairy

COLOR: silvery to green

SHAPE: elliptic to lance-shaped

FRAGRANCE: none

PESTS

COMMON DISEASES: root rot

OTHER PESTS: ants, mealybugs, scales

Harvesting considerations

WHAT IS HARVESTED: leaves, flower spikes

HARVESTING TECHNIQUES: cut

BEST TIME OF DAY TO HARVEST: early morning

BEST WAY TO TRANSPORT FROM PICKING AREA: brown paper bag

The lei shown also contains ʻaʻaliʻi, ʻōhiʻa lehua, palaʻā, and cup-and-saucer plant.

Notes on lei making

BEST FOR WHICH TYPE OF LEI: neck, head, wrist, ankle, horse

CLEANING OF PLANT MATERIALS: cold water soak

STORING RAW LEI MATERIALS: soak in water for 5 minutes, drip dry, wrap in dry newspaper, and refrigerate in paper box at 40°F for up to 10 days

PREPARING FOR USE IN LEI: clip off the wrinkled, limp, or poor quality areas before adding to lei

STORING A COMPLETED LEI BEFORE WEARING: soak lei in water, drip dry, place in paper box, and refrigerate

PRESERVING A LEI FOR LONG-TERM STORAGE OR DISPLAY: air-dry

References and further reading

Bornhorst, H.L., and F.D. Rauch. 1994. *Native Hawaiian Plants for Landscaping, Conservation, and Reforestation.* University of Hawaiʻi, CTAHR, Research Extension Series 142.

Hawaiʻi Plant Conservation Center. 1992. *Plant Information Sheets on Native Plants of Hawaiʻi.* Lawai, Hawaiʻi: National Tropical Botanical Garden.

Nagata, Kenneth M. 1992. *How to Plant a Native Hawaiian Garden.* Honolulu: State of Hawaiʻi, Office of Environmental Quality Control.

Wagner, Warren L., Derral R. Herbst, and S.H. Sohmer. 1990. *Manual of the Flowering Plants of Hawaiʻi.* 2 vols. Bishop Museum Special Publication 83. Honolulu: University of Hawaiʻi Press and Bishop Museum Press.

kupukupu / sword fern

OTHER COMMON NAMES: *ʻōkupukupu, niʻaniʻau*

SCIENTIFIC NAME: *Nephrolepis cordifolia*

FAMILY: Nephrolepidaceae (sword fern family)

NATURAL SETTING/LOCATION: tropics; indigenous to Hawaiian Islands in dry to wet forests and lava fields

CURRENT STATUS IN THE WILD IN HAWAIʻI: common

Growing your own

PROPAGATION

FORM: divisions; spores; tissue culture

PREPLANTING TREATMENT: remove old leaves and bulbs from division

PLANTING DEPTH: sow spores on surface; with divisions, keep root crown just below soil level

PREFERRED PRODUCTION CONDITIONS

GENERAL SOIL CHARACTERISTICS: moist, well drained; tolerates a range of soil and climatic conditions but generally likes cool, moist, shady locations; can grow in the soil or on lava, tree trunks, or *hāpuʻu*

SOIL PH: 5.5–6.5

LIGHT: full sun to partial shade

WATER: keep moist, tolerates occasional drought

TEMPERATURE: 40–90°F

ELEVATION: 10–4000'

SALT TOLERANCE: poor

WIND RESISTANCE: moderate

MANAGEMENT

FERTILIZER NEEDS: light; supplemental N may be beneficial

RECOMMENDED SPACING: 8–12" on center

ADAPTATION TO GROWING IN CONTAINERS: yes, 5-gallon tubs

SPECIAL CULTURAL HINTS: remove old fronds

SUGGESTED COMPANION PLANTINGS: *ʻōhiʻa lehua, koa, wiliwili*

kupukupu / sword fern

Plant characteristics

HEIGHT: 24"

SPREAD: 24–36"; may spread indefinitely

GROWTH RATE: slow to establish, then moderate

GROWTH HABIT: upright fern, spreading groundcover

FOLIAGE

TEXTURE: stiff

COLOR: yellowish green to dark green, glossy

SHAPE: pinately (once) divided and sword-shaped

FRAGRANCE: none

PESTS

COMMON DISEASES: none known

OTHER PESTS: ants, mealybugs, scales, slugs

Harvesting considerations

WHAT IS HARVESTED: fronds

HARVESTING TECHNIQUES: cut

BEST TIME OF DAY TO HARVEST: early morning

BEST WAY TO TRANSPORT FROM PICKING AREA: cloth bag

The lei shown also contains *kuluʻi*.

Notes on lei making

BEST FOR WHICH TYPE OF LEI: neck, head, wrist, ankle, horse

VASE LIFE: 5–7 days

CLEANING OF PLANT MATERIALS: cold water soak

STORING RAW LEI MATERIALS: wrap in several sheets of wet newspaper and store in plastic container in refrigerator at 40°F for up to 14 days

PREPARING FOR USE IN LEI: clip off the wrinkled, limp, or poor quality areas before adding to lei

STORING A COMPLETED LEI BEFORE WEARING: soak lei in water for 5 minutes, shake off excess water, wrap in wet newspaper, place in plastic container, and refrigerate

PRESERVING A LEI FOR LONG-TERM STORAGE OR DISPLAY: cannot be preserved

References and further reading

Bornhorst, Heidi L. 1996. *Growing Native Hawaiian Plants: A How-to Guide for the Gardener*. Honolulu: Bess Press.

Hoshizaki, Barbara J. 1976. *Fern Growers Manual*. New York: Alfred A. Knopf.

Keeble, T., H. Clay, D. Crater, and G. Smith. 1975. *Growing Ferns*. University of Georgia CES Bulletin 737.

Neal, Marie C. 1965. *In Gardens of Hawaii*. Bernice P. Bishop Museum Special Publication 50. Honolulu: Bishop Museum Press.

Valier, Kathy. 1995. *Ferns of Hawaiʻi*. Honolulu: University of Hawaii Press.

Wagner, Warren L., Derral R. Herbst, and S.H. Sohmer. 1990. *Manual of the Flowering Plants of Hawaiʻi*. 2 vols. Bishop Museum Special Publication 83. Honolulu: University of Hawaiʻi Press and Bishop Museum Press.

ma'o

OTHER COMMON NAMES: Hawaiian cotton, *huluhulu*

SCIENTIFIC NAME: *Gossypium tomentosum*

FAMILY: Malvaceae (mallow family)

NATURAL SETTING/LOCATION: endemic to Hawaiian Islands; found in arid, rocky, or clay coastal plains on all main islands except Hawai'i

CURRENT STATUS IN THE WILD IN HAWAI'I: uncommon to rare; most commonly used in landscaping

Growing your own

PROPAGATION

FORM: seeds; cuttings 6–7" long, ¼" diameter

PREPLANTING TREATMENT: remove seeds from lint; scarify seeds by scratching the seedcoat, or put them in water that has been brought to a boil and removed from heat, and soak for 24 hours; use medium rooting hormone on cuttings

PLANTING DEPTH: sow seeds ¼–½" deep in medium; insert base of cutting 1–2" into medium

GERMINATION TIME: 2 weeks or longer

CUTTING ROOTING TIME: 1–2 months

PREFERRED PRODUCTION CONDITIONS

GENERAL SOIL CHARACTERISTICS: well drained

SOIL PH: 6.5–7.5

LIGHT: full sun

WATER: keep dry

TEMPERATURE: 60–90°F

ELEVATION: 10–400'

SALT TOLERANCE: moderate to good

WIND RESISTANCE: good

MANAGEMENT

FERTILIZER NEEDS: medium; do not overfertilize with N

RECOMMENDED SPACING: 6–10' in rows

ADAPTATION TO GROWING IN CONTAINERS: yes, 2–5-gallon tubs, but grows better in the ground

PRUNING: plants may become straggly, therefore prune to manage size and shape and stimulate vigorous new shoots

SPECIAL CULTURAL HINTS: avoid water-logged soils

SUGGESTED COMPANION PLANTINGS: *kulu'ī, 'ilima,* other dry-forest or coastal scrubland plants

ma'o

Plant characteristics

HEIGHT: 2–5'

SPREAD: 5–7'

GROWTH RATE: moderate

GROWTH HABIT: sprawling shrub

FLOWERS

SIZE: 2–3" diameter

COLOR: bright yellow

SHAPE: cup-shaped

FRAGRANCE: none

FLOWERS IN FIRST YEAR: from cutting, yes; from seed, no

FLOWERING PERIOD: summer

TIME TO FLOWERING: 1–2 years (depending on culture)

INDUCING AND MAINTAINING FLOWERING: not known

FOLIAGE

TEXTURE: smooth to slight fuzz

COLOR: silvery-green to gray-green

SHAPE: leaves are wider than they are long

FRAGRANCE: none

PESTS

COMMON DISEASES: root rot, leaf spots, root-knot nematodes

OTHER PESTS: ants, aphids, mealybugs, rose beetle, whitefly, scales

The lei shown also contains *kupukupu*.

Harvesting considerations

WHAT IS HARVESTED: leaves and flowers

HARVESTING TECHNIQUES: cut

BEST TIME OF DAY TO HARVEST: early morning

BEST WAY TO TRANSPORT FROM PICKING AREA: cloth bag

Notes on lei making

BEST FOR WHICH TYPE OF LEI: neck, head, wrist, ankle, horse

CLEANING OF PLANT MATERIALS: cold water soak, except flowers, which need no water

STORING RAW LEI MATERIALS: refrigerate at 40°F for up to 10 days (leaves), 2 days (flowers)

PREPARING FOR USE IN LEI: clip off wrinkled, limp, or poor quality areas before adding to lei; also remove calyx (green, leafy base) from bud being sewn

STORING A COMPLETED LEI BEFORE WEARING: soak leaves, drip dry, and refrigerate in plastic container; place flowers dry in sealed plastic container and refrigerate

PRESERVING A LEI FOR LONG-TERM STORAGE OR DISPLAY: air-dry leaves; flowers cannot be preserved

References and further reading

Bornhorst, Heidi L. 1996. *Growing Native Hawaiian Plants: A How-to Guide for the Gardener.* Honolulu: Bess Press.

Culliney, John L., and Bruce P. Koebele. 1999. *A Native Hawaiian Garden: How to Grow and Care for Island Plants.* Honolulu: University of Hawai'i Press.

Nagata, Kenneth M. 1992. *How to Plant a Native Hawaiian Garden.* Honolulu: State of Hawai'i, Office of Environmental Quality Control.

Rauch, Fred D., Heidi L. Bornhorst, and David L. Hensley. 1997. *Ma'o (Hawaiian Cotton).* University of Hawai'i, CTAHR, OF-13.

Wagner, Warren L., Derral R. Herbst, and S.H. Sohmer. 1990. *Manual of the Flowering Plants of Hawai'i.* 2 vols. Bishop Museum Special Publication 83. Honolulu: University of Hawai'i Press and Bishop Museum Press.

maile

OTHER COMMON NAMES: none

SCIENTIFIC NAME: *Alyxia oliviformis*

FAMILY: Apocynaceae (dogbane family)

NATURAL SETTING/LOCATION: endemic to Hawaiian Islands; found in most vegetation zones on all main islands except Niʻihau and Kahoʻolawe

CURRENT STATUS IN THE WILD IN HAWAIʻI: occasional to common

Growing your own

HANDLING CAUTIONS: milky, sticky sap may cause allergic reaction, stain clothes

PROPAGATION

FORM: fresh seeds; hardwood cuttings 3" long with at least one node

PREPLANTING TREATMENT: remove seeds from pulp, soak in water for 12 hours or refrigerate in water for 3 days; use medium rooting hormone on cuttings

PLANTING DEPTH: sow seeds ¼–½" deep in medium; insert base of cutting 1–2" into medium, keeping node beneath surface of medium

GERMINATION TIME: 1–3 months

CUTTING ROOTING TIME: 8 weeks

PREFERRED PRODUCTION CONDITIONS

GENERAL SOIL CHARACTERISTICS: well drained

SOIL PH: 6.5–7.5

LIGHT: shade

WATER: keep moist

TEMPERATURE: 40–90°F

ELEVATION: 10–6000'

SALT TOLERANCE: poor

WIND RESISTANCE: moderate

MANAGEMENT

FERTILIZER NEEDS: medium

RECOMMENDED SPACING: 2–3' apart

ADAPTATION TO GROWING IN CONTAINERS: yes, 5-gallon tubs or larger

PRUNING: not necessary

SPECIAL CULTURAL HINTS: may be cultivated on arbor, trellis, or other support; can grow in lowlands if care is taken to provide shade

SUGGESTED COMPANION PLANTINGS: tree for climbing

maile

Plant characteristics

HEIGHT: to 15'

SPREAD: 6–8'

GROWTH RATE: moderate

GROWTH HABIT: vine to shrub; extremely variable, depending on variety

FOLIAGE

TEXTURE: glossy

COLOR: dark green

SHAPE: variable, sword-shaped to oval

FRAGRANCE: yes

PESTS

COMMON DISEASES: fungal leaf spots, rust spots, root-knot nematodes, damping off (seedlings)

OTHER PESTS: ants, aphids, scales

Harvesting considerations

WHAT IS HARVESTED: leaves with pliable bark of young stems

HARVESTING TECHNIQUES: *'u'u*—strip the bark from the woody stem

BEST TIME OF DAY TO HARVEST: early morning

BEST WAY TO TRANSPORT FROM PICKING AREA: plastic bag

AVOID CONTACT WITH THESE PRODUCTS: smoke, car exhaust, ripening fruits, and wilting flowers

Notes on lei making

BEST FOR WHICH TYPE OF LEI: neck, head, wrist, ankle, horse

CLEANING OF PLANT MATERIALS: quick cold water dip

STORING RAW LEI MATERIALS: soak, drip dry, place leaves and skin of young stems in plastic container, refrigerate at 40°F for up to 14 days

PREPARING FOR USE IN LEI: if *hipu'u* (tying together in the knotted pattern), strip bark and leaves from woody stem close to tip, then tie

STORING A COMPLETED LEI BEFORE WEARING: mist lei, shake excess water off, then place in plastic bag or container and refrigerate

PRESERVING A LEI FOR LONG-TERM STORAGE OR DISPLAY: air-dry

References and further reading

Bornhorst, Heidi L. 1996. *Growing Native Hawaiian Plants: A How-to Guide for the Gardener*. Honolulu: Bess Press.

Culliney, John L., and Bruce P. Koebele. 1999. *A Native Hawaiian Garden: How to Grow and Care for Island Plants*. Honolulu: University of Hawai'i Press.

Hawai'i Plant Conservation Center. 1992. *Plant Information Sheets on Native Plants of Hawai'i*. Lawai, Hawai'i: National Tropical Botanical Garden.

Ide, Laurie S. 1998. *Hawaiian Lei Making: Step-by-Step Guide*. Honolulu: Mutual Publishing.

Tanabe, M. 1979. Ecology of Maile. University of Hawai'i, Dept. of Horticulture. *Horticulture Digest* 117:3–5.

Tanabe, M. 1980. Effect of Depulping and Growth Regulators on Seed Germination of *Alyxia olivaeformis*. *HortScience* 15(2): 199–200.

Wagner, Warren L., Derral R. Herbst, and S.H. Sohmer. 1990. *Manual of the Flowering Plants of Hawai'i*. 2 vols. Bishop Museum Special Publication 83. Honolulu: University of Hawai'i Press and Bishop Museum Press.

māmane

OTHER COMMON NAMES: mamani

SCIENTIFIC NAME: *Sophora chrysophylla*

FAMILY: Fabaceae (pea family)

NATURAL SETTING/LOCATION: endemic to Hawaiian Islands, scattered in dry shrublands and forests to mesic (medium-wet) forests; dominant element of vegetation in the high peaks of east Maui and Hawai'i; not found on Ni'ihau and Kaho'olawe; rare on O'ahu

CURRENT STATUS IN THE WILD IN HAWAI'I: rare to common

Growing your own

PROPAGATION

FORM: seeds

PREPLANTING TREATMENT: scarify seeds by scraping seedcoat or soak in water for 24 hours or until swelling occurs

PLANTING DEPTH: sow ¼–½" deep in medium

GERMINATION TIME: 2–14 weeks; if no preplanting treatment, can take 1–6 months

PREFERRED PRODUCTION CONDITIONS

GENERAL SOIL CHARACTERISTICS: well drained

SOIL PH: 6.0–6.5

LIGHT: full sun

WATER: keep dry

TEMPERATURE: 40–80°F

ELEVATION: 500–8000'

SALT TOLERANCE: poor

WIND RESISTANCE: good

MANAGEMENT

FERTILIZER NEEDS: medium

RECOMMENDED SPACING: 3–5' (shrubs), 10–15' (trees)

ADAPTATION TO GROWING IN CONTAINERS: not recommended

PRUNING: not necessary

SPECIAL CULTURAL HINTS: propagate from seeds collected at elevation similar to the one where plant materials will be grown; numerous varieties and subspecies have been proposed; because there are island-specific varieties, it would be prudent not to grow different island stock without consideration of potential genetic effects (e.g., inadvertently crossing Hawai'i stock with Maui stock)

SUGGESTED COMPANION PLANTINGS: low-growing plants, ground cover

māmane

Plant characteristics

HEIGHT: to 45'

SPREAD: 3–20'

GROWTH RATE: slow

GROWTH HABIT: shrub to medium tree, depending on seed source and growing conditions

FLOWERS

SIZE: ¼–1" long, ⅓–¾" wide

COLOR: yellow or pale yellow

SHAPE: pea flower shape in small clusters

FRAGRANCE: none

FLOWERS IN FIRST YEAR: no

FLOWERING PERIOD: spring, summer

TIME TO FLOWERING: 2–5 years

INDUCING AND MAINTAINING FLOWERING: not known

PESTS

COMMON DISEASES: none

OTHER PESTS: ants, spider mites, thrips, Chinese rose beetle

Harvesting considerations

WHAT IS HARVESTED: flowers with 1–2" of stem

HARVESTING TECHNIQUES: snap

BEST TIME OF DAY TO HARVEST: early morning

BEST WAY TO TRANSPORT FROM PICKING AREA: plastic container

The lei shown also contains yarrow and protea.

Notes on lei making

BEST FOR WHICH TYPE OF LEI: neck, head, wrist, ankle, horse

CLEANING OF PLANT MATERIALS: cold water soak

STORING RAW LEI MATERIALS: place stems in water after picking, then place in sealed plastic container and refrigerate at 40°F for up to 3 days

PREPARING FOR USE IN LEI: clip off wrinkled, limp, or poor quality areas before adding to lei

STORING A COMPLETED LEI BEFORE WEARING: optional to soak and drip dry before placing lei on damp newspaper or paper towel in a sealed plastic container and refrigerating

PRESERVING A LEI FOR LONG-TERM STORAGE OR DISPLAY: cannot be preserved

References and further reading

Culliney, John L., and Bruce P. Koebele. 1999. *A Native Hawaiian Garden: How to Grow and Care for Island Plants.* Honolulu: University of Hawai'i Press.

Degener, O. 1973. *Plants of Hawaii National Parks Illustrative of Plants and Customs of the South Seas.* Ann Arbor, Michigan: Braun-Brumfield, Inc.

Little, Elbert L., Jr., and Roger G. Skolmen. 1989. *Common Forest Trees of Hawai'i (Native and Introduced).* Agriculture Handbook No. 679. Washingtron, D.C.: U.S. Department of Agriculture, Forest Service.

Scowcroft, Paul G. 1978. *Germination of Sophora Chrysophylla Increased by Presowing Treatment.* Research Note PSW–327. Berkeley, California: Pacific Southwest Forest and Range Experiment Station, Forest Service, United States Department of Agriculture.

Wagner, Warren L., Derral R. Herbst, and S.H. Sohmer. 1990. *Manual of the Flowering Plants of Hawai'i.* 2 vols. Bishop Museum Special Publication 83. Honolulu: University of Hawai'i Press and Bishop Museum Press.

moa

OTHER COMMON NAMES: whisk fern

SCIENTIFIC NAME: *Psilotum nudum*

FAMILY: Psilotaceae (whisk fern family)

NATURAL SETTING/LOCATION: indigenous to Hawaiian Islands, found in moderately dry to wet environments in rock crevices, on trees, and on the ground

CURRENT STATUS IN THE WILD IN HAWAI'I: common

Growing your own

PROPAGATION

FORM: spores or divisions

PREPLANTING TREATMENT: sow spores as soon as they are ripe; to tell if they are ripe, place a frond in a paper bag and hang it for 24 hours; the spores that fall to the bottom of the bag are ready for sowing; keep moist or use vermiculite and peat covered with moist paper towel to germinate spores

PLANTING DEPTH: surface-sow spores on black cinder or *hāpu'u*. keep root crown of division just below soil level

SPORE GERMINATION TIME: 3–6 months

PREFERRED PRODUCTION CONDITIONS

GENERAL SOIL CHARACTERISTICS: well drained, moist, rocky soil, or on *hāpu'u* trunks

SOIL PH: 6.0–7.5

LIGHT: full sun to shade

WATER: keep moist

TEMPERATURE: 60–90°F

ELEVATION: 10–4000'

SALT TOLERANCE: poor

WIND RESISTANCE: good

MANAGEMENT

FERTILIZER NEEDS: light

RECOMMENDED SPACING: 6" apart

ADAPTATION TO GROWING IN CONTAINERS: yes, pots with (or without) other plants, *hāpu'u* trunks, or rocks

PRUNING: remove older, dead stems

SPECIAL CULTURAL HINTS: keep divisions in moist shade for first 2 weeks; greener and more lush in humid areas and at specific times of year

SUGGESTED COMPANION PLANTINGS: trees and *hāpu'u*

moa

The top lei shown also contains *palapalai*, dusty miller, and bougainvillea. The bottom lei shown also contains *palapalai*.

Plant characteristics

HEIGHT: to 24"

SPREAD: clumps up to 24"

GROWTH RATE: moderate

GROWTH HABIT: clusters of slender, erect, bright green stalks

FOLIAGE

(no leaves; "naked," bright green, branching stems)

TEXTURE: coarse

COLOR: green to yellow-orange

SHAPE: thin branches

FRAGRANCE: none

PESTS

COMMON DISEASES: none known

OTHER PESTS: none known

Harvesting considerations

WHAT IS HARVESTED: branches (stems)

HARVESTING TECHNIQUES: cut, don't pull

BEST TIME OF DAY TO HARVEST: early morning

BEST WAY TO TRANSPORT FROM PICKING AREA: plastic bag

Notes on lei making

BEST FOR WHICH TYPE OF LEI: neck, head, wrist, ankle, horse

VASE LIFE: 7–14 days

CLEANING OF PLANT MATERIALS: cold water soak

STORING RAW LEI MATERIALS: soak stems in water for 5 minutes, drip dry, wrap in damp paper towel and store in a sealed plastic container, refrigerate at 40°F for up to 30 days

PREPARING FOR USE IN LEI: clip off the wrinkled, limp, or poor quality areas before adding to lei

STORING A COMPLETED LEI BEFORE WEARING: soak lei in water for 5 minutes, drip dry, wrap in damp paper towel, store in a sealed plastic container, and refrigerate

PRESERVING A LEI FOR LONG-TERM STORAGE OR DISPLAY: air-dry

References and further reading

Neal, Marie C. 1965. *In Gardens of Hawaii*. Bernice P. Bishop Museum Special Publication 50. Honolulu: Bishop Museum Press.

Valier, Kathy. 1995. *Ferns of Hawaiʻi*. Honolulu: University of Hawaiʻi Press.

'ōhi'a lehua

OTHER COMMON NAMES: *lehua, 'ōhi'a*

SCIENTIFIC NAME: *Metrosideros polymorpha*

FAMILY: Myrtaceae (myrtle family)

NATURAL SETTING/LOCATION: endemic to Hawaiian Islands in a wide range of habitats: lava fields, dry to wet forests, and bogs; found on all islands except Ni'ihau and Kaho'olawe

CURRENT STATUS IN THE WILD IN HAWAI'I: common in the rainforest

CULTIVARS: many plant forms (poly-morphic); also, other species can be used, such as *M. tremaloides, M. macropus, M. rugosa*

Growing your own

PROPAGATION

FORM: seeds, cuttings, or air layering (varies in ability to be propagated by cuttings; some types are harder to root than others)

PREPLANTING TREATMENT: seeds will keep if refrigerated, but fresh ones are best; no seed treatment needed; use medium or strong rooting hormone on cuttings

PLANTING DEPTH: scatter seeds on surface and cover with ¼" of medium; insert base of cutting 1–2" into medium

GERMINATION TIME: 1 week to 3 months

CUTTING ROOTING TIME: 2–4 months, or 4–6 weeks with rooting hormone under mist); air layers take 3–7 months to root but using 3% IBA on girdled area wrapped with sphagnum moss will produce roots in about 2 months

PREFERRED PRODUCTION CONDITIONS

GENERAL SOIL CHARACTERISTICS: well drained

SOIL PH: 6.5–7.5 (slightly acid)

LIGHT: sunny location

WATER: keep moist but well drained; do not allow to completely dry out

TEMPERATURE: 40–90°F

ELEVATION: 100–7000'

SALT TOLERANCE: poor (slight tolerance for coastal varieties); plant pohutukawa in low-elevation, saline conditions

WIND RESISTANCE: good

MANAGEMENT

FERTILIZER NEEDS: medium

RECOMMENDED SPACING: depends on type, generally 5' apart or more

ADAPTATION TO GROWING IN CONTAINERS: yes, 2–3-gallon plastic tubs

PRUNING: prune to reduce size, induce lower branches, and stimulate vigorous new shoots; prune after flower-ing

SPECIAL CULTURAL HINTS: young seedlings are very sensitive to transplanting; keep root disturbance to a minimum; best germination is in 50% shade; plant in fields when 1½–2 years old; fuzzy-leaf variety resists Chinese rose beetle; plants grown from seed vary in leaf size and shape, flower

color, etc.; some growers plant seeds on *hāpu'u* log

SUGGESTED COMPANION PLANTINGS: low-growing plants such as *maile, palapalai,* ferns

'ōhi'a lehua

Plant characteristics

HEIGHT: 3–80'

SPREAD: 10–30'

GROWTH RATE: slow

GROWTH HABIT: low shrub to tall tree

FLOWERS

SIZE: 1–2" clusters

COLOR: red, yellow, salmon, pink

SHAPE: pom-pom

FRAGRANCE: none

FLOWERS IN FIRST YEAR: no

FLOWERING PERIOD: year-round

TIME TO FLOWERING: takes 4–5 years to flower from seed; flowers faster from air layer and cutting

FOLIAGE

TEXTURE: extremely variable, from smooth and waxy to fuzzy

COLOR: reddish-gray to shiny green, silvery underneath, dull green to bright green

SHAPE: simple, oval to ovate

FRAGRANCE: none

PESTS

COMMON DISEASES: root rot, collar rot, leafspots, nematodes, damping off (seedling)

OTHER PESTS: ants, aphids, mealybugs, scales, twig borer, two-spotted leafhopper

The lei shown also contains *'a'ali'i, moa, pūkiawe,* and *wāwae'iole.*

Harvesting considerations

WHAT IS HARVESTED: young leaves at tips (*liko*), flowers, buds, seed pods

HARVESTING TECHNIQUES: cut

BEST TIME OF DAY TO HARVEST: early morning

BEST WAY TO TRANSPORT FROM PICKING AREA: paper or cloth bag

Notes on lei making

BEST FOR WHICH TYPE OF LEI: neck, head, wrist, ankle, horse

VASE LIFE: 2 days for flowers; 14 days for leaves and seed pods

CLEANING OF PLANT MATERIALS: cold water soak

STORING RAW LEI MATERIALS: soak flowers for 5 minutes and place face up in paper box or sealed plastic container; refrigerate at 40°F for up to 7 days; green *liko* can be placed in plastic container or paper box; red *liko* needs to be in paper box; seed pod can be placed in plastic or paper container; refrigerate at 40°F for up to 14 days

PREPARING FOR USE IN LEI: clip off wrinkled, limp, or poor quality areas before adding to lei

STORING A COMPLETED LEI BEFORE WEARING: soak lei in water, drip dry, wrap in wet newspaper, place in paper box, and refrigerate

PRESERVING A LEI FOR LONG-TERM STORAGE OR DISPLAY: air-dry

References and further reading

Bornhorst, Heidi L. 1996. *Growing Native Hawaiian Plants: A How-to Guide for the Gardener.* Honolulu: Bess Press.

Degener, O. 1973. *Plants of Hawaii National Parks Illustrative of Plants and Customs of the South Seas.* Ann Arbor, Michigan: Braun-Brumfield, Inc.

Little, Elbert L., Jr., and Roger G. Skolmen. 1989. *Common Forest Trees of Hawai'i (Native and Introduced).* Agriculture Handbook No. 679. Washingtron, D.C.: U.S. Department of Agriculture, Forest Service.

Rauch, Fred D., and David Hensley. 1997. *Ohia lehua.* University of Hawai'i, CTAHR, OF-11.

Rauch, F.D., K. Ninno and J. McEwen. 1997. *Vegetative Propagation of Yellow Ohia Lehua.* University of Hawai'i, CTAHR, Horticulture Research Note HRN-3. <http://www2.ctahr.hawaii.edu/freepubs>.

Wagner, Warren L., Derral R. Herbst, and S.H. Sohmer. 1990. *Manual of the Flowering Plants of Hawai'i.* 2 vols. Bishop Museum Special Publication 83. Honolulu: University of Hawai'i Press and Bishop Museum Press.

pa'iniu

OTHER COMMON NAMES: astelia, *kaluaha*

SCIENTIFIC NAME: *Astelia menziesiana*

FAMILY: Liliaceae (lily family)

NATURAL SETTING/LOCATION: endemic to Hawaiian Islands in moist to wet forests and bogs on all main islands except Ni'ihau and Kaho'olawe; epiphytic or terrestrial

CURRENT STATUS IN THE WILD IN HAWAI'I: common (rare on O'ahu)

Growing your own

PROPAGATION

FORM: seeds, division

PREPLANTING TREATMENT: remove seeds from pulp, put in water that has been brought to a boil and removed from heat, let soak for about 24 hours

PLANTING DEPTH: sow seeds ¼" deep in medium; for divisions, keep root crown just below soil level

GERMINATION TIME: 3–5 weeks

PREFERRED PRODUCTION CONDITIONS

GENERAL SOIL CHARACTERISTICS: well drained, potting soil, orchid mix, or *hāpu'u*

SOIL PH: epiphytic; terrestrial forms grow in bog conditions; preferred soil pH is not known, but likely acidic

LIGHT: part to full shade

WATER: keep moist

TEMPERATURE: 40–50°F

ELEVATION: 2000–5000'

SALT TOLERANCE: poor

WIND RESISTANCE: poor

MANAGEMENT

FERTILIZER NEEDS: light

RECOMMENDED SPACING: 2–3' apart

ADAPTATION TO GROWING IN CONTAINERS: yes, 5-gallon tubs

PRUNING: not necessary

SPECIAL CULTURAL HINTS: treat like an epiphytic orchid or bromeliad; male and female flowers occur on separate plants

SUGGESTED COMPANION PLANTINGS: *hāpu'u*

pa'iniu

Plant characteristics

HEIGHT: to 36"

SPREAD: to 36"

GROWTH RATE: slow to moderate

GROWTH HABIT: herbaceous, succulent

FOLIAGE

TEXTURE: waxy on top, sometimes fuzzy underneath

COLOR: green on top, sometimes white, golden, or silver underneath

SHAPE: long and tapered

FRAGRANCE: none

PESTS

COMMON DISEASES: none known

OTHER PESTS: mealybugs, spider mites

Harvesting considerations

WHAT IS HARVESTED: leaves

HARVESTING TECHNIQUES: cut the bottom leaves and leave the top ones

BEST TIME OF DAY TO HARVEST: early morning

BEST WAY TO TRANSPORT FROM PICKING AREA: paper or cloth bag

The lei shown also contains *pūkiawe*, *'ōhi'a lehua*, *wāwae'iole*, and *palapalai*.

Notes on lei making

BEST FOR WHICH TYPE OF LEI: neck, head, wrist, ankle, horse

VASE LIFE: 7 days

CLEANING OF PLANT MATERIALS: cold water soak

STORING RAW LEI MATERIALS: refrigerate at 40°F for up to 14 days or longer

PREPARING FOR USE IN LEI: clip off wrinkled, limp, or poor quality areas before adding to lei

STORING A COMPLETED LEI BEFORE WEARING: soak lei in water for 5 minutes, drip dry, wrap in damp newspaper, place in any type of container, and refrigerate

PRESERVING A LEI FOR LONG-TERM STORAGE OR DISPLAY: air-dry

References and further reading

Bornhorst, Heidi L. 1998. "Hawai'i Gardens: *Pa'iniu* Grows Nicely in Home Gardens." *The Honolulu Advertiser*, Sunday, 31 May 1998, D3.

Stone, Charles P., and Linda W. Pratt. 1994. *Hawai'i's Plants and Animals: Biological Sketches of Hawaii Volcanoes National Park*. Honolulu: Hawaii Natural History Association and University of Hawaii Press.

Wagner, Warren L., Derral R. Herbst, and S.H. Sohmer. 1990. *Manual of the Flowering Plants of Hawai'i*. 2 vols. Bishop Museum Special Publication 83. Honolulu: University of Hawai'i Press and Bishop Museum Press.

Native and Canoe Plants

pala'ā

OTHER COMMON NAMES: lace fern, *palae, palapala'ā*

SCIENTIFIC NAME: *Sphenomeris chinensis*

FAMILY: Lindsaeaceae (lace fern family)

NATURAL SETTING/LOCATION: indigenous to tropics, subtropics, and Hawaiian Islands, where it is likely to be found in road cuts and clearings on all main islands

CURRENT STATUS IN THE WILD IN HAWAI'I: common

Growing your own

PROPAGATION

FORM: division

PREPLANTING TREATMENT: remove old leaves

PLANTING DEPTH: keep root crown just below soil level

PREFERRED PRODUCTION CONDITIONS

GENERAL SOIL CHARACTERISTICS: well drained

SOIL PH: 6.0–7.0

LIGHT: can be grown in sun, but prefers shady areas

WATER: keep moist, tolerates some drought

TEMPERATURE: 60–90°F

ELEVATION: 10–4000'

SALT TOLERANCE: poor

WIND RESISTANCE: poor

MANAGEMENT

FERTILIZER NEEDS: light

RECOMMENDED SPACING: 1–2' apart

ADAPTATION TO GROWING IN CONTAINERS: yes, 5-gallon tubs

PRUNING: remove dead fronds

SPECIAL CULTURAL HINTS: plant close together to keep weeds out

SUGGESTED COMPANION PLANTINGS: other forest plants that provide shade

pala'ā

Native and Canoe Plants

Plant characteristics

HEIGHT: 3–4'

SPREAD: 3–4'

GROWTH RATE: fast

GROWTH HABIT: fern, groundcover

FOLIAGE

TEXTURE: smooth

COLOR: green

SHAPE: pointed lacy fronds

FRAGRANCE: none

PESTS

COMMON DISEASES: none known

OTHER PESTS: caterpillars, scales

The lei shown also contains *'ōhi'a lehua*, *wāwae'iole*, and *kulu'ī*.

Harvesting considerations

WHAT IS HARVESTED: mature fronds (fully expanded)

HARVESTING TECHNIQUES: cut, don't pull

BEST TIME OF DAY TO HARVEST: early morning

BEST WAY TO TRANSPORT FROM PICKING AREA: paper or cloth bag

Notes on lei making

BEST FOR WHICH TYPE OF LEI: neck, head, wrist, ankle, horse

VASE LIFE: 5 days

CLEANING OF PLANT MATERIALS: cold water soak

STORING RAW LEI MATERIALS: place in sealed plastic container and refrigerate at 40°F for up to 30 days

PREPARING FOR USE IN LEI: clip off wrinkled, limp, or poor quality areas before adding to lei

STORING A COMPLETED LEI BEFORE WEARING: soak lei, drip dry, wrap in damp newspaper, place in sealed plastic container, and refrigerate

PRESERVING A LEI FOR LONG-TERM STORAGE OR DISPLAY: cannot be preserved

References and further reading

Bornhorst, Heidi L. 1996. *Growing Native Hawaiian Plants: A How-to Guide for the Gardener.* Honolulu: Bess Press.

Hoshizaki, Barbara J. 1976. *Fern Growers Manual.* New York: Alfred A. Knopf.

Neal, Marie C. 1965. *In Gardens of Hawaii.* Bernice P. Bishop Museum Special Publication 50. Honolulu: Bishop Museum Press.

Valier, Kathy. 1995. *Ferns of Hawai'i.* Honolulu: University of Hawai'i Press.

palapalai

OTHER COMMON NAMES: *palai*

SCIENTIFIC NAME: *Microlepia strigosa*

FAMILY: Dennstaedtiaceae
(dicksoniaceae family)

NATURAL SETTING/LOCATION: indigenous to
the Hawaiian Islands in the
understory of rain forests on all
main islands; also native to India,
Malaysia, Taiwan, Japan, and
South Pacific islands

CURRENT STATUS IN THE WILD IN HAWAIʻI:
common

Growing your own

PROPAGATION

FORM: division of clumps

PREPLANTING TREATMENT: remove old
foliage

PLANTING DEPTH: keep root crown just
below soil level

PREFERRED PRODUCTION CONDITIONS

GENERAL SOIL CHARACTERISTICS:
well drained

SOIL PH: 6.5–7.5

LIGHT: can be grown in sun, but
prefers shady areas

WATER: keep moist

TEMPERATURE: 40–90°F

ELEVATION: 750–6000'

SALT TOLERANCE: poor

WIND RESISTANCE: moderate

MANAGEMENT

FERTILIZER NEEDS: light

RECOMMENDED SPACING: 2–4' apart

ADAPTATION TO GROWING IN CONTAINERS:
yes, 5-gallon tubs

PRUNING: remove dead fronds

SPECIAL CULTURAL HINTS: plant close
together to keep weeds out; fronds
resemble those of the leatherleaf fern

SUGGESTED COMPANION PLANTINGS: other
forest plants that provide shade

palapalai

Plant characteristics

HEIGHT: 2–5'

SPREAD: fronds grow to almost 5' long

GROWTH RATE: moderate to fast

GROWTH HABIT: clumping, trunkless fern

FOLIAGE

TEXTURE: delicate hairy fronds

COLOR: light green to dark green, depending on maturity

SHAPE: pointed, lacy fronds

FRAGRANCE: none

PESTS

COMMON DISEASES: none known

OTHER PESTS: none known

Harvesting considerations

WHAT IS HARVESTED: fronds

HARVESTING TECHNIQUES: cut, don't pull the mature fronds

BEST TIME OF DAY TO HARVEST: early morning

BEST WAY TO TRANSPORT FROM PICKING AREA: paper or cloth bag

Notes on lei making

BEST FOR WHICH TYPE OF LEI: neck, head, wrist, ankle, horse

VASE LIFE: 5 days

CLEANING OF PLANT MATERIALS: cold water soak

STORING RAW LEI MATERIALS: soak for 5 minutes, drip dry; either place whole fronds between paper in sealed plastic container or break fronds down, wrap in newspaper, then place in sealed plastic container and refrigerate at 40°F for up to 30 days

PREPARING FOR USE IN LEI: clip off wrinkled, limp, or poor quality areas before adding to lei

STORING A COMPLETED LEI BEFORE WEARING: soak lei, drip dry, store in sheets of damp newspaper, place in sealed container, and refrigerate

PRESERVING A LEI FOR LONG-TERM STORAGE OR DISPLAY: cannot be preserved

References and further reading

Bornhorst, Heidi L. 1996. *Growing Native Hawaiian Plants: A How-to Guide for the Gardener.* Honolulu: Bess Press.

Hoshizaki, Barbara J. 1976. *Fern Growers Manual.* New York: Alfred A. Knopf.

Nagata, Kenneth M. 1992. *How to Plant a Native Hawaiian Garden.* Honolulu: State of Hawai'i, Office of Environmental Quality Control.

Neal, Marie C. 1965. *In Gardens of Hawaii.* Bernice P. Bishop Museum Special Publication 50. Honolulu: Bishop Museum Press.

Stone, Charles P., and Linda W. Pratt. 1994. *Hawai'i's Plants and Animals: Biological Sketches of Hawaii Volcanoes National Park.* Honolulu: Hawaii Natural History Association and University of Hawaii Press.

Valier, Kathy. 1995. *Ferns of Hawai'i.* Honolulu: University of Hawai'i Press.

pōhinahina

OTHER COMMON NAMES: beach vitex, *kolokolo kahakai*

SCIENTIFIC NAME: *Vitex rotundifolia*

FAMILY: Verbenaceae (verbena family)

NATURAL SETTING/LOCATION: indigenous throughout the Pacific including the Hawaiian Islands, where it occurs on sandy beaches, rocky shores, and dunes on all islands except Kahoʻolawe.

CURRENT STATUS IN THE WILD IN HAWAIʻI: common

Growing your own

PROPAGATION

FORM: seeds, cuttings (matured terminal or upper piece of leafy, matured stem)

PREPLANTING TREATMENT: scarify seeds by scraping the seedcoat; use medium rooting hormone on cutting

PLANTING DEPTH: sow seeds ½" deep in medium; insert base of cutting 1–2" into medium

GERMINATION TIME: 15–30 days if scarified, 36 months if not scarified

CUTTING ROOTING TIME: 3–4 weeks

PREFERRED PRODUCTION CONDITIONS

GENERAL SOIL CHARACTERISTICS: well drained, rocky, sandy

SOIL PH: 6.0–7.0

LIGHT: sunny location

WATER: keep dry

TEMPERATURE: 60–90°F

ELEVATION: 10–1000'

SALT TOLERANCE: good

WIND RESISTANCE: good

MANAGEMENT

FERTILIZER NEEDS: light

RECOMMENDED SPACING: 2–3' in row, 4–6' between rows

ADAPTATION TO GROWING IN CONTAINERS: yes, 8" pots to 5-gallon tubs, but planting in the ground is better

PRUNING: prune to manage size and shape and to stimulate compactness

SPECIAL CULTURAL HINTS: plant close together to keep weeds out; thins out during winter months; can get leggy with too much water and fertilizer and not enough sun

SUGGESTED COMPANION PLANTINGS: dry-area plants or coastal plants (*maʻo, ʻūlei, hinahina*)

pōhinahina

Plant characteristics

HEIGHT: 1–4'

SPREAD: 3–6'

GROWTH RATE: fast

GROWTH HABIT: low growing, mat-forming shrub

FLOWERS

SIZE: inflorescence 1–3" long, flower less than ½"

COLOR: bluish-purple

SHAPE: funnel-shaped flowers in spikes

FRAGRANCE: none

FLOWERS IN FIRST YEAR: yes, from cuttings

FLOWERING PERIOD: year-round

TIME TO FLOWERING: 1–2 years from seed, faster from cuttings

INDUCING AND MAINTAINING FLOWERING: flowering can occur year-round without special treatment and if not under stress

FOLIAGE

TEXTURE: downy, fuzzy

COLOR: pale green

SHAPE: oval

FRAGRANCE: spicy when crushed

PESTS

COMMON DISEASES: powdery mildew, leaf spots

OTHER PESTS: ants, mealybugs, scales, whiteflies

The lei shown also contains bougainvillea and *palapalai*.

Harvesting considerations

WHAT IS HARVESTED: branch tips with or without fruit and flowers

HARVESTING TECHNIQUES: cut stems

BEST TIME OF DAY TO HARVEST: early morning

BEST WAY TO TRANSPORT FROM PICKING AREA: paper or cloth bag

Notes on lei making

BEST FOR WHICH TYPE OF LEI: neck, head, wrist, ankle, horse

CLEANING OF PLANT MATERIALS: cold water soak

STORING RAW LEI MATERIALS: store in sealed plastic container and refrigerate at 40°F for up to 14 days

PREPARING FOR USE IN LEI: clip off wrinkled, limp, or poor quality areas before adding to lei

STORING A COMPLETED LEI BEFORE WEARING: soak lei, drip dry, place in sealed plastic container and refrigerate

PRESERVING A LEI FOR LONG-TERM STORAGE OR DISPLAY: air-dry (fruit and leaves only)

References and further reading

Bornhorst, H.L. and F.D. Rauch. 1994. *Native Hawaiian Plants for Landscaping, Conservation, and Reforestation.* University of Hawai'i, CTAHR, Research Extension Series 142.

Nagata, Kenneth M. 1992. *How to Plant a Native Hawaiian Garden.* Honolulu: State of Hawai'i, Office of Environmental Quality Control.

Wagner, Warren L., Derral R. Herbst, and S.H. Sohmer. 1990. *Manual of the Flowering Plants of Hawai'i.* 2 vols. Bishop Museum Special Publication 83. Honolulu: University of Hawai'i Press and Bishop Museum Press.

pūkiawe

OTHER COMMON NAMES: *maiele*

SCIENTIFIC NAME: *Styphelia tameiameiae*

FAMILY: Epacridaceae (epacris family)

NATURAL SETTING/LOCATION: indigenous to Hawaiian Islands; scattered dominant vegetation in windswept coasts, deserts, rain forests, frost-prone mountain slopes, and bogs on all main islands except Niʻihau and Kahoʻolawe.

CURRENT STATUS IN THE WILD IN HAWAIʻI: scattered to common

Growing your own

PROPAGATION

FORM: seeds; air layering

PRETREATMENT: soak seeds in vinegar for several hours followed by hot-water (120°F) soak for several hours

PLANTING DEPTH: on surface of medium

GERMINATION TIME: 1–2 months

AIR LAYERING ROOTING TIME: 6–12 months

PREFERRED PRODUCTION CONDITIONS

GENERAL SOIL CHARACTERISTICS: well drained

SOIL PH: 6.5–7.5

LIGHT: sunny location

WATER: keep moist

TEMPERATURE: 60–75°F

ELEVATION: 50–10,000'

SALT TOLERANCE: moderate (coastal types)

WIND RESISTANCE: good

MANAGEMENT

FERTILIZER NEEDS: light

RECOMMENDED SPACING: 3–4' apart

ADAPTATION TO GROWING IN CONTAINERS: yes, 1-gallon tub or larger

PRUNING: prune to maintain size and shape

SPECIAL CULTURAL HINTS: size, shape, and growing conditions depend on propagation source; water well in good drainage conditions

pūkiawe

Plant characteristics

HEIGHT: 2–12'

SPREAD: 3–6'

GROWTH RATE: slow to moderate

GROWTH HABIT: erect, spreading shrub

FRUIT (flowers inconspicuous)

SIZE: fruit ⅛–¼" wide

COLOR: dark red to pink, sometimes white

SHAPE: round

FRAGRANCE: none

FOLIAGE

TEXTURE: leathery

COLOR: green

SHAPE: small and variable

FRAGRANCE: none

PESTS

COMMON DISEASES: none known

OTHER PESTS: none known

Harvesting considerations

WHAT IS HARVESTED: branch tips, with or without fruit

HARVESTING TECHNIQUES: snap or cut tips

BEST TIME OF DAY TO HARVEST: early morning

BEST WAY TO TRANSPORT FROM PICKING AREA: paper or cloth bag

The lei shown also contains crown flower and dusty miller.

Notes on lei making

BEST FOR WHICH TYPE OF LEI: neck, head, wrist, ankle, horse

VASE LIFE: 5–7 days

CLEANING OF PLANT MATERIALS: cold water soak

STORING RAW LEI MATERIALS: soak in water for 5 minutes, wrap in damp newspaper, then place in plastic container and refrigerate at 40°F for up to 14 days

PREPARING FOR USE IN LEI: clip off wrinkled, limp, or poor quality areas before adding to lei; make sure leaves are removed from lower stem so that when you *wili* (twist) it, it doesn't jab you or the wearer

STORING A COMPLETED LEI BEFORE WEARING: soak lei, drip dry, wrap in damp newspaper, place in paper or plastic container and refrigerate

PRESERVING A LEI FOR LONG-TERM STORAGE OR DISPLAY: air-dry

References and further reading

Stone, Charles P., and Linda W. Pratt. 1994. *Hawai'i's Plants and Animals: Biological Sketches of Hawaii Volcanoes National Park.* Honolulu: Hawaii Natural History Association and University of Hawaii Press.

Wagner, Warren L., Derral R. Herbst, and S.H. Sohmer. 1990. *Manual of the Flowering Plants of Hawai'i.* 2 vols. Bishop Museum Special Publication 83. Honolulu: University of Hawai'i Press and Bishop Museum Press.

Native and Canoe Plants

ti

OTHER COMMON NAMES: *kī, laʻi*

SCIENTIFIC NAME: *Cordyline fruticosa*

FAMILY: Agavaceae (agave family)

NATURAL SETTING/LOCATION: Polynesian introduction; extensively cultivated and common in mesic (medium-wet) valleys and mesic forests on all Hawaiian Islands except Kahoʻolawe

CURRENT STATUS IN THE WILD IN HAWAIʻI: common

CULTIVARS: tremendous variation in color and form, such as variegated, red, orange, pink, yellow

Growing your own

PROPAGATION

FORM: cuttings preferred (large stem pieces may be used); air layering; seeds (growing from seeds results in great variation in plant size and leaf color and shape)

PREPLANTING TREATMENT: use medium rooting hormone on cuttings, or none

PLANTING DEPTH: sow seeds ¼" deep in medium; insert base of cutting 3–5" into medium

GERMINATION TIME: 2–6 weeks

CUTTING ROOTING TIME: 2–4 weeks

PREFERRED PRODUCTION CONDITIONS

GENERAL SOIL CHARACTERISTICS: will grow in just about any soil as long as pH and salt levels are not too high.

SOIL PH: 5.5–6.5

LIGHT: green ti can be grown in full sun to partial shade

WATER: irrigation required in dry areas

TEMPERATURE: 60–90°F

ELEVATION: 10–2000'

SALT TOLERANCE: poor

WIND RESISTANCE: requires windbreaks in windy areas to prevent shredding

MANAGEMENT

FERTILIZER NEEDS: heavy

RECOMMENDED SPACING: 18–24" in rows, 18–24" between rows, with a larger 36" aisle every 3–6 rows

ADAPTATION TO GROWING IN CONTAINERS: yes, large containers

PRUNING: prune to about 1' height when main stem grows to point where harvesting becomes difficult; leave 3 new shoots to grow, and remove all smaller shoots

SPECIAL CULTURAL HINTS: plants can be cut back and 2 or 3 new shoots per stem allowed to grow; best grown in drier climates with irrigation to avoid fungus and bacterial leaf spots; remove inflorescences as they emerge to direct energy toward new leaves; the common green ti rarely if ever produces seeds; leaves can be harvested in first year

SUGGESTED COMPANION PLANTINGS: tall plants for shade and windbreak

ti

Plant characteristics

HEIGHT: to 20'

SPREAD: 3–4'

GROWTH RATE: moderately fast

GROWTH HABIT: upright shrub

FOLIAGE

TEXTURE: smooth and glossy

COLOR: green most common; red, pink, and orange variants occur

SHAPE: long and narrow

FRAGRANCE: none

PESTS

COMMON DISEASES: *Cercospora* fungus, *Pseudomonas* bacteria, leaf spots

OTHER PESTS: caterpillars, mites, pigs, rodents, rose beetles, scales, slugs, snails, stem borers, thrips, two-spotted leafhopper

Harvesting considerations

WHAT IS HARVESTED: leaves

HARVESTING TECHNIQUES: pull or snap leaf off stem; at least 3 leaves should be left on plant to produce energy for further growth

BEST TIME OF DAY TO HARVEST: early morning

BEST WAY TO TRANSPORT FROM PICKING AREA: large plastic bag

The lei shown also contains Geraldton waxflower.

Notes on lei making

BEST FOR WHICH TYPE OF LEI: neck, head, wrist, ankle, horse

VASE LIFE: 14 days

CLEANING OF PLANT MATERIALS: hand-wash under cold, running water; soapy water may be needed

STORING RAW LEI MATERIALS: fresh leaves can be stored in a plastic container with water and refrigerated at 40°F for 30 days or frozen for much longer

PREPARING FOR USE IN LEI: if traditional ti lei, then clean, tie, and strip leaves; if done in *wili* (twisting) or *hilo* (braiding) pattern, you need to freeze, boil, microwave, iron, or *pūlehu* the leaf to soften it

STORING A COMPLETED LEI BEFORE WEARING: if traditional ti lei, place in sealed container and refrigerate; if *wili* or *hilo* pattern, wipe down with cloth, wrap in dry newspaper, and store in freezer

PRESERVING A LEI FOR LONG-TERM STORAGE OR DISPLAY: air-dry or freeze

References and further reading

Brown, Frank. 1994. *The Cordyline: King of Tropical Foliage*. Valkaria, Florida: Valkaria Tropical Garden.

Ide, Laurie S. 1998. *Hawaiian Lei Making: Step-by-Step Guide*. Honolulu: Mutual Publishing.

Rauch, Fred D. 1996. *Tropical Landscape Plants*. 3rd ed. Battle Ground, Washington: Hawaii Floriculture.

Wagner, Warren L., Derral R. Herbst, and S.H. Sohmer. 1990. *Manual of the Flowering Plants of Hawai'i*. 2 vols. Bishop Museum Special Publication 83. Honolulu: University of Hawai'i Press and Bishop Museum Press.

Warren, William. 1997. *Tropical Plants for Home and Garden*. London: Thames and Hudson.

Watson D.P., and W.J. Yee. 1973. *Hawai'i Ti*. University of Hawai'i, Cooperative Extension Service Circular 481.

'ūlei

OTHER COMMON NAMES: *u'ūlei*

SCIENTIFIC NAME: *Osteomeles anthyllidifolia*

FAMILY: Rosaceae (rose family)

NATURAL SETTING/LOCATION: indigenous to Hawaiian Islands in a wide variety of habitats such as coastal cliffs, lava fields, dry shrublands, and semi-dry forests on all main islands except Ni'ihau and Kaho'olawe; also occurs in the Cook Islands and Tonga

CURRENT STATUS IN THE WILD IN HAWAI'I: scattered to locally common

Growing your own

PROPAGATION

FORM: cuttings 3–6" long; seeds (plants from seed will have varying amounts of flowers and fruits)

PREPLANTING TREATMENT: soak seeds in water for 48 hours; use strong rooting hormone on cuttings; mist is helpful

PLANTING DEPTH: sow seeds ¼" deep in medium; insert base of cutting 1–2" into medium

GERMINATION TIME: 1–3 months

CUTTING ROOTING TIME: 1–3 months

PREFERRED PRODUCTION CONDITIONS

GENERAL SOIL CHARACTERISTICS: well drained

SOIL PH: 5.5–6.5

LIGHT: sunny location

WATER: keep moist; tolerates drought once established

TEMPERATURE: 40–90°F

ELEVATION: 10–7600'

SALT TOLERANCE: moderate (coastal varieties)

WIND RESISTANCE: good

MANAGEMENT

FERTILIZER NEEDS: light

RECOMMENDED SPACING: 3–5' apart in rows

ADAPTATION TO GROWING IN CONTAINERS: 2-gallon tubs or larger, but planting in the ground is better

PRUNING: prune to reduce size, maintain shape, and to keep full and bushy; avoid cutting old growth

SPECIAL CULTURAL HINTS: provide room to spread; seed-produced plants result in variable growth forms

'ūlei

Plant characteristics

HEIGHT: 1–15'

SPREAD: 5–15'

GROWTH RATE: moderate

GROWTH HABIT: prostrate to slightly upright, spreading shrub

FLOWERS

SIZE: ½"

COLOR: white

SHAPE: round

FRAGRANCE: yes

FLOWERS IN FIRST YEAR: no

FLOWERING PERIOD: winter through spring

TIME TO FLOWERING: typically 1 year from cutting and 2–3 years from seed

INDUCING AND MAINTAINING FLOWERING: can be maintained under good light conditions; under shaded conditions, flowering is sparse to non-existent; prune for new growth on which flowers are borne

FOLIAGE

TEXTURE: leathery leaflets, shiny, smooth, fine

COLOR: green

SHAPE: divided into leaflets

FRAGRANCE: none

PESTS

COMMON DISEASES: none known

OTHER PESTS: ants, aphids, mealybugs, scales, thrips, twig borer

The lei shown also contains *'ākia, 'a'ali'i, pūkiawe*, and *'ōhi'a lehua*.

Harvesting considerations

WHAT IS HARVESTED: fruit, flowers, leaves

HARVESTING TECHNIQUES: break or cut

BEST TIME OF DAY TO HARVEST: early morning

BEST WAY TO TRANSPORT FROM PICKING AREA: paper or cloth bag

Notes on lei making

BEST FOR WHICH TYPE OF LEI: neck, head, wrist, ankle, horse

CLEANING OF PLANT MATERIALS: cold water soak

STORING RAW LEI MATERIALS: soak in water for 5 minutes, wrap flowers in paper towel and place in plastic container, wrap leaves and fruit in damp newspaper and place in plastic container, refrigerate at 40°F for up to 14 days

PREPARING FOR USE IN LEI: clip off wrinkled, limp, or poor quality areas before adding to lei

STORING A COMPLETED LEI BEFORE WEARING: soak lei, drip dry, wrap in damp newspaper, place in plastic container and refrigerate

PRESERVING A LEI FOR LONG-TERM STORAGE OR DISPLAY: air-dry leaves only

References and further reading

Bornhorst, Heidi L. 1996. *Growing Native Hawaiian Plants. A How-to Guide for the Gardener.* Honolulu: Bess Press.

Hawai'i Plant Conservation Center. 1992. *Plant Information Sheets on Native Plants of Hawai'i.* Lawai, Hawai'i: National Tropical Botanical Garden.

Nagata, Kenneth M. 1992. *How to Plant a Native Hawaiian Garden.* Honolulu: State of Hawai'i, Office of Environmental Quality Control.

Wagner, Warren L., Darrel R. Herbst, and S.H. Sohmer. 1990. *Manual of the Flowering Plants of Hawai'i.* 2 vols, Bishop Museum Special Publication 83. Honolulu: University of Hawai'i Press and Bishop Museum Press.

wiliwili

OTHER COMMON NAMES: coral tree, Hawaiian erythrina

SCIENTIFIC NAME: *Erythrina sandwicensis*

FAMILY: Fabaceae (pea family)

NATURAL SETTING/LOCATION: endemic to the Hawaiian Islands; found in arid lowlands and dry forests on leeward slopes of all main islands including Kahoʻolawe and Niʻihau

CURRENT STATUS IN THE WILD IN HAWAIʻI: locally common

Growing your own

HANDLING CAUTIONS: thorns on branches and trunks, but sometimes thornless; seeds reported to be poisonous

PROPAGATION

FORM: seeds; cuttings 2–4' long

PREPLANTING TREATMENT: put seeds in water that has been brought to a boil and removed from heat, let soak for 24 hours, discard floating, nonviable seeds; or, scarify seeds by scratching seedcoat

PLANTING DEPTH: sow seeds ½" deep in well drained medium, place in full sun; amount of cutting inserted into medium varies with its length

GERMINATION TIME: 7 days

CUTTING ROOTING TIME: 1 month

PREFERRED PRODUCTION CONDITIONS

GENERAL SOIL CHARACTERISTICS: well drained

SOIL PH: 5.5–7.5

LIGHT: sunny location

WATER: drought tolerant; deep and infrequent watering

TEMPERATURE: 50–90°F

ELEVATION: 10–1800'

SALT TOLERANCE: good

WIND RESISTANCE: moderate

MANAGEMENT

FERTILIZER NEEDS: medium

RECOMMENDED SPACING: 20' apart

ADAPTATION TO GROWING IN CONTAINERS: not recommended

PRUNING: prune when young to manage size and shape and direct growth

SPECIAL CULTURAL HINTS: give plenty of room, keep out of high-traffic areas, and keep dry; leaf drop usually coincides with flowering

SUGGESTED COMPANION PLANTINGS: low-growing, drought tolerant plants

wiliwili

Plant characteristics

HEIGHT: 18–50'

SPREAD: 25–30'

GROWTH RATE: generally fast; rapid in winter, slow in summer after leaves fall

GROWTH HABIT: tree

FLOWERS

SIZE: 1½"

COLOR: red, orange, white, pale green, pale yellow

SHAPE: beak-like in clusters

FRAGRANCE: none

FLOWERS IN FIRST YEAR: no

FLOWERING PERIOD: summer, right after leaves fall

TIME TO FLOWERING: more than 5 years from seeds; around 4 years from cuttings

INDUCING AND MAINTAINING FLOWERING: normally only flowers during the summer

FOLIAGE

TEXTURE: slightly hairy on underside

COLOR: green

SHAPE: compound leaf with large, triangular leaflets

FRAGRANCE: none

PESTS

COMMON DISEASES: powdery mildew, root-knot nematodes

OTHER PESTS: ants, aphids, Chinese rose beetle, leaf-eating caterpillars, mealybugs, spider mites, scales, seed borers, stinkbug, twig borer

The lei shown also contains globe amaranth, *'ōhi'a lehua,* and bougainvillea.

Harvesting considerations

WHAT IS HARVESTED: flowers with 1–2" stem (seeds are not discussed here)

HARVESTING TECHNIQUES: cut or snap

BEST TIME OF DAY TO HARVEST: early morning

BEST WAY TO TRANSPORT FROM PICKING AREA: paper bag

Notes on lei making

BEST FOR WHICH TYPE OF LEI: neck

CLEANING OF PLANT MATERIALS: no water

STORING RAW LEI MATERIALS: place in paper box and refrigerate at 40°F for up to 3 days; no water

PREPARING FOR USE IN LEI: clip stem off, then sew

STORING A COMPLETED LEI BEFORE WEARING: store lei in paper box without refrigeration or water

PRESERVING A LEI FOR LONG-TERM STORAGE OR DISPLAY: cannot be preserved

References and further reading

Bornhorst, H.L., and F.D. Rauch. 1994. *Native Hawaiian Plants for Landscaping, Conservation, and Reforestation.* University of Hawai'i, CTAHR, Research Extension Series 142.

Culliney, John L., and Bruce P. Koebele. 1999. *A Native Hawaiian Garden: How to Grow and Care for Island Plants.* Honolulu: University of Hawai'i Press.

Nagata, Kenneth M. 1992. *How to Plant a Native Hawaiian Garden.* Honolulu: State of Hawai'i, Office of Environmental Quality Control.

Rauch, Fred D., and David Hensley. 1997. *Wiliwili.* University of Hawai'i, CTAHR, OF-10. <http://www2.ctahr.hawaii.edu/freepubs>.

Stone, Charles P., and Linda W. Pratt. 1994. *Hawai'i's Plants and Animals: Biological Sketches of Hawaii Volcanoes National Park.* Honolulu: Hawaii Natural History Association and University of Hawaii Press.

Wagner, Warren L., Derral R. Herbst, and S.H. Sohmer. 1990. *Manual of the Flowering Plants of Hawai'i.* 2 vols. Bishop Museum Special Publication 83. Honolulu: University of Hawai'i Press and Bishop Museum Press.

agapanthus

OTHER COMMON NAMES: African lily, blue lily, lily of the Nile

SCIENTIFIC NAME: *Agapanthus africanus*

FAMILY: Liliaceae (lily family)

NATURAL SETTING/LOCATION: native to South Africa

CURRENT STATUS IN THE WILD IN HAWAI'I: introduced garden plant

CULTIVARS: 'Albus', 'Flore Pleno'

Growing your own

PROPAGATION

FORM: division (easiest and fastest; use 6" clumps); seeds (seedlings take longer to flower than plants from divisions)

PREPLANTING TREATMENT: soak seeds in water for 24 hours

PLANTING DEPTH: sow seeds ¼" deep in medium; keep root crown just below soil level for divisions

GERMINATION TIME: slow and erratic

PREFERRED PRODUCTION CONDITIONS

GENERAL SOIL CHARACTERISTICS: well drained, moisture-retentive

SOIL PH: 5.0–6.5

LIGHT: full sun to partial shade

WATER: moderate; tolerates drought once established

TEMPERATURE: tolerates temperatures down to 25°F, but prefers temperatures above 50°F

ELEVATION: 10–4500'

SALT TOLERANCE: moderate

WIND RESISTANCE: moderate

MANAGEMENT

FERTILIZER NEEDS: medium

RECOMMENDED SPACING: 12–18" apart

ADAPTATION TO GROWING IN CONTAINERS: yes, 12" pots or larger (prefers crowded conditions)

SPECIAL CULTURAL HINTS: divide every 5–6 years

agapanthus

Plant characteristics

HEIGHT: foliage 1½–2' tall; flower stalks 2–5' tall; dwarf cultivars are available

SPREAD: 2'

GROWTH RATE: moderate

GROWTH HABIT: clumps of arching, evergreen leaves

FLOWERS

SIZE: 1½–3"

COLOR: dark blue to pale blue to white

SHAPE: tubular

FRAGRANCE: none

FLOWERS IN FIRST YEAR: yes, if propagated from large divisions

FLOWERING PERIOD: summer

TIME TO FLOWERING: 2–3 years from seed, less if from division

INDUCING AND MAINTAINING FLOWERING: not known

PESTS

COMMON DISEASES: none serious

OTHER PESTS: slugs, snails

Harvesting considerations

WHAT IS HARVESTED: flowers, buds with 1–2" stem

HARVESTING TECHNIQUES: cut, don't pull

BEST TIME OF DAY TO HARVEST: early morning

BEST WAY TO TRANSPORT FROM PICKING AREA: paper or cloth bag

AVOID CONTACT WITH THESE PRODUCTS: smoke, car exhaust, ripening fruits, and wilting flowers

Notes on lei making

BEST FOR WHICH TYPE OF LEI: neck, head, wrist, ankle

VASE LIFE: to 7 days

CLEANING OF PLANT MATERIALS: place stems in water

STORING RAW LEI MATERIALS: refrigerate at 40°F for up to 7 days

PREPARING FOR USE IN LEI: if sewing, cut flower with ⅛" of stem

STORING A COMPLETED LEI BEFORE WEARING: mist lei, shake off excess water, place in sealed plastic container and refrigerate

PRESERVING A LEI FOR LONG-TERM STORAGE OR DISPLAY: cannot be preserved

References and further reading

Ide, Laurie S. 1998. *Hawaiian Lei Making: Step-by-Step Guide*. Honolulu: Mutual Publishing.

Joffe, Pitta. 1993. *The Gardener's Guide to South African Plants*. Cape Town, South Africa: Tafelberg Publishers Ltd.

Nowack, Joanna and Ryszard M. Rudnicki. 1990. *Postharvest Handling and Storage of Cut Flowers, Florist Greens, and Potted Plants*. Portland, Oregon: Timber Press.

Still, Steven M. 1994. *Manual of Herbaceous Ornamental Plants*. Champaign, Illinois: Stipes Publishing Co.

Introduced Perennials

akulikuli-lei

OTHER COMMON NAMES: *akulikuli*, ice plant, noon flower

SCIENTIFIC NAME: *Lampranthus glomeratus* (magenta), *Lampranthus* sp.

FAMILY: Aizoaceae (fig-marigold family)

NATURAL SETTING/LOCATION: native to coasts of South Africa along the Sahara

CURRENT STATUS IN THE WILD IN HAWAIʻI: not found

Growing your own

PROPAGATION

FORM: cuttings from stems with spent flowers

PREPLANTING TREATMENT: allow cut end to air-dry 1–2 days, treat with mild rooting hormone

PLANTING DEPTH: insert base of cutting 1–1½" into medium

CUTTING ROOTING TIME: 1 month

PREFERRED PRODUCTION CONDITIONS

GENERAL SOIL CHARACTERISTICS: well drained

SOIL PH: 5.5–6.5

LIGHT: full sun

WATER: sparingly; tolerates drought

TEMPERATURE: 40–70°F

ELEVATION: common magenta form 300–3200', orange form 3000–4000'

SALT TOLERANCE: good

WIND RESISTANCE: good

MANAGEMENT

FERTILIZER NEEDS: medium; apply after flowering and in late summer

RECOMMENDED SPACING: 18–24" apart

ADAPTATION TO GROWING IN CONTAINERS: not recommended

PRUNING: not necessary

SPECIAL CULTURAL HINTS: likes hot days and cold nights (Kula, Waimea climates are ideal); do not overwater

akulikuli-lei

Plant characteristics

HEIGHT: to 18"

SPREAD: to 36"

GROWTH RATE: moderate

GROWTH HABIT: low groundcover

FLOWERS

SIZE: 1½–2½"

COLOR: magenta, white, orange to brownish orange

SHAPE: daisy-like

FRAGRANCE: very light

FLOWERS IN FIRST YEAR: yes

FLOWERING PERIOD: depends on transplanting time

TIME TO FLOWERING: cuttings flower in less than 9 months

INDUCING AND MAINTAINING FLOWERING: if attempting to produce flowers for graduation time (May–June), transplant or make cuttings for planting in August through October (depending on elevation); flowers will emerge starting in early May; natural flowering will be later by 1 month

PESTS

COMMON DISEASES: nematodes, root rot, southern blight

OTHER PESTS: scales

The lei shown also contains cymbidium orchid and anthurium.

Harvesting considerations

WHAT IS HARVESTED: flower buds with 1–2" stem

HARVESTING TECHNIQUES: cut or break by hand

BEST TIME OF DAY TO HARVEST: early morning before flowers open

BEST WAY TO TRANSPORT FROM PICKING AREA: metal can

AVOID CONTACT WITH THESE PRODUCTS: smoke, car exhaust, ripening fruits, and wilting flowers.

Notes on lei making

BEST FOR WHICH TYPE OF LEI: neck, head, wrist, ankle, horse

CLEANING OF PLANT MATERIALS: no water

STORING RAW LEI MATERIALS: store in paper box and refrigerate at 40°F for up to 10 days

PREPARING FOR USE IN LEI: clip stems at different sizes, then sew; for *poepoe* (circular) style, sew closed flowers—open flowers not usually used; no water

STORING A COMPLETED LEI BEFORE WEARING: place lei in paper box and refrigerate; no water

PRESERVING A LEI FOR LONG-TERM STORAGE OR DISPLAY: cannot be preserved

References and further reading

Ide, Laurie S. 1998. *Hawaiian Lei Making: Step-by-Step Guide*. Honolulu: Mutual Publishing.

Joffe, Pitta. 1993. *The Gardener's Guide to South African Plants*. Cape Town, South Africa: Tafelberg Publishers Ltd.

Mathias, Mildred E. 1973. *Color for the Landscape: Flowering Plants for Subtropical Climates*. Los Angeles: Los Angeles Beautiful, Inc.

Introduced Perennials

asparagus fern

OTHER COMMON NAMES: asparagus

SCIENTIFIC NAME: *Asparagus setaceus* var. *plumosus*; *Asparagus densiflorus* var. *sprengeri, myersii*

FAMILY: Liliaceae (lily family)

NATURAL SETTING/LOCATION: southern and eastern Africa

CURRENT STATUS IN THE WILD IN HAWAI'I: not found

CULTIVARS: *A. densiflorus* var. *sprengeri* is light yellow-green, coarse, and has recurving spines; *A. densiflorus* var. *myersii* has elongated, foxtail-like shoots; *A. setaceous* var. *plumosus* has dark green, finely divided branches and looks fern-like

Growing your own

HANDLING CAUTIONS: some have thorns

PROPAGATION

FORM: seeds; division

PREPLANTING TREATMENT: remove seeds from fleshy pulp, plant fresh, germinate at 85/70°F (day/night)

PLANTING DEPTH: sow seeds on surface of medium or slightly below (¼"); keep division root crown just below soil level

GERMINATION TIME: 60–90 days

PREFERRED PRODUCTION CONDITIONS

GENERAL SOIL CHARACTERISTICS: well drained, light, sandy; in pots, 1:1 peat:perlite

SOIL pH: 6.0–7.0

LIGHT: full sun to partial shade (best quality with up to 50% shade)

WATER: high quality best, though tolerant of slightly brackish water. irrigate deeply about once a week—more frequently in light soils during dry weather.

TEMPERATURE: 70–80°F (day), 60–70°F (night)

ELEVATION: 10–1000'

SALT TOLERANCE: avoid direct salt spray; tolerates slightly brackish water

WIND RESISTANCE: tolerant, but *S. setaceus* varieties develop brown leaf tips when dehydrated by wind

MANAGEMENT

FERTILIZER NEEDS: medium

RECOMMENDED SPACING: *A. densiflorus*: 3' apart; *A. setaceus*: 1–2' apart

ADAPTATION TO GROWING IN CONTAINERS: yes, pots or planter boxes, container size 8" or larger and 8–12" deep; plants can split plastic and cement containers as they grow

PRUNING: harvest recently matured shoots twice a week; old shoots lose their leaves quickly after harvest, and young shoots wilt; experience will determine the best stage to cut; allow at least 6–8 developing shoots per plant to remain

SPECIAL CULTURAL HINTS: may become weedy if left unchecked

SUGGESTED COMPANION PLANTINGS: could be used as an underplanting or border plant in landscape; *sprengeri* and *myersii* varieties are useful accent plants in the landscape

asparagus fern

Plant characteristics

HEIGHT: *A. setaceus* to 8–10', *A. densiflorus* to 36"

SPREAD: *A. setaceus* to 6–8', *A. densiflorus* to 5–6'

GROWTH RATE: fast

GROWTH HABIT: erect, climbing, or trailing woody herb

FOLIAGE

TEXTURE: fine

COLOR: green

SHAPE: needle-like

FRAGRANCE: none

PESTS

COMMON DISEASES: leaf spot and root rot

OTHER PESTS: mites, scales, thrips

Harvesting considerations

WHAT IS HARVESTED: mature stems

HARVESTING TECHNIQUES: break or cut; leave 6–8 shoots per plant

BEST TIME OF DAY TO HARVEST: early morning

BEST WAY TO TRANSPORT FROM PICKING AREA: paper or cloth bag

The lei shown also contains *pakalana*, globe amaranth, plumeria, bougainvillea, and Spanish moss.

Notes on lei making

BEST FOR WHICH TYPE OF LEI: neck, head, wrist, ankle, horse

VASE LIFE: 16 days, depending on cultivar

CLEANING OF PLANT MATERIALS: cold water soak

STORING RAW LEI MATERIALS: place stems in water immediately after harvesting, refrigerate at 45°F for up to 10 days

PREPARING FOR USE IN LEI: clip off wrinkled, limp, or poor quality areas before adding to lei; stem length should be 3–4"

STORING A COMPLETED LEI BEFORE WEARING: soak lei, drip dry, wrap in damp newspaper, place in sealed plastic bag or container, and refrigerate

PRESERVING A LEI FOR LONG-TERM STORAGE OR DISPLAY: cannot be preserved

References and further reading

Bredmose, N. 1976. Blueprint Cropping of Asparagus Fern. *Scientia Horticulturae* 4:201–210.

Clay, Horace F., and James C. Hubbard. 1977. *The Hawai'i Garden: Tropical Exotics*. Honolulu: University of Hawai'i Press.

Introduced Perennials

aster

OTHER COMMON NAMES: koniaka, Michaelmas daisy, New York aster (*Aster novi-belgii*)

SCIENTIFIC NAME: *Aster novi-belgii* and *A. ericoides*

FAMILY: Asteraceae (formerly Compositae), (aster family)

NATURAL SETTING/LOCATION: North America

CURRENT STATUS IN THE WILD IN HAWAI'I: not found

CULTIVARS: *A. novi-belgii*: 'Alert', 'Bonningale White', 'Crimson Brocade', 'Eventide'; *A. ericoides*: 'Monte Casino', 'Pink Casino'

Growing your own

PROPAGATION

FORM: division or cuttings (most growers purchase rooted cuttings from plant propagators)

PLANTING DEPTH: insert base of cutting 1–2" into medium, use mild rooting hormone; keep division root crown just below soil level

PREFERRED PRODUCTION CONDITIONS

GENERAL SOIL CHARACTERISTICS: adapted to most soils

SOIL PH: 5.5–7.0

LIGHT: full sun to light shade

WATER: moist

TEMPERATURE: 68–70°F

MANAGEMENT

FERTILIZER NEEDS: medium; do not fertilize once flowers begin to open

RECOMMENDED SPACING: 12–18"

ADAPTATION TO GROWING IN CONTAINERS: yes, 1–2-gallon pots

PRUNING: remove dead and old flowers to promote development of new ones

SPECIAL CULTURAL HINTS: plants spread through underground rhizomes; often self-sown; does not reproduce true from seed

aster

Plant characteristics

HEIGHT: 1–3'

SPREAD: 12"

GROWTH RATE: fast

GROWTH HABIT: short shrub

FLOWERS

SIZE: 12"

COLOR: red, pink, purple, white, and mixtures

SHAPE: round, daisy-like

FRAGRANCE: none

TIME TO FLOWERING: 16–18 weeks

INDUCING AND MAINTAINING FLOWERING: requires short days (less than 12 hours) for consistent and abundant flowering

PESTS

COMMON DISEASES: *Botrytis*, leaf spots, powdery and downy mildew, *Rhizoctonia* foliage blight

OTHER PESTS: aphids, mites, thrips, and whiteflies

Harvesting considerations

WHAT IS HARVESTED: flowers and buds

HARVESTING TECHNIQUES: cut

BEST TIME OF DAY TO HARVEST: early morning

BEST WAY TO TRANSPORT FROM PICKING AREA: cooler or plastic container with water

AVOID CONTACT WITH THESE PRODUCTS: smoke, car exhaust, ripening fruits, and wilting flowers

The lei shown also contains bleeding heart, bougainvillea, and globe amaranth.

Notes on lei making

BEST FOR WHICH TYPE OF LEI: neck, head, wrist, ankle, horse

VASE LIFE: 5–7 days

CLEANING OF PLANT MATERIALS: cold water soak for 2 minutes to get dust off; foliage wilts quickly so should be removed

STORING RAW LEI MATERIALS: store in plastic container with water and refrigerate at 35–40°F for up to 7 days

PREPARING FOR USE IN LEI: clip the wrinkled, limp, or poor quality areas before adding to lei

STORING A COMPLETED LEI BEFORE WEARING: sprinkle with water, drip dry, wrap in newspaper, and place in plastic container

PRESERVING A LEI FOR LONG-TERM STORAGE OR DISPLAY: cannot be preserved

References and further reading

Faber, Willie, and Jeff McGrew. 1998. *The Ball Redbook*. 16th ed., p. 372–385. Batavia, Illinois: Ball Publishing.

Hessayon, D.G. 1995. *The Flower Expert*. London: Transworld Publishers.

Nau, Jim. 1993. *Ball Culture Guide: The Encyclopedia of Seed Germination*. 2nd ed. Batavia, Illinois: Ball Publishing.

Sascalis, John N. 1993. *Cut Flowers Prolonging Freshness*. Batavia, Illinois: Ball Publishing.

Introduced Perennials

baby's breath

SCIENTIFIC NAME: *Gypsophila paniculata*

FAMILY: Caryophyllaceae (pink family)

NATURAL SETTING/LOCATION: native to central Asia, central and eastern Europe

CURRENT STATUS IN THE WILD IN HAWAI'I: not found

CULTIVARS: 'Bristol Fairy', 'Double Snowflake', 'Pink Fairy', 'Red Sea', 'Klamingo'

Growing your own

PROPAGATION

FORM: cuttings; seeds of named cultivars

PREPLANTING TREATMENT: none

PLANTING DEPTH: sow seeds on surface or slightly below (⅛"); use medium rooting hormone on cutting and insert base 1–2" into medium

GERMINATION TIME: 5–10 days

CUTTING ROOTING TIME: 10–14 days during summer

PREFERRED PRODUCTION CONDITIONS

GENERAL SOIL CHARACTERISTICS: well drained; in fields, loam to sandy soils; in pots, 1:1 peat:perlite

SOIL PH: 7.0

LIGHT: full sun, long daylength

WATER: keep moist

TEMPERATURE: requires 55°F nights followed by long days (14–16 hours); preferred daytime temperature range is 60–70°F

ELEVATION: 500–3500'

SALT TOLERANCE: poor

WIND RESISTANCE: poor

MANAGEMENT

FERTILIZER NEEDS: medium; amend field soils with Ca and Mg if analysis is low

RECOMMENDED SPACING: 18–24" apart

ADAPTATION TO GROWING IN CONTAINERS: yes, 3-gallon tubs, but planting in the ground is better

PRUNING: remove old flower stalks

SPECIAL CULTURAL HINTS: most cultivars propagated vegetatively due to variability of seedlings; seed is used for only a few cultivars; better production in 2nd year; don't overwater

SUGGESTED COMPANION PLANTINGS: statice or sweet william (*Dianthus barbadus*)

baby's breath

Plant characteristics

HEIGHT: 2–4'

SPREAD: 36"

GROWTH RATE: slow to moderate

GROWTH HABIT: short, mound-like

FLOWERS

SIZE: ¼–⅜"

COLOR: white, pink

SHAPE: round, flat

FRAGRANCE: none

FLOWERS IN FIRST YEAR: requires cool temperatures before flowering

FLOWERING PERIOD: natural flowering occurs in late spring to late summer; lights are needed for winter production; can be treated as perennial or annual

TIME TO FLOWERING: once flowering has started, wait about another 10 weeks to harvest

INDUCING AND MAINTAINING FLOWERING: lighting may be necessary during summer months in Hawai'i and is necessary during winter months for good flower production, as it requires 14–16 hours of light

PESTS

COMMON DISEASES: damping off, root rot, nematodes, crown gall, *Botrytis* (on flowers)

OTHER PESTS: spider mites, thrips

The lei shown also contains bougainvillea, Geraldton waxflower, chysanthemum, bleeding heart, globe amaranth, and joyweed.

Harvesting considerations

WHAT IS HARVESTED: flowering branches

HARVESTING TECHNIQUES: for fresh flowers, cut 1–2" stems when 60–70% of flowers are open; for drying, cut when 80–90% are open

BEST TIME OF DAY TO HARVEST: early morning

BEST WAY TO TRANSPORT FROM PICKING AREA: paper box

AVOID CONTACT WITH THESE PRODUCTS: smoke, car exhaust, ripening fruits, and wilting flowers

Notes on lei making

BEST FOR WHICH TYPE OF LEI: neck, head, wrist, ankle, horse

VASE LIFE: 57 days

CLEANING OF PLANT MATERIALS: none; do not wet flower heads

STORING RAW LEI MATERIALS: place stems in water and refrigerate at 40°F for up to 7 days

PREPARING FOR USE IN LEI: clip off wrinkled, limp, or poor quality areas before adding to lei; boil water and placed cut stems in hot water to force flowering if not all have bloomed

STORING A COMPLETED LEI BEFORE WEARING: mist lei, shake off excess water, place on damp paper towel, place in sealed plastic container, and refrigerate

PRESERVING A LEI FOR LONG-TERM STORAGE OR DISPLAY: air-dry

References and further reading

Anonymous. 1995. *Gypsophila: Cultivation Practices in Israel*. Beit Dagan, Israel: Danziger 'Dan' Flower Farm.

Armitage, A.M. 1993. *Specialty Cut Flowers*. Portland, Oregon: Varsity Press and Timber Press.

Nowack, Joanna and Ryszard M. Rudnicki. 1990. *Postharvest Handling and Storage of Cut Flowers, Florist Greens, and Potted Plants*. Portland, Oregon: Timber Press.

Sascalis, John N. 1993. *Cut Flowers Prolonging Freshness*. Batavia, Illinois: Ball Publishing.

Introduced Perennials

bleeding heart

OTHER COMMON NAMES: clerodendrum, glorybower, *hōʻehapuʻuwai*

SCIENTIFIC NAME: *Clerodendrum thomsoniae* and *Clerodendrum* x *speciosum*

FAMILY: Verbenaceae (verbena family)

NATURAL SETTING/LOCATION: native to tropical West Africa

CURRENT STATUS IN THE WILD IN HAWAIʻI: not found

Growing your own

PROPAGATION

FORM: soft wood or semi-ripe cuttings under mist; commercially propagated from single-node cuttings; also grown from root cuttings and rooted suckers

PRETREATMENT: treat cutting with medium rooting hormone

PLANTING DEPTH: insert base of cutting 1–1½" into medium

CUTTING ROOTING TIME: 6–8 weeks

PREFERRED PRODUCTION CONDITIONS

GENERAL SOIL CHARACTERISTICS: rich, well drained

SOIL PH: 5.5–6.5 (avoid high-pH soils)

LIGHT: full sun for best bloom

WATER: keep moist; over-watering can cause leaf drop

TEMPERATURE: tolerates temperatures down to 35°F, but temperatures below 60°F inhibit growth

ELEVATION: 10–2000'

SALT TOLERANCE: moderate

WIND RESISTANCE: moderate

MANAGEMENT

FERTILIZER NEEDS: medium

RECOMMENDED SPACING: 36" apart

ADAPTATION TO GROWING IN CONTAINERS: yes, will flower in 6" pot, but larger containers are easier to maintain

PRUNING: prune after flowering; can be maintained as a shrub or high ground cover 24–36" high (6–7 nodes above the roots); pruning shorter than this will delay flowering

SPECIAL CULTURAL HINTS: provide support if vining is desired

bleeding heart

Plant characteristics

HEIGHT: 10–15'

SPREAD: 36"

GROWTH RATE: fast

GROWTH HABIT: evergreen, twining shrub

FLOWERS

SIZE: calyx (leafy base of flower) ½–¾"

COLOR: *C. thomsoniae* calyx is white with red corolla; *C. x speciosum* calyx is pink, corolla deep rose to red

SHAPE: flowers consist of bell-shaped calyx and narrow tubular corolla; the calyx stands out and is used in lei

FRAGRANCE: none

FLOWERS IN FIRST YEAR: yes

FLOWERING PERIOD: year-round under high-light conditions, heaviest in winter through spring

TIME TO FLOWERING: 3–5 months; terminal cuttings flower soonest, and seed-propagated plants take at least 1 month longer than cuttings to flower

INDUCING AND MAINTAINING FLOWERING: both types are short-day plants; nights longer than 10 hours promote flowering; high light intensity also promotes flowering and can minimize the need for long nights

PESTS

COMMON DISEASES: none serious

OTHER PESTS: none serious

The lei shown also contains shinobu.

Harvesting considerations

WHAT IS HARVESTED: flower calyx (leafy base)

HARVESTING TECHNIQUES: plant has long internodes; cut close to nodes to avoid leaving long pieces of dying stem

BEST TIME OF DAY TO HARVEST: early morning

BEST WAY TO TRANSPORT FROM PICKING AREA: paper or cloth bag

AVOID CONTACT WITH THESE PRODUCTS: smoke, car exhaust, ripening fruits, and wilting flowers

Notes on lei making

BEST FOR WHICH TYPE OF LEI: neck, head, wrist, ankle, horse

VASE LIFE: 2 days

CLEANING OF PLANT MATERIALS: cold water soak

STORING RAW LEI MATERIALS: store in sealed container and refrigerate at 40°F for up to 14 days

PREPARING FOR USE IN LEI: clip off wrinkled, limp, or poor quality areas before adding to lei; true flowers are most often removed, as well as the leaves

STORING A COMPLETED LEI BEFORE WEARING: soak lei in water for 5 minutes, drip dry, place in sealed container, and refrigerate

PRESERVING A LEI FOR LONG-TERM STORAGE OR DISPLAY: cannot be preserved

References and further reading

Sanderson, K.C., and W.C. Martin Jr. 1975. Cultural Concepts for Growing *Clerodendrum thomsoniae* Balf. as a Pot Plant. Proceedings of the Florida State Horticultural Society 88: 439–441.

Shillo, Ruth, and Ronnie Engel. 1985. "*Clerodendrum speciosum*." In: *CRC Handbook of Flowering*. vol. II, ed. A.H. Halevy, p. 302–307. Boca Raton, Florida: CRC Press.

Stromme, E., and H. Hildrum. 1985. "*Clerodendrum thomsoniae*." In: *CRC Handbook of Flowering*. vol. II, ed. A.H. Halevy, p. 299–301. Boca Raton, Florida: CRC Press.

Introduced Perennials

blue jade vine

OTHER COMMON NAMES: green jade vine, jade vine

SCIENTIFIC NAME: *Strongylodon macrobotrys*

FAMILY: Fabaceae (pea family)

NATURAL SETTING/LOCATION: Philippines

CURRENT STATUS IN THE WILD IN HAWAI'I: not found

Growing your own

HANDLING CAUTIONS: may stain some fabrics

PROPAGATION

FORM: air layering; semi-woody cuttings 9" long; fresh seeds

PREPLANTING TREATMENT: use fresh seeds, plant immediately upon opening of capsule, scarify seeds by scratching seedcoat or put in water that has been brought to a boil and removed from heat and soak for about 24 hours; use strong rooting hormone on cuttings

PLANTING DEPTH: sow seeds ½–1" deep in medium; insert cutting ½ its length into medium

GERMINATION TIME: 10–14 days at 80–85°F

AIR LAYERING ROOTING TIME: 4–8 months

PREFERRED PRODUCTION CONDITIONS

GENERAL SOIL CHARACTERISTICS: rich, moist, well drained

SOIL PH: 6.0–7.0

LIGHT: full sun to partial shade

WATER: moderate

TEMPERATURE: 60–90°F

ELEVATION: 10–800'

SALT TOLERANCE: poor

WIND RESISTANCE: moderate

MANAGEMENT

FERTILIZER NEEDS: medium; apply after flowering and in spring

RECOMMENDED SPACING: 8' apart

ADAPTATION TO GROWING IN CONTAINERS: not recommended

PRUNING: prune to manage spread of plant

SPECIAL CULTURAL HINTS: provide strong arbor, trellis, or other support; stem is too weak to support itself in an upright position

blue jade vine

Plant characteristics

HEIGHT: twining vine to 40'

SPREAD: 20–30'

GROWTH RATE: fast

GROWTH HABIT: perennial, evergreen, woody, flowering vine

FLOWERS

SIZE: 2½–3" clusters to 36" long

COLOR: aquamarine to jade green

SHAPE: beak-like

FRAGRANCE: none

FLOWERS IN FIRST YEAR: no

FLOWERING PERIOD: late summer, fall

TIME TO FLOWERING: air layering quicker than seed-propagated plants, with first flowering in 3 years

INDUCING AND MAINTAINING FLOWERING: remove old flowers and seed pods

PESTS

COMMON DISEASES: root rot, leaf spot, root-knot nematodes

OTHER PESTS: black stink bugs, mealybugs, scales

Harvesting considerations

WHAT IS HARVESTED: flowers

HARVESTING TECHNIQUES: snap

BEST TIME OF DAY TO HARVEST: early morning

BEST WAY TO TRANSPORT FROM PICKING AREA: paper or cloth bag

AVOID CONTACT WITH THESE PRODUCTS: smoke, car exhaust, ripening fruits, and wilting flowers

The lei shown also contains tuberose.

Notes on lei making

BEST FOR WHICH TYPE OF LEI: neck, head

VASE LIFE: 4 days

CLEANING OF PLANT MATERIALS: spray with water

STORING RAW LEI MATERIALS: place in a sealed plastic container and refrigerate at 40°F for up to 4 days

PREPARING FOR USE IN LEI: clip off wrinkled, limp, or poor quality areas before adding to lei

STORING A COMPLETED LEI BEFORE WEARING: mist lei, place in sealed plastic container, and refrigerate

PRESERVING A LEI FOR LONG-TERM STORAGE OR DISPLAY: cannot be preserved

References and further reading

Ide, Laurie S. 1998. *Hawaiian Lei Making: Step-by-Step Guide*. Honolulu: Mutual Publishing.

Riffle, Robert L. 1998. *The Tropical Look: An Encyclopedia of Dramatic Landscape Plants*. Portland, Oregon: Timber Press.

Teho, Fortunato G. 1971. *Plants of Hawaii: How to Grow Them*. Hilo, Hawaii: Petroglyph Press.

Warren, William. 1997. *Tropical Plants for Home and Garden*. London: Thames and Hudson.

Introduced Perennials

bougainvillea

OTHER COMMON NAMES: *kepalo, pukanawila*

SCIENTIFIC NAME: *Bougainvillea* cultivars

FAMILY: Nyctaginaceae (four-o'clock family)

NATURAL SETTING/LOCATION: native to Brazil

CURRENT STATUS IN THE WILD IN HAWAI'I: not naturalized but often found in public areas

CULTIVARS: many, including "double-bract" forms that are particularly useful in lei making

Growing your own

HANDLING CAUTIONS: most cultivars have thorny stems

PROPAGATION

FORM: cuttings (semi-soft wood, ⅛" thick)

PREPLANTING TREATMENT: treat cuttings with strong rooting hormone

PLANTING DEPTH: insert cutting 1–2" into medium

CUTTING ROOTING TIME: semi-soft cuttings root in 4 weeks, woody cuttings root in 4–8 weeks, depending on variety and rooting treatment

PREFERRED PRODUCTION CONDITIONS

GENERAL SOIL CHARACTERISTICS: well drained soil is best; tolerates many soil types

SOIL PH: 5.5–6.0

LIGHT: full sun

WATER: keep relatively dry after plant is established

TEMPERATURE: 50–90°F

ELEVATION: 10–2500'

SALT TOLERANCE: good

WIND RESISTANCE: good

MANAGEMENT

FERTILIZER NEEDS: light

RECOMMENDED SPACING: 5' apart or more

ADAPTATION TO GROWING IN CONTAINERS: yes, 3-gallon tubs or larger

PRUNING: prune back vigorous, vining growth and allow shorter side branches to develop

SPECIAL CULTURAL HINTS: provide trellis or other support; variety of growth habits possible

bougainvillea

Plant characteristics

HEIGHT: to 20'

SPREAD: to 20'

GROWTH RATE: fast

GROWTH HABIT: vine, sprawling shrub

FLOWERS

SIZE: bracts: ½–2"

COLOR: magenta, rose, pink, red, orange, gold, white, bicolor

SHAPE: bracts are triangular to almost round

FRAGRANCE: none

FLOWERS IN FIRST YEAR: yes

FLOWERING PERIOD: heaviest from September through April

TIME TO FLOWERING: rooted cuttings flower in 7–10 weeks

INDUCING AND MAINTAINING FLOWERING: flowers occur on new growth; short daylengths enhance flowering; keep N and water on the low side; plants in heavy shade or pruned too frequently will not flower

PESTS

COMMON DISEASES: *Phytopthora* foliar blight, leaf spots, *Pythium* root rot, reniform nematodes

OTHER PESTS: aphids, caterpillars, grasshoppers, mites, soft scales, whiteflies

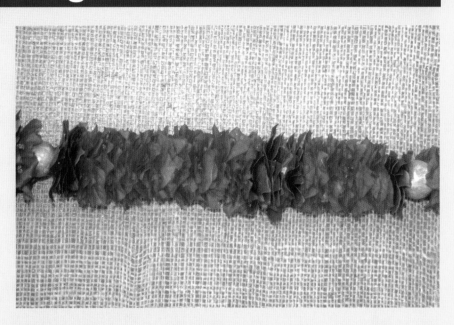

The lei shown also contains mock orange leaves.

Harvesting considerations

WHAT IS HARVESTED: clusters of bracts with or without flowers

HARVESTING TECHNIQUES: clip

BEST TIME OF DAY TO HARVEST: early morning

BEST WAY TO TRANSPORT FROM PICKING AREA: paper or cloth bag

AVOID CONTACT WITH THESE PRODUCTS: smoke, car exhaust, ripening fruits, and wilting flowers

Notes on lei making

BEST FOR WHICH TYPE OF LEI: neck, head, wrist, ankle, horse

VASE LIFE: 7 days

CLEANING OF PLANT MATERIALS: cold water soak

STORING RAW LEI MATERIALS: wrap in damp newspaper in plastic container or paper box and refrigerate at 40°F for up to 14 days

PREPARING FOR USE IN LEI: clip off the wrinkled, limp, or poor quality areas before adding to lei

STORING A COMPLETED LEI BEFORE WEARING: mist lei, shake off excess water, wrap in damp newspaper in plastic container or paper box, and refrigerate

PRESERVING A LEI FOR LONG-TERM STORAGE OR DISPLAY: air-dry

References and further reading

Criley, Richard A. 1997. Bougainvillea. In: *Tips on Growing Specialty Potted Crops*. eds. M.L. Gaston, S.A. Carver, and C.A. Irwin. Columbus, Ohio: Ohio Florists' Assoc.

Ide, Laurie S. 1998. *Hawaiian Lei Making: Step-by-Step Guide*. Honolulu: Mutual Publishing.

Iredell, Jan. 1990. *The Bougainvillea Growers Handbook*. Brookvale, Australia: Simon & Schuster Australia.

Watson, Donald P., and Richard A. Criley. 1973. *Bougainvilleas*. University of Hawai'i, Cooperative Extension Service, Circular 469.

Introduced Perennials

carnation

OTHER COMMON NAMES: pink, *ponimō'ī*

SCIENTIFIC NAME:
Dianthus caryophyllus

FAMILY:
Caryophyllaceae (pink family)

NATURAL SETTING/LOCATION: native to the Mediterranean

CURRENT STATUS IN THE WILD IN HAWAI'I: not found

CULTIVARS: many; some pot types available from seed

Growing your own

PROPAGATION

FORM: tip cuttings (most growers purchase rooted cuttings); seeds (purchase from seed source)

PRETREATMENT: treat cutting with mild rooting hormone; chill seeds for 1–2 weeks at 30–35°F before sowing

PLANTING DEPTH: sow seeds on surface with a light covering; insert base of cutting 1" into medium

GERMINATION TIME: 1–2 weeks

CUTTING ROOTING TIME: 2–4 weeks

PREFERRED PRODUCTION CONDITIONS

GENERAL SOIL CHARACTERISTICS: rich, well drained, loamy soil

SOIL PH: 5.5–6.5

LIGHT: full sun to partial shade

WATER: keep moist

TEMPERATURE: 80°F days, 50–60°F nights

ELEVATION: 10–3000'

SALT TOLERANCE: poor

WIND RESISTANCE: poor

MANAGEMENT

FERTILIZER NEEDS: medium

RECOMMENDED SPACING: 4–8" apart

ADAPTATION TO GROWING IN CONTAINERS: yes, 6" pots or larger

PRUNING: many different techniques used; pinching or pruning is a strategy used to time flowering around periods of high demand; spray types for lei production are usually not pruned

SPECIAL CULTURAL HINTS: good planting time is at the end of summer; flowering will first occur in mid-December and then continuously; calyx (green, leafy base) splitting is a major problem, particularly for single-stem flower types; nonsplitting types are available; requires soil free of disease and nematodes where carnation hasn't been grown before; container culture will avoid soil-borne problems; mostly grown under cover

carnation

Plant characteristics

HEIGHT: 36"

SPREAD: 1'

GROWTH RATE: relatively fast

GROWTH HABIT: sprawling herb

FLOWERS

SIZE: large-flowered types 2½–4" in diameter, smaller-flowered (spray types) 1½–3" in diameter, miniature-flowered 1½–2" in diameter

COLOR: red, white, pink, yellow, orange, white, purple

SHAPE: round

FRAGRANCE: varies from nonfragrant to spicy

FLOWERS IN FIRST YEAR: yes

FLOWERING PERIOD: year-round; more flowers in summer

TIME TO FLOWERING: plants flower 3–4 months after transplanting; peak production in 6 months

INDUCING AND MAINTAINING FLOWERING: remove first flower; remove spent flowers, and harvest flowers regularly

PESTS

COMMON DISEASES: rootknot nematodes, *Botrytis* on flowers; fungal problems including *Fusarium* rust, stem rot (*Rhizoctonia*), *Alternaria* blight, leaf spot, or branch rot; at least four viruses are found in carnation; bacterial diseases include bacterial and *Fusarium* wilt, both of which can persist in the soil for several years

OTHER PESTS: caterpillars, Hawaiian flower thrips (infest flowers), spider mites

Harvesting considerations

WHAT IS HARVESTED: open flowers plus 1–2" of stem

HARVESTING TECHNIQUES: cut

BEST TIME OF DAY TO HARVEST: early morning while flowers are turgid

BEST WAY TO TRANSPORT FROM PICKING AREA: brown paper box or bag

AVOID CONTACT WITH THESE PRODUCTS: smoke, car exhaust, ripening fruits, and wilting flowers

Notes on lei making

BEST FOR WHICH TYPE OF LEI: neck, head, wrist, ankle, horse

VASE LIFE: 6–9 days

CLEANING OF PLANT MATERIALS: no water

STORING RAW LEI MATERIALS: refrigerate at 40–48°F for up to 14 days; don't wet flowers; store in covered box, lay flowers on dry newspaper (to absorb moisture) over polyethylene liner, put layers of newspaper between layers of flowers, and don't allow flowers to contact the plastic; box should have vents to prevent ethylene build-up and should be spaced away from each other to allow for circulation around box

PREPARING FOR USE IN LEI: for single lei, cut flower close to the clayx (green, leafy base), leaving little or no stem; for double lei, remove calyx of each blossom or split open

STORING A COMPLETED LEI BEFORE WEARING: soak lei, shake off excess water, place on dry newspaper in paper box, and refrigerate

PRESERVING A LEI FOR LONG-TERM STORAGE OR DISPLAY: cannot be preserved

References and further reading

Boodley, James W. 1998. *The Commercial Greenhouse*. 2nd ed. Albany, New York: Demar Publishing.

Gardenier, Phil, and Van Staaveren. 1998. "*Dianthus* (Carnation)." In: *Ball Red Book*. 16th ed., p. 473–477. Batavia, Illinois: Ball Publishing.

Holley, Winfred D., and Ralph Baker. 1963. *Carnation Production, Including the History, Breeding, Culture and Marketing of Carnations*. Dubuque, Iowa: Brown.

Ide, Laurie S. 1998. *Hawaiian Lei Making: Step-by-Step Guide*. Honolulu: Mutual Publishing.

Nau, Jim. 1993. *Ball Culture Guide: The Encyclopaedia of Seed Germination*. 2nd ed. Batavia, Illinois: Ball Publishing.

Neal, Marie C. 1965. *In Gardens of Hawaii*. Bernice P. Bishop Museum Special Publication 50. Honolulu: Bishop Museum Press.

Trujillo, Eduardo E. 1989. *Diseases and Pests of Carnation*. University of Hawai‘i, CTAHR, Research Extension Series 107.

cigar flower

OTHER COMMON NAMES: *pua kīkā*

SCIENTIFIC NAME: *Cuphea ignea*

FAMILY: Lythraceae (loosestrife family)

NATURAL SETTING/LOCATION: native to Mexico

CURRENT STATUS IN THE WILD IN HAWAIʻI: not found

CULTIVARS: other species and cultivars available.

Growing your own

PROPAGATION

FORM: cuttings or seeds (purchase from seed source)

PREPLANTING TREATMENT: treat cuttings with mild rooting hormone.

PLANTING DEPTH: sow seed ⅛" deep in medium; insert base of cutting 1–2" into medium

GERMINATION TIME: 2 weeks at 70°F; temperature-sensitive

CUTTING ROOTING TIME: 3–4 weeks

PREFERRED PRODUCTION CONDITIONS

GENERAL SOIL CHARACTERISTICS: silty loam, or soil with a high organic matter content

SOIL PH: 6.0–6.5

LIGHT: full sun

WATER: drought tolerant

TEMPERATURE: 60–95°F

ELEVATION: 10–2000'

SALT TOLERANCE: moderate

WIND RESISTANCE: moderate

MANAGEMENT

FERTILIZER NEEDS: medium

RECOMMENDED SPACING: 1' apart within rows, 4–6' between rows

ADAPTATION TO GROWING IN CONTAINERS: yes, 3-gallon tubs

PRUNING: prune to reduce size, maintain shape, and keep full and bushy

SPECIAL CULTURAL HINTS: plant in a well drained area to avoid root rot problems

SUGGESTED COMPANION PLANTINGS: mixed border or mixed bedding planting

cigar flower

Plant characteristics

HEIGHT: 1–3'

SPREAD: 2–5'

GROWTH RATE: moderate

GROWTH HABIT: low, dense, evergreen shrub

FLOWERS

SIZE: 1" long

COLOR: orange, red (other types available in purple and pink)

SHAPE: tubular

FRAGRANCE: none

FLOWERS IN FIRST YEAR: yes

FLOWERING PERIOD: year-round

TIME TO FLOWERING: seedlings flower about 3½ months after germination; cuttings produce flowers 6–8 weeks after rooting

INDUCING AND MAINTAINING FLOWERING: avoid drastic pruning and excessive N fertilizer

PESTS

COMMON DISEASES: fungal root rots, foliar blights

OTHER PESTS: aphids, beetles, grasshoppers, sunflower spittle bug

Harvesting considerations

WHAT IS HARVESTED: flowers with ½" of stem

HARVESTING TECHNIQUES: pluck flowers

BEST TIME OF DAY TO HARVEST: early morning or evening

BEST WAY TO TRANSPORT FROM PICKING AREA: paper bag

AVOID CONTACT WITH THESE PRODUCTS: smoke, car exhaust, ripening fruits, and wilting flowers

Notes on lei making

BEST FOR WHICH TYPE OF LEI: neck, head, wrist, ankle

CLEANING OF PLANT MATERIALS: cold water soak

STORING RAW LEI MATERIALS: place in sealed container and refrigerate at 40°F for up to 7 days

PREPARING FOR USE IN LEI: clip off stem then sew; for other styles of lei, remove leaves from stem before using

STORING A COMPLETED LEI BEFORE WEARING: soak lei, shake off excess water, place in sealed container, and refrigerate; lei may be revived by soaking in water and placing in plastic bag in refrigerator for 3 hours

PRESERVING A LEI FOR LONG-TERM STORAGE OR DISPLAY: air-dry

References and further reading

Holttum, R.E., and Ivan Enoch. 1991. *Gardening in the Tropics*. Portland, Oregon: Timber Press.

Ide, Laurie S. 1998. *Hawaiian Lei Making: Step-by-Step Guide*. Honolulu: Mutual Publishing.

Moggi, Guido, and Luciano Giugnolini. 1983. *Simon and Schuster's Guide to Garden Flowers*. New York: Simon and Schuster.

Introduced Perennials

crown flower

OTHER COMMON NAMES: giant milk-weed, *pua kalaunu*

SCIENTIFIC NAME: *Calotropis gigantea*

FAMILY: Asclepiadaceae (milkweed family)

NATURAL SETTING/LOCATION: native to India and the East Indies

CURRENT STATUS IN THE WILD IN HAWAI'I: typically not found

CULTIVARS: small-flowered type available (*Calotropis procera*)

Growing your own

HANDLING CAUTIONS: all plant parts are poisonous; milky sap in eyes may cause blindness, on skin may cause considerable irritation

PROPAGATION

FORM: seeds; cuttings

PREPLANTING TREATMENT: soak seeds in water for 4–6 hours; use medium rooting hormone on cuttings

PLANTING DEPTH: sow seeds ¼" in medium; insert base of cutting 1–2" into medium

GERMINATION TIME: 1–2 weeks

CUTTING ROOTING TIME: 6–8 weeks

PREFERRED PRODUCTION CONDITIONS

GENERAL SOIL CHARACTERISTICS: well drained

SOIL PH: 6.0–6.5

LIGHT: full sun

WATER: requires irrigation during dry periods

TEMPERATURE: >70°F

ELEVATION: 10–1000'

SALT TOLERANCE: moderate

WIND RESISTANCE: moderate

MANAGEMENT

FERTILIZER NEEDS: light

RECOMMENDED SPACING: 8–12' apart

ADAPTATION TO GROWING IN CONTAINERS: yes, 2–5-gallon tubs

PRUNING: pruning to keep within picking height will temporarily reduce flower production; thinning out old branches induces vigorous new growth

SPECIAL CULTURAL HINTS: grow in dry and hot areas; keep low for harvesting

SUGGESTED COMPANION PLANTINGS: low annuals

crown flower

Plant characteristics

HEIGHT: to 12'

SPREAD: 15'

GROWTH RATE: fast

GROWTH HABIT: erect, evergreen, rounded shrub

FLOWERS

SIZE: 1" diameter

COLOR: pale lavender, pink, or white

SHAPE: five curled-back petals and a prominent crown

FRAGRANCE: faint

FLOWERS IN FIRST YEAR: yes, from cuttings

FLOWERING PERIOD: year-round

TIME TO FLOWERING: maturity after 3–4 years (from seed)

INDUCING AND MAINTAINING FLOWERING: not known

PESTS

COMMON DISEASES: none

OTHER PESTS: caterpillars (monarch butterfly)

Harvesting considerations

WHAT IS HARVESTED: flowers

HARVESTING TECHNIQUES: break off; gloves and eye protection advised to avoid contact with sap while harvesting

BEST TIME OF DAY TO HARVEST: early morning

BEST WAY TO TRANSPORT FROM PICKING AREA: paper or cloth bag

AVOID CONTACT WITH THESE PRODUCTS: smoke, car exhaust, ripening fruits, and wilting flowers

Notes on lei making

BEST FOR WHICH TYPE OF LEI: neck, head, wrist, ankle, horse

VASE LIFE: 3 days for purple flowers, 2 days for white flowers

CLEANING OF PLANT MATERIALS: cold water soak for 5 minutes

STORING RAW LEI MATERIALS: store purple flowers for up to 5 days in refrigerator at 40°F; white flowers for up to 4 days

PREPARING FOR USE IN LEI: for crown lei, separate blossoms and buds; for bud lei, use buds of same size; for whole crown lei, use all of the newly opened and fully developed blossoms; for crown flower petal lei, use petals in best condition

STORING A COMPLETED LEI BEFORE WEARING: mist lei, shake off excess water, place on dry paper towel in sealed plastic container, and refrigerate

PRESERVING A LEI FOR LONG-TERM STORAGE OR DISPLAY: air-dry

References and further reading

Bird, Adren J., and Josephine P.K. Bird. 1987. *Hawaiian Flower Lei Making*. Honolulu: Unversity of Hawai‘i Press.

Clay, Horace F., and James C. Hubbard. 1977. *The Hawai‘i Garden: Tropical Exotics*. Honolulu: University of Hawai‘i Press.

Ide, Laurie S. 1998. *Hawaiian Lei Making: Step-by-Step Guide*. Honolulu: Mutual Publishing.

Rauch, Fred D. 1996. *Tropical Landscape Plants*. 3rd ed. Battle Ground, Washington: Hawaii Floriculture.

Riffle, Robert L. 1998. *The Tropical Look: An Encyclopedia of Dramatic Landscape Plants*. Portland, Oregon: Timber Press.

Warren, William. 1997. *Tropical Plants for Home and Garden*. London: Thames and Hudson.

cup-and-saucer plant

OTHER COMMON NAMES: Chinaman's hat, parasol flower

SCIENTIFIC NAME: *Holmskioldia sanguinea, H. sanguinea* f. *citrina, H. tettensis*

FAMILY: Labiatae (mint family)

NATURAL SETTING/LOCATION: foothills of Indian Himalayas *(H. sanguinea)*; southeast Africa *(H. tettensis)*

CURRENT STATUS IN THE WILD IN HAWAI'I: not found

Growing your own

PROPAGATION

FORM: woody cuttings

PREPLANTING TREATMENT: treat cuttings with medium rooting hormone

PLANTING DEPTH: insert base of cutting 1–1½" into medium

CUTTING ROOTING TIME: 6–8 weeks

PREFERRED PRODUCTION CONDITIONS

GENERAL SOIL CHARACTERISTICS: well drained loam

SOIL PH: 6.0–6.5

LIGHT: full sun

WATER: keep dry

TEMPERATURE: 55–90°F

ELEVATION: 10–3200'

SALT TOLERANCE: moderate

WIND RESISTANCE: moderate

MANAGEMENT

FERTILIZER NEEDS: medium

RECOMMENDED SPACING: 4–6' apart

ADAPTATION TO GROWING IN CONTAINERS: yes, 2-gallon tubs or larger

PRUNING: vigorous pruning recommended to manage shape and induce new growth and flowering; *H. tettensis* best pruned to tall, linear form during the winter after main flowering period

cup-and-saucer plant

Plant characteristics

HEIGHT: *H. sanguinea* to 10', *H. tettensis* to 15'

SPREAD: *H. sanguinea* to 6', *H. tettensis* up to 4'

GROWTH RATE: *H. sanguinea* fast, *H. tettensis* moderate

GROWTH HABIT: *H. sanguinea,* rounded shrub; *H. tettensis,* upright shrub

FLOWERS

SIZE: ¾–1"

COLOR: orange to red (*H. sanguinea*), yellow-green (*H. sanguinea* f. *citrina*), purplish (*H. tettensis*)

SHAPE: round, funnel-shaped

FRAGRANCE: none

FLOWERS IN FIRST YEAR: yes

FLOWERING PERIOD: year-round, heaviest in winter and spring

TIME TO FLOWERING: 6–8 months, but 2–3 years for full maturity

INDUCING AND MAINTAINING FLOWERING: flowers on new wood, so pruning is essential to stimulate new growth

PESTS

COMMON DISEASES: *Pythium* root rot, nematodes

OTHER PESTS: ants, mealybugs, scales, thrips

The lei shown also contains baby's breath, globe amaranth, dusty miller, feverfew, and galphimia.

Harvesting considerations

WHAT IS HARVESTED: flowers with 1–2" of stem

HARVESTING TECHNIQUES: pinch

BEST TIME OF DAY TO HARVEST: early morning

BEST WAY TO TRANSPORT FROM PICKING AREA: paper or cloth bag

AVOID CONTACT WITH THESE PRODUCTS: smoke, car exhaust, ripening fruits, and wilting flowers

Notes on lei making

BEST FOR WHICH TYPE OF LEI: neck, head, wrist, ankle, horse

VASE LIFE: 3–5 days

CLEANING OF PLANT MATERIALS: cold water soak for 5 minutes

STORING RAW LEI MATERIALS: place on damp newspaper in paper or plastic container and refrigerate at 40°F for up to 10 days

PREPARING FOR USE IN LEI: clip off wrinkled, limp, or poor quality areas before adding to lei

STORING A COMPLETED LEI BEFORE WEARING: soak lei, drip dry, place in paper or plastic container, and refrigerate

PRESERVING A LEI FOR LONG-TERM STORAGE OR DISPLAY: air-dry

References and further reading

Clay, Horace F., and James C. Hubbard. 1977. *The Hawai'i Garden: Tropical Shrubs.* Honolulu: University of Hawai'i Press.

Holttum, Richard E., and Ivan Enoch. 1991. *Gardening in the Tropics.* Singapore: Times Editions.

dracaena tricolor

OTHER COMMON NAMES: money tree

SCIENTIFIC NAME: *Dracaena marginata* var. *tricolor*

FAMILY: Agavaceae (agave family)

NATURAL SETTING/LOCATION: *D. marginata* is from tropical West Africa; var. *tricolor* is only found in cultivation

CURRENT STATUS IN THE WILD IN HAWAI'I: not found

Growing your own

PROPAGATION

FORM: cuttings (minimum 6" long)

PREPLANTING TREATMENT: treat with medium rooting hormone

PLANTING DEPTH: insert base of cutting 3–4" into medium

CUTTING ROOTING TIME: 1–3 months

PREFERRED PRODUCTION CONDITIONS

GENERAL SOIL CHARACTERISTICS: well drained; tolerant of various soil types

SOIL PH: 5.5–6.5

LIGHT: full sun to partial shade

WATER: moderate

TEMPERATURE: 65–90°F

ELEVATION: 10–2000'

SALT TOLERANCE: moderate

WIND RESISTANCE: moderate

MANAGEMENT

FERTILIZER NEEDS: heavy

RECOMMENDED SPACING: 2–4' apart

ADAPTATION TO GROWING IN CONTAINERS: yes, 1–5-gallon tubs

PRUNING: prune tips back to induce new, thin shoots with smaller leaves and to control size

SUGGESTED COMPANION PLANTINGS: low-growing plants

dracaena tricolor

Plant characteristics

HEIGHT: to 15'

SPREAD: 3–5'

GROWTH RATE: fast

GROWTH HABIT: erect, angular, woody, evergreen

FOLIAGE

TEXTURE: leathery, pliable

COLOR: from emerald to gray-green, sometimes variegated

SHAPE: lance-shaped

FRAGRANCE: none

PESTS

COMMON DISEASES: *Fusarium* and other leaf-spot fungi, root rot, bacterial soft rot, nematodes (root-knot, reniform, spiral)

OTHER PESTS: caterpillar (banana moth), mealybugs, scales

Harvesting considerations

WHAT IS HARVESTED: leaves

HARVESTING TECHNIQUES: pull or snap leaf off of stem; don't cut

BEST TIME OF DAY TO HARVEST: early morning

BEST WAY TO TRANSPORT FROM PICKING AREA: plastic bag

The lei shown also contains dusty miller.

Notes on lei making

BEST FOR WHICH TYPE OF LEI: neck, head, wrist, ankle, horse

CLEANING OF PLANT MATERIALS: hand wash under cold, running water

STORING RAW LEI MATERIALS: place in sealed plastic container and refrigerate at 40°F for up to 14 days

PREPARING FOR USE IN LEI: clip off wrinkled, limp, or poor quality areas before adding to lei

STORING A COMPLETED LEI BEFORE WEARING: mist lei, shake off excess water, wrap in paper towels, place in sealed plastic container, and refrigerate

PRESERVING A LEI FOR LONG-TERM STORAGE OR DISPLAY: air-dry

References and further reading

Clay, Horace F., and James C. Hubbard. 1977. *The Hawai'i Garden: Tropical Shrubs.* Honolulu: University of Hawai'i Press.

Poole, R.T., A.R. Chase, and L.S. Osborne. *Dracaena Production Guide.* University of Florida, IFAS. <www.ifas.ufl.edu/~apkweb/folnotes/dracaena.htm>.

Rauch, Fred D. 1996. *Tropical Landscape Plants.* 3rd ed. Battle Ground, Washington: Hawaii Floriculture.

Introduced Perennials

dusty miller

SCIENTIFIC NAME: *Senecio cineraria; Centaurea cineraria*

FAMILY: Asteraceae (formerly Compositae) (aster family)

NATURAL SETTING/LOCATION: western and southern Mediterranean

CURRENT STATUS IN THE WILD IN HAWAI'I: not found

CULTIVARS: 'Silver Lace', 'Silver Dust', 'Silver Storm'

Growing your own

PROPAGATION

FORM: tip cuttings; seeds (purchase from seed source)

PREPLANTING TREATMENT: treat cuttings with mild rooting hormone

PLANTING DEPTH: sow seeds ⅛" deep in medium; insert base of cutting 1–2" into medium

GERMINATION TIME: 2–3 weeks

CUTTING ROOTING TIME: 3 weeks

PREFERRED PRODUCTION CONDITIONS

GENERAL SOIL CHARACTERISTICS: well drained, rich soil

SOIL PH: 6.0–7.0

LIGHT: full sun

WATER: moderate

TEMPERATURE: 50–90°F

ELEVATION: 10–4000'

SALT TOLERANCE: moderate

WIND RESISTANCE: moderate

MANAGEMENT

FERTILIZER NEEDS: light; amend field soils with Ca and Mg if analysis is low

RECOMMENDED SPACING: 15" apart

ADAPTATION TO GROWING IN CONTAINERS: yes, 6–8" pots

PRUNING: pinch flower buds as they appear in order to maintain foliage quality

SPECIAL CULTURAL HINTS: treat as an annual in Hawai'i; avoid waterlogged and poorly drained soils

dusty miller

Plant characteristics

HEIGHT: 1–2'

SPREAD: 1–2'

GROWTH RATE: fast

GROWTH HABIT: compact, mounding herb

FOLIAGE

TEXTURE: fuzzy

COLOR: gray-green to silvery

SHAPE: feathery lobes

FRAGRANCE: none

PESTS

COMMON DISEASES: *Phytophthora* blight, root rot, root-knot nematodes

OTHER PESTS: caterpillars

Harvesting considerations

WHAT IS HARVESTED: leaves

HARVESTING TECHNIQUES: cut or pinch off

BEST TIME OF DAY TO HARVEST: early morning

BEST WAY TO TRANSPORT FROM PICKING AREA: paper or cloth bag

The lei shown also contains rose, *'ōhi'a lehua, pa'iniu*, and *palapalai*.

Notes on lei making

BEST FOR WHICH TYPE OF LEI: neck, head, wrist, ankle, horse

CLEANING OF PLANT MATERIALS: hand wash under cold, running water

STORING RAW LEI MATERIALS: place in plastic container and refrigerate at 40°F for up to 14 days

PREPARING FOR USE IN LEI: clip off wrinkled, limp, or poor quality areas before adding to lei

STORING A COMPLETED LEI BEFORE WEARING: soak lei, shake off excess water, wrap in damp newspaper, place in plastic or paper box, and refrigerate

PRESERVING A LEI FOR LONG-TERM STORAGE OR DISPLAY: air-dry

References and further reading

Nau, Jim. 1998. "*Senecio* (Dusty Miller)." In: *Ball Red Book.* 16th ed., p. 750–751. Batavia, Illinois: Ball Publishing.

Still, Steven M. 1994. *Manual of Herbaceous Ornamental Plants.* Champaign, Illinois: Stipes Publishing Co.

Introduced Perennials

feverfew

SCIENTIFIC NAME: *Tanacetum parthenium*

FAMILY: Asteraceae (formerly Compositae) (aster family)

NATURAL SETTING/LOCATION: native to southeast Europe and Caucasus mountains

CURRENT STATUS IN THE WILD IN HAWAI'I: not found

Growing your own

PROPAGATION

FORM: seeds (purchase from seed source); division; cuttings

PREPLANTING TREATMENT: use mild rooting hormone on cuttings

PLANTING DEPTH: sow seeds on surface of medium or slightly below (⅛"); for divisions, keep root crown just below soil level; insert base of cutting 1–2" into medium

GERMINATION TIME: 10–15 days at 70°F

CUTTING ROOTING TIME: 3–4 weeks

PREFERRED PRODUCTION CONDITIONS

GENERAL SOIL CHARACTERISTICS: sandy, loamy

SOIL PH: 6.0–6.5

LIGHT: full sun

WATER: moderate to light

TEMPERATURE: 60–70°F (day), 55°F (night)

ELEVATION: 500–3500'

SALT TOLERANCE: moderate

WIND RESISTANCE: moderate

MANAGEMENT

FERTILIZER NEEDS: medium

RECOMMENDED SPACING: 1' apart

ADAPTATION TO GROWING IN CONTAINERS: yes, 1–2-gallon tubs

PRUNING: prune to generate new shoots from crown; pinching generally not needed for branching

SPECIAL CULTURAL HINTS: cuttings from vegetative shoots result in a more uniform plant; avoid wet growing conditions, as plants die out from root rot in wet soils

SUGGESTED COMPANION PLANTINGS: baby's breath

feverfew

The lei shown also contains baby's breath, hydrangea, rose, ageratum, statice, and chrysanthemum.

Plant characteristics

HEIGHT: 15–24"

SPREAD: clump size 10–15"

GROWTH RATE: fast

GROWTH HABIT: clumping herb

FLOWERS

SIZE: ¾" diameter

COLOR: white, cream, yellow

SHAPE: round, flat (daisy-type flower) singles, doubles

FRAGRANCE: none

FLOWERS IN FIRST YEAR: from division, yes; from seed, yes; from cutting, yes (if propagated in spring)

FLOWERING PERIOD: late spring, summer; provide lights for better year-round flowering

TIME TO FLOWERING: 10–12 weeks from established seedling during spring or summer; 10 weeks after start of light treatment

INDUCING AND MAINTAINING FLOWERING: flowering duration is 8 weeks; can be pruned and renewed

PESTS

COMMON DISEASES: *Botrytis* on flowers, mildew on foliage, root rot; may be susceptible to aster yellows

OTHER PESTS: aphids, spider mites, thrips

Harvesting considerations

WHAT IS HARVESTED: flowers

HARVESTING TECHNIQUES: cut stems low to encourage branching from crown of the plant

BEST TIME OF DAY TO HARVEST: early morning

BEST WAY TO TRANSPORT FROM PICKING AREA: brown paper bag

AVOID CONTACT WITH THESE PRODUCTS: smoke, car exhaust, ripening fruits, and wilting flowers

Notes on lei making

BEST FOR WHICH TYPE OF LEI: neck, head, wrist, ankle, horse

VASE LIFE: 4 days

CLEANING OF PLANT MATERIALS: put stem bases in water; do not wet flower heads

STORING RAW LEI MATERIALS: store in sealed plastic container and refrigerate at 40°F for up to 10 days

PREPARING FOR USE IN LEI: clip off wrinkled, limp, or poor quality areas before adding to lei; remove leaves

STORING A COMPLETED LEI BEFORE WEARING: mist lei, shake off excess water, wrap in damp newspaper, place in sealed plastic container, and refrigerate

PRESERVING A LEI FOR LONG-TERM STORAGE OR DISPLAY: air-dry

References and further reading

Ball, Vic, ed. 1998. "Feverfew." In: *Ball Red Book*. 16 ed., p. 250–251. Batavia, Illinois: Ball Publishing.

Still, Steven M. 1994. *Manual of Herbaceous Ornamental Plants*. Champaign, Illinois: Stipes Publishing Co.

Introduced Perennials

gardenia

OTHER COMMON NAMES: *kiele*

SCIENTIFIC NAME: *Gardenia augusta*

FAMILY: Rubiaceae (coffee family)

NATURAL SETTING/LOCATION: native to China

CURRENT STATUS IN THE WILD IN HAWAI'I: *G. augusta* not found in the wild; three native species (*G. brighamii, G. remyi, G. mannii*) are either rare or endangered

CULTIVARS: there are many, but only a few are available with a consistently used name: 'Enchantress', 'Mystery', 'Amy Yoshioka', 'Veitchii'

Growing your own

PROPAGATION

FORM: seeds; cuttings 6–7" long; air layering; grafting

PREPLANTING TREATMENT: soak seeds in water for 24 hours; treat cuttings with medium rooting hormone

PLANTING DEPTH: sow seeds ¼" deep in medium; insert base of cutting 1–2" into medium

GERMINATION TIME: 3 months

CUTTING ROOTING TIME: 3–6 weeks

PREFERRED PRODUCTION CONDITIONS

GENERAL SOIL CHARACTERISTICS: rich, well drained

SOIL PH: 5.0–5.5 (avoid high pH)

LIGHT: sunny location

WATER: heavy soaking

TEMPERATURE: 60–75°F

ELEVATION: 10–2500'

SALT TOLERANCE: poor

WIND RESISTANCE: moderate (wind damages fragile flowers)

MANAGEMENT

FERTILIZER NEEDS: medium; to correct chlorosis, apply acidifying fertilizer such as iron sulfate

RECOMMENDED SPACING: 5' apart

ADAPTATION TO GROWING IN CONTAINERS: yes, 2–5-gallon tubs, but growing in the ground is best

PRUNING: remove weak wood; head back (cut back) vigorous stems; avoid pruning late in the year; prune

to keep within picking height and to produce new shoots for flowering

SPECIAL CULTURAL HINTS: under high-pH conditions, new growth will turn yellow: give iron; remove spent flowers; regular irrigation important to keep plant strong and healthy

SUGGESTED COMPANION PLANTINGS: low herbs or annuals requiring partial sun or shade

gardenia

Plant characteristics

HEIGHT: 2–6'

SPREAD: 4–5'

GROWTH RATE: moderate

GROWTH HABIT: upright, oval shrub

FLOWERS

SIZE: 2–5"

COLOR: white to cream

SHAPE: round

FRAGRANCE: highly scented

FLOWERS IN FIRST YEAR: yes, from cuttings or air layering

FLOWERING PERIOD: late spring, early summer

TIME TO FLOWERING: less than 1 year from cutting and air layering, 2–3 years from seed

INDUCING AND MAINTAINING FLOWERING: can induce by pruning

PESTS

COMMON DISEASES: leaf spots, stem canker, root-knot nematode, sooty mold (a problem when ants, aphids, and scales are not controlled)

OTHER PESTS: ants, aphids, mealybugs, mites, scales, thrips

Harvesting considerations

WHAT IS HARVESTED: flowers and calyx (green, leafy base); harvesting only from cultivated plants is recommended due to scarcity of the native *Gardenia* species

HARVESTING TECHNIQUES: cut, don't pull

BEST TIME OF DAY TO HARVEST: morning for buds, afternoon for open flowers

The lei shown also contains agapanthus, bougainvillea, and lantern 'ilima.

BEST WAY TO TRANSPORT FROM PICKING AREA: plastic bag or container

AVOID CONTACT WITH THESE PRODUCTS: smoke, car exhaust, ripening fruits, and wilting flowers

Notes on lei making

BEST FOR WHICH TYPE OF LEI: neck, head, wrist, ankle

VASE LIFE: 2 days

CLEANING OF PLANT MATERIALS: spray with water

STORING RAW LEI MATERIALS: place on wet paper towel in a bowl and refrigerate at 40°F for up to 1 day for flowers and 3 days for buds

PREPARING FOR USE IN LEI: for flower lei, remove calyx, then sew; if calyx is sewn into lei, clip bottom; for *wili* (twisting pattern) lei, remove calyx

STORING A COMPLETED LEI BEFORE WEARING: soak lei, shake off excess water, place in sealed container, and refrigerate

PRESERVING A LEI FOR LONG-TERM STORAGE OR DISPLAY: cannot be preserved

References and further reading

Baird, Eugene, and Alex Laurie. 1942. Studies of the Effect of Environmental Factors and Cultural Practices on Bud Initiation, Bud Abscission, and Bud Development of the Gardenia. *Proceedings of the American Society for Horticultural Science* 40:585–588.

Burkhart, Leland, and H.N. Biekart. 1937. Gardenia Nutrition in Relation to Flower Bud Development. *Proceedings of the American Society for Horticultural Science* 35:768–769.

Hasek, Raymond F. 1948. Observation on Gardenia Flower Production at High Air and Soil Temperatures. *Proceedings of the American Society for Horticultural Science* 51:610–612.

Ide, Laurie S. 1998. *Hawaiian Lei Making: Step-by-Step Guide*. Honolulu: Mutual Publishing.

Rauch, Fred D. 1996. *Tropical Landscape Plants*. 3rd ed. Battle Ground, Washington: Hawaii Floriculture.

Watkins, J.V. 1950. *Gardenias in Florida*. University of Florida, Agriculture Extension Service Bulletin 145.

Wilkins, H.F. 1986. "*Gardenia jasminoides.*" In: *CRC Handbook of Flowering*. vol V., ed. by A. H. Halevy, p. 127–131. Boca Raton, Florida: CRC Press.

ginger (white and yellow)

OTHER COMMON NAMES: *'awapuhi ke'oke'o* (white ginger), *'awapuhi melemele* (yellow ginger)

SCIENTIFIC NAME: *Hedychium coronarium, H. flavescens* and other species

FAMILY: Zingiberaceae (ginger family)

NATURAL SETTING/LOCATION: southwest China and northeast India

CURRENT STATUS IN THE WILD IN HAWAI'I: has potential to be invasive in wet areas

CULTIVARS: a number of hybrids exist with different colors and flower sizes; few are readily available

Growing your own

PROPAGATION

FORM: division of rhizomes is best; seeds

PREPLANTING TREATMENT: remove any diseased portion of the division and dust the cuts with fungicide before planting

PLANTING DEPTH: sow seeds on surface or slightly below (¼"); keep root crown of division just below soil level

GERMINATION TIME: 1 month

RHIZOME ROOTING TIME: 3–4 weeks

PREFERRED PRODUCTION CONDITIONS

GENERAL SOIL CHARACTERISTICS: high organic matter

SOIL PH: 5.5–6.5

LIGHT: full sun to partial shade

WATER: heavy watering

TEMPERATURE: 50–75°F

ELEVATION: 10–6000'

SALT TOLERANCE: poor

WIND RESISTANCE: poor

MANAGEMENT

FERTILIZER NEEDS: heavy

RECOMMENDED SPACING: 3–5' apart

ADAPTATION TO GROWING IN CONTAINERS: yes, 2–5-gallon tubs

PRUNING: remove old canes after flowering

SPECIAL CULTURAL HINTS: divide and replant after 5 years

SUGGESTED COMPANION PLANTINGS: can be grown under light shade of tall trees

ginger (white and yellow)

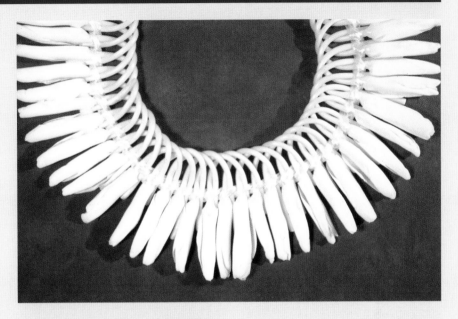

Plant characteristics

HEIGHT: to 5–6'

SPREAD: depends on age of clump (3–5' for 2–3-year-old plants)

GROWTH RATE: clump size increases 10% per year

GROWTH HABIT: upright, sprawling, herbaceous

FLOWERS

SIZE: 2½–3"

COLOR: white, yellow, orange

SHAPE: tubular

FRAGRANCE: yes, strong

FLOWERS IN FIRST YEAR: from divisions, yes; seeds take 2–3 years

FLOWERING PERIOD: white forms flower in late summer, yellow forms flower year-round

TIME TO FLOWERING: 3 months minimum, depending on size of division and time of year the division is taken; spring is the best time to make divisions

INDUCING AND MAINTAINING FLOWERING: in winter, use of flood lamps to interrupt dark period causes mature plants to flower 8–10 weeks later

PESTS

COMMON DISEASES: bacterial leaf spots, root rot, nematodes (root-knot, burrowing, lesion, reniform)

OTHER PESTS: ants, aphids, mealybugs, scales, thrips

Harvesting considerations

WHAT IS HARVESTED: flower buds

HARVESTING TECHNIQUES: pull buds from stalk

BEST WAY TO TRANSPORT FROM PICKING AREA: brown paper bag, or wrap in ti leaf and put in sealed container

AVOID CONTACT WITH THESE PRODUCTS: smoke, car exhaust, ripening fruits, and wilting flowers

Notes on lei making

BEST FOR WHICH TYPE OF LEI: neck, head, wrist, ankle

CLEANING OF PLANT MATERIALS: cold water soak

STORING RAW LEI MATERIALS: depends on lei pattern; for single or double, place buds in water to slightly open flowers; for Micronesian pattern, do not place in water, keep in bud form, and place on ti leaf sealed in cellophane; refrigerate at 40°F for up to 3 days

PREPARING FOR USE IN LEI: depends on lei pattern; for single or double, gently open up flowers; for Micronesian, leave bud covering on until lei is completed

STORING A COMPLETED LEI BEFORE WEARING: mist lei, place in sealed plastic container, and refrigerate

PRESERVING A LEI FOR LONG-TERM STORAGE OR DISPLAY: cannot be preserved

References and further reading

Chapman, Timothy S. 1995. *Ornamental Gingers: A Guide to Selection and Cultivation.* St. Gabriel, Louisiana: T.S. Chapman.

Clay, Horace F., and James C. Hubbard. 1977. *The Hawai'i Garden: Tropical Exotics.* Honolulu: University of Hawai'i Press.

Ide, Laurie S. 1998. *Hawaiian Lei Making: Step-by-Step Guide.* Honolulu: Mutual Publishing.

Riffle, Robert L. 1998. *The Tropical Look: An Encyclopedia of Dramatic Landscape Plants.* Portland, Oregon: Timber Press.

Introduced Perennials

hoya

OTHER COMMON NAMES: honey plant, *pua-hōkū-hihi*, star flower, wax plant

SCIENTIFIC NAME: *Hoya* species

FAMILY: Asclepiadaceae (milkweed family)

NATURAL SETTING/LOCATION: Asia, Oceanea

CURRENT STATUS IN THE WILD IN HAWAI'I: not found

CULTIVARS: many cultivars and species available: 'Exotica', 'Krinkle Kurl', 'Variegata'

Growing your own

PROPAGATION

FORM: cuttings; seeds (seeds rarely available)

PREPLANTING TREATMENT: allow cuttings to dry for 7 days before planting, treat with medium rooting hormone

PLANTING DEPTH: insert base of cutting 1" into medium

GERMINATION TIME: unknown

CUTTING ROOTING TIME: 2–3 weeks

PREFERRED PRODUCTION CONDITIONS

GENERAL SOIL CHARACTERISTICS: well drained, loose

SOIL PH: 6.0–6.5

LIGHT: full sun to partial shade

WATER: keep dry

TEMPERATURE: 45–105°F

ELEVATION: 10–2000'

SALT TOLERANCE: moderate

WIND RESISTANCE: good

MANAGEMENT

FERTILIZER NEEDS: medium

RECOMMENDED SPACING: 2' in rows

ADAPTATION TO GROWING IN CONTAINERS: yes, with a well drained and nematode-free medium; hanging baskets preferred; support needed when grown in pots

SPECIAL CULTURAL HINTS: spray whole plant when watering; highly susceptible to burrowing nematodes; provide trellis or other support

hoya

The lei shown also contains aster, rose, bleeding heart, globe amaranth, ageratum, bougainvillea, and 'ākia.

Plant characteristics

HEIGHT: 10', depending on support height

SPREAD: 36"

GROWTH RATE: fast to slow, depending on species

GROWTH HABIT: moderately compact vine

FLOWERS

SIZE: ¼–¾"

COLOR: white, pink, peach

SHAPE: flat with fleshy crown, star-shaped

FRAGRANCE: sweet

FLOWERS IN FIRST YEAR: possibly 3 clusters of flowers with stalks of nearly equal length

FLOWERING PERIOD: year-round

TIME TO FLOWERING: 6 months

INDUCING AND MAINTAINING FLOWERING: continual, minimal fertilizer

PESTS

COMMON DISEASES: fungal root rot, root-knot and burrowing nematodes

OTHER PESTS: mealybugs, scales

Harvesting considerations

WHAT IS HARVESTED: individual flowers and flower clusters

HARVESTING TECHNIQUES: do not remove persistent stalk (that which remains attached to the plant)

BEST TIME OF DAY TO HARVEST: early morning

BEST WAY TO TRANSPORT FROM PICKING AREA: paper bag

AVOID CONTACT WITH THESE PRODUCTS: smoke, car exhaust, ripening fruits, and wilting flowers

Notes on lei making

BEST FOR WHICH TYPE OF LEI: neck, head, wrist, ankle

CLEANING OF PLANT MATERIALS: cold water soak

STORING RAW LEI MATERIALS: keep damp with wet paper towels and refrigerate at 40°F for up to 10 days

PREPARING FOR USE IN LEI: clip off the wrinkled, limp, or poor quality areas before adding to lei. stem length should be ¼"

STORING A COMPLETED LEI BEFORE WEARING: soak lei, drip dry, wrap in damp paper towel in sealed plastic container, and refrigerate

PRESERVING A LEI FOR LONG-TERM STORAGE OR DISPLAY: air-dry

References and further reading

Elbert, Virginie F., and George A. Elbert. 1975. *Fun with Growing Odd and Curious House Plants*. New York: Crown Publishers Inc.

Heintze, Steven. 1981. Hoyas. *American Horticulturist* 60 (12): 2428, 35.

Hirsch, Doris F. 1977. *Indoor Plants: Comprehensive Care and Culture*. Radnor, Pennsylvania: Chilton Book Co.

hydrangea

OTHER COMMON NAMES: ajisai, hortensia, mil flores, *pōpōhau*

SCIENTIFIC NAME: *Hydrangea macrophylla*

FAMILY: Hydrangeaceae (hydrangea family)

NATURAL SETTING/LOCATION: native to Japan

CURRENT STATUS IN THE WILD IN HAWAIʻI: occasionally found but not naturalized

CULTIVARS: 'Bottstein', 'Jennifer', 'Rose Supreme', 'Sister Therese'

Growing your own

HANDLING CAUTIONS: all parts of the plant are poisonous if eaten

PROPAGATION

FORM: cuttings

PREPLANTING TREATMENT: treat with medium rooting hormone

PLANTING DEPTH: plant base 1–2" into medium

CUTTING ROOTING TIME: 3–5 weeks with mist and bottom heat (72°F)

PREFERRED PRODUCTION CONDITIONS

GENERAL SOIL CHARACTERISTICS: well drained loam or sandy loam

SOIL PH: pink flowers are produced at pH >6.0–6.5, blue flowers are produced with the addition of aluminum sulfate and a lower pH of 5.0–5.5

LIGHT: full sun to partial shade

WATER: keep moist

TEMPERATURE: for flower initiation, night temperature in the 65–70°F range is necessary; an exposure to 52°F for a period of 6–8 weeks will improve flowering

ELEVATION: 500–3500' (flowering is erratic at lower elevations)

SALT TOLERANCE: poor

WIND RESISTANCE: poor

MANAGEMENT

FERTILIZER NEEDS: medium

RECOMMENDED SPACING: 3–5' apart

ADAPTATION TO GROWING IN CONTAINERS: yes, 3–5-gallon tubs or large planter boxes

PRUNING: pinch shoots back to 2 nodes in late May and early July; thin out weak growth early in the year; don't prune late in the year or you may lose next year's flowers

SPECIAL CULTURAL HINTS: pinch through early summer to produce many branches; plants under long-day conditions remain vegetative, while short-day conditions encourage flower initiation; for pink flowers, avoid acidic soils high in aluminum (Al); for blue flowers, high-Al soils are good, or aluminum sulfate can be added to lower pH; if Al is added to pots with pink flowers, they may gradually turn to a mauve-blue color; some cultivars have stable flower color

SUGGESTED COMPANION PLANTINGS: azalea

hydrangea

The lei shown also contains feverfew, baby's breath, rose, ageratum, statice, and chrysanthemum.

Plant characteristics

HEIGHT: to 10'

SPREAD: to 5–6'

GROWTH RATE: fast

GROWTH HABIT: spreading shrub

FLOWERS

SIZE: inflorescences are 4–8" in diameter

COLOR: white, pink, red, blue, lavender, mauve

SHAPE: inflorescence spherical, individual florets squarish

FRAGRANCE: none

FLOWERS IN FIRST YEAR: yes if forced, but normally flowering occurs during the second year

FLOWERING PERIOD: spring

TIME TO FLOWERING: floral development requires 8–10 weeks from initiation

INDUCING AND MAINTAINING FLOWERING: for plants grown in covered areas, 6–10 weeks of short days (8–12 hours) and 65°F nights in late summer are needed to stimulate flower initiation; for potted plants, provide 6 weeks of temperature below 55°F and force at 60–65°F; no good control system for open field–grown plants

FOLIAGE

TEXTURE: coarse

COLOR: dark green

SHAPE: ovate with serrated margins and accuminate tip

FRAGRANCE: none

PESTS

COMMON DISEASES: powdery mildew, root rot, various leaf spots, viruses

OTHER PESTS: aphids, mites, scales, slugs, snails, thrips, whiteflies

Harvesting considerations

WHAT IS HARVESTED: inflorescence or parts of one

HARVESTING TECHNIQUES: pluck individual inflorescence

BEST TIME OF DAY TO HARVEST: early morning

BEST WAY TO TRANSPORT FROM PICKING AREA: paper bag

AVOID CONTACT WITH THESE PRODUCTS: smoke, car exhaust, ripening fruits, and wilting flowers

Notes on lei making

BEST FOR WHICH TYPE OF LEI: neck, head, wrist, ankle, horse

VASE LIFE: 4 days

CLEANING OF PLANT MATERIALS: cold water soak

STORING RAW LEI MATERIALS: wrap individual flowers in wet paper towel, place in plastic or paper container, and refrigerate at 40°F for up to 10 days.

PREPARING FOR USE IN LEI: clip off the wrinkled, limp, or poor quality areas before adding to lei

STORING A COMPLETED LEI BEFORE WEARING: soak lei, drip dry, wrap in wet paper towel, place in plastic or paper container, and refrigerate

PRESERVING A LEI FOR LONG-TERM STORAGE OR DISPLAY: air-dry when flowers are older (in the green color stage)

References and further reading

Bailey, Douglas A. 1989. *Hydrangea Production.* Portland, Oregon: Timber Press.

Miller, Robert O. 1998. "*Hydrangea.*" In: *Ball Red Book,* 16th ed., p. 553–564. Batavia, Illinois: Ball Publishing.

Introduced Perennials

ixora

OTHER COMMON NAMES: *pōpōlehua*

SCIENTIFIC NAME: *Ixora coccinea*; *I. chinensis*; *I. casei*

FAMILY: Rubiaceae (coffee family)

NATURAL SETTING/LOCATION: Southeast Asia and China

CURRENT STATUS IN THE WILD IN HAWAI'I: not found

CULTIVARS: many cultivars are available, in dwarf and standard sizes; 'Nora Grant' is very popular

Growing your own

PROPAGATION

FORM: terminal cuttings; air layering

PREPLANTING TREATMENT: treat cuttings with medium rooting hormone

PLANTING DEPTH: insert base of cutting 1–2" into medium

CUTTING ROOTING TIME: 2–3 months

PREFERRED PRODUCTION CONDITIONS

GENERAL SOIL CHARACTERISTICS: well drained, loamy to sandy loam; in pots, 1:2:2 soil:peat:perlite or volcanic cinders

SOIL PH: 5.0–5.5; considerable chlorosis develops at higher pH

LIGHT: full sun (tolerates partial shade but does not flower as profusely)

WATER: keep moist

TEMPERATURE: 55–90°F

ELEVATION: 10–1000'

SALT TOLERANCE: moderate

WIND RESISTANCE: good

MANAGEMENT

FERTILIZER NEEDS: medium; to correct chlorosis, apply acidifying fertilizer such as iron sulfate

RECOMMENDED SPACING: larger type should be planted about 5' on center unless grown as a hedge, in which case 8–36", depending on type

ADAPTATION TO GROWING IN CONTAINERS: yes, 2-gallon tubs or larger with drainage

PRUNING: cut back to leave 3–4 leaf pairs on a branch; thin out weak branches

ixora

Plant characteristics

HEIGHT: 2–12'

SPREAD: 2–5'

GROWTH RATE: moderate

GROWTH HABIT: spreading to erect, evergreen, woody shrub

FLOWERS

SIZE: terminal clusters up to 10" across; a double red form exists

COLOR: white, red, pink, orange, yellow

SHAPE: individual flowers with long tube and 4-lobed petals

FRAGRANCE: none

FLOWERS IN FIRST YEAR: yes

FLOWERING PERIOD: year-round, heaviest in summer

TIME TO FLOWERING: from transplanted cuttings, allow 4–6 months; seedlings have a juvinility period and take longer to flower than do cuttings

INDUCING AND MAINTAINING FLOWERING: flowers occur on new growth; prune as needed to produce new shoots; pruning back to old wood stimulates small axillary flower clusters; use of a growth retardant stimulates flowering

PESTS

COMMON DISEASES: root rot in wet soils, *Botrytis* on flowers in wet weather, leaf spots, nematodes, sooty mold with high insect populations, susceptible to nutrient imbalances

OTHER PESTS: ants, aphids, mealybugs, scales, whiteflies

The lei shown also contains bougainvillea, epidendrum orchid, panax, aster, *moa*, and ti.

Harvesting considerations

WHAT IS HARVESTED: flowers

HARVESTING TECHNIQUES: pluck indiviudal flowers

BEST TIME OF DAY TO HARVEST: early morning

BEST WAY TO TRANSPORT FROM PICKING AREA: paper or cloth bag

AVOID CONTACT WITH THESE PRODUCTS: smoke, car exhaust, ripening fruits, and wilting flowers

Notes on lei making

BEST FOR WHICH TYPE OF LEI: neck, head, wrist, ankle

VASE LIFE: 2 days

CLEANING OF PLANT MATERIALS: cold water soak

STORING RAW LEI MATERIALS: store in water and refrigerate at 40°F for up to 4 days

PREPARING FOR USE IN LEI: clip off wrinkled, limp, or poor quality areas before adding to lei

STORING A COMPLETED LEI BEFORE WEARING: soak lei, drip dry, place on wet paper towel in sealed plastic container, and refrigerate

PRESERVING A LEI FOR LONG-TERM STORAGE OR DISPLAY: cannot be preserved

References and further reading

Clay, Horace F., and James C. Hubbard. 1977. *The Hawaii Garden: Tropical Shrubs*. Honolulu: University of Hawai'i Press.

Odenwald, Neil G., and James R. Turner. 1980. *Plants for the South: A Guide to Landscape Design*. Baton Rouge, Louisiana: Claitor's Publishing Division.

Rauch, Fred D. 1996. *Tropical Landscape Plants*. 3rd ed. Battle Ground, Washington: Hawaii Floriculture.

Shillo, Ruth, and Hadas Tsook. 1989. "*Ixora*." In: *CRC Handbook of Flowering*, vol. VI, p. 379–386. Boca Raton, Florida: CRC Press.

joyweed

OTHER COMMON NAMES: Joseph's coat, *palewāwae*

SCIENTIFIC NAME: *Alternanthera tenella*

FAMILY: Amaranthaceae (amaranth family)

NATURAL SETTING/LOCATION: tropical and subtropical America

CURRENT STATUS IN THE WILD IN HAWAI'I: not found

CULTIVARS: other species of the genus *Alternanthera* can be used; review seed catalogs for available color forms and leaf varieties

Growing your own

PROPAGATION

FORM: cuttings (2–3" cuttings root rapidly); division

PREPLANTING TREATMENT: rooting hormone not needed

PLANTING DEPTH: insert base of cutting 1" into medium; keep division root crown just below soil level

CUTTING ROOTING TIME: 7–14 days

PREFERRED PRODUCTION CONDITIONS

GENERAL SOIL CHARACTERISTICS: well drained, moisture-retentive

SOIL PH: 5.5–6.5

LIGHT: full sun produces the best leaf color; tolerates partial shade

WATER: moderate

TEMPERATURE: frost-tender; low temperatures reduce foliage color

ELEVATION: 10–2000'

SALT TOLERANCE: poor

WIND RESISTANCE: poor

MANAGEMENT

FERTILIZER NEEDS: medium; fertilize lightly after shearing

RECOMMENDED SPACING: 4–6" apart

ADAPTATION TO GROWING IN CONTAINERS: yes, ½–1-gallon pots, but planting in the ground is better

PRUNING: responds well to clipping and shearing and can be maintained at 4–6" height; plants become weak and thin when allowed to grow too tall

joyweed

Plant characteristics

HEIGHT: 6–12"

SPREAD: 10–12"

GROWTH RATE: fast

GROWTH HABIT: low, creeping, mat-like shrub

FOLIAGE

TEXTURE: smooth

COLOR: multicolored in yellow, red, orange, green, and white

SHAPE: spoon shaped or ovoid

FRAGRANCE: none

PESTS

COMMON DISEASES: root rot, foliar blights, southern blight, rootknot nematodes

OTHER PESTS: broad mite, mealybugs, slugs, snails

Harvesting considerations

WHAT IS HARVESTED: branch tips

HARVESTING TECHNIQUES: cut, don't pull

BEST TIME OF DAY TO HARVEST: early morning

BEST WAY TO TRANSPORT FROM PICKING AREA: paper or cloth bag

AVOID CONTACT WITH THESE PRODUCTS: smoke, car exhaust, ripening fruits, and wilting flowers

The lei shown also contains crown flower, liriope, *moa*, baby's breath, and pentas.

Notes on lei making

BEST FOR WHICH TYPE OF LEI: neck, head, wrist, ankle, horse

VASE LIFE: 3 days

CLEANING OF PLANT MATERIALS: cold water soak

STORING RAW LEI MATERIALS: refrigerate in plastic container at 40°F for up to 14 days

PREPARING FOR USE IN LEI: clip off wrinkled, limp, or poor quality areas before adding to lei

STORING A COMPLETED LEI BEFORE WEARING: soak lei in water for 5 minutes, drip dry, wrap in damp newspaper, place in sealed plastic container, and refrigerate

PRESERVING A LEI FOR LONG-TERM STORAGE OR DISPLAY: air-dry

References and further reading

Holttum, Richard E., and Ivan Enoch. 1991. *Gardening in the Tropics.* Singapore: Times Editions.

Odenwald, Neil G., and James R. Turner. 1980. *Plants for the South: A Guide to Landscape Design.* Baton Rouge, Louisiana: Claitor's Publishing Division.

Still, Steven M. 1994. *Manual of Herbaceous Ornamental Plants.* Champaign, Illinois: Stipes Publishing Co.

Warren, William. 1997. *Tropical Plants for Home and Garden.* London: Thames and Hudson.

Introduced Perennials

kalanchoe

SCIENTIFIC NAME: *Kalanchoe* species, and cultivars of *K. blossfeldiana*

FAMILY: Crassulaceae (orpine family)

NATURAL SETTING/LOCATION: native to Madagascar

CURRENT STATUS IN THE WILD IN HAWAI'I: not found

CULTIVARS: many available from commercial sources: 'Pumila', 'Tetra Vulcan'

Growing your own

PROPAGATION

FORM: stem cuttings 2–3 nodes long; leaf cuttings used for some species; preferred propagation material varies among species; seeds available from some seed sources

PREPLANTING TREATMENT: cuttings can be dried for 3–4 days before propagating; use mild rooting hormone

PLANTING DEPTH: insert base of cutting 1–2" into medium; sow seeds on surface of medium, do not cover

GERMINATION TIME: 15 days

CUTTING ROOTING TIME: 3 weeks for stem cuttings; leaf cuttings may require 8–10 weeks to generate roots and shoots

PREFERRED PRODUCTION CONDITIONS

GENERAL SOIL CHARACTERISTICS: well drained; in pots, 2:1:1 peat:perlite:sand; plant has fine root system and needs a fine medium, so commercial mixes that are mostly peat and perlite are satisfactory

SOIL PH: 5.8–6.5

LIGHT: 50–60% shade to full sun; plants are photoperiod-sensitive: long days promote vegetative growth, while short days (9–10 hours of light) are required for flowering

WATER: drought tolerant; do not over-water; allow the soil to dry slightly before watering

TEMPERATURE: flowering delayed below 65°F or above 75°F

ELEVATION: 1000–3500'; some cultivars adapted to low elevations

SALT TOLERANCE: moderate

WIND RESISTANCE: good

MANAGEMENT

FERTILIZER NEEDS: medium

RECOMMENDED SPACING: a 6" potted plant would require 12–15" space from its center to the center of the adjacent plant

ADAPTATION TO GROWING IN CONTAINERS: yes, 4–8" plastic or clay pots

PRUNING: about 3 weeks after potting, pinch out one set of leaves from tip of plant to induce more branches; pinching delays flower development by 4 weeks

SPECIAL CULTURAL HINTS: avoid oil-based or emulsifiable sprays

SUGGESTED COMPANION PLANTINGS: begonia

kalanchoe

Introduced Perennials

Plant characteristics

HEIGHT: to 40" (depending on species)

SPREAD: to 12" (depending on species)

GROWTH RATE: slow to moderate

GROWTH HABIT: compact, succulent herb

FLOWERS

SIZE: clusters to 4" in diameter

COLOR: red, yellow, orange, pink, rose, white (some species with two-tone flowers)

SHAPE: round to irregular cluster of 4-petalled flowers

FRAGRANCE: none

FLOWERS IN FIRST YEAR: yes

FLOWERING PERIOD: during and following the short-day period of the year

TIME TO FLOWERING: from seed: about 10–11 months; from cuttings: 12–16 weeks, depending on variety and daylength treatments

INDUCING AND MAINTAINING FLOWERING: provide rooted transplants with 2–4 weeks of long days (minimum 12 hours of light) both before and after pinching; to time of flowering, provide 3–6 weeks of short days (11–11½ hours of light); flower development requires 5–8 weeks from the end of short days, depending on the variety

PESTS

COMMON DISEASES: bacterial soft rot, *Botrytis* on the flowers, mildew on the foliage, fungal leafspot, crown rot, rootknot nematodes

OTHER PESTS: aphids, caterpillars, mealybugs, thrips, whiteflies

The lei shown also contains panax and shinobu.

Harvesting considerations

WHAT IS HARVESTED: flower spikes

HARVESTING TECHNIQUES: pinch flowers off

BEST TIME OF DAY TO HARVEST: early morning

BEST WAY TO TRANSPORT FROM PICKING AREA: cloth or paper bag or container

AVOID CONTACT WITH THESE PRODUCTS: smoke, car exhaust, ripening fruits, and wilting flowers

Notes on lei making

BEST FOR WHICH TYPE OF LEI: neck, head, wrist, ankle, horse

CLEANING OF PLANT MATERIALS: stick stems in water

STORING RAW LEI MATERIALS: store in sealed plastic container and refrigerate at 40–45°F for up to 7 days

PREPARING FOR USE IN LEI: *haku* (mounting against a background) pattern requires about 3–4" of stem with a cluster tied together; clip off wrinkled, limp, or poor quality areas before adding to lei

STORING A COMPLETED LEI BEFORE WEARING: soak lei, shake off excess water, place in sealed plastic container, and refrigerate

PRESERVING A LEI FOR LONG-TERM STORAGE OR DISPLAY: cannot be preserved

References and further reading

Ball, V., ed. 1998. "*Kalanchoe.*" In: *Ball Redbook,* 16 ed., p. 586–591. Batavia, Illinois: Ball Publishing Co.

Pertuit, A.J. 1997. "*Kalanchoe.*" In: *Tips on Growing Specialty Crops.* Columbus, Ohio: Ohio Floral Association.

kīkānia

SCIENTIFIC NAME:
Solanum capsicoides

FAMILY: Solanaceae
(nightshade family)

NATURAL SETTING/LOCATION: native to Brazil

CURRENT STATUS IN THE WILD IN HAWAI'I: common weed in disturbed areas such as pastures, trails, and pond banks

Growing your own

HANDLING CAUTIONS: fruits are used in lei but are poisonous if eaten; stems and foliage have thorns

PROPAGATION

FORM: seeds

PRETREATMENT: remove seeds from pulp, soak in water for 24 hours

PLANTING DEPTH: sow ¼" deep in medium

GERMINATION TIME: 2 weeks

PREFERRED PRODUCTION CONDITIONS

GENERAL SOIL CHARACTERISTICS: well drained

SOIL PH: 5.5–6.5

LIGHT: sunny location

WATER: keep dry

TEMPERATURE: 60–80°F

ELEVATION: 10–2500'

SALT TOLERANCE: poor

WIND RESISTANCE: moderate

MANAGEMENT

FERTILIZER NEEDS: medium

RECOMMENDED SPACING: 4' apart

ADAPTATION TO GROWING IN CONTAINERS: not recommended

SPECIAL CULTURAL HINTS: pick spent flowers; for larger fruits, remove new flowers after first fruits have set

kīkānia

Plant characteristics

HEIGHT: to 36"

SPREAD: to 36"

GROWTH RATE: fast

GROWTH HABIT: short-lived shrub

FRUIT

SIZE: ⅜–1"

COLOR: orange at maturity

SHAPE: round

TYPE: smooth, hard berry

FRAGRANCE: none

FLOWERS IN FIRST YEAR: yes

FLOWERING PERIOD: year-round

TIME TO FLOWERING: 4 months

INDUCING AND MAINTAINING FLOWERING: plant is always flowering

PESTS

COMMON DISEASES: alternaria and other foliar diseases affecting nightshade plants

OTHER PESTS: mealybugs, mites, whiteflies

Harvesting considerations

WHAT IS HARVESTED: mature fruits

HARVESTING TECHNIQUES: pick fruit by hand; gloves advised due to thorns on stems and foliage

BEST TIME OF DAY TO HARVEST: early morning

BEST WAY TO TRANSPORT FROM PICKING AREA: glass jar

The lei shown also contains bird of paradise and *kuhuna o ka lā* (mangrove).

Notes on lei making

BEST FOR WHICH TYPE OF LEI: neck, head, wrist, ankle, horse

CLEANING OF PLANT MATERIALS: no water

STORING RAW LEI MATERIALS: store in glass or plastic container and refrigerate at 40°F for up to 20 days; no water

PREPARING FOR USE IN LEI: remove calyx (green, leafy base) and stem before sewing

STORING A COMPLETED LEI BEFORE WEARING: place in glass or plastic container and refrigerate; no water

PRESERVING A LEI FOR LONG-TERM STORAGE OR DISPLAY: cannot be preserved

References and further reading

Haselwood, E.L., and G.G. Motter. 1983. *Handbook of Hawaiian Weeds*. 2nd ed., revised and expanded by Robert Hirano, Harold L. Lyon Arboretum. Honolulu: University of Hawai'i Press.

Ide, Laurie S. 1998. *Hawaiian Lei Making: Step-by-Step Guide*. Honolulu: Mutual Publishing.

McDonald, Marie A. 1989. *Ka Lei: the Leis of Hawaii*. Honolulu: Ku Pa'a Inc., and Press Pacifica.

Introduced Perennials

lantern *'ilima* and royal *'ilima*

OTHER COMMON NAMES: abutilon, *mao* (lantern *'ilima*); triple *'ilima* (royal *'ilima*)

SCIENTIFIC NAME: *Abutilon pictum* (lantern *'ilima*); *A. grandiflorum* (royal *'ilima*)

FAMILY: Malvaceae (mallow family)

NATURAL SETTING/LOCATION: Brazil, Uruguay, and Argentina

CURRENT STATUS IN THE WILD IN HAWAI'I: *A. pictum* not found; *A. grandiflorum* naturalized in dry areas

Growing your own

PROPAGATION

FORM: cuttings; seeds

PREPLANTING TREATMENT: soak seeds in water for 24 hours; treat cuttings with medium rooting hormone, place under mist

PLANTING DEPTH: sow seeds ¼" deep in medium; insert base of cutting 1–2" into medium

GERMINATION TIME: 1–3 months

CUTTING ROOTING TIME: 3–5 weeks

PREFERRED PRODUCTION CONDITIONS

GENERAL SOIL CHARACTERISTICS: well drained

SOIL PH: 6.0–7.5

LIGHT: full sun

WATER: apply ½" every other day in dry areas once established

TEMPERATURE: 45–90°F

ELEVATION: 10–2500'

SALT TOLERANCE: poor

WIND RESISTANCE: very poor

MANAGEMENT

FERTILIZER NEEDS: medium

RECOMMENDED SPACING: 4' apart

ADAPTATION TO GROWING IN CONTAINERS: yes, 10-gallon tubs

PRUNING: prune to manage size and shape and keep full and bushy

SPECIAL CULTURAL HINTS: plant in raised beds or mounds in areas with poor drainage; stake in areas where winds are strong; a beneficial virus (abutilon mosaic virus) causes leaves to be mottled and rugose (bumpy); plants without the virus have smooth leaves and grow vigorously but produce flowers that are not desirable and are few in number; royal *'ilima* grown from seed varies in size, shape, and growing characteristics

lantern *'ilima* and royal *'ilima*

Plant characteristics

HEIGHT: 8'

SPREAD: 4'

GROWTH RATE: fast

GROWTH HABIT: sprawling shrub

FLOWERS

SIZE: 1"

COLOR: yellow with red veins and stamens *(A. pictum)*; yellow-orange *(A. grandiflorum)*

SHAPE: bell-shaped *(A. pictum)*; tight cluster, roundish *(A. grandiflorum)*

FRAGRANCE: none

FLOWERS IN FIRST YEAR: yes

FLOWERING PERIOD: year-round

TIME TO FLOWERING: some flower at 4–6 months; maturity after 12–18 months

PESTS

COMMON DISEASES: root rot, rust fungi *(A. grandiflorum)*; *A. pictum* is affected by abutilon mosaic virus (causing mottled leaves) but it is not a problem; nematodes

OTHER PESTS: Chinese rose beetle, mealybugs, thrips, whiteflies

Harvesting considerations

WHAT IS HARVESTED: flowers

HARVESTING TECHNIQUES: pull or snap

BEST TIME OF DAY TO HARVEST: early morning

BEST WAY TO TRANSPORT FROM PICKING AREA: paper or cloth bag

AVOID CONTACT WITH THESE PRODUCTS: smoke, car exhaust, ripening fruits, and wilting flowers

Notes on lei making

BEST FOR WHICH TYPE OF LEI: neck, head, wrist, ankle

VASE LIFE: 8–24 hours

CLEANING OF PLANT MATERIALS: no water

STORING RAW LEI MATERIALS: store in shallow, stackable open trays until flowers open. don't pack in boxes; refrigerator temperature should be less than 40°F (38°F is good); no water

PREPARING FOR USE IN LEI: remove calyx (green, leafy base) before stringing

STORING A COMPLETED LEI BEFORE WEARING: place lei in sealed container and refrigerate; no water

PRESERVING A LEI FOR LONG-TERM STORAGE OR DISPLAY: cannot be preserved

References and further reading

Ide, Laurie S. 1998. *Hawaiian Lei Making: Step-by-Step Guide*. Honolulu: Mutual Publishing.

Odenwald, Neil G., and James R. Turner. 1980. *Plants for the South: A Guide to Landscape Design*. Baton Rouge, Louisiana: Claitor's Publishing Division.

Still, Steven M. 1994. *Manual of Herbaceous Ornamental Plants*. Champaign, Illinois: Stipes Publishing Co.

Introduced Perennials

laua'e

OTHER COMMON NAMES: *lauwa'e, maile*-scented fern

SCIENTIFIC NAME: *Phymatosorus grossus (Microsorum scolopendria)*

FAMILY: Polypodiaceae (polypody family)

NATURAL SETTING/LOCATION: Old World tropics, Polynesia

CURRENT STATUS IN THE WILD IN HAWAI'I: common; naturalized, especially in disturbed areas, from coastal to shaded moist lowland forests and windswept ridges

CULTIVARS: *laua'e iki* (dwarf cultivar)

Growing your own

HANDLING CAUTIONS: may cause skin irritation

PROPAGATION

FORM: spores; division; rhizome cuttings (with at least one node)

PREPLANTING TREATMENT: rooting hormone not needed for cuttings

PLANTING DEPTH: sow spores on surface of medium; keep division root crown just below soil level; insert base of cutting 1–2" into medium

CUTTING ROOTING TIME: 6–8 weeks

PREFERRED PRODUCTION CONDITIONS

GENERAL SOIL CHARACTER-ISTICS: rich, well drained

SOIL PH: 5.5–6.5

LIGHT: full sun to light shade

WATER: moderate to wet

TEMPERATURE: 55–90°F

ELEVATION: 10–1500'

SALT TOLERANCE: moderate

WIND RESISTANCE: poor to moderate

MANAGEMENT

FERTILIZER NEEDS: medium

RECOMMENDED SPACING: 1' apart

ADAPTATION TO GROWING IN CONTAINERS: yes, 3-gallon tubs or larger

PRUNING: remove old fronds

SPECIAL CULTURAL HINTS: keep in contained area to keep it from taking

over unplanted areas; full sun will cause fronds to be lighter green

SUGGESTED COMPANION PLANTINGS: plants that provide shade

laua'e

Plant characteristics

HEIGHT: 2–3'

SPREAD: 6–10'

GROWTH RATE: slow at first, fast when established

GROWTH HABIT: fern, groundcover

FOLIAGE

TEXTURE: smooth

COLOR: green to black

SHAPE: large, pinnately lobed

FRAGRANCE: spicy, *maile*-like

PESTS

COMMON DISEASES: fungal root rot, root-knot and lesion nematodes

OTHER PESTS: fern weevil, mites, scales, slugs, snails

Harvesting considerations

WHAT IS HARVESTED: leaves

HARVESTING TECHNIQUES: cut, don't pull

BEST TIME OF DAY TO HARVEST: early morning

BEST WAY TO TRANSPORT FROM PICKING AREA: paper or cloth bag

The lei shown also contains asparagus fern and dusty miller.

Notes on lei making

BEST FOR WHICH TYPE OF LEI: neck, head, wrist, ankle, horse

VASE LIFE: 14 days

CLEANING OF PLANT MATERIALS: cold water soak

STORING RAW LEI MATERIALS: store in sealed plastic container and refrigerate at 40°F for up to 30 days

PREPARING FOR USE IN LEI: leave fronds out overnight to soften, then braid with ti leaf

STORING A COMPLETED LEI BEFORE WEARING: soak lei, drip dry, wrap in damp newspaper, place in sealed plastic container, and refrigerate

PRESERVING A LEI FOR LONG-TERM STORAGE OR DISPLAY: air-dry

References and further reading

Hoshizaki, Barbara J. 1976. *Fern Grower's Manual*. New York: Alfred A. Knopf.

Neal, Marie C. 1965. *In Gardens of Hawaii*. Bernice P. Bishop Museum Special Publication 50. Honolulu: Bishop Museum Press.

Valier, Kathy. 1995. *Ferns of Hawai'i*. Honolulu: University of Hawai'i Press.

Introduced Perennials

maunaloa

SCIENTIFIC NAME:
Canavalia cathartica

FAMILY: Fabaceae (pea family)

NATURAL SETTING/LOCATION: East Africa, India, Malaysia, Polynesia

CURRENT STATUS IN THE WILD IN HAWAI'I: naturalized in dry to mesic (medium-wet) disturbed sites

Growing your own

PROPAGATION

FORM: seeds

PLANTING DEPTH: sow seeds ½" deep in medium

GERMINATION TIME: 7 days

PREFERRED PRODUCTION CONDITIONS

GENERAL SOIL CHARACTERISTICS: tolerant of many soil types

SOIL PH: 6.0–7.0

LIGHT: sunny location

WATER: drought tolerant

TEMPERATURE: 50–90°F

ELEVATION: 10–1000'

SALT TOLERANCE: moderate

WIND RESISTANCE: moderate

MANAGEMENT

FERTILIZER NEEDS: light

RECOMMENDED SPACING: 4' apart

ADAPTATION TO GROWING IN CONTAINERS: not recommended

PRUNING: prune to keep plant manageable for easy harvesting

SPECIAL CULTURAL HINTS: provide a trellis or other support; may become weedy if left unchecked

maunaloa

Plant characteristics

HEIGHT: limited to height of support

SPREAD: 20'

GROWTH RATE: fast

GROWTH HABIT: rampant vine

FLOWERS

SIZE: 1½"

COLOR: lavender, pink, purple

SHAPE: bilaterally symmetrical, like a pea flower

FRAGRANCE: none

FLOWERS IN FIRST YEAR: yes

FLOWERING PERIOD: year-round, heaviest in spring and summer

TIME TO FLOWERING: 3 months

INDUCING AND MAINTAINING FLOWERING: remove spent flowers and pods

PESTS

COMMON DISEASES: fungal root rot

OTHER PESTS: black stink bug

Harvesting considerations

WHAT IS HARVESTED: flowers

HARVESTING TECHNIQUES: pinch flowers off

BEST TIME OF DAY TO HARVEST: early morning

BEST WAY TO TRANSPORT FROM PICKING AREA: paper or cloth container

AVOID CONTACT WITH THESE PRODUCTS: smoke, car exhaust, ripening fruits, and wilting flowers

Notes on lei making

BEST FOR WHICH TYPE OF LEI: neck, head, wrist, ankle

CLEANING OF PLANT MATERIALS: spray with water.

STORING RAW LEI MATERIALS: store in sealed plastic bag or container and refrigerate at 40°F for up to 3 days; no water

PREPARING FOR USE IN LEI: clip off wrinkled, limp, or poor quality areas before adding to lei

STORING A COMPLETED LEI BEFORE WEARING: place lei on wax paper in sealed plastic bag or container and refrigerate; no water

PRESERVING A LEI FOR LONG-TERM STORAGE OR DISPLAY: cannot be preserved

References and further reading

Ide, Laurie S. 1998. *Hawaiian Lei Making: Step-by-Step Guide*. Honolulu: Mutual Publishing.

Kuck, Loraine E., and Richard C. Tongg. 1955. *The Modern Tropical Garden: Its Design, Plant Materials, and Horticulture*. Honolulu: Tongg Publishing Co.

Neal, Marie C. 1965. *In Gardens of Hawaii*. Bernice P. Bishop Museum Special Publication 50. Honolulu: Bishop Museum Press.

Introduced Perennials

'ohai ali'i

OTHER COMMON NAMES: dwarf poinciana, pride of Barbados

SCIENTIFIC NAME:
Caesalpinia pulcherrima

FAMILY: Fabaceae (pea family)

NATURAL SETTING/LOCATION:
tropical America

CURRENT STATUS IN THE WILD IN HAWAI'I: not found

CULTIVARS: none named; red-orange, yellow, pink, cream, and rose types are grown

Growing your own

HANDLING CAUTIONS: thorns on stems

PROPAGATION

FORM: seeds

PREPLANTING TREATMENT: soak seeds in water for 24 hours

PLANTING DEPTH: sow in well drained medium (1 seed per container, ¼" deep in medium) and put in full sun

GERMINATION TIME: 7 days

PREFERRED PRODUCTION CONDITIONS

GENERAL SOIL CHARACTERISTICS: rich, well drained

SOIL PH: 5.5–6.5

LIGHT: sunny location

WATER: drought tolerant

TEMPERATURE: 50–90°F

ELEVATION: 10–1500' or more

SALT TOLERANCE: moderate

WIND RESISTANCE: good

MANAGEMENT

FERTILIZER NEEDS: light

RECOMMENDED SPACING: 6–8' apart

ADAPTATION TO GROWING IN CONTAINERS: yes, 3-gallon tubs or larger

PRUNING: thin out weak growth and head back (cut back) vigorous shoots to induce branching; prune branch tips to old wood after flowering

SPECIAL CULTURAL HINTS: plants can be variable when grown from seed; may become weedy if left unchecked

SUGGESTED COMPANION PLANTINGS: ferns

'ohai ali'i

Plant characteristics

HEIGHT: 10'

SPREAD: 10'

GROWTH RATE: fast

GROWTH HABIT: rounded shrub or small tree

FLOWERS

SIZE: 1" diameter, 2" long

COLOR: red-orange, yellow, pink, rose, cream

SHAPE: round, with long stamens

FRAGRANCE: none

FLOWERS IN FIRST YEAR: yes

FLOWERING PERIOD: year-round

TIME TO FLOWERING: 6–12 months

INDUCING AND MAINTAINING FLOWERING: remove seed pods as they form to maintain flowering

PESTS

COMMON DISEASES: fungal stem rot, root rot

OTHER PESTS: caterpillars, scales

Harvesting considerations

WHAT IS HARVESTED: flowers with 1–2" of stem

HARVESTING TECHNIQUES: pinch flowers

BEST TIME OF DAY TO HARVEST: early morning

BEST WAY TO TRANSPORT FROM PICKING AREA: paper or cloth container

AVOID CONTACT WITH THESE PRODUCTS: smoke, car exhaust, ripening fruits, and wilting flowers

The lei shown also contains dracaena tricolor and Mexican creeper.

Notes on lei making

BEST FOR WHICH TYPE OF LEI: neck, head, wrist, ankle

CLEANING OF PLANT MATERIALS: cold water soak

STORING RAW LEI MATERIALS: store in sealed plastic container in refrigerator at 40°F for up to 4 days

PREPARING FOR USE IN LEI: for sewing, clip stem when picking; for *haku* (mounting against a background) or *wili* (twisting pattern), leave stem; mist with water frequently while making lei

STORING A COMPLETED LEI BEFORE WEARING: mist lei, place on dry tissue paper in sealed plastic container, and refrigerate

PRESERVING A LEI FOR LONG-TERM STORAGE OR DISPLAY: cannot be preserved

References and further reading

Clay, Horace F., and James C. Hubbard. 1977. *The Hawaii Garden: Tropical Shrubs*. Honolulu: University of Hawai'i Press.

Ide, Laurie S. 1998. *Hawaiian Lei Making: Step-by-Step Guide*. Honolulu: Mutual Publishing.

Rauch, Fred D. 1996. *Tropical Landscape Plants*. 3rd ed. Battle Ground, Washington: Hawaii Floriculture.

Warren, William. 1997. *Tropical Plants for Home and Garden*. London: Thames and Hudson.

Introduced Perennials

orchid: cymbidium

OTHER COMMON NAMES: *'okika*

SCIENTIFIC NAME: *Cymbidium* species

FAMILY: Orchidaceae (orchid family)

NATURAL SETTING/LOCATION: Southeast Asia to India

CURRENT STATUS IN THE WILD IN HAWAI'I: not found

CULTIVARS: many large and miniature species and varieties

Growing your own

PROPAGATION

FORM: seeds; mericloning (commercial growers purchase tissue-cultured plantlets in sterile flasks); division

PREPLANTING TREATMENT: pods are sterilized before aseptic culture; remove old foliage and bulbs from divisions

PLANTING DEPTH: sow seeds on surface of aseptic medium; keep division root crown just below soil level

GERMINATION TIME: 2–3 months

PREFERRED PRODUCTION CONDITIONS

GENERAL SOIL CHARACTERISTICS: soilless media, gravel, cinder, *hāpu'u*, wood bark

SOIL PH: 5.5–6.5

LIGHT: full sun to partial shade

WATER: keep moist

TEMPERATURE: 55°F at night during summer

ELEVATION: 1500–4000'

SALT TOLERANCE: poor

WIND RESISTANCE: poor

MANAGEMENT

FERTILIZER NEEDS: light to medium; varies among types

RECOMMENDED SPACING: 2 ft^2 per plant

ADAPTATION TO GROWING IN CONTAINERS: yes, 2-gallon plastic pots or larger

PRUNING: not necessary; remove old flower stalks and yellow or dead leaves

SPECIAL CULTURAL HINTS: sterilize tools between cuttings and remove old medium when deflasking; sanitation is important

SUGGESTED COMPANION PLANTINGS: other orchids

orchid: cymbidium

Plant characteristics

HEIGHT: 3–4'

SPREAD: gets large if left undivided

GROWTH RATE: moderate

GROWTH HABIT: vertical, epiphytic

FLOWERS

SIZE: 2–4"

COLOR: white, green, red, yellow, pink, orange

SHAPE: star-shaped

FRAGRANCE: faint, sweet

FLOWERS IN FIRST YEAR: yes, but flowers are small until the following season, when they become larger and more numerous

FLOWERING PERIOD: spring through early summer

TIME TO FLOWERING: 8 months from divisions, about 2–3 years from seed

INDUCING AND MAINTAINING FLOWERING: summer night temperature must remain at or below 55°F for consistent flower initiation for most varieties; miniature types can flower with warmer temperatures

PESTS

COMMON DISEASES: *Pythium* and *Phytophthora* root rot, black rot, *Colletotrichum* leaf spot (fungus), petal and blossom spot (fungi), bacterial stem rot, cymbidium mosaic and odontoglossum ringspot viruses

OTHER PESTS: aphids, mice, mites, slugs, snails, thrips

The lei shown also contains cup-and-saucer plant, kangaroo paw, kalanchoe, Peruvian lily, and ʻōhiʻa lehua.

Harvesting considerations

WHAT IS HARVESTED: spray (raceme with flowers) or individual flower on 2" of stem

HARVESTING TECHNIQUES: cut or snap spray close to the base

BEST TIME OF DAY TO HARVEST: early morning

BEST WAY TO TRANSPORT FROM PICKING AREA: place cut end of spray in a container with water; individual flower stems can be placed in water in a plastic tube sealed with a rubber band or plastic cover

AVOID MIXING WITH THESE MATERIALS: smoke, car exhaust, ripening fruits, and wilting flowers; avoid extremes of heat and cold

Notes on lei making

BEST FOR WHICH TYPE OF LEI: neck, head, wrist, ankle, horse

VASE LIFE: 14 days

CLEANING OF PLANT MATERIALS: soak flowers in clean water for 5 minutes after harvesting; check for insects in throat of flower

STORING RAW LEI MATERIALS: spray can be stored for up to 14 days in water; individual flower can be stored for up to 14 days if stem is wrapped with a piece of moist paper in a plastic bag; refrigerate both at 40°F

PREPARING FOR USE IN LEI: clip stem if sewing lei, keep stem if using in other lei patterns

STORING A COMPLETED LEI BEFORE WEARING: mist lei, shake off excess water, place in sealed plastic container or bag, and refrigerate

PRESERVING A LEI FOR LONG-TERM STORAGE OR DISPLAY: cannot be preserved

References and further reading

Leonhardt, K.W. 1980. *Simple Orchid Culture*. University of Hawaiʻi, CTAHR, CES Circular 452.

Sacalis, John N. 1993. *Cut Flowers Prolonging Freshness*. Batavia, Illinois: Ball Publishing.

Introduced Perennials

orchid: dendrobium

OTHER COMMON NAMES: *'okika*

SCIENTIFIC NAME: *Dendrobium* species

FAMILY: Orchidaceae (orchid family)

NATURAL SETTING/LOCATION: found worldwide

CURRENT STATUS IN THE WILD IN HAWAI'I: not found

CULTIVARS: many UH-CTAHR cultivars available; newest are 'Splendor' and 'White Cascade'

Growing your own

PROPAGATION

FORM: seeds; aerial offshoots; division; mericloning (commercial growers purchase tissue-cultured plantlets in sterile flasks)

PREPLANTING TREATMENT: green pods or seeds are sterilized before aseptic culture; remove old foliage and bulbs from divisions

PLANTING DEPTH: sow seeds on surface of aseptic medium; keep division root crown just below soil level

GERMINATION TIME: 2–4 months

PREFERRED PRODUCTION CONDITIONS

GENERAL SOIL CHARACTERISTICS: soilless media, gravel, cinder, wood bark, *hāpu'u*

SOIL PH: 5.5–6.5

LIGHT: 30% shade

WATER: prefers high humidity; water 3–4 times per week

TEMPERATURE: 75–85°F (day) / 65°F (night)

ELEVATION: 10–1000'

SALT TOLERANCE: poor

WIND RESISTANCE: poor

MANAGEMENT

FERTILIZER NEEDS: light to medium; varies among types

RECOMMENDED SPACING: 1 ft² per plant

ADAPTATION TO GROWING IN CONTAINERS: yes; plastic, clay, or cement pots; polybags

PRUNING: not necessary; remove old flower stalks and yellow or dead leaves

SPECIAL CULTURAL HINTS: sterilize tools between cuts and remove old medium when deflasking; sanitation is important

SUGGESTED COMPANION PLANTINGS: other orchids

orchid: dendrobium

Plant characteristics

HEIGHT: to 6'

SPREAD: 24"

GROWTH RATE: fast

GROWTH HABIT: upright, epiphytic

FLOWERS

SIZE: 2–4"

COLOR: white, purple, blush-pink, yellow

SHAPE: star-shaped, 3 petals, 3 sepals

FRAGRANCE: yes, varies

FLOWERS IN FIRST YEAR: no

FLOWERING PERIOD: heaviest during summer

TIME TO FLOWERING: 18 months from flask

INDUCING AND MAINTAINING FLOWERING: maintain good plant health and provide adequate fertilizer

PESTS

COMMON DISEASES: *Pythium* and *Phytophthora* root rot, black rot, *Colletotrichum* leaf spot (fungus), petal and blossom spot (fungi), bacterial stem rot, cymbidium mosaic and odontoglossum ringspot viruses

OTHER PESTS: aphids, blossom midge, mealybugs, mice, mites, orchid weevil, scales, slugs, snails, thrips

Harvesting considerations

WHAT IS HARVESTED: spray (raceme with flowers), or individual flower on 2" of stem

HARVESTING TECHNIQUES: cut or snap spray close to the stem

BEST TIME OF DAY TO HARVEST: early morning

BEST WAY TO TRANSPORT FROM PICKING AREA: cut end of spray under water in a plastic container or pick flowers and carry in plastic, paper, or cloth bag

AVOID CONTACT WITH THESE PRODUCTS: smoke, car exhaust, ripening fruits, and wilting flowers; avoid extremes of heat and cold

Notes on lei making

BEST FOR WHICH TYPE OF LEI: neck, head, wrist, ankle, horse

VASE LIFE: to 7 days

CLEANING OF PLANT MATERIALS: soak flowers in clean water for 5 minutes after harvesting; check for insects inside throat of flower

STORING RAW LEI MATERIALS: spray can be stored for up to 14 days with cut end in water; individual flower can be stored for up to 14 days if stem is wrapped with a piece of moist paper in a plastic bag; refrigerate both at 40°F

PREPARING FOR USE IN LEI: clip stem if sewing lei, keep stem if using other lei patterns

STORING A COMPLETED LEI BEFORE WEARING: mist lei, shake off excess water, place in sealed plastic bag or container, and refrigerate

PRESERVING A LEI FOR LONG-TERM STORAGE OR DISPLAY: cannot be preserved

References and further reading

Ide, Laurie S. 1998. *Hawaiian Lei Making: Step-by-Step Guide*. Honolulu: Mutual Publishing.

Leonhardt, K.W. 1980. *Simple Orchid Culture*. University of Hawai'i, CTAHR, CES Circular 452.

Leonhardt, K.W., and Kelvin Sewake. 1999. *Growing Dendrobium Orchids in Hawai'i: Production and Pest Management Guide*. University of Hawai'i, CTAHR.

Northen, Rebecca T. 1990. *Home Orchid Growing*. 4th rev. ed. New York: Prentice Hall Press.

Orchid Society of South East Asia. 1993. *Orchid Growing in theTropics*. Singapore: Times Editions.

Teoh, Eng Soon. 1989. *Orchids of Asia*. Singapore: Times Books International.

Introduced Perennials

orchid: epidendrum

OTHER COMMON NAMES: baby orchid, butterfly orchid, buttonhole orchid, epis, ʻokika, reed orchid

SCIENTIFIC NAME: *Epidendrum* species

FAMILY: Orchidaceae (orchid family)

NATURAL SETTING/LOCATION: tropical America and tropical West Africa

CURRENT STATUS IN THE WILD IN HAWAIʻI: only one species has become naturalized in Hawaiʻi: *Epidendrum* x *Obrienianum*

CULTIVARS: over 1000 species and numerous hybrids and cultivars

Growing your own

PROPAGATION

FORM: aerial offshoot; seeds; division; mericloning (commercial growers purchase tissue-cultured plantlets in sterile flasks)

PRETREATMENT: pods are sterilized before aseptic culture; remove old leaves and bulbs from divisions

PLANTING DEPTH: sow seeds on surface of aseptic medium; keep division root crown just below soil level

GERMINATION TIME: 2–4 months

PREFERRED PRODUCTION CONDITIONS

GENERAL SOIL CHARACTERISTICS: rock, orchid bark, *hāpuʻu*, cinder

SOIL PH: 5.5–6.5

LIGHT: full sun

WATER: most prefer high humidity and daily irrigation

TEMPERATURE: 55–90°F

ELEVATION: 10–1000'

SALT TOLERANCE: poor

WIND RESISTANCE: moderate to poor

MANAGEMENT

FERTILIZER NEEDS: light to medium; varies among types

RECOMMENDED SPACING: varies with plant size; generally 6–18" apart

ADAPTATION TO GROWING IN CONTAINERS: yes; beds, bags, plastic or clay pots

PRUNING: not necessary; remove old flower stalks and yellow or dead leaves

SPECIAL CULTURAL HINTS: if grown in a pot, repot every 1–2 years; sterilize tools between cuttings and remove old medium; sanitation is important

SUGGESTED COMPANION PLANTINGS: other orchids and bromeliads

orchid: epidendrum

Plant characteristics

HEIGHT: to 4'

SPREAD: 8"

GROWTH RATE: fast

GROWTH HABIT: upright, epiphytic

FLOWERS

SIZE: 1–2½"

COLOR: white, pink, purple, yellow, green, red, orange

SHAPE: star-shaped, 3 petals and 3 sepals

FRAGRANCE: varies

FLOWERS IN FIRST YEAR: yes, from cuttings and divisions

FLOWERING PERIOD: year-round

TIME TO FLOWERING: 18–24 months from flask for some

INDUCING AND MAINTAINING FLOWERING: keep healthy and give adequate light

PESTS

COMMON DISEASES: *Pythium* and *Phytophthora* root rot, black rot, *Colletotrichum* leaf spot (fungus), petal and blossom spot (fungi), bacterial stem rot, cymbidium mosaic and odontoglossum ringspot viruses

OTHER PESTS: blossom midge, mites, orchid weevil, thrips

Harvesting considerations

WHAT IS HARVESTED: flower with 1–2" of stem

HARVESTING TECHNIQUES: pluck flower heads

BEST TIME OF DAY TO HARVEST: early morning

The lei shown also contains Peruvian lily, oncidium orchid, and a fern.

BEST WAY TO TRANSPORT FROM PICKING AREA: paper or cloth bag

AVOID CONTACT WITH THESE PRODUCTS: smoke, car exhaust, ripening fruits, and wilting flowers; avoid extremes of heat and cold

Notes on lei making

BEST FOR WHICH TYPE OF LEI: neck, head, wrist, ankle, horse

VASE LIFE: 7 days

CLEANING OF PLANT MATERIALS: soak flowers in clean water for 5 minutes after harvesting; check for insects stuck in lip

STORING RAW LEI MATERIALS: place in sealed plastic container and refrigerate at 40°F for up to 14 days

PREPARING FOR USE IN LEI: clip stems if sewing lei, keep stem if using other lei patterns

STORING A COMPLETED LEI BEFORE WEARING: soak lei, shake off excess water, place in sealed plastic container, and refrigerate

PRESERVING A LEI FOR LONG-TERM STORAGE OR DISPLAY: cannot be preserved

References and further reading

Ide, Laurie S. 1998. *Hawaiian Lei Making: Step-by-Step Guide*. Honolulu: Mutual Publishing.

Leonhardt, K.W. 1980. *Simple Orchid Culture*. University of Hawai‘i CTAHR, CES Circular 452.

Northen, Rebecca T. 1990. *Home Orchid Growing*. 4th rev. ed. New York: Prentice Hall Press.

Orchid Society of South East Asia. 1993. *Orchid Growing in the Tropics*. Singapore: Times Editions.

Sessler, G.J. 1978. *Orchids and How to Grow Them*. New York: Prentice Hall Press.

Teoh, Eng Soon. 1989. *Orchids of Asia*. Singapore: Times Books International.

Introduced Perennials

orchid: vanda

OTHER COMMON NAMES: 'Miss Joaquim', *'okika*, vanda

SCIENTIFIC NAME: *Vanda* species

FAMILY: Orchidaceae (orchid family)

NATURAL SETTING/LOCATION: found worldwide

CURRENT STATUS IN THE WILD IN HAWAI'I: not found

CULTIVARS: many readily available: 'Miss Joaquim' varieties include Rose Marie, Josephine, John Laycoch; inbred cultivars include Diane, Atherton, Shimomishi

Growing your own

PROPAGATION

FORM: cuttings; tissue culture; mericloning; seeds (seeded plants are not generally used in lei flower production)

PREPLANTING TREATMENT: pods are sterilized before aseptic culture

PLANTING DEPTH: sow seeds on surface of aseptic medium; insert base of cutting 1–2" into medium

GERMINATION TIME: 1–4 months

CUTTING ROOTING TIME: 2–4 months

PREFERRED PRODUCTION CONDITIONS

GENERAL SOIL CHARACTERISTICS: soilless media, *hāpu'u*, gravel, cinder

SOIL PH: 5.5–6.5

LIGHT: full sun

WATER: high humidity, daily irrigation

TEMPERATURE: 75–85°F (day), 65°F (night)

ELEVATION: 10–1000'

SALT TOLERANCE: poor

WIND RESISTANCE: poor

MANAGEMENT

FERTILIZER NEEDS: light to medium; varies among types

RECOMMENDED SPACING: 8–12 plants per ft²

ADAPTATION TO GROWING IN CONTAINERS: yes; *hāpu'u* logs, plastic pots, polybags, or similar

PRUNING: as needed when plant becomes too tall for harvesting; some growers remove summer and fall flower spikes before they flower

to encourage stronger winter flowering

SPECIAL CULTURAL HINTS: replant when 6' tall; sterilize tools between cuttings and remove old medium; sanitation is important

SUGGESTED COMPANION PLANTINGS: other orchids

orchid: vanda

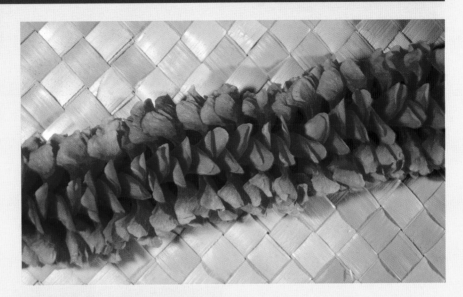

Plant characteristics

HEIGHT: indeterminate, but cut and replant when plant reaches 6'

SPREAD: very confined; grows straight upward

GROWTH RATE: fast

GROWTH HABIT: epiphytic

FLOWERS

SIZE: 2–3"

COLOR: purple

SHAPE: star-shaped, 3 petals and 3 sepals

FRAGRANCE: yes, light

FLOWERS IN FIRST YEAR: yes, from cuttings

FLOWERING PERIOD: summer

TIME TO FLOWERING: 8–12 months from cuttings

INDUCING AND MAINTAINING FLOWERING: provide full sun and keep healthy

PESTS

COMMON DISEASES: *Pythium* and *Phytophthora* root rot, black rot, *Colletotrichum* leafspot (fungus), petal and blossom spot (fungi), bacterial stem rot, cymbidium mosaic and odontoglossum ringspot viruses, foliar nematodes

OTHER PESTS: mites, orchid weevil, scales, stink bugs, thrips

Harvesting considerations

WHAT IS HARVESTED: flower with 1–2" of stem

HARVESTING TECHNIQUES: don't remove pollinia while hand picking; ethylene gas from detached pollinia, fruits, and exhaust from internal combustion engines can cause flowers to turn white prematurely

BEST TIME OF DAY TO HARVEST: early morning

BEST WAY TO TRANSPORT FROM PICKING AREA: paper or cloth bag

AVOID CONTACT WITH THESE PRODUCTS: smoke, car exhaust, ripening fruits, and wilting flowers; avoid extremes of heat and cold

Notes on lei making

BEST FOR WHICH TYPE OF LEI: neck, head, wrist, ankle, horse

CLEANING OF PLANT MATERIALS: soak flowers in clean water for 5 minutes after harvesting; check for insects in throat of flower

STORING RAW LEI MATERIALS: lay flowers on top of damp newspaper and cover with dry tissue; place in paper box and refrigerate at 40°F for up to 5 days

PREPARING FOR USE IN LEI: clip stem if sewing lei, keep stem if not; check to make sure pollinia is intact, otherwise discard flower if it is missing

STORING A COMPLETED LEI BEFORE WEARING: mist lei, shake off excess water, place on top of damp newspaper in paper box, and refrigerate

PRESERVING A LEI FOR LONG-TERM STORAGE OR DISPLAY: cannot be preserved

References and further reading

Ide, Laurie S. 1998. *Hawaiian Lei Making: Step-by-Step Guide*. Honolulu: Mutual Publishing.

Leonhardt, K.W. 1980. *Simple Orchid Culture*. University of Hawai'i CTAHR, CES Circular 452.

Northen, Rebecca T. 1990. *Home Orchid Growing*. 4th rev. ed. New York: Prentice Hall Press.

Orchid Society of South East Asia. 1993. *Orchid Growing in theTropics*. Singapore: Times Editions.

Teoh, Eng Soon. 1989. *Orchids of Asia*. Singapore: Times Books International.

Introduced Perennials

pakalana

OTHER COMMON NAMES: Chinese violet

SCIENTIFIC NAME:
Telosma cordata

FAMILY: Asclepiadaceae
(milkweed family)

NATURAL SETTING/LOCATION: native to
Southeast Asia

CURRENT STATUS IN THE WILD IN HAWAI'I:
not found

Growing your own

PROPAGATION

FORM: cuttings with 2–3 nodes; seeds;
air layering

PREPLANTING TREATMENT: treat cuttings
with medium rooting hormone

PLANTING DEPTH: sow seeds on surface
of medium or slightly (⅛") below;
insert base of cutting 1–2" into
medium

GERMINATION TIME: 1 month

CUTTING ROOTING TIME: 4–5 weeks

PREFERRED PRODUCTION CONDITIONS

GENERAL SOIL CHARACTERISTICS: rich, well
drained

SOIL PH: 6.0–6.5

LIGHT: sunny location

WATER: keep moist; water deeply
twice a week

TEMPERATURE: 70–90°F for rapid
flowering

ELEVATION: 10–300'

SALT TOLERANCE: poor

WIND RESISTANCE: poor

MANAGEMENT

FERTILIZER NEEDS:
medium

RECOMMENDED SPACING:
24–36" apart

**ADAPTATION TO GROWING
IN CONTAINERS:** yes, 2–
3-gallon tubs with
support

PRUNING: thin out old
shoots to induce
new growth

SPECIAL CULTURAL HINTS:
provide a trellis or
other support; can
also be grown in a
large pot raised
above ground with
room for vines to
hang down around it
to allow for easy
flower picking;
flowers occur on
new growth

SUGGESTED COMPANION PLANTINGS: grows
best without competition from other
plants; in particular, it does not
compete well with other vines

pakalana

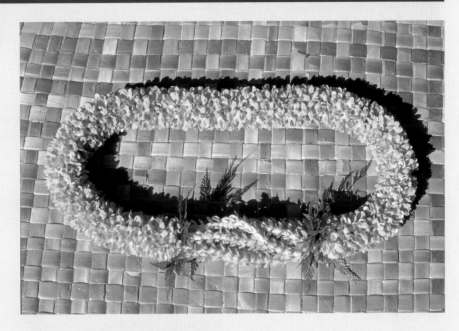

Plant characteristics

HEIGHT: 8–10'

SPREAD: will spread to 3–4' wide if not supported

GROWTH RATE: fast

GROWTH HABIT: vine

FLOWERS

SIZE: about ½"

COLOR: greenish yellow upon opening, turning orange with age

SHAPE: 5-lobed corolla on short tubes

FRAGRANCE: similar to violets

FOLIAGE

TEXTURE: smooth

COLOR: dark green

SHAPE: broad, heart-shaped

FRAGRANCE: none

PESTS

COMMON DISEASES: root rots in wet soils, nematodes, mosaic virus

OTHER PESTS: mites, soft scales, stink bugs, thrips, whiteflies

Harvesting considerations

WHAT IS HARVESTED: flowers and sometimes leaves (depending on lei type)

HARVESTING TECHNIQUES: cut or pinch (don't pull) individual flowers from cluster, leaving unopened buds

BEST TIME OF DAY TO HARVEST: early morning

BEST WAY TO TRANSPORT FROM PICKING AREA: glass jar

AVOID CONTACT WITH THESE PRODUCTS: smoke, car exhaust, ripening fruits, and wilting flowers

Notes on lei making

BEST FOR WHICH TYPE OF LEI: neck, head, wrist, ankle

CLEANING OF PLANT MATERIALS: cold water soak

STORING RAW LEI MATERIALS: wrap in a damp paper towel, place in plastic or glass container, and refrigerate at 40°F for up to 5 days

PREPARING FOR USE IN LEI: clip stem and sew, unless making other styles, then leave flowers on cluster

STORING A COMPLETED LEI BEFORE WEARING: soak lei, shake off excess water, wrap in a damp paper towel, place in plastic or glass container, and refrigerate

PRESERVING A LEI FOR LONG-TERM STORAGE OR DISPLAY: cannot be preserved

References and further reading

Criley, Richard A. 1995. Temperature Influences Flowering of Pakalana (*Telosma cordata* Merrill) under Long Days. *HortScience* 30(3):482–483.

Criley, Richard A. 1989. Some Advances in Lei Flower Production. Univ. of Hawaii, CTAHR, *Horticulture Digest* 89:68.

Ide, Laurie S. 1998. *Hawaiian Lei Making: Step-by-Step Guide*. Honolulu: Mutual Publishing.

McDonald, Marie A. 1989. *Ka Lei: the Leis of Hawaii*. Honolulu: Ku Pa'a Inc., and Press Pacifica.

Introduced Perennials

panax

OTHER COMMON NAMES: fern leaf aralia, parsley panax

SCIENTIFIC NAME: *Polyscias* species

FAMILY: Araliaceae (ginseng family)

NATURAL SETTING/LOCATION: India to Polynesia

CURRENT STATUS IN THE WILD IN HAWAI'I: not found

CULTIVARS: 'Golden Prince', 'Ming Aralia'

Growing your own

PROPAGATION

FORM: cuttings; can also be grafted onto common hedge panax

PREPLANTING TREATMENT: treat with medium rooting hormone

PLANTING DEPTH: insert base 1–2" into medium

CUTTING ROOTING TIME: 4–6 weeks

PREFERRED PRODUCTION CONDITIONS

GENERAL SOIL CHARACTERISTICS: well drained; tolerates various soil types

SOIL pH: 5.5–6.5

LIGHT: full sun to partial shade

WATER: moderate

TEMPERATURE: 45–90°F

ELEVATION: 10–3000'

SALT TOLERANCE: good

WIND RESISTANCE: good

MANAGEMENT

FERTILIZER NEEDS: heavy

RECOMMENDED SPACING: 24–36" apart

ADAPTATION TO GROWING IN CONTAINERS: yes, 2-gallon tubs or larger

PRUNING: prune to reduce size, maintain shape, and keep full and bushy

SPECIAL CULTURAL HINTS: older plants can be habitats for termites

SUGGESTED COMPANION PLANTINGS: short, shade-loving plants

panax

Plant characteristics

HEIGHT: to 12'

SPREAD: to 3–4'

GROWTH RATE: fast

GROWTH HABIT: erect, evergreen, woody shrub

FOLIAGE

TEXTURE: smooth, bumpy, feathery

COLOR: dark green or variegated

SHAPE: finely divided, compound with leaflets; various sizes and shapes

FRAGRANCE: none

PESTS

COMMON DISEASES: fungal root and stem rots, bacterial leaf spots, root-knot and reniform nematodes

OTHER PESTS: borers, mealybugs, rats, scales, termites (in older plants)

Harvesting considerations

WHAT IS HARVESTED: foliage

HARVESTING TECHNIQUES: cut

BEST TIME OF DAY TO HARVEST: early morning

BEST WAY TO TRANSPORT FROM PICKING AREA: paper or cloth bag

The lei shown also contains dracaena and a fern.

Notes on lei making

BEST FOR WHICH TYPE OF LEI: neck, head, wrist, ankle, horse

VASE LIFE: 14 days

CLEANING OF PLANT MATERIALS: cold water soak

STORING RAW LEI MATERIALS: wrap in damp newspaper and place in sealed plastic container; refrigerate at 40°F for up to 30 days

PREPARING FOR USE IN LEI: clip off wrinkled, limp, or poor quality areas before adding to lei

STORING A COMPLETED LEI BEFORE WEARING: soak lei, drip dry, wrap in damp newspaper, place in sealed plastic container, and refrigerate

PRESERVING A LEI FOR LONG-TERM STORAGE OR DISPLAY: air-dry

References and further reading

Clay, Horace F., and James C. Hubbard. 1977. *The Hawaii Garden: Tropical Shrubs.* Honolulu: University of Hawai'i Press.

Rauch, Fred D. 1996. *Tropical Landscape Plants.* 3rd ed. Battle Ground, Washington: Hawaii Floriculture.

Introduced Perennials

pentas

OTHER COMMON NAMES: Egyptian starflower

SCIENTIFIC NAME: *Pentas lanceolata*

FAMILY: Rubiaceae (coffee family)

NATURAL SETTING/LOCATION: Madagascar, tropical South Africa

CURRENT STATUS IN THE WILD IN HAWAI'I: not found

CULTIVARS: none named, but red, rose, violet, and pink types have been selected

Growing your own

PROPAGATION

FORM: seeds (purchase from seed source); cuttings

PREPLANTING TREATMENT: treat cuttings with mild rooting hormone

PLANTING DEPTH: sow seeds on surface or slightly (⅛") below; insert base of cutting 1–2" into medium

GERMINATION TIME: 5–12 days

CUTTING ROOTING TIME: 3–4 weeks

PREFERRED PRODUCTION CONDITIONS

GENERAL SOIL CHARACTERISTICS: well drained loam or sandy loam; in pots, 1:1 peat:perlite

SOIL PH: 5.5–6.5

LIGHT: full sun

WATER: keep moist

TEMPERATURE: 50–90°F

ELEVATION: 10–2000'

SALT TOLERANCE: poor

WIND RESISTANCE: moderate–poor

MANAGEMENT

FERTILIZER NEEDS: medium

RECOMMENDED SPACING: 12–18" apart

ADAPTATION TO GROWING IN CONTAINERS: yes, 1–3-gallon tubs

PRUNING: cut back to 12–18" but not back to hard wood

SUGGESTED COMPANION PLANTINGS: globe amaranth

pentas

Plant characteristics

HEIGHT: to 36"

SPREAD: to 36"

GROWTH RATE: fast

GROWTH HABIT: spreading, woody, evergreen shrub

FLOWERS

SIZE: clusters of about 30 flowers 2–4" across; individual flower about ⅜"

COLOR: white, pink, red, red and pink, lilac

SHAPE: 5-petalled, star-shaped

FRAGRANCE: none

FLOWERS IN FIRST YEAR: yes

FLOWERING PERIOD: year-round, heaviest in summer

TIME TO FLOWERING: about 8–10 weeks from rooted cutting, about 4 months from seed

INDUCING AND MAINTAINING FLOWERING: to induce more flowering shoots, pinch the young shoots to leave 2 or 3 pairs of nodes; remove spent flowers

PESTS

COMMON DISEASES: *Botrytis* on the flowers, southern blight

OTHER PESTS: aphids, caterpillars, mites, whiteflies

The lei shown also contains ti, panax, and aster.

Harvesting considerations

WHAT IS HARVESTED: flower cluster with 1–2" of stem

HARVESTING TECHNIQUES: pluck flowers

BEST TIME OF DAY TO HARVEST: early morning

BEST WAY TO TRANSPORT FROM PICKING AREA: plastic bag

AVOID CONTACT WITH THESE PRODUCTS: smoke, car exhaust, ripening fruits, and wilting flowers

Notes on lei making

BEST FOR WHICH TYPE OF LEI: neck, head, wrist, ankle, horse

CLEANING OF PLANT MATERIALS: stick stem in water.

STORING RAW LEI MATERIALS: store in sealed container and refrigerate at 40°F for up to 4 days

PREPARING FOR USE IN LEI: clip off wrinkled, limp, or poor quality areas before adding to lei

STORING A COMPLETED LEI BEFORE WEARING: soak for 30 minutes, drip dry, store in sealed container, and refrigerate

PRESERVING A LEI FOR LONG-TERM STORAGE OR DISPLAY: cannot be preserved

Reference and further reading

Nau, Jim. 1993. *Ball Culture Guide: The Encyclopedia of Seed Germination.* 2nd ed., p. 50–51. Batavia, Illinois: Ball Publishing.

Introduced Perennials

pīkake

OTHER COMMON NAMES: jasmine, *lei-pīkake*, sampaguita (Philippines), single-flowered star jasmine

SCIENTIFIC NAME: *Jasminum sambac*

FAMILY: Oleaceae (olive family)

NATURAL SETTING/LOCATION: native to tropical Asia

CURRENT STATUS IN THE WILD IN HAWAI'I: typically not found

CULTIVARS: 'Grand Duke' is a double form used in *haku* lei

Growing your own

PROPAGATION

FORM: cuttings from 1-year-old wood

PREPLANTING TREATMENT: treat with mild rooting hormone

PLANTING DEPTH: insert base 1–2" into medium

CUTTING ROOTING TIME: 2–3 weeks under mist

PREFERRED PRODUCTION CONDITIONS

GENERAL SOIL CHARACTERISTICS: well drained, silty clay loam

SOIL PH: 6–6.5

LIGHT: full sun; long days produce more flowers

WATER: moderate irrigation (1"/week); allow to dry between waterings; water entire root system

TEMPERATURE: 80–90°F (days), 70–80°F (nights); if night temperatures drop below 70s, flower number and size will be adversely affected; temperatures in low 60s will cause plants to cease flowering until higher temperatures return; one night of low temperature may shut down flowering for as long as 1–2 weeks

ELEVATION: 10–25' ideal; cool night breezes in valleys may retard flowering and reduce amount and size of blossoms; can be grown at higher elevations (500')

SALT TOLERANCE: moderate

WIND RESISTANCE: moderate (wind may damage flowers)

MANAGEMENT

FERTILIZER NEEDS: medium

RECOMMENDED SPACING: 1–1½' within rows, 5–6' between rows; grown as a hedge

ADAPTATION TO GROWING IN CONTAINERS: not recommended

PRUNING: prune to increase branching and flowering (flowers emerge from terminal tips) and to facilitate easy harvesting; suckers should be pruned, because they are unproductive

SPECIAL CULTURAL HINTS: long days and high temperature favor high production and large flowers, while short days and cold temperature reduce flower size and amount of flowering

pīkake

Plant characteristics

HEIGHT: 6'

SPREAD: 24–36" wide

GROWTH RATE: moderate to slow in winter

GROWTH HABIT: shrub with some runners or suckers

FLOWERS

SIZE: ½–¾"

COLOR: cream-white

SHAPE: oval bud (unopened), star-shaped (open)

FRAGRANCE: distinctive, very strong, sweet; used for flavoring teas (jasmine tea) and as a perfume

FLOWERS IN FIRST YEAR: yes

FLOWERING PERIOD: under natural conditions, moderate flowering can be expected during the months of March–September; long days produce more flowers

TIME TO FLOWERING: bushes are pruned back with hedge trimmers to 1-year-old wood, or leaves are stripped by hand, causing plants to flower in 30 days during the hottest months and 45 days during spring and late summer; this flowering will continue for 7–12 days, and if plants are very healthy, it will continue for up to 20 days

INDUCING AND MAINTAINING FLOWERING: force flowering during winter months by enclosing plants in a plastic structure to increase temperature; warm air is captured in the structure, inducing flowering by increasing night temperatures; covering should be closed at least 1–2 hours before sunset; covering should be opened by early to mid-morning to avoid over-heating; flowers grown in covered area will be larger and whiter than open field–grown plants

PESTS

COMMON DISEASES: powdery mildew, mosaic virus, nematodes; root rot and southern blight can be a problem with clay soil, poor drainage, and high rainfall

OTHER PESTS: Hawaiian flower thrips, blossom midge, broad mite, carmine spider mite, whiteflies; because buds are produced at tips, broad mite damage can severely decrease the amount of flowers produced; flower thrips and blossom midge attack buds and can affect postharvest quality

Harvesting considerations

WHAT IS HARVESTED: flower buds (opened flowers are not usually sold for lei)

HARVESTING TECHNIQUES: pick at bud stage; avoid handling too much (the delicate flowers are easily bruised)

BEST TIME OF DAY TO HARVEST: early to mid-morning, depending on time of year

BEST WAY TO TRANSPORT FROM PICKING AREA: cloth, paper bag, or paper box

AVOID CONTACT WITH THESE PRODUCTS: smoke, car exhaust, ripening fruits, and wilting flowers

Notes on lei making

BEST FOR WHICH TYPE OF LEI: neck, head, wrist, ankle

CLEANING OF PLANT MATERIALS: no water

STORING RAW LEI MATERIALS: store in sealed plastic container and refrigerate at 40°F for up to 3 days

PREPARING FOR USE IN LEI: remove calyx (green, leafy base), then sew

STORING A COMPLETED LEI BEFORE WEARING: wrap lei in wax paper, place in sealed plastic container, and refrigerate; no water

PRESERVING A LEI FOR LONG-TERM STORAGE OR DISPLAY: cannot be preserved

References and further reading

Ide, Laurie S. 1998. *Hawaiian Lei Making: Step-by-Step Guide.* Honolulu: Mutual Publishing.

Leonhardt, K.W., and G.I. Teves. 2002. Pīkake, *a Fragrant-Flowered Plant for Landscapes and Lei Production.* University of Hawai'i, CTAHR, OF-29.

pincushion protea

OTHER COMMON NAMES: sunburst, Hawaiian sunflower

SCIENTIFIC NAME: *Leucospermum saxosum, L. erubescens, L. bolusii, L. oleifolium, L. mundii, L. muirii, L. parile, L. rodolentum*

FAMILY: Proteaceae (protea family; includes macadamia)

NATURAL SETTING/LOCATION: South Africa; adapted to cool, dry areas of Maui and Hawai'i above 1500 feet elevation

CURRENT STATUS IN THE WILD IN HAWAI'I: not found

Growing your own

PROPAGATION

FORM: tip cuttings 6" long, taken in Sept.–Oct. after growth stops

PREPLANTING TREATMENT: use a medium strength rooting hormone

PLANTING DEPTH: insert base of cuttings 1½–2" into medium

CUTTING ROOTING TIME: 2–3 months under mist

PREFERRED PRODUCTION CONDITIONS

GENERAL SOIL CHARACTERISTICS: well drained

SOIL PH: 5.5–6.5

LIGHT: sunny location

WATER: twice weekly for established plants, more often for new plantings

TEMPERATURE: 40–90°F

ELEVATION: 1500–4000'

SALT TOLERANCE: poor

WIND RESISTANCE: moderate to good

MANAGEMENT

FERTILIZER NEEDS: light; fertilize sparingly; sensitive to P

RECOMMENDED SPACING: 4–6' apart in field, depending on species

ADAPTATION TO GROWING IN CONTAINERS: yes, 5-gallon tubs

PRUNING: prune after flowering to maintain size, remove dead or diseased wood, and stimulate vigorous new shoots

SPECIAL CULTURAL HINTS: cuttings are slow to root, and intermittent mist is essential for successful propagation; rooted cuttings are moved to 4–6" pots and grown for 4–6 months before transplanting; in the field, specialized "proteoid" roots are matted near the soil surface and can be damaged by shallow cultivation

SUGGESTED COMPANION PLANTINGS: any low growing, cool climate perennials

pincushion protea

Plant characteristics

HEIGHT: 2–3', depending on species

SPREAD: 3–5', depending on species

GROWTH RATE: reaches ideal production size 3 years after transplanting

GROWTH HABIT: mounding shrub

FLOWERS

SIZE: single flowers up to 2½" for *L. saxosum*; other species have 1–1½" flowers singly or in clusters

COLOR: much variation among species; yellow-orange, pink, red, yellow-green, and cream-white can occur

SHAPE: most species have "pincushion" shape

FRAGRANCE: in *L. bolusii, muirii, parile, rodolentum*

FLOWERS IN FIRST YEAR: under optimal conditions, flowers within 1 year after transplanting to the field

FLOWERING PERIOD: fall–winter–spring

INDUCING AND MAINTAINING FLOWERING: 3–4 weeks of 50°F winter night temperature results in best flowering

PESTS

COMMON DISEASES: root rot, collar rot, leaf spots, *Botrytis*, root-knot nematode

OTHER PESTS: aphids and scales if plant is under stress, otherwise relatively free of insects and mites

Harvesting considerations

WHAT IS HARVESTED: flowers

HARVESTING TECHNIQUE: cut or pluck

BEST TIME OF DAY TO HARVEST: early morning

BEST WAY TO TRANSPORT FROM PICKING AREA: plastic bag

The protea used in the lei shown is *Leucospermum oleifolium*; the lei also contains flowers of *Grevillea wilsonii* and *Lambertia inermis*.

Introduced Perennials

Notes on lei making

BEST FOR WHICH TYPE OF LEI: neck, head, wrist, ankle, horse, hat

CLEANING OF PLANT MATERIALS: for single-strand lei, trim off stems close to flower head; for *haku* or *wili* style, remove stems if too thick or stiff

STORING RAW LEI MATERIALS: cover flowers with moist paper towels or stick stems in water-soaked "oasis," refrigerate at 40°F, store for 5–14 days, depending on species

PREPARING FOR USE IN LEI: for single-strand lei, stringing can be easier after drilling through center of flowerhead; for *haku* or *wili* style, wire flowers together for easier handling

STORING A COMPLETED LEI BEFORE WEARING: wrap in moist paper towels and refrigerate

PRESERVING A LEI FOR LONG-TERM STORAGE OR DISPLAY: cannot be preserved

References and further reading

Kepler, Angela K., and Jacob Mau. 1988. *Proteas in Hawaii.* Honolulu: Mutual Publishing.

Rousseau, F. 1970. *The Proteaceae of South Africa.* Cape Town: Purnell and Sons, Ltd.

plumeria

OTHER COMMON NAMES: frangipani, *make*-man, *melia, pua melia,* temple tree

SCIENTIFIC NAME: *Plumeria* species and cultivars

FAMILY: Apocynaceae (dogbane family)

NATURAL SETTING/LOCATION: native to tropical America

CURRENT STATUS IN THE WILD IN HAWAI'I: not found

CULTIVARS: many named cultivars, some with better flower shelflife than others

Growing your own

HANDLING CAUTIONS: milky sap may irritate eyes and skin

PROPAGATION

FORM: tip cuttings 6–36" long; seeds (seedlings take longer to flower)

PREPLANTING TREATMENT: allow end of cutting to air-dry at least 24 hours; mild rooting hormone speeds rooting

PLANTING DEPTH: sow seeds ¼–½" deep in medium; insert base of cutting 2–4" into medium, or more if large

GERMINATION TIME: 2 weeks

CUTTING ROOTING TIME: 2 months

PREFERRED PRODUCTION CONDITIONS

GENERAL SOIL CHARACTERISTICS: well drained

SOIL PH: 6.0–6.5

LIGHT: full sun

WATER: keep moist

TEMPERATURE: 60–90°F

ELEVATION: 10–2000'

SALT TOLERANCE: moderate

WIND RESISTANCE: good (if tree is healthy)

MANAGEMENT

FERTILIZER NEEDS: medium to heavy; varies among cultivars

RECOMMENDED SPACING: 6–10' within the row and 12–15' between rows

ADAPTATION TO GROWING IN CONTAINERS: yes, large containers

PRUNING: easiest in winter, but it sacrifices spring flowering; prune back for easier flower harvest

SPECIAL CULTURAL HINTS: keep on dry side, especially in container; in field, plant branched cuttings with axils set low to the ground for low branching and easier flower harvest; provide 5–7 gallons/day irrigation water per tree, covering whole root system

SUGGESTED COMPANION PLANTINGS: during the first few years, annuals can be planted between trees

plumeria

Plant characteristics

HEIGHT: to 30'

SPREAD: 30'

GROWTH RATE: fast

GROWTH HABIT: round-headed, small tree

FLOWERS

SIZE: average 2–3" in diameter

COLOR: white, red, yellow, pink, multiple

SHAPE: tubular flower with 5 petals

FRAGRANCE: most varieties highly fragrant, with different scents

FLOWERS IN FIRST YEAR: from cutting: 1 year; from seed: 3 years

FLOWERING PERIOD: most cultivars flower March–October

TIME TO FLOWERING: maturity after about 5 years

INDUCING AND MAINTAINING FLOWERING: in dry areas, irrigation will promote flowering; defoliation in fall with ethephon will stimulate emergence of inflorescences as early as December

PESTS

COMMON DISEASES: plumeria rust, *Colletotrichum* leafspot and shoot blight, powdery mildew on leaves, fungal rots

OTHER PESTS: ants, blossom midge, long-horned beetles, mites, scales, thrips, whiteflies

Harvesting considerations

WHAT IS HARVESTED: open flowers

HARVESTING TECHNIQUES: grasp individual flowers at base and tug gently

BEST TIME OF DAY TO HARVEST: early morning

The lei shown also contains dendrobium orchid.

BEST WAY TO TRANSPORT FROM PICKING AREA: paper box or bag

AVOID CONTACT WITH THESE PRODUCTS: smoke, car exhaust, ripening fruits, and wilting flowers

Notes on lei making

BEST FOR WHICH TYPE OF LEI: neck, head, wrist, ankle, horse

CLEANING OF PLANT MATERIALS: soak the flower in clean water for no more than 10 minutes

STORING RAW LEI MATERIALS: place flowers in a bowl or sink, cover container with a light-weight, damp towel; can be refrigerated or left at room temperature

PREPARING FOR USE IN LEI: clip off wrinkled, limp, or poor quality areas before adding to lei

STORING A COMPLETED LEI BEFORE WEARING: soak lei, shake off all excess water, drip dry, then place in paper box; can be refrigerated for 2 days or left at room temperature for 1 day

PRESERVING A LEI FOR LONG-TERM STORAGE OR DISPLAY: cannot be preserved

References and further reading

Chinn, James T., and Richard A. Criley. 1982. *Plumeria Cultivars in Hawaii.* University of Hawai'i, CTAHR Research Bulletin 158.

Criley, Richard. 1998. *Plumeria.* University of Hawai'i, CTAHR, OF-24.

Criley, Richard. 1994. Enhanced Winter Flowering of Plumeria with Ethephon. Acta Horticulturae 394: 325–330.

Eggenberger, Richard M., and Mary H. Eggenberger. 1994. *Handbook on Plumeria Culture.* 3rd ed. Houston, Texas: The Plumeria People.

Ide, Laurie S. 1998. *Hawaiian Lei Making: Step-by-Step Guide.* Honolulu: Mutual Publishing.

Watson, Donald P., James T. Chinn, Horace F. Clay, and James L. Brewbaker. 1965. *Hawaiian Plumerias.* University of Hawai'i, CTAHR, CES Circular 410.

Introduced Perennials

pohutukawa (New Zealand maori)

OTHER COMMON NAMES: New Zealand Christmas tree

SCIENTIFIC NAME:
Metrosideros excelsus

FAMILY: Myrtaceae (myrtle family)

NATURAL SETTING/LOCATION: coastal zones of New Zealand

CURRENT STATUS IN THE WILD IN HAWAI'I: not found

CULTIVARS: various

Growing your own

PROPAGATION

FORM: seeds; semi-hardwood cuttings; air layering

PREPLANTING TREATMENT: air-dry capsules, allow seeds to fall from them; use medium to strong rooting hormone on cuttings

PLANTING DEPTH: sow seeds on surface; insert base of cutting 1–2" into medium

GERMINATION TIME: 30–60 days at 60–70°F

CUTTING ROOTING TIME: 9 months or more; best results with bottom heat

PREFERRED PRODUCTION CONDITIONS

GENERAL SOIL CHARACTERISTICS: tolerates most soil types

SOIL PH: less than 6.5

LIGHT: full sun

WATER: keep moist; somewhat drought-tolerant once established

TEMPERATURE: 40–90°F

ELEVATION: 10–3000'; best along coast; sensitive to dry air

SALT TOLERANCE: good; will tolerate both salt spray and saline soil

WIND RESISTANCE: good

MANAGEMENT

FERTILIZER NEEDS: medium

RECOMMENDED SPACING: 20' apart if tree form is desired

ADAPTATION TO GROWING IN CONTAINERS: yes, when young, in large containers

PRUNING: prune to reduce size and induce low branches; prune after flowering

SUGGESTED COMPANION PLANTINGS: low-growing plants

pohutukawa (New Zealand maori)

Plant characteristics

HEIGHT: more than 30'

SPREAD: 20–30'

GROWTH RATE: slow

GROWTH HABIT: broad, oval, evergreen tree or large shrub

FLOWERS

SIZE: 1½"

COLOR: dark crimson (rare yellow and white forms exist)

SHAPE: staminate, pompom-like

FRAGRANCE: none

FLOWERS IN FIRST YEAR: no

FLOWERING PERIOD: summer

TIME TO FLOWERING: from seed, 5–7 years; from air layer, 1 year; no information for cutting

FOLIAGE

TEXTURE: extremely variable, from smooth and waxy to fuzzy

COLOR: dark gray-green on top, silvery underneath

SHAPE: simple, oval to ovate

FRAGRANCE: none

PESTS

COMMON DISEASES: none serious

OTHER PESTS: none serious

The lei shown also contains goldenrod.

Harvesting considerations

WHAT IS HARVESTED: branch tips (*liko*), flowers, and bud clusters

HARVESTING TECHNIQUES: cut

BEST TIME OF DAY TO HARVEST: early morning

BEST WAY TO TRANSPORT FROM PICKING AREA: plastic bag

AVOID CONTACT WITH THESE PRODUCTS: smoke, car exhaust, ripening fruits, and wilting flowers

Notes on lei making

BEST FOR WHICH TYPE OF LEI: neck, head, wrist, ankle, horse

VASE LIFE: 7 days

CLEANING OF PLANT MATERIALS: cold water soak

STORING RAW LEI MATERIALS: store in paper box in refrigerator at 40°F for up to 14 days

PREPARING FOR USE IN LEI: clip off wrinkled, limp, or poor quality areas before adding to lei

STORING A COMPLETED LEI BEFORE WEARING: soak lei for 5 minutes, drip dry, place in paper box, and refrigerate

PRESERVING A LEI FOR LONG-TERM STORAGE OR DISPLAY: air-dry flowers; *liko* and bud clusters cannot be preserved

References and further reading

Editors of Sunset Books and Sunset Magazine. 1995. *Sunset Western Garden Book.* 6th ed. Menlo Park, California: Sunset Pub. Corp.

Metcalf, Lawrie. 1995. *The Propagation of New Zealand Native Plants.* Auckland, New Zealand: Godwit Publishing Ltd.

Neal, Marie C. 1965. *In Gardens of Hawaii.* Bernice P. Bishop Museum Special Publication 50. Honolulu: Bishop Museum Press.

Introduced Perennials

pua kenikeni

OTHER COMMON NAMES: ten-cent flower

SCIENTIFIC NAME: *Fagraea berterana*

FAMILY: Loganiaceae (logania family)

NATURAL SETTING/LOCATION: native to South Pacific islands

CURRENT STATUS IN THE WILD IN HAWAI'I: not found

Growing your own

PROPAGATION

FORM: air layering (most commonly used); seeds

PLANTING DEPTH: sow seeds ½" deep in medium

GERMINATION TIME: 30–90 days

AIR LAYERING ROOTING TIME: 6–8 weeks

PREFERRED PRODUCTION CONDITIONS

GENERAL SOIL CHARACTERISTICS: rich, well drained

SOIL PH: 5.5–6.5

LIGHT: full sun

WATER: keep moist

TEMPERATURE: 60–90°F

ELEVATION: 10–1000'

SALT TOLERANCE: moderate

WIND RESISTANCE: moderate

MANAGEMENT

FERTILIZER NEEDS: medium

RECOMMENDED SPACING: 15' x 15'

ADAPTATION TO GROWING IN CONTAINERS: yes, 5-gallon tubs or larger

PRUNING: prune to keep within picking height and to produce new shoots for flowering

SPECIAL CULTURAL HINTS: flowers on new growth; don't overfertilize

SUGGESTED COMPANION PLANTINGS: low-growing shade plants

pua kenikeni

Plant characteristics

HEIGHT: up to 25'

SPREAD: 15'

GROWTH RATE: fast

GROWTH HABIT: upright, small tree or shrub

FLOWERS

SIZE: 2½" long to 1" wide

COLOR: cream colored, changing to orange

SHAPE: tubular

FRAGRANCE: sweet

FLOWERS IN FIRST YEAR: yes, from air layering

FLOWERING PERIOD: year-round, heaviest in summer

TIME TO FLOWERING: 9 months from air layering, at least 5 years from seed

INDUCING AND MAINTAINING FLOWERING: withold water to induce flowering

PESTS

COMMON DISEASES: leaf spots, fungal root rots, root-knot nematode

OTHER PESTS: mealybugs, scales, thrips

Harvesting considerations

WHAT IS HARVESTED: flowers and calyx (green, leafy base)

HARVESTING TECHNIQUES: break stem with flower, leaving calyx on the blossom

BEST TIME OF DAY TO HARVEST: early morning

BEST WAY TO TRANSPORT FROM PICKING AREA: basket lined with ti leaf

AVOID CONTACT WITH THESE PRODUCTS: smoke, car exhaust, ripening fruits, and wilting flowers

Notes on lei making

BEST FOR WHICH TYPE OF LEI: neck, head, wrist, ankle

CLEANING OF PLANT MATERIALS: no water

STORING RAW LEI MATERIALS: store at room temperature for up to 1 day for orange flower, 2 days for yellow, and 3 days for white; no water; to remove thrips from flowers, wrap in wet newspaper, then seal in plastic container and place in ice-cold water

PREPARING FOR USE IN LEI: depends on style; clip bottom at 45° angle, then sew lei, or clip calyx and sew

STORING A COMPLETED LEI BEFORE WEARING: lay wet cloth or paper towel over lei or put lei in plastic bag and float over cold water; do not refrigerate

PRESERVING A LEI FOR LONG-TERM STORAGE OR DISPLAY: cannot be preserved

References and further reading

Ide, Laurie S. 1998. *Hawaiian Lei Making: Step-by-Step Guide*. Honolulu: Mutual Publishing.

Neal, Marie C. 1965. *In Gardens of Hawaii*. Bernice P. Bishop Museum Special Publication 50. Honolulu: Bishop Museum Press.

Rauch, Fred D. 1996. *Tropical Landscape Plants*. 3rd ed. Battle Ground, Washington: Hawaii Floriculture.

Introduced Perennials

rose

OTHER COMMON NAMES: *loke, lokelani, loke-lau* (green rose), *roselani* (heavenly rose)

SCIENTIFIC NAME: *Rosa* cultivars

FAMILY: Rosaceae (rose family)

NATURAL SETTING/LOCATION: Asia, Asia Minor

CURRENT STATUS IN THE WILD IN HAWAI'I: not found

CULTIVARS: many new cultivars can out-perform old-fashioned standards; choose from miniature roses, floribunda, shrub roses, polyantha, and landscape types for lei flower use; check commercial catalogs for available cultivars

Growing your own

HANDLING CAUTIONS: thorns on stems

PROPAGATION

FORM: cuttings; air layering; grafting

PRETREATMENT: treat cuttings with medium rooting hormone

PLANTING DEPTH: insert base of cutting 1–2" into medium; set grafted plants with graft union above soil level

CUTTING ROOTING TIME: 1 month or longer, depending on type

PREFERRED PRODUCTION CONDITIONS

GENERAL SOIL CHARACTERISTICS: rich in organic matter, well drained, sandy to sandy loam; in pots, medium in 1:1:1 ratio of soil, sphagnum or peat moss, and perlite or coarse cinder

SOIL PH: 6.0–6.5

LIGHT: full sunlight to partial shade

WATER: keep moist

TEMPERATURE: 50–90°F

ELEVATION: 10–3500'

SALT TOLERANCE: poor

WIND RESISTANCE: moderate (strong winds dehydrate plants)

MANAGEMENT

FERTILIZER NEEDS: medium to heavy; varies among types

RECOMMENDED SPACING: 2' apart in rows

ADAPTATION TO GROWING IN CONTAINERS: yes, 3-gallon tubs or larger

PRUNING: as flowers are harvested, the stem usually is cut back to the second 5-leaflet leaf above its point of origin; when plants get too tall or aisles too narrow, renewal pruning is practiced by heading them back; pruning to keep the plant's center open lets sunlight in and prevents black spot and other blights

SPECIAL CULTURAL HINTS: various production difficulties; a crop for the experienced grower

rose

Plant characteristics

HEIGHT: to 6'

SPREAD: to 4'

GROWTH RATE: depends on cultivar

GROWTH HABIT: shrub

FLOWERS

SIZE: buds are from ⅜–1¼"; flowers borne 1 per stem or in clusters

COLOR: pink, white, red, yellow, lavender, green bi-color

SHAPE: bud pointed to urn-shaped

FRAGRANCE: yes, varies

FLOWERS IN FIRST YEAR: yes

FLOWERING PERIOD: year-round

TIME TO FLOWERING: from transplants and cuttings, flowers are produced on new shoots about 45–55 days after the shoot develops from a pruning cut

INDUCING AND MAINTAINING FLOWERING: approximately 55 days from pruning to flower

PESTS

COMMON DISEASES: powdery mildew, downy mildew, blackspot, root rot, rust, anthracnose, nematodes, viruses, *Botrytis* blight (flowers), stem canker

OTHER PESTS: aphids, caterpillars, Chinese rose beetle, flower thrips, grasshoppers, mealybugs, spider mites, scales

The lei shown also contains heliconia and *'ōhi'a lehua*.

Harvesting considerations

WHAT IS HARVESTED: buds or partially open flowers, with or without stems

HARVESTING TECHNIQUES: cut

BEST TIME OF DAY TO HARVEST: early morning

BEST WAY TO TRANSPORT FROM PICKING AREA: paper bag

AVOID MIXING WITH THESE PRODUCTS/CONDITIONS: smoke, car exhaust, ripening fruits, and wilting flowers; avoid excessive heat

Notes on lei making

BEST FOR WHICH TYPE OF LEI: neck, head, wrist, ankle, horse

VASE LIFE: 6 days

CLEANING OF PLANT MATERIALS: place in clean, warm water (105–110°F) after harvesting

STORING RAW LEI MATERIALS: place in sealed plastic bag or container and refrigerate at 32–35°F for up to 14 days

PREPARING FOR USE IN LEI: clip off wrinkled, limp, or poor quality areas before adding to lei; pick off damaged outer petals

STORING A COMPLETED LEI BEFORE WEARING: soak lei, shake off excess water, store in sealed plastic bag or container, and refrigerate

PRESERVING A LEI FOR LONG-TERM STORAGE OR DISPLAY: air-dry buds only

References and further reading

There are many cultural guides for cut rose production. The American Rose Society publishes a monthly magazine and annual yearbook, available in some libraries.

Ide, Laurie S. 1998. *Hawaiian Lei Making: Step-by-Step Guide*. Honolulu: Mutual Publishing.

Pemberton, H. B., J. W. Kelly, and J. Ferare. 1997. *Production of Pot Roses*. Portland, Oregon: Timber Press.

Sascalis, John N. 1993. *Cut Flowers, Prolonging Freshness*. Batavia, Illinois: Ball Publishing.

Watson, D.P., P.E. Parvin, and R.A. Criley. 1972. *Rose Growing in Hawaii*. University of Hawai'i, CTAHR, CES Circular 468.

shinobu

OTHER COMMON NAMES: davallia, rabbit's foot fern

SCIENTIFIC NAME: *Davallia* species

FAMILY: Davalliaceae (fern family)

NATURAL SETTING/LOCATION: Eastern Hemisphere tropics

CURRENT STATUS IN THE WILD IN HAWAI'I: not found

Growing your own

PROPAGATION

FORM: rhizome cuttings

PREPLANTING TREATMENT: rooting hormone not needed

PLANTING DEPTH: place on surface

CUTTING ROOTING TIME: 8 weeks

PREFERRED PRODUCTION CONDITIONS

GENERAL SOIL CHARACTERISTICS: well drained, organic soil

SOIL PH: 5.5–6.5

LIGHT: partial shade

WATER: regular, deep watering

TEMPERATURE: 50–90°F

ELEVATION: 10–2000'

SALT TOLERANCE: poor

WIND RESISTANCE: poor

MANAGEMENT

FERTILIZER NEEDS: light

RECOMMENDED SPACING: 2–3' apart

ADAPTATION TO GROWING IN CONTAINERS: yes, baskets with *hāpuʻu* or sphagnum moss

PRUNING: remove old fronds

SPECIAL CULTURAL HINTS: mature fronds last longer than if the delicate, immature ones are used

SUGGESTED COMPANION PLANTINGS: tall trees for shade

shinobu

Plant characteristics

HEIGHT: 20"

SPREAD: 5–8'

GROWTH RATE: moderate

GROWTH HABIT: running fern

FOLIAGE

TEXTURE: fine

COLOR: dark green

SHAPE: fern-like

FRAGRANCE: none

PESTS

COMMON DISEASES: crown and foot rot, lesion nematodes

OTHER PESTS: fern caterpillar

The lei shown also contains cup-and-saucer plant and statice.

Harvesting considerations

WHAT IS HARVESTED: fronds

HARVESTING TECHNIQUES: cut, don't pull

BEST TIME OF DAY TO HARVEST: early morning

BEST WAY TO TRANSPORT FROM PICKING AREA: paper or cloth bag

AVOID CONTACT WITH THESE PRODUCTS: none known

Notes on lei making

BEST FOR WHICH TYPE OF LEI: neck, head, wrist, ankle, horse

VASE LIFE: 7 days

CLEANING OF PLANT MATERIALS: cold water soak

STORING RAW LEI MATERIALS: either refrigerate in sealed container at 40°F for up to 14 days or soak stems in water without refrigeration

PREPARING FOR USE IN LEI: clip off wrinkled, limp, or poor quality areas before adding to lei

STORING A COMPLETED LEI BEFORE WEARING: soak lei, drip dry, place in sealed container, and refrigerate or place in damp newspaper and store in room temperature

PRESERVING A LEI FOR LONG-TERM STORAGE OR DISPLAY: air-dry (becomes brittle)

References and further reading

Hoshizaki, Barbara J. 1976. *Fern Growers Manual*. New York: Alfred A. Knopf.

Keeble, T., H. Clay, D. Crater, and G. Smith. 1975. *Growing Ferns*. University of Georgia, CES Bulletin 737.

shrimp plant (white and yellow)

OTHER COMMON NAMES: squirrel's tail

SCIENTIFIC NAME: *Justicia betonica* (white); *J. brandegeana* (yellow and red)

FAMILY: Acanthaceae (acanthus family)

NATURAL SETTING/LOCATION: Malaysia westward to Africa

CURRENT STATUS IN THE WILD IN HAWAI'I: *J. betonica* found naturalized along roadsides, *J. brandegeana* not found

Growing your own

PROPAGATION

FORM: cuttings; seeds (only *J. betonica*)

PRETREATMENT: none

PLANTING DEPTH: sow seeds on surface or slightly (⅛") below; insert base of cutting 1–2" into medium, use mild rooting hormone

GERMINATION TIME: undetermined

CUTTING ROOTING TIME: 10–21 days

PREFERRED PRODUCTION CONDITIONS

GENERAL SOIL CHARACTERISTICS: rich, well drained soils; tolerant of many soil types

SOIL PH: 6.0–7.0

LIGHT: full sun to partial shade

WATER: keep moist

TEMPERATURE: 60–90°F

ELEVATION: 10–500'

SALT TOLERANCE: poor

WIND RESISTANCE: poor

MANAGEMENT

FERTILIZER NEEDS: medium

RECOMMENDED SPACING: 2–3' apart

ADAPTATION TO GROWING IN CONTAINERS: yes, 1-gallon tubs or larger

PRUNING: established plants will tolerate severe cutback

SPECIAL CULTURAL HINTS: white shrimp plant has potential of becoming a serious weed if left unchecked; do not plant near native landscapes

shrimp plant (white and yellow)

Plant characteristics

HEIGHT: 2–5'

SPREAD: 2–3'

GROWTH RATE: moderate

GROWTH HABIT: weak-stemmed shrub

FLOWERS

SIZE: flower spike to 6" long

COLOR: *J. betonica* has green and white bracts, *J. brandegeana* has red or yellow bracts

SHAPE: oval, pointed

FRAGRANCE: none

FLOWERS IN FIRST YEAR: yes

FLOWERING PERIOD: year-round, heaviest in summer

TIME TO FLOWERING: from cutting, 3–4 months

INDUCING AND MAINTAINING FLOWERING: flowers on terminals or new growth; prune to keep plants in bounds and encourage new growth

PESTS

COMMON DISEASES: none

OTHER PESTS: none serious

The lei shown also contains bougainvillea.

Harvesting considerations

WHAT IS HARVESTED: new, short inflorescences or tips of longer ones

HARVESTING TECHNIQUES: the plant is brittle; use snips to cut the flower spikes

BEST TIME OF DAY TO HARVEST: early morning

BEST WAY TO TRANSPORT FROM PICKING AREA: paper bag

AVOID CONTACT WITH THESE PRODUCTS: smoke, car exhaust, ripening fruits, and wilting flowers

Notes on lei making

BEST FOR WHICH TYPE OF LEI: neck, head, wrist, ankle, horse

CLEANING OF PLANT MATERIALS: cold water soak

STORING RAW LEI MATERIALS: wrap in damp newspaper and refrigerate at 40°F for up to 5 days

PREPARING FOR USE IN LEI: clip off wrinkled, limp, or poor quality areas before adding to lei

STORING A COMPLETED LEI BEFORE WEARING: soak lei, drip dry, wrap in damp newspaper, store in sealed plastic container, and refrigerate

PRESERVING A LEI FOR LONG-TERM STORAGE OR DISPLAY: air-dry

References and further reading

Rauch, Fred D. 1996. *Tropical Landscape Plants*. 3rd ed. Battle Ground, Washington: Hawaii Floriculture.

Odenwald, Neil G., and James R. Turner. 1980. *Plants for the South: A Guide to Landscape Design*. Baton Rouge, Louisiana: Claitor's Publishing Division.

Spanish moss

OTHER COMMON NAMES: Dole's beard, *hinahina, 'umi'umi-o-Dole*

SCIENTIFIC NAME: *Tillandsia usneoides*

FAMILY: Bromeliaceae (pineapple family)

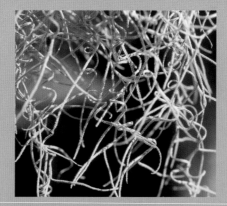

NATURAL SETTING/LOCATION: Florida, Central and South America

CURRENT STATUS IN THE WILD IN HAWAI'I: typically not found

Growing your own

PROPAGATION

FORM: vegetative clump divisions

PLANTING DEPTH: none; drape on tree branches or hangers

PREFERRED PRODUCTION CONDITIONS

GENERAL SOIL CHARACTERISTICS: none; an epiphyte (air plant)

LIGHT: full sun to partial shade

WATER: daily misting

TEMPERATURE: 40–90°F

ELEVATION: 10–3000'

SALT TOLERANCE: moderate

WIND RESISTANCE: moderate

MANAGEMENT

FERTILIZER NEEDS: none required, but a very diluted liquid fertilizer can be applied occasionally as a foliar spray

RECOMMENDED SPACING: on hangers spaced 18" apart

ADAPTATION TO GROWING IN CONTAINERS: can be grown on trees or hanging from artificial supports such as clothes hangers

SPECIAL CULTURAL HINTS: provide good air movement and daily misting; can be harvested in 3–6 months

SUGGESTED COMPANION PLANTINGS: can be hung on trees or grown above smaller plants

Spanish moss

Plant characteristics

HEIGHT: hanging clusters up to 15' long

SPREAD: up to 1' in diameter

GROWTH RATE: fast

GROWTH HABIT: mosslike, herbaceous

FOLIAGE

TEXTURE: fuzzy

COLOR: silver with bluish cast

SHAPE: short, needle-like

FRAGRANCE: none

PESTS

COMMON DISEASES: rot can develop in thick bunches where there is poor air circulation; fungal root rot

OTHER PESTS: none known

Harvesting considerations

WHAT IS HARVESTED: clumps

HARVESTING TECHNIQUES: cut or pull

BEST TIME OF DAY TO HARVEST: any time

BEST WAY TO TRANSPORT FROM PICKING AREA: brown paper or cloth bag

The lei shown also contains *pua kenikeni*.

Notes on lei making

BEST FOR WHICH TYPE OF LEI: neck, head, wrist, ankle, horse

CLEANING OF PLANT MATERIALS: spray with water.

STORING RAW LEI MATERIALS: place clumps on damp newspaper in paper or plastic container and refrigerate at 40°F for up to 30 days

PREPARING FOR USE IN LEI: clip off wrinkled, limp, or poor quality areas before adding to lei

STORING A COMPLETED LEI BEFORE WEARING: soak, drip dry, place on damp newspaper in paper or plastic container, and refrigerate; or, leave hanging outside in well ventilated area, spray with water

PRESERVING A LEI FOR LONG-TERM STORAGE OR DISPLAY: air-dry

References and further reading

Clay, Horace F., and James C. Hubbard. 1977. *The Hawaii Garden: Tropical Exotics*. Honolulu: University of Hawai'i Press.

Ide, Laurie S. 1998. *Hawaiian Lei Making: Step-by-Step Guide*. Honolulu: Mutual Publishing.

Rauh, Wermer. 1979. *Bromeliads for Home, Garden and Greenhouse.* Dorset, England: Blandford Press.

Introduced Perennials

statice

OTHER COMMON NAMES: sea lavender

SCIENTIFIC NAME: *Limonium latifolium* (perennial); *L. sinuatum* (annual)

FAMILY: Plumbaginaceae (plumbago family)

NATURAL SETTING/LOCATION: southeast and central Europe, Mediterranean

CURRENT STATUS IN THE WILD IN HAWAI'I: not found

CULTIVARS: Fortress series, 'Avignon'

Growing your own

PROPAGATION

FORM: seeds (purchase from a seed source); division (of perennial form)

PLANTING DEPTH: sow seeds on medium surface (or slightly below); keep division root crown just below soil level

GERMINATION TIME: 5–15 days at 65–70°F for *L. latifolium* and 60°F for *L. sinuatum*

PREFERRED PRODUCTION CONDITIONS

GENERAL SOIL CHARACTERISTICS: well drained and high in calcium

SOIL PH: 6.5–7.5

LIGHT: full sun

WATER: keep moist

TEMPERATURE: 60–90°F

ELEVATION: 10–3500'

SALT TOLERANCE: poor

WIND RESISTANCE: poor

MANAGEMENT

FERTILIZER NEEDS: medium

RECOMMENDED SPACING: 14–18" apart

ADAPTATION TO GROWING IN CONTAINERS: yes, 2-gallon tubs or larger, but planting in the ground is better

PRUNING: not necessary

SPECIAL CULTURAL HINTS: start with seedlings with 5–6 leaves; good

drainage is critical; cool temperature will induce flowering in *L. sinuatum*

SUGGESTED COMPANION PLANTINGS: bedding plants

statice

Plant characteristics

HEIGHT: *L. latifolium* to 24",
L. sinuatum to 24–36" at flowering

SPREAD: 12–24"

GROWTH RATE: *L. latifolium* slow, *L. sinuatum* fast

GROWTH HABIT: upright clumps

FLOWERS

SIZE: ¼", borne in 3–5" clusters

COLOR: *L. latifolium*: blue, white, pink; *L. sinuatum*: blue, lavender, white-pink

SHAPE: cup-shaped

FRAGRANCE: none

FLOWERS IN FIRST YEAR: *L. latifolium*, few flowers first year (3–4 years to maturity); *L. sinuatum* will flower in first year

FLOWERING PERIOD: *L. latifolium* summer; *L. sinuatum* April–October

TIME TO FLOWERING: *L. sinuatum* 3–5 months after sowing

INDUCING AND MAINTAINING FLOWERING: cool temperature required for young plants to flower

PESTS

COMMON DISEASES: root rot in wet soils; leaf spots (various diseases); *Botrytis* in flowers in wet areas

OTHER PESTS: aphids, chewing insects

The lei shown also contains hydrangea, baby's breath, panax, and bougainvillea.

Harvesting considerations

WHAT IS HARVESTED: flowering stems from base of plant

HARVESTING TECHNIQUES: harvest when most flowers are open and showing color

BEST TIME OF DAY TO HARVEST: early morning

BEST WAY TO TRANSPORT FROM PICKING AREA: plastic container with water

AVOID CONTACT WITH THESE PRODUCTS: smoke, car exhaust, ripening fruits, and wilting flowers

Notes on lei making

BEST FOR WHICH TYPE OF LEI: neck, head, wrist, ankle, horse

CLEANING OF PLANT MATERIALS: place stems in water; dust off field dust and clip off wrinkled, limp, or poor quality areas before adding to lei

STORING RAW LEI MATERIALS: refrigerate at 40°F for up to 14 days

PREPARING FOR USE IN LEI: cut flowers with stems about 1–2" long and place in paper container with no water; do not wet heads

STORING A COMPLETED LEI BEFORE WEARING: mist lei, shake off excess water, place on dry newspaper in paper box, and refrigerate

PRESERVING A LEI FOR LONG-TERM STORAGE OR DISPLAY: air-dry

References and further reading

Armitage, Allan M. 1993. *Specialty Cut Flowers, The Production of Annuals, Perennials, Bulbs, and Woody Plants for Fresh and Dried Cut Flowers*. Portland, Oregon: Varsity Press and Timber Press.

Harada, Daijiro. 1998. "*Limonium*." In: *The Ball Redbook*, 16th ed., p. 630–633. Batavia, Illinois: Ball Publishing.

Sascalis, John N. 1993. *Cut Flowers, Prolonging Freshness*. Batavia, Illinois: Ball Publishing.

Stevens, Alan B. 1997. *Field Grown Cut Flowers, A Practical Guide and Sourcebook; Commercial Field Grown, Fresh and Dried Cut Flower Production*. Edgerton, Wisconsin: Avatar's World.

Still, Steven M. 1994. *Manual of Herbaceous Ornamental Plants*. Champaign, Illinois: Stipes Publishing Co.

stephanotis

OTHER COMMON NAMES: floradora, Madagascar jasmine, *pua male*, waxflower

SCIENTIFIC NAME: *Marsdenia floribunda*

FAMILY: Asclepiadaceae (milkweed family)

NATURAL SETTING/LOCATION: native to Madagascar

CURRENT STATUS IN THE WILD IN HAWAIʻI: not found

Growing your own

PROPAGATION

FORM: seeds; cuttings of semi-mature wood (roots form at nodes)

PRETREATMENT: remove fiber from seeds; treat cuttings with medium rooting hormone

PLANTING DEPTH: sow seeds ¼" deep in medium; insert base of cutting 1–2" into medium

GERMINATION TIME: 2 weeks

CUTTING ROOTING TIME: 4–6 weeks

PREFERRED PRODUCTION CONDITIONS

GENERAL SOIL CHARACTERISTICS: rich, well drained

SOIL PH: 5.5–6.5

LIGHT: full sun

WATER: keep moist

TEMPERATURE: 65–90°F

ELEVATION: 10–1000'

SALT TOLERANCE: moderate

WIND RESISTANCE: good

MANAGEMENT

FERTILIZER NEEDS: medium

RECOMMENDED SPACING: 36" apart in rows

ADAPTATION TO GROWING IN CONTAINERS: yes, large containers

PRUNING: older plants may become straggly, therefore prune to manage size and shape and to induce flowering

SPECIAL CULTURAL HINTS: provide trellis or other support; let dry between waterings

stephanotis

Plant characteristics

HEIGHT: limited to height of support

SPREAD: 6–15', limited by length of support

GROWTH RATE: slow to establish, fast when established

GROWTH HABIT: vine

FLOWERS

SIZE: to 2" long

COLOR: white

SHAPE: tubular

FRAGRANCE: sweet, strong

FLOWERS IN FIRST YEAR: from cutting, yes; from seed, no

FLOWERING PERIOD: April–July and sporadically during the rest of the year; flowering can be forced with lights

TIME TO FLOWERING: 10–12 weeks after pruning if night temperature remains above 72°F

INDUCING AND MAINTAINING FLOWERING: to induce winter flowering, provide light as a night-break interruption for 4–6 hours at 20 watts per square yard of vine for 8 weeks in October–November

PESTS

COMMON DISEASES: root-knot nematode

OTHER PESTS: aphids, mealybugs, spider mites, scale, thrips

Harvesting considerations

WHAT IS HARVESTED: flowers

HARVESTING TECHNIQUES: pinch from vine

BEST TIME OF DAY TO HARVEST: early morning

BEST WAY TO TRANSPORT FROM PICKING AREA: paper bag

AVOID CONTACT WITH THESE PRODUCTS: smoke, car exhaust, ripening fruits, and wilting flowers

Notes on lei making

BEST FOR WHICH TYPE OF LEI: neck, head, wrist, ankle, horse

CLEANING OF PLANT MATERIALS: cold water soak

STORING RAW LEI MATERIALS: store in sealed plastic container and refrigerate at 40°F for up to 7 days

PREPARING FOR USE IN LEI: cut blossom stem to length desired for lei fullness

STORING A COMPLETED LEI BEFORE WEARING: mist lei, shake off excess water, place in sealed plastic container, and refrigerate

PRESERVING A LEI FOR LONG-TERM STORAGE OR DISPLAY: cannot be preserved

References and further reading

Anonymous. 1979. Seasonable Suggestions. *Florists' Review* 164 (4259):97–98.

Evans, Michael, 1993. Stephanotis. *GrowerTalks* 57(1):17.

Ide, Laurie S. 1998. *Hawaiian Lei Making: Step-by-Step Guide*. Honolulu: Mutual Publishing.

Kofranek, Anton M., and John Kubota. 1981. The Influence of Pruning and of Extending the Photoperiod on the Winter Flowering of *Stephanotis floribunda*. *Acta Horticulturae* 128:69–78.

Kofranek, Anton M., and Richard A. Criley. 1983. Photoperiod and Temperature Effects on Stephanotis Flowering. *Acta Horticulturae* 147:211–218.

Wikesjo, Karl. 1982. Cultivation of the Stephanotis. *Florists' Review* 170 (4409):44, 156.

tree heliotrope

OTHER COMMON NAMES:
messerschmidia, *tahinu*, beach
heliotrope

SCIENTIFIC NAME:
Tournefortia argentea

FAMILY: Boraginaceae
(borage family)

NATURAL SETTING/LOCATION: Indian and
Pacific Ocean coastal areas

CURRENT STATUS IN THE WILD IN HAWAI'I:
common in coastal areas

Growing your own

PROPAGATION

FORM: seeds; cuttings 6–12" long
(hardened wood or green wood, but
green wood is more prone to
rotting); air layering

PREPLANTING TREATMENT: use medium
rooting hormone on cuttings

PLANTING DEPTH: sow seeds ¼" deep in
medium; insert base of cutting 2–4"
into medium

GERMINATION TIME: 2–4 weels

CUTTING ROOTING TIME: 3–6 weeks

PREFERRED PRODUCTION CONDITIONS

GENERAL SOIL CHARACTERISTICS: sandy,
well drained

SOIL PH: 6.0–7.5

LIGHT: full sun

WATER: drought tolerant

TEMPERATURE: 65–95°F

ELEVATION: 10–50'

SALT TOLERANCE: good

WIND RESISTANCE: good

MANAGEMENT

FERTILIZER NEEDS: medium

RECOMMENDED SPACING: 15' apart

ADAPTATION TO GROWING IN CONTAINERS:
not recommended

PRUNING: prune to keep within picking
height and induce branching; do not
prune into old wood

SPECIAL CULTURAL HINTS: do not
overwater

SUGGESTED COMPANION PLANTINGS: low-
growing beach plants

tree heliotrope

Plant characteristics

HEIGHT: 10–15'

SPREAD: 15'

GROWTH RATE: slow at maturity

GROWTH HABIT: round-headed, small tree

FLOWERS

SIZE: small (individually), forming clusters

COLOR: white

SHAPE: tubular

FRAGRANCE: none

FLOWERS IN FIRST YEAR: from cutting, yes; no information for seed or air layer

FLOWERING PERIOD: year-round

TIME TO FLOWERING: several years from seed, 1–2 years from cutting and air layer

INDUCING AND MAINTAINING FLOWERING: always flowering

FRUITS

SIZE: ⅕"

COLOR: pale green to brown

SHAPE: round

FRAGRANCE: none

TIME TO FRUITING: many years from seed

FRUITING PERIOD: late summer

PESTS

COMMON DISEASES: root rots if too wet, leaf and flower spots

OTHER PESTS: ants, mealybugs

The lei shown also contains aster, rose, and ʻūlei.

Harvesting considerations

WHAT IS HARVESTED: flowers and fruit clusters

BEST TIME OF DAY TO HARVEST: early morning

BEST WAY TO TRANSPORT FROM PICKING AREA: paper or cloth bag

AVOID CONTACT WITH THESE PRODUCTS: smoke, car exhaust, ripening fruits, and wilting flowers

Notes on lei making

BEST FOR WHICH TYPE OF LEI: neck, head, wrist, ankle, horse

VASE LIFE: 7 days

CLEANING OF PLANT MATERIALS: cold water soak

STORING RAW LEI MATERIALS: put stems in water and refrigerate at 40°F for up to 10 days

PREPARING FOR USE IN LEI: clip off wrinkled, limp, or poor quality areas before adding to lei

STORING A COMPLETED LEI BEFORE WEARING: soak lei, drip dry, wrap in damp newspaper, place in sealed plastic container, and refrigerate

PRESERVING A LEI FOR LONG-TERM STORAGE OR DISPLAY: cannot be preserved

Reference and further reading

Rauch, Fred D. 1996. *Tropical Landscape Plants*. 3rd ed. Battle Ground, Washington: Hawaii Floriculture.

tuberose

OTHER COMMON NAMES: azucena, *kupaloke*, nardo

SCIENTIFIC NAME: *Polianthes tuberosa*

FAMILY: Agavaceae (agave family)

NATURAL SETTING/LOCATION: native to Mexico

CURRENT STATUS IN THE WILD IN HAWAI'I: not found

CULTIVARS: 'Excelsior', 'Pearl'

Growing your own

PROPAGATION

FORM: corms (1½–2" diameter)

PREPLANTING TREATMENT: dip corms in insecticide for corm mealybugs

PLANTING DEPTH: plant corm 1½" deep in medium

CORM ROOTING TIME: 10 days

PREFERRED PRODUCTION CONDITIONS

GENERAL SOIL CHARACTERISTICS: well drained, loamy soil to minimize incidence of soil-borne fungi and damping off organisms

SOIL PH: 6.0–6.5

LIGHT: full sun

WATER: high water requirement; don't allow corms to dry out

TEMPERATURE: 68–90°F to develop flowers of large size, amount, and good keeping quality; for optimum root growth, average soil temperature should be above 68°F

ELEVATION: 10–1000'; prefers moderate elevations, such as conditions found on slopes of Haleakalā on Maui or in Waimea on Hawai'i; has done well in lowlands, such as 300' in Ho'olehua during winter and spring months

SALT TOLERANCE: poor

WIND RESISTANCE: moderate (but flower stalks can be blown over in strong winds)

MANAGEMENT

FERTILIZER NEEDS: medium

RECOMMENDED SPACING: 6–8" in rows, 8" between rows, or 1' square or triangle; many different planting systems are used for production

ADAPTATION TO GROWING IN CONTAINERS: yes, pots 8" or larger

PRUNING: cut stalk to base after flowering

SPECIAL CULTURAL HINTS: grow on mounds for good drainage to avoid root rot; sterilize soil to avoid nematodes; use corms 1" or larger in diameter

tuberose

Plant characteristics

HEIGHT: plant: up to 2'; flower stalk: 2–5'

SPREAD: 12"

GROWTH RATE: fast in summer, slow in winter

GROWTH HABIT: low growing, herbaceous

FLOWERS

SIZE: 2–3" long, 1–1½" diameter

COLOR: white

SHAPE: star-shaped tubular flower with rounded petals (only double-petalled flowers used for lei)

FRAGRANCE: very sweet

FLOWERS IN FIRST YEAR: yes

FLOWERING PERIOD: year-round, heaviest in spring and summer

TIME TO FLOWERING: 4–6 months, depending on temperature and time of year

INDUCING AND MAINTAINING FLOWERING: regular fertilizer and irrigation

PESTS

COMMON DISEASES: *Pythium* root rot fungus, bacterium, southern blight, *Botrytis* blossom rot, foliar and root-knot nematodes

OTHER PESTS: ants, aphids, blossom midge, carmine spider mite, mealy-bugs, slugs, thrips

The lei shown also contains shinobu.

Harvesting considerations

WHAT IS HARVESTED: majority of flowers open

HARVESTING TECHNIQUES: grasp individual flowers at base and give a gentle tug

BEST TIME OF DAY TO HARVEST: early morning

BEST WAY TO TRANSPORT FROM PICKING AREA: brown paper bag

AVOID CONTACT WITH THESE PRODUCTS: smoke, car exhaust, ripening fruits, and wilting flowers

Notes on lei making

BEST FOR WHICH TYPE OF LEI: neck, head, wrist, ankle, horse

VASE LIFE: 7 days if flowers on stalk

CLEANING OF PLANT MATERIALS: cold water soak

STORING RAW LEI MATERIALS: store flowers in paper box and refrigerate at 40°F for up to 4 days

PREPARING FOR USE IN LEI: clip off wrinkled, limp, or poor quality areas before adding to lei

STORING A COMPLETED LEI BEFORE WEARING: mist lei, wrap in damp paper towel, place in paper box, and refrigerate

PRESERVING A LEI FOR LONG-TERM STORAGE OR DISPLAY: cannot be preserved

References and further reading

Armitage, Allan M. 1993. *Specialty Cut Flowers, The Production of Annuals, Perennials, Bulbs, and Woody Plants for Fresh and Dried Cut Flowers*. Portland, Oregon: Varsity Press and Timber Press.

Benschop, M. 1993. "*Polianthes*." In: *The Physiology of Flower Bulbs*. A. Deltertogh and M. LeNard, eds., p. 589–601.

Horton, Alvin, and James McNair, 1987. *All About Bulbs*. San Ramon, California: Ortho Books.

Trujillo, E. 1961. *Diseases of Tuberose in Hawaii*. University of Hawai'i, CTAHR, CES Circular 427.

Yadav, L.P., and R.G. Maity. 1989. "Tuberose." In: *Commercial Flowers*. L.P. Bose and L.P. Yadav, eds., p. 519–543. Calcutta, India: Naya Prokash.

violet

OTHER COMMON NAMES: Australian violet (*Viola hederacea*), sweet violet (*V. odorata*), waioleka

SCIENTIFIC NAME: *Viola hederacea, V. odorata*

FAMILY: Violaceae (violet family)

NATURAL SETTING/LOCATION: *V. odorata*: Eurasia and Africa; *V. hederacea*: Australia

CURRENT STATUS IN THE WILD IN HAWAI'I: *V. odorata* naturalized in some wet areas on Lāna'i and Kaua'i

Growing your own

PROPAGATION

FORM: seeds (*V. odorata*); division; cuttings (taken in spring, rooted in sand)

PREPLANTING TREATMENT: none

PLANTING DEPTH: sow seeds ¹⁄₁₆–¹⁄₈" deep, barely covering with medium; keep division root crown just below soil level; insert base of cutting 1–2" into medium

GERMINATION TIME: 10–20 days at 70°F

CUTTING ROOTING TIME: 3–4 weeks

PREFERRED PRODUCTION CONDITIONS

GENERAL SOIL CHARACTERISTICS: light, sandy soil, well drained

SOIL PH: 6.0–7.0

LIGHT: partial to heavy shade

WATER: high quality water, applied deeply once a week

TEMPERATURE: 60°F (day), 50°F (night); tolerates warmer

ELEVATION: 1000–3000' (*V. odorata*); 200–500' (*V. hederacea*)

SALT TOLERANCE: poor

WIND RESISTANCE: poor

MANAGEMENT

FERTILIZER NEEDS: very light

RECOMMENDED SPACING: 6–8" apart

ADAPTATION TO GROWING IN CONTAINERS: yes, raised beds

PRUNING: not necessary; remove old leaves

SPECIAL CULTURAL HINTS: plants vegetate at high temperature, so keep cool; *V. hederacea* grows and flowers year-round in Hawai'i, while *V. odorata* flowers in spring only; too much sunlight causes burning; mulch to keep soil cool and moist; becomes chlorotic at high soil pH; water from bottom rather than from top to protect fragile flowers

violet

Plant characteristics

HEIGHT: 4–6"

SPREAD: 12–20"; forms mat or runners

GROWTH RATE: 6–10" a year

GROWTH HABIT: low growing, herbaceous

FLOWERS

SIZE: ½–1¼"

COLOR: violet, white, yellow; *V. hederacea*: blue-violet and white

SHAPE: 5-petalled

FRAGRANCE: sweet (*V. odorata*), none (*V. hederacea*)

FLOWERS IN FIRST YEAR: yes, depending on when propagated; *V. odorata* flowers in first year if started from seed in early spring

FLOWERING PERIOD: *V. odorata*: 8–12 weeks in spring; *V. hederacea*: year-round

TIME TO FLOWERING: perennial; less likely to flower in long days of summer and early fall

PESTS

COMMON DISEASES: root rot (*Phytophthora, Pythium, Rhizoctonia*), leaf spots (*Colletotrichum, Spaceloma*), black root (*Thielaviopsis basicola*), root-knot nematode

OTHER PESTS: aphids, mealybugs, mites, slugs

The lei shown also contains leatherleaf fern, goldenrod, German statice, baby's breath, and statice.

Harvesting considerations

WHAT IS HARVESTED: flowers with 1–2" of stem

HARVESTING TECHNIQUES: pinch stems

BEST TIME OF DAY TO HARVEST: early morning

BEST WAY TO TRANSPORT FROM PICKING AREA: plastic container

AVOID CONTACT WITH THESE PRODUCTS: smoke, car exhaust, ripening fruits, wilting flowers

Notes on lei making

BEST FOR WHICH TYPE OF LEI: neck, head, wrist, ankle

VASE LIFE: 3–7 days

CLEANING OF PLANT MATERIALS: stick stems in water

STORING RAW LEI MATERIALS: place in sealed plastic container or glass vase and refrigerate at 40°F for up to 7 days

PREPARING FOR USE IN LEI: clip off wrinkled, limp, or poor quality areas before adding to lei

STORING A COMPLETED LEI BEFORE WEARING: mist lei, shake off excess water, place in sealed plastic container, and refrigerate

PRESERVING A LEI FOR LONG-TERM STORAGE OR DISPLAY: cannot be preserved

References and further reading

Post, Kenneth. 1950. *Florist Crop Production and Marketing.* New York: Orange Judd Publishing Co. Inc.

Rowell, Raymond J. 1992. *Ornamental Plants in Australia: Annuals, Soft-wooded Perennials, Bulbous and Climbing Plants.* Kensington, Australia: New South Wales University Press.

Introduced Perennials

ageratum

OTHER COMMON NAMES: floss flower, *maile-hohono*

SCIENTIFIC NAME:
Ageratum houstonianum

FAMILY: Asteraceae (formerly Compositae), (aster family)

NATURAL SETTING/LOCATION:
Central America

CURRENT STATUS IN THE WILD IN HAWAI'I: naturalized in some areas, but its rangy form of growth in the wild generally precludes wild-collected flowers being used in lei

CULTIVARS: 'Blue Blazer', 'Blue Bouquet', 'Blue Chip', Blue Mink', 'Fairy Pink', 'Florist's Blue', 'Violet Cloud', 'Pinky Improved', 'Hawaii Royal'

Growing your own

HANDLING CAUTIONS: the plant contains coumarin and is toxic if eaten; contact can irritate mucous membranes in people sensitive to it

PROPAGATION

FORM: seeds

PLANTING DEPTH: broadcast seeds; do not cover with any soil or medium; light aids germination

GERMINATION TIME: 7–10 days

PREFERRED PRODUCTION CONDITIONS

GENERAL SOIL CHARACTERISTICS: best in rich, moist, well drained media; generally produced in pots

LIGHT: full sun to partial shade

WATER: irrigate abundantly

SOIL TEMPERATURE: 75–82°F

SALT TOLERANCE: poor

MANAGEMENT

FERTILIZER NEEDS: light

RECOMMENDED SPACING: 6–10"

ADAPTATION TO GROWING IN CONTAINERS: yes, 3–4" pots

SPECIAL CULTURAL HINTS: liberally reseeds itself and may become a pest

ageratum

Plant characteristics

HEIGHT: 6–9" (dwarfs); 2–2½' (other varieties)

SPREAD: 6–20"

GROWTH HABIT: loose, spreading, herbaceous

FLOWERS

SIZE: ¼–½"

COLOR: shades of blue, light purple, pink, white

SHAPE: tassel-like flowers in dense clusters

FRAGRANCE: none

TIME TO FLOWERING: 12–13 weeks for dwarf varieties; others take several weeks longer

INDUCING AND MAINTAINING FLOWERING: remove dead and old flowers to promote development of new ones

PESTS

COMMON DISEASES: powdery mildew, root rot

OTHER PESTS: aphids, slugs, snails, spider mites, whiteflies

The lei shown also contains agapanthus and hydrangea.

Harvesting considerations

WHAT IS HARVESTED: flower with 1–2" of stem free of leaves

HARVESTING TECHNIQUES: cut

BEST TIME OF DAY TO HARVEST: early morning

BEST WAY TO TRANSPORT FROM PICKING AREA: plastic bag

AVOID CONTACT WITH THESE PRODUCTS: smoke, car exhaust, ripening fruits, wilting flowers

Notes on lei making

BEST FOR WHICH TYPE OF LEI: neck, head, wrist, ankle

VASE LIFE: 1 day

CLEANING OF PLANT MATERIALS: cut stem, remove old foliage; avoid wetting flower heads

STORING RAW LEI MATERIALS: put stems in water with flower heads above water; flower heads tend to blacken with overwatering and being covered with paper; refrigerate at 40°F for up to 5 days

PREPARING FOR USE IN LEI: clip wrinkled, limp, or poor quality areas before adding to lei

STORING A COMPLETED LEI BEFORE WEARING: spray lightly, store in sealed plastic container, and refrigerate

PRESERVING A LEI FOR LONG-TERM STORAGE OR DISPLAY: cannot be preserved

References and further reading

Heitz, Halina. 1992. *Container Plants for Patios, Balconies, and Window Boxes.* Hauppauge, New York: Barron's Educational Series, Inc.

Nau, Jim. 1993. *Ball Culture Guide: The Encyclopedia of Seed Germination.* 2nd ed. Batavia, Illinois: Ball Publishing.

Nau, Jim. 1998. "*Ageratum.*" In: *The Ball Redbook.* 16th ed., p. 339–340. Batavia, Illinois: Ball Publishing.

Ortho Books. 1999. *Ortho's All About Annuals.* Des Moines, Iowa: Meredith Publishing Group.

Smith and Hawken. 1996. *The Book Of Outdoor Gardening.* New York: Workman Publishing Company, Inc.

Sunset. 1998. *Western Garden Book.* Menlo Park, California: Sunset Publishing Corp.

Introduced Annuals

alyssum

OTHER COMMON NAMES: sweet alyssum, sweet alison

SCIENTIFIC NAME: *Lobularia maritima* (L.) Desv.

FAMILY: Brassicaceae (mustard family)

NATURAL SETTING/LOCATION: Mediterranean

CURRENT STATUS IN THE WILD IN HAWAI'I: naturalized in Kula, Maui

CULTIVARS: 'Apricot Shades', 'Rosie O'Day', 'Wonderland', 'Oriental Night', 'Carpet of Snow', 'Snow Crystals', 'Basket-of-Gold'

Growing your own

PROPAGATION

FORM: primarily seeds; has a low level of self-sowing from one year to the next

PLANTING DEPTH: broadcast seeds; do not cover with any soil or medium; light aids germination; best to water seeds with warm water

GERMINATION TIME: 7–10 days

PREFERRED PRODUCTION CONDITIONS

GENERAL SOIL CHARACTERISTICS: well drained, average fertility; will grow in poor soils

LIGHT: full sun to partial shade

WATER: moderately

SOIL TEMPERATURES: 78–80°F

MANAGEMENT

FERTILIZER NEEDS: light

RECOMMENDED SPACING: 8"

ADAPTATION TO GROWING IN CONTAINERS: yes, 5" pots

SPECIAL CULTURAL HINTS: can be cut back repeatedly and fertilized lightly after each cut; may stop flowering in periods of extreme heat; can be produced in pots

alyssum

Plant characteristics

HEIGHT: 4–8"

SPREAD: 10–15"

GROWTH RATE: medium

GROWTH HABIT: low, branching, trailing

FLOWERS

SIZE: tiny

COLOR: white, pink, lavender

SHAPE: 4-petaled (with the petals of equal size)

FRAGRANCE: honey-like

TIME TO FLOWERING: 10–11 weeks

INDUCING AND MAINTAINING BLOOMING: to prolong flowering season, cut them down by half after the first flush of flowers and they will bloom again; flowers profusely under cool (60–68°F) temperature

PESTS

COMMON DISEASES: sensitive to damping off, powdery and downy mildew

COMMON INSECT PESTS: aphids, thrips

Harvesting considerations

WHAT IS HARVESTED: flowers

HARVESTING TECHNIQUES: cut

BEST TIME OF DAY TO HARVEST: early morning

BEST WAY TO TRANSPORT FROM PICKING AREA: cooler or wet newspaper

AVOID CONTACT WITH THESE PRODUCTS: smoke, car exhaust, ripening fruits, wilting flowers

The lei shown also contains asparagus fern, ageratum, dusty miller, and ʻōhiʻa lehua.

Notes on lei making

BEST FOR WHICH TYPE OF LEI: neck, head, wrist, ankle

VASE LIFE: 1 day

CLEANING OF PLANT MATERIALS: cold water soak

STORING RAW LEI MATERIALS: refrigerate at 40°F for up to 10 days

PREPARING FOR USE IN LEI: clean leaves and old seed pods, cut 2", place stem in water

STORING A COMPLETED LEI BEFORE WEARING: immerse whole lei in water and drip dry; place in wet tissue, then place in sealed plastic container and refrigerate

PRESERVING A LEI FOR LONG-TERM STORAGE OR DISPLAY: cannot be preserved

References and further reading

Heitz, Halina. 1992. *Container Plants for Patios, Balconies, and Window Boxes.* Hauppauge, New York: Barron's Educational Series, Inc.

Nau, Jim. 1993. *Ball Culture Guide: The Encyclopedia of Seed Germination.* 2nd ed. Batavia, Illinois: Ball Publishing.

Nau, Jim. 1998. *Lobularia.* In: *The Ball Redbook.* 16th ed., p. 635–636. Batavia, Illinois: Ball Publishing.

Smith and Hawken. 1996. *The Book Of Outdoor Gardening.* New York: Workman Publishing Company, Inc.

Introduced Annuals

celosia

OTHER COMMON NAMES: cockscomb, *lepe-a-moa*

SCIENTIFIC NAME: *Celosia argentea* var. *cristata* and var. *plumosa*

FAMILY: Amaranthaceae (amaranth family)

NATURAL SETTING/LOCATION: tropical Africa

CURRENT STATUS IN THE WILD IN HAWAI'I: not found

CULTIVARS: *C. argentea* var. *cristata*: Chief hybrids, Coral Garden hybrids, 'Fireglow', 'Toreador'; var. *plumosa*: Castle hybrids, Kimono hybrids, 'Apricot Brandy', 'Fiery Feather'

Growing your own

PROPAGATION

FORM: seeds

PLANTING DEPTH: broadcast; do not cover with any soil or medium; light aids germination

GERMINATION TIME: 11–12 days

PREFERRED PRODUCTION CONDITIONS

GENERAL SOIL CHARACTERISTICS: rich, well drained, high in organic matter; tolerates dry soil

LIGHT: full sun to partial shade

WATER: abundantly

SOIL TEMPERATURE: 75–78°F

MANAGEMENT

FERTILIZER NEEDS: light

RECOMMENDED SPACING: 8–18" (8" for single harvests, 18" for continual harvests)

ADAPTATION TO GROWING IN CONTAINERS: yes, 6" pots

PRUNING: cut off spent flowers regularly

SPECIAL CULTURAL HINTS: control damping off by limiting moisture and applying preventative fungicides; both types of celosia are extremely sensitive to high soluble-salt levels in media; symptoms of salt damage include reduced leaf size and plant height, leaf chlorosis at tips or margins, and increased variability among the plants

celosia

Plant characteristics

HEIGHT: 6–20"

SPREAD: 8–12"

GROWTH RATE: fast

GROWTH HABIT: erect, branching, herbaceous

FLOWERS

SIZE: large if they are at the apex of the plant, smaller if they arise from the axillary shoots

COLOR: solid colors of red, yellow, orange, gold, pink

SHAPE: either spire-like plumes of flowers (var. *cristata)* or Y-shaped, convoluted, flat-topped flowers resembling a "rooster's comb" (var. *plumosa)*

FRAGRANCE: none

TIME TO FLOWERING: 12–15 weeks

INDUCING AND MAINTAINING BLOOMING: remove dead and old flowers to promote development of new ones

PESTS

COMMON DISEASES: damping off, leaf spots, nematodes

OTHER PESTS: aphids, spider mites

Harvesting considerations

WHAT IS HARVESTED: half-open flower spike

HARVESTING TECHNIQUES: cut

BEST TIME OF DAY TO HARVEST: early morning

BEST WAY TO TRANSPORT FROM PICKING AREA: cooler

AVOID CONTACT WITH THESE PRODUCTS: smoke, car exhaust, ripening fruits, wilting flowers

The lei shown also contains *paʻiniu,* strawflower, globe amaranth, and rose.

Notes on lei making

BEST FOR WHICH TYPE OF LEI: neck, head, wrist, ankle, horse

VASE LIFE: to 6 days

CLEANING OF PLANT MATERIALS: cut stem, remove all foliage; avoid wetting flower heads

STORING RAW LEI MATERIALS: store in container with water and refrigerate at 40°F for up to 6 days

PREPARING FOR USE IN LEI: clip wrinkled, limp, or poor quality areas before adding to lei

STORING A COMPLETED LEI BEFORE WEARING: place in sealed plastic container and refrigerate

PRESERVING A LEI FOR LONG-TERM STORAGE OR DISPLAY: place on hat and let dry naturally in cool, dark area; red flowers give the best results

References and further reading

Heitz, Halina. 1992. *Container Plants for Patios, Balconies, and Window Boxes.* Hauppauge, New York: Barron's Educational Series, Inc.

Hessayon, D.G. 1995. *The Flower Expert.* London: Transworld Publishers.

Nau, Jim. 1993. *Ball Culture Guide, The Encyclopedia of Seed Germination.* 2nd ed. Batavia, Illinois: Ball Publishing.

Styer, R.C., and D.S. Koranski. 1997. *Plug and Transplant Production, A Grower's Guide.* Batavia, Illinois: Ball Publishing.

Introduced Annuals

chrysanthemum

OTHER COMMON NAMES: mum (florist mum, garden mum), feverfew, *pua pākē*

SCIENTIFIC NAME: *Chrysanthemum* species and hybrids

FAMILY: Asteraceae (formerly Compositae), (aster family)

NATURAL SETTING/LOCATION: China, Japan, Europe

CURRENT STATUS IN THE WILD IN HAWAI'I: not found

CULTIVARS: many cultivars are available from commercial sources; new ones are developed frequently

Growing your own

HANDLING CAUTIONS: flowers of some types contain pollen to which some people are allergic

PROPAGATION

FORM: cuttings; seeds (takes longer); division (runner plants)

PLANTING DEPTH: keep runner root crown just below soil level

GERMINATION TIME: 5–14 days

PREFERRED PRODUCTION CONDITIONS

GENERAL SOIL CHARACTERISTICS: well drained, all-purpose

LIGHT: full sun

WATER: keep damp

SOIL TEMPERATURE: 60–70°F

MANAGEMENT

FERTILIZER NEEDS: light to medium

RECOMMENDED SPACING: 8–12" apart

ADAPTATION TO GROWING IN CONTAINERS: yes, 6" pots

PRUNING: cut off spent flowers regularly

SPECIAL CULTURAL HINTS: blooms with short days; there are specific budding and flowering times for various mums; colors differ in the second blooming, so a variety of colors can be obtained by allowing a second crop to flower after cutting back the fall crop

chrysanthemum

Plant characteristics

HEIGHT: 8–12"

SPREAD: 10–12"

GROWTH RATE: moderate to fast

GROWTH HABIT: erect, branching, herbaceous

FLOWERS

SIZE: small-flowered types (1–2") best for use in lei

COLOR: pink, orange-bronze, yellow, cream

SHAPE: pompon, daisy, button

FRAGRANCE: yes, but not sweet

TIME TO FLOWERING: 11–12 weeks

INDUCING AND MAINTAINING BLOOMING: short-day types require covering to shorten long summer days; covering must completely block light

PESTS

COMMON DISEASES: foliar diseases, petal blight, stunt virus

OTHER PESTS: aphids, spider mites, thrips

Harvesting considerations

WHAT IS HARVESTED: flowers

HARVESTING TECHNIQUES: cut when flower is open but center is still tight

BEST TIME OF DAY TO HARVEST: early morning

BEST WAY TO TRANSPORT FROM PICKING AREA: plastic bag

AVOID CONTACT WITH THESE PRODUCTS: smoke, car exhaust, ripening fruits, wilting flowers

The lei shown also contains *moa*, *kīkānia*, and rondeletia.

Notes on lei making

BEST FOR WHICH TYPE OF LEI: neck, head, wrist, ankle, horse

VASE LIFE: 7–10 days, depending on the cultivar

CLEANING OF PLANT MATERIALS: remove all leaves; cut above base of stem where hard and woody to assist water uptake

STORING RAW LEI MATERIALS: store in container with water and refrigerate at 40°F for up to 10 days

PREPARING FOR USE IN LEI: clip off wrinkled, limp, or poor quality areas

STORING A COMPLETED LEI BEFORE WEARING: soak in water, drip dry, wrap in dry paper towel, and refrigerate in sealed plastic container

PRESERVING A LEI FOR LONG-TERM STORAGE OR DISPLAY: *C. parthenium* is suitable for drying

References and further reading

Ball, Vic. 1998. "Chrysanthemum." In: *The Ball Redbook*. 16th ed, p. 425–426. Batavia, Illinois: Ball Publishing.

Halpin, Anne Moyer. 1990. *Foolproof Planting*. New York: Roundtable Press, Inc.

Heitz, Halina. 1992. *Container Plants for Patios, Balconies, and Window Boxes*. Hauppauge, New York: Barron's Educational Series, Inc.

Hessayon, D.G. 1995. *The Flower Expert*. London: Transworld Publishers.

Hodge, Peggy Hicock. 1996. *Gardening in Hawaii*. Honolulu: Mutual Publishing.

Sascalis, John N. 1993. *Cut Flowers, Prolonging Freshness*. Batavia, Illinois: Ball Publishing.

Sturdivant, Lee. 1992. *Flowers for Sale*. Friday Harbor, Washington: San Juan Naturals.

Introduced Annuals

cornflower

OTHER COMMON NAMES: bachelor's button

SCIENTIFIC NAME: *Centaurea cyanus*

FAMILY: Asteraceae (formerly Compositae), (aster family)

NATURAL SETTING/LOCATION: native to Europe

CURRENT STATUS IN THE WILD IN HAWAI'I: not found

CULTIVARS: 'Florence Pink', 'Pink Ball', 'Blue Diadem', 'Ultra Dwarf Blue'

Growing your own

PROPAGATION

FORM: seeds

PLANTING DEPTH: cover seeds ¼" deep with fine medium

GERMINATION TIME: 12–14 days

PREFERRED PRODUCTION CONDITIONS

GENERAL SOIL CHARACTERISTICS: dry to moist

LIGHT: full sun

WATER: moderate

SOIL TEMPERATURES: 65–70°F

MANAGEMENT

FERTILIZER NEEDS: light

RECOMMENDED SPACING: 6–9"

ADAPTATION TO GROWING IN CONTAINERS: yes, dwarf cultivars in 3–5-gallon tubs

SPECIAL CULTURAL HINTS: very sensitive to being root-bound; does not transplant well and is best seeded directly into the garden; grows best by starting under short days, followed by long days; acts as a perennial by reseeding itself; provide supplementary lighting to increase daylength during short winter days

cornflower

Plant characteristics

HEIGHT: 12–36"

SPREAD: 6–12"

GROWTH HABIT: erect, branching, herbaceous

FLOWERS

SIZE: 1–1½" wide flowerheads

COLOR: blue, white, pink, purple

SHAPE: long-stalked

FRAGRANCE: none

TIME TO FLOWERING: 5–6 months

INDUCING AND MAINTAINING BLOOMING: remove dead and old flowers to promote development of new ones

PESTS

COMMON DISEASES: *Botrytis*, aster yellows, downey mildew

COMMON INSECT PESTS: leafhoppers, aphids

Harvesting considerations

WHAT IS HARVESTED: flowers beginning to open

HARVESTING TECHNIQUES: cut

BEST TIME OF DAY TO HARVEST: early morning

BEST WAY TO TRANSPORT FROM PICKING AREA: cooler

AVOID CONTACT WITH THESE PRODUCTS: smoke, car exhaust, ripening fruits, wilting flowers

The lei shown also contains hydrangea, baby's breath, asparagus fern, and *pa'iniu*.

Notes on lei making

BEST FOR WHICH TYPE OF LEI: neck, head, wrist, ankle

VASE LIFE: 6–10 days

CLEANING OF PLANT MATERIALS: cut stem off at 2"

STORING RAW LEI MATERIALS: store in container with water and refrigerate at 40°F for up to 3 days; do not cover flower heads

PREPARING FOR USE IN LEI: clip off wrinkled, limp, or poor quality areas before adding to lei

STORING A COMPLETED LEI BEFORE WEARING: sprinkle with water, drip dry, place in sealed plastic container, and refrigerate

PRESERVING A LEI FOR LONG-TERM STORAGE OR DISPLAY: cannot be air dried; sand and borax methods used

References and further reading

Nau, Jim. 1993. *Ball Culture Guide: The Encyclopedia of Seed Germination.* 2nd ed. Batavia, Illinois: Ball Publishing.

Halpin, Anne Moyer. 1990. *Foolproof Planting.* New York: Roundtable Press, Inc.

Hessayon, D.G. 1995. *The Flower Expert.* London: Transworld Publishers.

Nowack, Joanna, and Ryszard M. Rudnicki. 1990. *Postharvest Handling and Storage of Cut Flowers, Florist Greens, and Potted Plants.* Portland, Oregon: Timber Press.

Styer, R.C., and D.S. Koranski. 1997. *Plug and Transplant Production, A Grower's Guide.* Batavia, Illinois: Ball Publishing.

Introduced Annuals

dianthus

OTHER COMMON NAMES: sweet william, *ponimo'i-li'ili'i*

SCIENTIFIC NAME: *Dianthus* species and hybrids

FAMILY: Caryophyllaceae (carnation family)

NATURAL SETTING/LOCATION: Europe

CURRENT STATUS IN THE WILD IN HAWAI'I: not found

CULTIVARS: 'Wee Willie Mix', 'Roundabout', 'Summer Beauty', 'Indian Carpet'

Growing your own

PROPAGATION

FORM: seeds; stem cuttings; division; air layering

PLANTING DEPTH: sow seeds ⅛" deep; keep division root crown just below soil level

GERMINATION TIME: 7–12 days

CUTTING ROOTING TIME: 10–15 days

PREFERRED PRODUCTION CONDITIONS

GENERAL SOIL CHARACTERISTICS: best in well drained, preferably sandy soil

LIGHT: full sun to partial shade

WATER: moderate

SOIL TEMPERATURE: 70–75°F

MANAGEMENT

FERTILIZER NEEDS: light

RECOMMENDED SPACING: 10–12" in the ground

ADAPTATION TO GROWING IN CONTAINERS: yes, 6" pots

SPECIAL CULTURAL HINTS: very sensitive to salt; for early flowering, increase light; acts as a perennial by reseeding itself; avoid standing water

dianthus

Plant characteristics

HEIGHT: 6–18"

SPREAD: 10–12"

GROWTH RATE: fast

GROWTH HABIT: upright, herbaceous

FLOWERS

SIZE: ½–1" across

COLOR: red, white, pink, purple, bicolors

SHAPE: fringed or toothed petals

FRAGRANCE: sweetly scented

TIME TO FLOWERING: 15–16 weeks

INDUCING AND MAINTAINING BLOOMING: remove dead and old flowers to promote development of new ones

PESTS

COMMON DISEASES: bacterial spot, fasciation, stem rot, leaf spot, branch blight, *Fusarium* wilt

OTHER PESTS: aphids, mites

Harvesting considerations

WHAT IS HARVESTED: half-open flowers

HARVESTING TECHNIQUES: cut

BEST TIME OF DAY TO HARVEST: early morning

BEST WAY TO TRANSPORT FROM PICKING AREA: plastic bag

AVOID CONTACT WITH THESE PRODUCTS: smoke, car exhaust, ripening fruits, wilting flowers

The lei shown also contains rose, statice, Peruvian lily, *moa*, agapanthus, shinobu, and ʻōhiʻa lehua.

Notes on lei making

BEST FOR WHICH TYPE OF LEI: neck, head, wrist, ankle

VASE LIFE: 5–9 days

CLEANING OF PLANT MATERIALS: cold water soak; clip all leaves and cut stem 2" below base of calyx

STORING RAW LEI MATERIALS: refrigerate at 45°F for up to 4 days

PREPARING FOR USE IN LEI: clip off wrinkled, limp, or poor quality areas before adding to lei

STORING A COMPLETED LEI BEFORE WEARING: soak lei in water, drip dry, wrap in newspaper, place in plastic bag, and refrigerate

PRESERVING A LEI FOR LONG-TERM STORAGE OR DISPLAY: cannot be preserved

References and further reading

Halpin, Anne Moyer. 1990. *Foolproof Planting*. New York: Roundtable Press, Inc.

Heitz, Halina. 1992. *Container Plants for Patios, Balconies, and Window Boxes*. Hauppauge, New York: Barron's Educational Series, Inc.

Nowack, Joanna, and Ryszard M. Rudnicki. 1990. *Postharvest Handling and Storage of Cut Flowers, Florist Greens, and Potted Plants*. Portland, Oregon: Timber Press.

Introduced Annuals

globe amaranth

OTHER COMMON NAMES: bozu, clover, *lehua-pepe*, *lei-hua*; also sometimes called by the misnomer "bachelor button"

SCIENTIFIC NAME: *Gomphrena globosa*

FAMILY: Amaranthaceae (amaranth family)

NATURAL SETTING/LOCATION: tropics of the Eastern Hemisphere

CURRENT STATUS IN THE WILD IN HAWAIʻI: not found

CULTIVARS: 'Buddy', 'Cissy', 'Strawberry Fields'

Growing your own

PROPAGATION

FORM: seeds

PRETREATMENT: soak seeds in water overnight.

PLANTING DEPTH: sow $\frac{1}{16}$ to $\frac{1}{8}$" deep (barely covered with medium)

GERMINATION TIME: 10–14 days

PREFERRED PRODUCTION CONDITIONS

GENERAL SOIL CHARACTERISTICS: light, well drained

LIGHT: full sun

WATER: lightly

SOIL TEMPERATURE: 72–75°F

MANAGEMENT

FERTILIZER NEEDS: light

RECOMMENDED SPACING: 6–9"

ADAPTATION TO GROWING IN CONTAINERS: yes, 6–10" pots

SPECIAL CULTURAL HINTS: taller varieties may need to be staked; avoid overwatering for best germination, root growth, and control of disease; very sensitive to most pesticides

globe amaranth

Plant characteristics

HEIGHT: 24–36"

SPREAD: 12–15"

GROWTH RATE: fast, once established

GROWTH HABIT: upright, herbaceous

FLOWERS

SIZE: ¾"

COLOR: pink, purple, white, lavender, orange, red, yellow

SHAPE: clover-like

FRAGRANCE: none

TIME TO FLOWERING: 10–14 weeks

INDUCING AND MAINTAINING BLOOMING: remove dead and old flowers to promote production of new ones

PESTS

COMMON DISEASES: mildew

OTHER PESTS: few, if any

Harvesting considerations

WHAT IS HARVESTED: flowers

HARVESTING TECHNIQUES: cut

BEST TIME OF DAY TO HARVEST: early morning

BEST WAY TO TRANSPORT FROM PICKING AREA: plastic bag

AVOID CONTACT WITH THESE PRODUCTS: smoke, car exhaust, ripening fruits, wilting flowers

The lei shown also contains crownflower and epidenrum orchid.

Notes on lei making

BEST FOR WHICH TYPE OF LEI: neck, head, wrist, ankle, horse

VASE LIFE: 7–10 days

CLEANING OF PLANT MATERIALS: cold water soak; clip stems to 2" and place in water

STORING RAW LEI MATERIALS: refrigerate at 40°F for up to 10 days

PREPARING FOR USE IN LEI: clip off wrinkled, limp, or poor quality areas before adding to lei

STORING A COMPLETED LEI BEFORE WEARING: soak lei in water, drip dry, place in paper bag or paper box, and refrigerate

PRESERVING A LEI FOR LONG-TERM STORAGE OR DISPLAY: air-dry

References and further reading

Heitz, Halina. 1992. *Container Plants for Patios, Balconies, and Window Boxes*. Hauppauge, New York: Barron's Educational Series, Inc.

Hutson, J., and B. Ward. 1995. *Annual Gardening*. New York: Pantheon Books.

Nau, Jim. 1993. *Ball Culture Guide: The Encyclopedia of Seed Germination*. 2nd ed. Batavia, Illinois: Ball Publishing.

Neal, Marie C. 1965. *In Gardens of Hawaii*. Bernice P. Bishop Museum Special Publication 50. Honolulu: Bishop Museum Press.

Styer, R.C., and D.S. Koranski. 1997. *Plug and Transplant Production, A Grower's Guide*. Batavia, Illinois: Ball Publishing.

Introduced Annuals

marguerite daisy

OTHER COMMON NAMES: *'okika*

SCIENTIFIC NAME:
Argyranthemum frutescens

FAMILY: Asteraceae (formerly
Compositae), (aster family)

NATURAL SETTING/LOCATION:
found worldwide

CURRENT STATUS IN THE WILD IN HAWAI'I:
not found

CULTIVARS: many are available

Growing your own

PROPAGATION

FORM: cuttings (non-flowering side
shoots) or purchased liners

PREPLANTING TREATMENT: use a medium
rooting hormone

PLANTING DEPTH: insert base of cutting
1–2" into medium

PREFERRED PRODUCTION
CONDITIONS

GENERAL SOIL CHARACTERISTICS: well
drained; use peat-perlite medium
when growing in containers

LIGHT: full sun

WATER: keep evenly damp

SOIL TEMPERATURE: 45–85°F

MANAGEMENT

FERTILIZER NEEDS: light

RECOMMENDED SPACING: 3–4'

ADAPTATION TO GROWING IN CONTAINERS:
yes, 1-gallon pots or larger

PRUNING: pinching will cause more
branching and more flowers but will
delay flowering period

SPECIAL CULTURAL HINTS: drench with
broad-spectrum fungicide when
planting liners

marguerite daisy

Plant characteristics

HEIGHT: 40–48", new dwarf varieties are 14–18"

SPREAD: 48–60", new dwarf varieties, 18–24"

GROWTH RATE: moderate

GROWTH HABIT: bushy, herbaceous

FLOWERS

SIZE: 1–1½"

COLOR: large yellow disc with white or yellow petals; also, new cultivars with pink hues are available

SHAPE: daisy-like; new cultivars with double flowers are available

FRAGRANCE: none

TIME TO FLOWERING: 5 months from liners

INDUCING AND MAINTAINING BLOOMING: remove dead and old flowers to promote production of new ones

PESTS

COMMON DISEASES: root rots in wet soils, several viruses

OTHER PESTS: aphids, thrips, whiteflies

Harvesting considerations

WHAT IS HARVESTED: flowers

HARVESTING TECHNIQUES: cut individual flowers at the base

BEST TIME OF DAY TO HARVEST: early morning

BEST WAY TO TRANSPORT FROM PICKING AREA: plastic bags

AVOID CONTACT WITH THESE PRODUCTS: smoke, car exhaust, ripening fruits, wilting flowers

The lei shown also contains Mexican creeper, ʻākia, *palapalai*, crown flower, bleeding heart, and *moa*.

Notes on lei making

BEST FOR WHICH TYPE OF LEI: neck, head, wrist, ankle

VASE LIFE: 4–7 days

CLEANING OF PLANT MATERIALS: cut stems, strip leaves, and place in water; do not cover heads.

STORING RAW LEI MATERIALS: store dry in a plastic container and refrigerate at 40°F for up to 8 days

PREPARING FOR USE IN LEI: clip off the wrinkled, limp, or poor quality areas before adding to lei

STORING A COMPLETED LEI BEFORE WEARING: sprinkle with water, drip dry, wrap in dry tissue, store in plastic container, and refrigerate

PRESERVING A LEI FOR LONG-TERM STORAGE OR DISPLAY: cannot be preserved

References and further reading

Ball, Vic. 1998. "*Argeranthemum.*" In: *The Ball Redbook.* 16th ed., p. 370–371. Batavia, Illinois: Ball Publishing.

Sascalis, John N. 1993. *Cut Flowers, Prolonging Freshness.* Batavia, Illinois: Ball Publishing.

Introduced Annuals

marigold

OTHER COMMON NAMES: French marigold (*Tagetes patula*) or American marigold (sometimes listed as African) (*Tagetes erecta*), 'ōkole-'oi'oi

SCIENTIFIC NAME: *Tagetes* cultivars

FAMILY: Asteraceae (formerly Compositae), (aster family)

NATURAL SETTING/LOCATION: Mexico and Guatemala

CURRENT STATUS IN THE WILD IN HAWAI'I: not found

CULTIVARS: *T. patula*: Aurora series, Bonanza series, Safari series, 'Bolero'; *T. erecta*: Antigua series, 'Apollo', 'Snowdrift'

Growing your own

HANDLING CAUTIONS: the plant contains substances that may induce photodermatitis

PROPAGATION

FORM: seeds

PLANTING DEPTH: sow ¼–½" deep in medium

GERMINATION TIME: 9–12 days

PREFERRED PRODUCTION CONDITIONS

GENERAL SOIL CHARACTERISTICS: well drained, moist, fertile

LIGHT: full sun to partial shade

WATER: keep evenly damp

SOIL TEMPERATURE: 70–75°F

MANAGEMENT

FERTILIZER NEEDS: light

RECOMMENDED SPACING: 6–12", depending on variety

ADAPTATION TO GROWING IN CONTAINERS: yes, 6–10" pots

SPECIAL CULTURAL HINTS: mulching between plants helps conserve soil moisture; keep soil pH above 6.0 to avoid micronutrient toxicities

marigold

The lei shown also contains bougainvillea and epidendrum orchid.

Plant characteristics

HEIGHT: 12–36"

SPREAD: 12"

GROWTH RATE: fast

GROWTH HABIT: branching, herbaceous

FLOWERS

SIZE: ½–4"

COLOR: yellow, gold shades, crimson, orange

SHAPE: flat to globular

FRAGRANCE: pungent

TIME TO FLOWERING: 8–12 weeks

INDUCING AND MAINTAINING BLOOMING: remove dead and old flowers to promote development of new ones

PESTS

COMMON DISEASES: *Botrytis*, powdery mildew, wilt and stem rots, leaf spot

COMMON INSECT PESTS: aphids, slugs, spider mites, whiteflies

Harvesting considerations

WHAT IS HARVESTED: fully open flowers

HARVESTING TECHNIQUES: cut

BEST TIME OF DAY TO HARVEST: early morning

BEST WAY TO TRANSPORT FROM PICKING AREA: plastic bag

AVOID CONTACT WITH THESE PRODUCTS: smoke, car exhaust, ripening fruits, wilting flowers

Notes on lei making

BEST FOR WHICH TYPE OF LEI: neck, head, wrist, ankle, horse

VASE LIFE: 5 days

CLEANING OF PLANT MATERIALS: cold water soak

STORING RAW LEI MATERIALS: refrigerate at 40°F for up to 7 days

PREPARING FOR USE IN LEI: clip off wrinkled, limp, or poor quality areas before adding to lei

STORING A COMPLETED LEI BEFORE WEARING: soak in water, drip dry, place in newspaper then in plastic bag, and refrigerate

PRESERVING A LEI FOR LONG-TERM STORAGE OR DISPLAY: hang and air-dry

References and further reading

Heitz, Halina. 1992. *Container Plants for Patios, Balconies, and Window Boxes.* Hauppauge, New York: Barron's Educational Series, Inc.

Hessayon, D.G. 1995. *The Flower Expert.* London: Transworld Publishers.

Nau, Jim. 1993. *Ball Culture Guide: The Encyclopedia of Seed Germination.* 2nd ed. Batavia, Illinois: Ball Publishing.

Nau, Jim. 1998. "*Tagetes* (Marigold)." In: *The Ball Redbook.* 16th ed., p. 763–766. Batavia, Illinois: Ball Publishing.

Styer, R.C., and D.S. Koranski. 1997. *Plug and Transplant Production, A Grower's Guide.* Batavia, Illinois: Ball Publishing.

Introduced Annuals

pansy

OTHER COMMON NAMES: *pāneki, poʻo-kanaka*

SCIENTIFIC NAME: *Viola* x *Wittrockiana*

FAMILY: Violaceae (violet family)

NATURAL SETTING/LOCATION: Europe, including Britain; North Africa

CURRENT STATUS IN THE WILD IN HAWAIʻI: not found

CULTIVARS: 'Imperial Antique Shades', 'Romeo and Juliet', 'Black Devil', 'Maxima Marina', 'Universal Melodys', 'Crystal Bowls', 'Rosy Cheeks'

Growing your own

PROPAGATION

FORM: seeds

PLANTING DEPTH: sow ¼–⅜" deep, barely covered with medium; light aids germination

GERMINATION TIME: 7–9 days

PREFERRED PRODUCTION CONDITIONS

GENERAL SOIL CHARACTERISTICS: moist, fertile, well drained

LIGHT: full sun to partial shade

WATER: keep evenly damp; don't allow to dry out

SOIL TEMPERATURE: 65–75°F

MANAGEMENT

FERTILIZER NEEDS: very light

RECOMMENDED SPACING: 10–12" apart on raised bed

ADAPTATION TO GROWING IN CONTAINERS: yes, 6" pots

PRUNING: remove faded flowers to keep the plants blooming

SPECIAL CULTURAL HINTS: reduce moisture after about 5 days for best germination; control root rot by limiting moisture, lowering pH, and applying fungicides; often reseeds itself

pansy

Plant characteristics

HEIGHT: 6–8"

SPREAD: to 12"

GROWTH RATE: slow to moderate

GROWTH HABIT: low growing, herbaceous

FLOWERS

SIZE: 1–2"

COLOR: usually 2 or 3 colors with "smiling face" (yellow, gold shades, crimson, orange, blue, purple, white)

SHAPE: round

FRAGRANCE: sweet

TIME TO FLOWERING: 15–17 weeks

INDUCING AND MAINTAINING BLOOMING: remove dead and old flowers to promote development of new ones

PESTS

COMMON DISEASES: *Botrytis*, powdery and downy mildew, root rot

COMMON INSECT PESTS: aphids, brown caterpillar, cutworm

Harvesting considerations

WHAT IS HARVESTED: almost-open flowers

HARVESTING TECHNIQUES: cut

BEST TIME OF DAY TO HARVEST: early morning

BEST WAY TO TRANSPORT FROM PICKING AREA: coffee can

AVOID CONTACT WITH THESE PRODUCTS: smoke, car exhaust, ripening fruits, wilting flowers

The lei shown also contains dusty miller.

Notes on lei making

BEST FOR WHICH TYPE OF LEI: neck, head, wrist, ankle

VASE LIFE: 2 days

CLEANING OF PLANT MATERIALS: cut stems, place in water

STORING RAW LEI MATERIALS: refrigerate at 40°F for up to 5 days

PREPARING FOR USE IN LEI: clip off wrinkled, limp, or poor quality areas before adding to lei

STORING A COMPLETED LEI BEFORE WEARING: sprinkle with water, place in sealed container with ti leaf bottom, and refrigerate

PRESERVING A LEI FOR LONG-TERM STORAGE OR DISPLAY: cannot be preserved

References and further reading

Healy, Will. 1998. "*Viola* x *Wittrockiana* (Pansy)." In: *The Ball Redbook*. 16th ed., p. 777–782. Batavia, Illinois: Ball Publishing.

Heitz, Halina. 1992. *Container Plants for Patios, Balconies, and Window Boxes*. Hauppauge, New York: Barron's Educational Series, Inc.

Hessayon, D.G. 1995. *The Flower Expert*. London: Transworld Publishers.

Hutson, J., and B. Ward. 1995. *Annual Gardening*. New York: Pantheon Books.

Nau, Jim. 1993. *Ball Culture Guide: The Encyclopedia of Seed Germination*. 2nd ed. Batavia, Illinois: Ball Publishing.

Styer, R.C., and D.S. Koranski. 1997. *Plug and Transplant Production, A Grower's Guide*. Batavia, Illinois: Ball Publishing.

Introduced Annuals

salvia

OTHER COMMON NAMES: scarlet sage (*Salvia splendens*); blue sage, mealycup sage (*S. farinacea*)

SCIENTIFIC NAME: *Salvia splendens*, *S. farinacea*

FAMILY: Lamiaceae (mint family)

NATURAL SETTING/LOCATION: *S. splendens* native to South America, *S. farinacea* native to Texas

CURRENT STATUS IN THE WILD IN HAWAIʻI: may be found in the wild

CULTIVARS: *S. farinacea*: 'Argent Blanche', 'Rhea Dark Blue', 'Signum'; *S. splendens*: 'Red Hot Sally', 'Scarlet Queen', 'Fuego', 'Victoria'

Growing your own

PROPAGATION

FORM: seeds; cuttings (soft wood taken from young shoots, 3–4" long)

PREPLANTING TREATMENT: use a mild rooting compound on cuttings, or none

PLANTING DEPTH: sow seeds on surface of medium, do not cover; light aids germination; insert base of cutting 1" into medium

GERMINATION TIME: 12–14 days

PREFERRED PRODUCTION CONDITIONS

GENERAL SOIL CHARACTERISTICS: moist, well drained

LIGHT: full sun

WATER: keep evenly damp

SOIL TEMPERATURE: 70–78°F

MANAGEMENT

FERTILIZER NEEDS: light

RECOMMENDED SPACING: 10–12"

ADAPTATION TO GROWING IN CONTAINERS: yes, 4–8" pots

SPECIAL CULTURAL HINTS: sensitive to salts in early stages and if salt-injured will take longer to bloom (especially *S. farinacea*); avoid standing water

salvia

Plant characteristics

HEIGHT: 8–36"

SPREAD: 6–12"

GROWTH RATE: fast

GROWTH HABIT: erect, bushy, herbaceous

FLOWERS

SIZE: 1"

COLOR: *S. splendens*: red, lilac, salmon, burgundy;
S. farinacea: blue, purple, white

SHAPE: tubular

FRAGRANCE: none

TIME TO FLOWERING: 11–16 weeks, depending on variety

PESTS

COMMON DISEASES: *Botrytis*, damping-off of seedlings, powdery mildew, downy mildew

OTHER PESTS: aphids, slugs, spider mites, whiteflies

Harvesting considerations

WHAT IS HARVESTED: flowers

HARVESTING TECHNIQUES: cut

BEST TIME OF DAY TO HARVEST: early morning

BEST WAY TO TRANSPORT FROM PICKING AREA: plastic container

AVOID CONTACT WITH THESE PRODUCTS: smoke, car exhaust, ripening fruits, wilting flowers

The lei shown also contains cup-and-saucer plant, dusty miller, and asparagus fern.

Notes on lei making

BEST FOR WHICH TYPE OF LEI: neck, head, wrist, ankle, horse

VASE LIFE: 5 days

CLEANING OF PLANT MATERIALS: cut stem, remove all foliage; avoid wetting flower heads

STORING RAW LEI MATERIALS: refrigerate at 40°F for up to 7 days

PREPARING FOR USE IN LEI: clip off wrinkled, limp, or poor quality areas before adding to lei

STORING A COMPLETED LEI BEFORE WEARING: soak, drip dry, place in sealed plastic container, and refrigerate

PRESERVING A LEI FOR LONG-TERM STORAGE OR DISPLAY: some cultivars will preserve ('Empire Lilac')

References and further reading

Halpin, Anne Moyer. 1990. *Foolproof Planting.* New York: Roundtable Press, Inc.

Heitz, Halina. 1992. *Container Plants for Patios, Balconies, and Window Boxes.* Hauppauge, New York: Barron's Educational Series, Inc.

Hutson, J., and B. Ward. 1995. *Annual Gardening.* New York: Pantheon Books.

Nau, Jim.1998. "*Salvia.*" In: *The Ball Redbook.* 16th ed, p. 730–733. Batavia, Illinois: Ball Publishing.

Styer, R.C., and D.S. Koranski. 1997. *Plug and Transplant Production, A Grower's Guide.* Batavia, Illinois: Ball Publishing.

Introduced Annuals

strawflower

OTHER COMMON NAMES: everlasting, *pua-pepa*

SCIENTIFIC NAME:
Helichrysum bracteatum

FAMILY: Asteraceae (formerly Compositae), (aster family)

NATURAL SETTING/LOCATION: Australia

CURRENT STATUS IN THE WILD IN HAWAI'I: not found

CULTIVARS: 'Hot Bikini', 'Bright Bikini', 'Swiss Giant Mix'

Growing your own

PROPAGATION

FORM: seeds

PLANTING DEPTH: sow seeds 1/16" deep, barely covering with medium; light aids germination

GERMINATION TIME: 7–12 days

PREFERRED PRODUCTION CONDITIONS

GENERAL SOIL CHARACTERISTICS: well drained

LIGHT: full sun

WATER: moderate

SOIL TEMPERATURE: 70–75°F

MANAGEMENT

FERTILIZER NEEDS: light

RECOMMENDED SPACING: 10–12"

ADAPTATION TO GROWING IN CONTAINERS: yes, 4–6" pots

PRUNING: pinch shoots of young plant when 6" tall to induce branching

SPECIAL CULTURAL HINTS: flowers appear dry, even when picked fresh from the plant; avoid high light and temperature, which promote premature flowering; needs some support (especially tetraploid types)

strawflower

Plant characteristics

HEIGHT: 18–36"

SPREAD: 10–12"

GROWTH RATE: fast

GROWTH HABIT: upright, herbaceous

FLOWERS

SIZE: 1–3"

COLOR: white, yellow, orange, red, pink, purple

SHAPE: round

FRAGRANCE: none

TIME TO FLOWERING: 3–4 months

PESTS

COMMON DISEASES: aster yellows, root rot, *Verticillium* wilt

OTHER PESTS: aphids, leafhoppers

Harvesting considerations

WHAT IS HARVESTED: flowers, before fully open, when bracts are unfolding and centers are visible (if picked when open, petals turn backward as they dry, resulting in an unattractive blossom)

HARVESTING TECHNIQUES: cut

BEST TIME OF DAY TO HARVEST: early morning

BEST WAY TO TRANSPORT FROM PICKING AREA: plastic container

AVOID CONTACT WITH THESE PRODUCTS: smoke, car exhaust, ripening fruits, wilting flowers

The lei shown also contains ti.

Notes on lei making

BEST FOR WHICH TYPE OF LEI: neck, head, wrist, ankle, horse

VASE LIFE: 7–10 days for fresh flowers, 2 years for dry flowers

CLEANING OF PLANT MATERIALS: cut stem, remove old foilage; avoid wetting flower heads

STORING RAW LEI MATERIALS: refrigerate at 40°F for up to 10 days

PREPARING FOR USE IN LEI: clip off wrinkled, limp, or poor quality areas before adding to lei

STORING A COMPLETED LEI BEFORE WEARING: spray lightly and store in paper bag or box and refrigerate

PRESERVING A LEI FOR LONG-TERM STORAGE OR DISPLAY: air-dry; for an entire lei of strawflowers, first dry flowers in bunches by stripping leaves and hanging upside down in a warm, well ventilated area; for single flowers, leave ½–1" stem and stand them straight up in a shallow container

References and further reading

Ball, Vic. 1998. Strawflower. In: *The Ball Redbook*. 16th ed, p. 266–267. Batavia, Illinois: Ball Publishing.

Hessayon, D.G. 1995. *The Flower Expert*. London: Transworld Publishers.

Hutson, J., and B. Ward. 1995. *Annual Gardening*. New York: Pantheon Books.

Introduced Annuals

torenia

OTHER COMMON NAMES: *ōlaʻa* beauty, wishbone flower, bluewings

SCIENTIFIC NAME: *Torenia fournieri*

FAMILY: Scrophulariaceae (figwort family)

NATURAL SETTING/LOCATION: Southeast Asia

CURRENT STATUS IN THE WILD IN HAWAIʻI: not found

CULTIVARS: Clown series

Growing your own

PROPAGATION

FORM: seeds

PLANTING DEPTH: sow on surface of medium, do not cover; light aids germination

GERMINATION TIME: 7–15 days

PREFERRED PRODUCTION CONDITIONS

GENERAL SOIL CHARACTERISTICS: medium, well drained, compost-enriched

LIGHT: shade to partial shade

WATER: keep moist

SOIL TEMPERATURE: 75–80°F

MANAGEMENT

FERTILIZER NEEDS: light

RECOMMENDED SPACING: 10–12"

ADAPTATION TO GROWING IN CONTAINERS: yes, 4–6" pots

PRUNING: pinch shoots of young plants to encourage bushy form

SPECIAL CULTURAL HINTS: leggy plants indicate poor light; the plant likes moisture and should not be allowed to dry out

torenia

Plant characteristics

HEIGHT: 6–8"

SPREAD: 8"

GROWTH RATE: slow at first

GROWTH HABIT: erect, bushy, herbaceous

FLOWERS

SIZE: 1–1½"

COLOR: bright blue, burgundy, orchid, rose, violet

SHAPE: asymmetrical bell-shape

FRAGRANCE: none

TIME TO FLOWERING: 13–15 weeks

INDUCING AND MAINTAINING BLOOMING: remove dead and old flowers to promote development of new ones

PESTS

COMMON DISEASES: powdery mildew, Scrophulariaceae virus

OTHER PESTS: aphids, slugs, whiteflies

Harvesting considerations

WHAT IS HARVESTED: flowers

HARVESTING TECHNIQUES: cut

BEST TIME OF DAY TO HARVEST: early morning

BEST WAY TO TRANSPORT FROM PICKING AREA: plastic container

AVOID CONTACT WITH THESE PRODUCTS: smoke, car exhaust, ripening fruits, wilting flowers

The lei shown also contains baby's breath, asparagus fern, and shinobu.

Notes on lei making

BEST FOR WHICH TYPE OF LEI: neck

VASE LIFE: 2–4 days

CLEANING OF PLANT MATERIALS: spray with water

STORING RAW LEI MATERIALS: refrigerate at 40°F for up to 2 days

PREPARING FOR USE IN LEI: clip off wrinkled, limp, or poor quality areas before adding to lei

STORING A COMPLETED LEI BEFORE WEARING: mist and refrigerate in sealed plastic container

PRESERVING A LEI FOR LONG-TERM STORAGE OR DISPLAY: cannot be preserved

References and further reading

Ball, Vic. 1998. "*Torenia*." In: *The Ball Redbook*. 16th ed, p. 767–769. Batavia, Illinois: Ball Publishing.

Hutson, J., and B. Ward. 1995. *Annual Gardening*. New York: Pantheon Books.

Nau, Jim. 1993. *Ball Culture Guide: The Encyclopedia of Seed Germination*. 2nd ed. Batavia, Illinois: Ball Publishing.

Styer, R.C., and D.S. Koranski. 1997. *Plug and Transplant Production, A Grower's Guide*. Batavia, Illinois: Ball Publishing.

Introduced Annuals

zinnia

OTHER COMMON NAMES: *pua-pihi*, thumbelina

SCIENTIFIC NAME: *Zinnia elegans*, *Z. angustifolia*

FAMILY: Asteraceae (formerly Compositae), (aster family)

NATURAL SETTING/LOCATION: Southwest USA, Mexico, Central America

CURRENT STATUS IN THE WILD IN HAWAIʻI: not found

CULTIVARS: *Z. elegans*: 'Big Red', 'Candy Cane Mix', 'Persian Carpet Mix', 'State Fair Mix', Ruffles series; *Z. angustifolia*: 'Classic Golden Orange', 'Crystal White', Star series

Growing your own

PROPAGATION

FORM: seeds

PLANTING DEPTH: lightly cover with medium

GERMINATION TIME: 7–10 days

PREFERRED PRODUCTION CONDITIONS

GENERAL SOIL CHARACTERISTICS: well drained; tolerates dry conditions

LIGHT: full sun

WATER: keep evenly and slightly damp, never wet

SOIL TEMPERATURE: 68–70°F

MANAGEMENT

FERTILIZER NEEDS: light

RECOMMENDED SPACING: 9–12"

ADAPTATION TO GROWING IN CONTAINERS: yes, 4–6" pots

PRUNING: pinch the tops of young plants when they are 4–6" high to encourage branching

SPECIAL CULTURAL HINTS: best germination if cool and dry; days of 12 hours or less stimulate flowering; seeds may be sown directly to the field or final growing container

zinnia

Plant characteristics

HEIGHT: 24–36"

SPREAD: 5–6"

GROWTH RATE: fast

GROWTH HABIT: upright, herbaceous

FLOWERS

SIZE: 1–3"

COLOR: any color except blue

SHAPE: classified according to flower type (single, double, cactus, dahlia type)

FRAGRANCE: none

TIME TO FLOWERING: 12–13 weeks

INDUCING AND MAINTAINING BLOOMING: remove dead and old flowers to promote development of new ones

PESTS

COMMON DISEASES: *Alternaria* blight, powdery mildew, bacterial leaf-spot

OTHER PESTS: aphids, beetles, slugs, spider mites

Harvesting considerations

WHAT IS HARVESTED: fully open flowers

HARVESTING TECHNIQUES: cut

BEST TIME OF DAY TO HARVEST: early morning

BEST WAY TO TRANSPORT FROM PICKING AREA: plastic container

AVOID CONTACT WITH THESE PRODUCTS: smoke, car exhaust, ripening fruits, wilting flowers

The lei shown also contains *moa*, statice, bougainvillea, asparagus fern, and *'ōhi'a lehua*.

Notes on lei making

BEST FOR WHICH TYPE OF LEI: neck, head, wrist, ankle, horse

VASE LIFE: 6–10 days in deionized water (without salts)

CLEANING OF PLANT MATERIALS: cut stem, remove all foliage; avoid wetting flower heads

STORING RAW LEI MATERIALS: refrigerate at 40°F for up to 7 days

PREPARING FOR USE IN LEI: clip off wrinkled, limp, or poor quality areas before adding to lei

STORING A COMPLETED LEI BEFORE WEARING: spray lightly, store in plastic container, and refrigerate

PRESERVING A LEI FOR LONG-TERM STORAGE OR DISPLAY: air-dry

References and further reading

Ball, Vic. 1998. "*Zinnia.*" In: *The Ball Redbook.* 16th ed., p. 785–787. Batavia, Illinois: Ball Publishing.

Heitz, Halina. 1992. *Container Plants for Patios, Balconies, and Window Boxes.* Hauppauge, New York: Barron's Educational Series, Inc.

Sascalis, John N. 1993. *Cut Flowers, Prolonging Freshness.* Batavia, Illinois: Ball Publishing.

Introduced Annuals

Section 2

Those who make lei *can play a vital role in preserving both native plant communities and native Hawaiian culture.*

Growing Plants for *Lei* Helps to Preserve Hawai'i's Natural and Cultural Heritage

Puanani O. Anderson-Fung and Kepā Maly

For most people in Hawai'i today, making a *lei* and giving it to someone is a gesture of *aloha* (love and respect) that is a distinctive part of the islands' contemporary social culture. The Hawaiian *lei* (a garland, usually of plant leaves, flowers, or seeds) has come to be recognized around the world as an expression of greeting and farewell, honor, congratulations, and love. But few people are

aware that the *lei* and the plant materials it is made of have deeper meanings in Hawaiian culture—and this was especially so before the modern era. More than today's decorative social token, a *lei* and its making, giving, and wearing embody—in the Hawaiian cultural perspective—a profoundly felt personal and spiritual significance.

Nature provided the islands of Hawai'i with an extraordinarily rich assemblage of native organisms, and Hawai'i's native people formed a deeply spiritual relationship with these non-human inhabitants. This section explores that relationship and summarizes the changes that have occurred both to Hawai'i's natural areas and to the human culture as it relates to them, changes that now threaten the integrity of the native plant communities with which Hawaiian culture is so deeply interconnected.

Those who make *lei* can play a vital role in preserving both native plant communities and native Hawaiian culture. This can be done simply by growing the plants needed for *lei* rather than gathering the materials from natural areas. We hope the following section makes clear why this is such an important choice.

[The views expressed in this section are those of the authors named above and not necessarily those of the book's other authors and contributors, the College of Tropical Agriculture and Human Resources, the University of Hawai'i, or the agencies that funded production of this book. The orthography of the Hawaiian quotations and their translations is exactly as given in the original sources, except where noted otherwise. Many statements and concepts included here were drawn from the writings of other students of Hawaiian culture and ecology, but for ease of reading they have not been attributed with in-text citations; some of these works are listed in the *Selected Bibliography* at the end of this book. The scenic photos in this section are by Clyde T. Imada.]

Part 1
A historical perspective on *lei* and native plant communities

The tradition of *lei* making was brought to the Hawaiian Islands by the Polynesian ancestors of those who would become the native Hawaiian people. As their culture developed over the centuries, so did the artistry and cultural significance of their *lei*.

In old Hawai'i, *lei* could have important ceremonial functions, such as in religious offerings and for chiefly regalia, but *lei* were also enjoyed as personal adornment by Hawaiians of all levels of society. The *ali'i* (chiefs) and the *maka'ainana* (the common people who tended the land) all wore *lei*. Even the *akua* (gods, deities, spirits), it was believed, sometimes wore *lei* when they walked the land in human form. The following observation by the French botanist Gaudichaud, who visited the islands in 1819, paints a picture of Hawai'i as a place where the *lei* was an integral part of everyday life:

> "It is indeed rare to encounter one of the natives of this archipelago who does not have an ornamental plant on his head or neck or some other part of his body…[The] women … change [the plants they wear] according to the seasons, [and for them] all the fragrant plants, all flowers, and even the colored fruits, serve as attire, one after another. …The young girls of the people, those of the island of Hawai'i especially, seem to be fond of the [*kou, Cordia subcordata*], a tree very abundant in all the cultivated areas… The young girls of the mountains, who live near the forests, give their preference to the flowers of the [*Erythrina* (*wiliwili*) and a species of *Canavalia,* called '*awikiwiki*], the lively color of which makes magnificent garlands. Such natural attire is much more rich, much more striking, than all the dazzling creations of the elegant European ladies."

This account and others like it suggest that *lei* worn for personal adornment were fashioned from the favorite plant materials that were readily available and abundant in the *lei* maker's environment. Unfortunately, in the period after Gaudichaud wrote, native plant materials gradually became more difficult to acquire, as the native forests receded into the uplands and Hawaiians began moving to cities and towns near the shore. Still, *lei* giving remained popular with Hawai'i's residents, an increasing number of whom were from diverse cultural groups that had come from various parts of the world. Soon *lei* were considered a "must-have" for many occasions in the new, cosmopolitan society, including such events as high school and college graduations, proms, retirement parties, and legislative openings. But it was largely the introduced ornamental plants, such as plumeria, carnation, *pakalana*, and *pīkake* (jasmine), that met the increased demand for such ceremonial *lei* in Hawai'i's growing population.

This reliance on introduced plants for *lei* material began to change in the 1970s, when Hawai'i began to experience a resurgence of interest in "things Hawaiian." This long-overdue development is welcome, but one consequence has been that things made from native plants, including jewelry, furniture, and *lei,* have recently gained in popularity and acquired considerable prestige. To meet the demand for authentic Hawaiian products, many more people began to gather native materials from acces-

Loss of native vegetation due to human habitation of the Hawaiian Islands

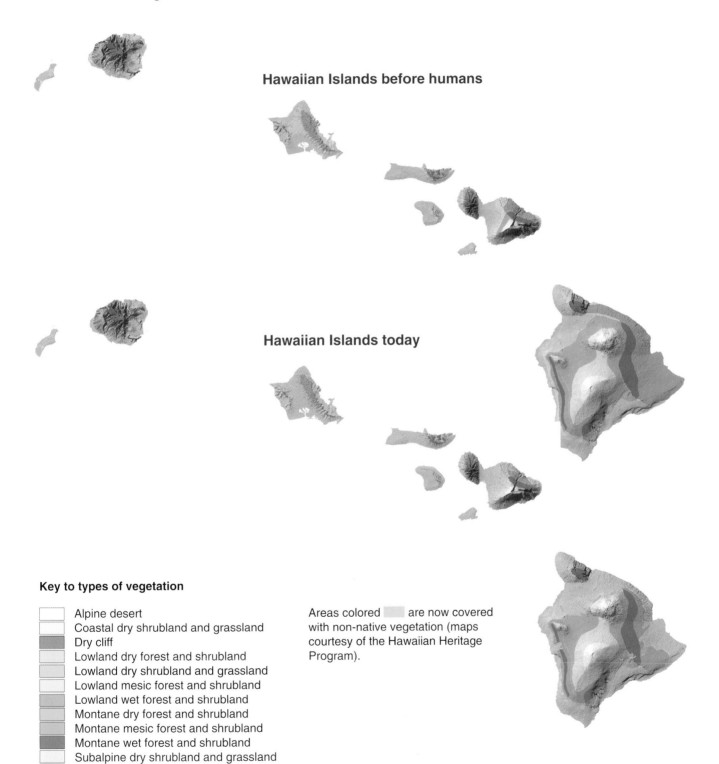

Hawaiian Islands before humans

Hawaiian Islands today

Key to types of vegetation

- Alpine desert
- Coastal dry shrubland and grassland
- Dry cliff
- Lowland dry forest and shrubland
- Lowland dry shrubland and grassland
- Lowland mesic forest and shrubland
- Lowland wet forest and shrubland
- Montane dry forest and shrubland
- Montane mesic forest and shrubland
- Montane wet forest and shrubland
- Subalpine dry shrubland and grassland
- Wet cliff
- Wetland
- Non-native vegetation

Areas colored ▆ are now covered with non-native vegetation (maps courtesy of the Hawaiian Heritage Program).

sible public lands. This brought much additional stress to native plant communities that were already greatly diminished and damaged by the activities of humans and the non-native plants and animals that have been brought to the islands.

Ironically, many of these gatherers were motivated by a well intentioned desire to do things in a "real Hawaiian way." They did not realize the potentially serious environmental damage they were causing, or that their collecting was threatening the future of the very native species they sought to bring to the attention of others. Thus what has been referred to as "the flowering of the 'Hawaiian Renaissance' in the 1970s" contributed to an unfortunate "de-flowering" of our native forests.

Lei making was a very real part of this problem, as native plant materials were needed in large quantities for *hula* competitions, *lei* making competitions, Hawaiian award ceremonies, and other events. Many of those who routinely worked or spent their recreational time in Hawaiʻi's natural plant environments began to notice that extensive damage was being done to certain native species used in *lei,* and this often occurred just before major *hula* competitions. Eventually, some people began to publicly express concern for the health of native plant communities.

Many native Hawaiians and conservationists are now working together to educate people about the serious, irreparable damage that is done to native Hawaiian ecosystems when we continue treating them as "inexhaustible free resources." Today's *lei* makers can become an important part of the solution to the problem of loss of native plant ecosystems by growing the plants they need rather than taking them from the wild. Like all those who reap benefits from nature in Hawaiʻi, *lei* makers owe it to themselves to learn more about Hawaiʻi's native plants and the effects of human actions on them. Through such learning, and guided by conscience, we each can choose to practice and promote only those actions that protect and preserve our natural heritage.

Part 2
Hawaiʻi's many native organisms and their relationship to human culture before 1778

The Hawaiian Islands have existed in the middle of the Pacific Ocean for millions of years, during which time nature has gradually covered them with a diverse assemblage of unique life forms. A group of human immigrants arrived in the islands from Polynesia hundreds of years ago, and eventually their descendents became intimately familiar with many of the species nature had provided the islands—especially the plants. Ultimately these people, who became known as the Hawaiian people, developed a deeply spiritual and loving relationship with Hawaiʻi's native plants and their habitats.

The emotional connection with nature felt by the Hawaiians was manifested in virtually every aspect of their lives. It was the guiding principle in their resource management ethics and practices, and it was always woven into their *moʻolelo* (stories), *ʻoli* (chants), *mele* (songs), and their *lei*. Before exploring this relationship more fully, however, it is important that we begin by gaining some insight into the rich legacy of native species and plant communities that are found in the Hawaiian Islands—for this was the environment in which native Hawaiian culture evolved.

Hawai'i's first natives

When Hawai'i's early human immigrants began to explore their new homeland, they discovered that it was already inhabited by millions of other natives—not human natives, but other life forms including animals, plants, fungi, and *limu,* a Hawaiian category of organisms that included seaweeds and freshwater algae, mosses, liverworts, lichens, and certain small, delicate ferns.

Scientists believe that the earliest ancestors of Hawai'i's native species were carried to the islands by birds, strong winds, or ocean currents.

The number and nature of native species in Hawai'i

When biologists talk about "non-human" natives, they refer to organisms that arrived in a place "naturally," that is, without any help (deliberate or accidental) from human beings. Scientists believe that the earliest ancestors of Hawai'i's native species were carried to the islands by birds, strong winds, or ocean currents. Those that survived the trip and also managed to become established, produce offspring, and increase in number are the ancestors of today's native Hawaiian species. These native organisms existed in Hawai'i for millions of years before the first humans arrived.

How many native species are there in Hawai'i? It has been estimated that there were approximately 8500 native species on land at the time the first humans arrived—and this includes only the mosses, ferns, flowering plants, mammals, birds, snails, insects, and spiders, not the fungi or the algae, for which reliable estimates of the number of native species are not yet available.

Remarkably, about 96 percent of these native species evolved in the islands and could be found nowhere else in the world! Biologists refer to native species that are found nowhere else as endemic species. The term *endemic* tells us the following things about a Hawaiian endemic species:

- Sometime in the ancient past, it arrived in these remote islands unaided by humans and became established.
- It managed to reproduce and spread.
- Over millions of years, some of its descendents underwent so many changes that they could be considered a new species distinct from the original, ancestral species.
- These new species cannot be found anywhere else in the world for two reasons—because they evolved in Hawai'i, and they have not naturally dispersed to other parts of the world.

A second type of native species is the indigenous species, those native to an area but also native elsewhere. The word *indigenous* (when applied to living things other than humans) tells us three things:

- The species is native—it got here naturally, without help from humans.
- Since the time that it first arrived, it has not changed enough to be considered a new, different species.
- The species is pretty much the same in Hawai'i as in other places where it is found (although slight differences may occur).

Even more remarkable is the fact that Hawai'i's 8150 endemic, land-dwelling species are thought to have evolved from only about 1000 original colonizing species. Thus about eight new species evolved from each one that successfully inhabited the islands. There is no other group of islands in the world where such a large number of new species evolved from such a small number of ancestral colonizing species.

A good example of the evolutionary principles just described is the group of plants named *naupaka* by the Hawaiians and internationally known as *Scaevola* (pronounced SKE-vole-uh) by botanists, who use a globally standardized system for naming plants. Each species in this group has flowers that look like "half-flowers," and each is thought to have evolved from one of three ancestral species, which we call "A," "B," and "C" in the table below.

Scaevola taccada

S. glabra

Ancestral species	Hawaiian name, [descriptive notes]	Meaning of Hawaiian name	Scientific name
A	*naupaka kahakai* [the white-flowered "beach *naupaka*" common throughout Hawai'i]	(*naupaka* of the seashore)	*Scaevola taccada*
B	*ohe naupaka* [yellow, tubular flowers; found in very wet forests on O'ahu and Kaua'i]	(*naupaka* with the tube-shaped flower)	*Scaevola glabra*
C	*naupaka* [a smaller, rarely encountered beach species with white flowers]	(no unique Hawaiian name is known)	*Scaevola coriacea*
C	*naupaka kuahiwi* [white flowers; occurs only on Kaua'i and O'ahu]	(*naupaka* of the mountains)	*Scaevola gaudichaudiana*
C	*naupaka kuahiwi* [white flowers; occurs on Moloka'i, Lana'i, Maui, and Hawai'i]	(*naupaka* of the mountains)	*Scaevola chamissoniana*
C	*naupaka kuahiwi* [purplish flowers; occurs on Kaua'i, O'ahu, and Moloka'i]	(*naupaka* of the mountains)	*Scaevola mollis*
C	*naupaka kuahiwi* [purplish flowers; occurs only on Hawai'i]	(*naupaka* of the mountains)	*Scaevola kilaueae*
C	*naupaka kuahiwi* [yellow flowers; occurs from Kaua'i to Hawai'i]	(*naupaka* of the mountains)	*Scaevola gaudichaudii*

S. coriacea

S. gaudichaudiana

S. chamissoniana

S. mollis

S. kilaueae

S. gaudichaudii

The most commonly encountered *naupaka* is the beach *naupaka* (*Scaevola taccada*), which is indigenous, meaning that it is considered to be the same as the *Scaevola taccada* found throughout tropical and subtropical Pacific and Indian Ocean coastal regions. It is thought to be the only species that resulted from the colonization of one of the ancestral species ("A" in the table), and thus we conclude that ancestor A was *Scaevola taccada*. A second ancestral *naupaka* (B) eventually gave rise to the endemic *'ohe naupaka* (*Scaevola glabra*), which has very distinctive, tubular, yellow half-flowers about an inch long. A third ancestor (C) is thought to have given rise to six endemic species—one coastal species, commonly known as the "dwarf *naupaka*" (currently listed as endangered) and five mountain species, all of which are commonly known as "mountain *naupaka*" or *naupaka kuahiwi*. Each Hawaiian island had, at most, three species of mountain *naupaka*, each with a different flower color—white, purple, or yellow. Thus the different species of mountain *naupaka* could be distinguished easily in the Hawaiian system of naming plants by also giving the flower color and the island on which it occurred.

So we see that both the Hawaiian plant experts of old and contemporary botanists used the same system—binomial nomenclature—for naming plants. One name (*naupaka* or *Scaevola*), indicates the group to which the species belongs. The second name (e.g., *kahakai* or *taccada*) indicates which particular *naupaka* is being referred to.

Effects of time, habitat diversity, and isolation on Hawai'i's native species

The type of evolution demonstrated by the *naupaka* also occurred in many other groups of plants, birds, land snails, insects, and spiders (to name only the most well known examples). This is why many people consider the Hawaiian Islands to be the best place in the world to see and study evolution! Three factors, discussed further below, help to explain how so many species were able to evolve in Hawai'i:

- There was lots of time for evolution to take place.
- There are many different types of habitats.
- The islands are isolated, and new species were rarely able to successfully colonize these islands.

Time
The native Hawaiian people developed a unique culture during the centuries that they lived in Hawai'i prior to 1778. How many centuries is uncertain; archaeologists do not agree when humans first arrived in Hawai'i. Some believe this occurred between 0 and 100 A.D., while others think it was later, between 600 and 700 A.D.

In contrast to the brief occupation by humans, Hawai'i's native plants and animals have inhabited these islands for *millions* of years. Scientists now believe that species could have been evolving in the archipelago for up to 70 million years—that's 700,000 centuries during which native species could have been evolving, as compared with only 11–17 centuries for the evolution of a unique human culture! Of course, not all the species arrived 70 million years ago; ancestral, colonizing species continued to arrive at different times throughout the entire period.

The native Hawaiian people developed a unique culture during the centuries that they lived in Hawai'i prior to 1778.

Habitat diversity

Most people who live outside of Hawai'i probably think of these islands as having a very mild climate that varies little throughout the year. However, closer inspection reveals that each of our "high islands" (from Kaua'i to Hawai'i) contains many different types of habitats, and these habitats often have very different climates. The naturalist Sherwin Carlquist described this well:

> Despite their small total area, the Islands have places which are desert dry and others which may be the wettest places on earth. Temperatures can go below freezing on high mountains, or can be above 90°F at sea level. Humidity can stand at virtually zero in alpine areas, yet be 100% nearly all of the time in wet mountain areas. In short, the Hawaiian Islands are a climatic showcase in which equable conditions co-exist with some of the most severe extremes in the world.

Habitats with very different climates can exist quite near one another, as do the Ka'ū Desert and the lush tree-fern forests of Kīlauea on Hawai'i.

Even a relative newcomer to the islands will notice the change in climate that occurs as they move from the wet windward coast of one of the islands, up into the cool mountains, and then back down toward the sea on the drier leeward side. An observant traveler will also notice a number of different habitats along the way, each of which is occupied by different types of plants and animals.

Isolation

The Hawaiian Islands are the most isolated major group of islands in the world. They lie more than 2000 miles from the nearest continent (North America) and about 1000 miles from the closest Pacific atolls (to the south). This means that successful colonization by any immigrant species was probably a very rare event! As a result, Hawai'i's diverse habitats were colonized mostly by the offspring of the few species that had become established in the islands, and rarely by new species from elsewhere. Some of these populations were, just by chance, isolated from others (by such barriers as expanses of ocean or mountain ridges). Over time, these isolated populations of a certain species changed in different ways—generally in ways that made them better suited to the different habitats in which they had become established. Given enough time, some of these populations became so different from their ancestral species that they became distinct species.

An excellent example of the effects of time, habitat diversity, and isolation is provided by the group of birds known as the Hawaiian honey creepers. Scientists now believe that a single ancestral species arrived in the islands about 20 million years ago, and its descendents evolved into 47 new endemic species. These birds vary remarkably in the colors of their plumage and the shapes of their bills, which scientists theorize to be the result of different environments and food sources.

Most people who live outside of Hawai'i probably think of these islands as having a very mild climate that varies little throughout the year.

Despite the small extent of land area in Hawai'i, nearly all of the world's major plant formation types can be found in the islands.

Evolution's legacy: unique plant communities rich with native species

Evolution, combined with the physical characteristics of the Hawaiian Islands, eventually led to the formation of many unique native plant communities, each with its own characteristic sets of plants, birds, snails, insects, spiders, and other creatures. Biologists have named 106 unique plant communities still found in Hawai'i. The following examples help to demonstrate how very different these special places are. Hawai'i has:

- Dry, coastal herb-lands, with extremely hot, dry conditions, and plants like *nama* (*Nama sandwicensis*) in sandy areas and '*ākulikuli* (*Sesuvium portulacastrum*) on mud.
- Montane wet forests, on the windward sides of some mountains, between 4000 and 7200 ft elevation, with a warm, wet climate, frequent afternoon fogs, and lots of *lehua* (*Metrosideros*) and *koa* (*Acacia koa*) trees and *hāpu'u* (*Cibotium*) tree ferns.
- Alpine dry shrublands on Maui and Hawai'i, above 9850 ft elevation, with extremely dry, cold conditions and frequent frosts, and silversword ('*āhinahina*, *Argyroxiphium sandwicense*) and na'ena'e (*Dubautia*), which grow on gravel and cinders.

Despite the small extent of land area in Hawai'i, nearly all of the world's major plant formation types can be found in the islands. This is particularly impressive considering that only about 20 percent of the land is still covered with "natural" plant communities (those that are not being actively managed by humans). The early Hawaiians were very much aware of the rich legacy of natural communities that surrounded them. They identified the various vegetation zones using some of the same criteria as today's scientists: the elevation, moisture received, and types of plants most commonly found. David Malo demonstrated this in discussing the Hawaiian concept of *wao*, the inland (mountain) regions that were generally forested and usually uninhabited:

> The belt below the *kuāmauna*, in which small trees grow, is called *kuāhea*, and the belt below the *kuāhea*, where the larger sized forest trees grow, is called *wao*, or *wao-nahele*, or *wao-eiwa*. The belt below the *wao-eiwa* was the one in which the monarchs of the forests grew, and was called *wao-maukele*, and the belt below that, in which again trees of smaller size grew was called *wao-akua*, and below the *wao-akua* comes the belt called *wao-kanaka* or *mau*. Here grows the *amau* fern and here men cultivate the land.

The "natural" universe of the early Hawaiian people

These natural communities were more than just vegetation zones to the early Hawaiians. They were also the homes of their gods, and places where they could *feel* the vitality—*ke ola* (the life)—that flowed through the Hawaiian universe.

This universe of the early Hawaiians was made up of the *honua* (earth), the *lani* (sky), and all things upon, within, and between these places. To the Hawaiian mind, all of nature's embodiments—including rocks, trees, and bodies of water—were thought to possess *ola* (life). As a result, they were thought to be aware of—and able to interact with—one another. The *lani* fertilized the *honua* with its rains and mists, and as a result, life sprang forth from the earth. Similarly, Hawaiians believed that all life (*ke ola*) was perpetuated through the sexual interactions of its members.

The Hawaiian people considered themselves a part of this universe—not apart from it. Modern English dictionaries define nature as "the external world in its entirety." Hawaiians had no equivalent word, despite the fact that they organized their universe into "paired opposites," such as *lani* and *honua* (sky and earth) or *uka* and *kai* (mountain and sea).

In the traditional Hawaiian society, people were bound affectionately to the land that nurtured their families and, in most cases, had been their homeland for many generations. As they worked on, learned of, and loved their homelands, Hawaiians understood that the land was simultaneously transforming them, for each place was thought to develop a population with a distinctive general character and cultural style.

And, as Hawaiians responded to the universe around them, nature responded to humans. The Hawaiians believed that nature's many forms could be called upon for inspiration, guidance, assistance, reassurance, or for their life-giving powers. The *'oli* at right, recorded in one of the Hawaiian language newspapers of the 19th century, illustrates this principle. It describes the upland forest and evokes (calls upon to appear) a goddess of that forest and the materials that are to be made into a *lei*.

To the Hawaiian mind, humans were the *malihini* (newcomers) in this universe, which was the place where they would be born, live, die, and where their spirits would remain after death. As such, their universe had to be nurtured carefully and was never considered expendable. The Hawaiians further believed that everything in their universe was related and that they were the youngest members of this extended family. As a result, they treated the rest of nature with love and the kind of respect that should be afforded an elder family member.

Hawaiians also believed that people should learn as much as possible about the things that they loved. This attitude is at the heart of an *'ōlelo no'eau* (wise saying), telling us that we should seek a deep knowledge of the things we love:

Hana no'eau ke aloha.

Love is wise work.

(from John Charlot)

Thus it is not surprising that the Hawaiians developed so much scientific knowledge about the natural world around them. Simply stated, science happens whenever we explore nature for the purpose of understanding it better. We have described how early Hawaiians were keen observers of nature and were often just as accurate as modern scientists when it came to identifying, classifying, and naming the plants, animals, and vegetation zones around them. Moreover, they also employed what we now know as "the scientific method" to learn more about the things in their environment. This method involves three basic steps: careful observations are made; a simple, reasonable explanation for these observations is proposed (a hypothesis); and experi-

E o ka wahine i loko o ka ohu...

I ae ka wahine nona ka lei

I uo ia e Hinaulu ohia

O ka hala me ka lehua i ka nahele...

Respond, O woman who is there in the mists...

The woman for whom the *lei* was made speaks

Her *lei* was made by Hina of the *'ōhi'a* grove

[It is made] of the *hala* and *lehua* of the forest...

(translated by Mary Kawena Puku'i; chant in the collection of K. Maly)

ments are designed to test the explanation. The results of the experiments indicate whether the investigator is on the right track.

Using this approach, Hawaiians developed a vast body of knowledge about the other species living in their environment. This included how different plant species and varieties were related to one another, where and how they were best grown, when they should be harvested, how they could be used, and how best to ensure an ample supply for current and future needs. Hawaiian natural medicinal therapy has been described as "very systematic" and "more scientific in many ways, at the time of discovery, than that of their European 'discoverers'." Hawaiians have also been called "true experimental horticulturalists" who developed hundreds of varieties of *kalo* (taro, *Colocasia esculenta*) and *'uala* (sweetpotato, *Ipomoea batatas*).

The intimacy of the relationship between the Hawaiians and their natural world went far beyond mere knowledge of the things around them: there was also a spiritual connection. The basis of this spiritual connection is beautifully and effectively communicated by one of the Hawaiian creation stories about the origin of the Hawaiian islands and its people. The story begins with a group of god-beings, or "creative forces of nature," two of whom were Wākea (the expanse of the sky) and Papa, also known as Papa *hānau moku* (Papa the Earth Mother who gave birth to the islands) and Haumea *nui hānau wāwā* (Great Haumea, Woman Earth, born time and time again). The sexual unions of Wākea and Papa—with each other and with various other closely-related creative forces of nature—resulted in the birth of each of the Hawaiian islands. Hawai'i, the largest of the islands, was the firstborn of these island children.

As the Hawaiian genealogical account continues, we find that these same god-beings came together again to populate the islands with people. The next-born child, however, did not survive and was buried. From the child's body grew the first *kalo* plant, which was named Hāloa, the ancestor of all of Hawai'i's *kalo* plants. Their next child, whom they also named Hāloa, was the first human being to live on the islands, and from him all of the native Hawaiian people are descended.

Two aspects of the story are important to our discussion. First, the Hawaiians believed that all of nature (including humankind) is descended from a small group of closely related deities; Hawai'i's human and non-human natives were members of one extended family. Second, the Hawaiian people considered themselves genealogically subordinate to the land and the *kalo*, since humans were descendents of the child born *after* the islands and the first taro plant were born. Handy and Puku'i explained this attitude, stating that "precedence or status was determined by genealogical seniority, not by generation or age, or by sex. Persons stemming from a genealogically elder branch outrank older generations of junior branches." Thus to the Hawaiian the natural world was genealogically precedent, and the appropriate attitude toward it was one of love and respect.

An extension of the various Hawaiian beliefs about creation is the concept of *kinolau* (body forms of the gods). Nature's many forms, from the skies and mountain peaks, to the watered valleys and plains, to the shore line and ocean depths, were considered to be embodiments of Hawaiian gods and deities. Puku'i and Elbert described *kinolau* as "the many forms [that might be] taken by a supernatural body." It is derived from the words *kino*, meaning "form or embodiment," and *lau*, meaning "many." Some believe that virtually every plant species known to the Hawaiians was considered *kinolau* of some spirit or deity. This concept helped to link the Hawaiian people to their gods.

Nature's many forms, from the skies and mountain peaks, to the watered valleys and plains, to the shore line and ocean depths, were considered to be embodiments of Hawaiian gods and deities.

Thus Hawaiians might call upon the *kinolau* of their deities as demonstrated in the closing of the *'oli* at right, below. The chanter speaks of the beauty of a waterfall and calls upon various nature forms for inspiration. Lau-ka-'ie'ie has been described as a "beautiful demigoddess who was transformed into an *'ie'ie* vine." The *palai* fern was a *kinolau* of Hi'iakia, a sister of Pele. The *kī*, or ti plant, was "not regarded as the *kinolau* of any forest god," and yet its leaves were considered essential for decorating the altar of Laka in the *hālau hula* (dancers' house).

Kinolau could also be worn. Wearing a *lei* made of materials from a *kinolau* would allow Hawaiians to touch their gods in a literal sense, and be touched by them, since the plants were bodily forms of the *akua*. Sometimes, Hawaiians wore *lei* to show the *akua* their appreciation for the beauty of the plants that were their *kinolau*. Other times, these lei were worn in hopes of being enlightened or inspired by the deity.

Kinolau were also placed on the altar (*kuahu*) of a *hālau hula*. Their presence on the *kuahu* was meant to honor the gods and goddesses of the hula and to inspire the *haumāna* (students) as they learned their art. *Kūpuna* (elder Hawaiians) born in the period between approximately 1885 and 1915 told us that the chants used in obtaining these offerings were so strong that the plants never wilted on the *kuahu* but remained green and fragrant. If any of the students broke one of the many strict rules of the *hālau* while in training, the plants would wilt, to show their disapproval. This example demonstrates that these *kinolau* (body form) offerings were not just decorative symbols but were powerful entities that were not to be taken lightly or treated with disrespect.

Six plants commonly placed on the altar of the *hālau hula*

Hawaiian name	Scientific name	Diety of which the plant was *kinolau*
lama wood	*Diospyros* species	Laka (a female deity)
lehua	*Metrosideros* species	Kūka'ōhi'alaka (a male Laka deity)
halapēpē	*Pleomele* species	Kapo and Laka
palai (*palapalai*) fern	*Sphenomeris chinensis*	Hi'iaka
'ie'ie	*Freycinetia arborea*	Lau-ka-'ie'ie
maile	*Alyxia oliviformis*	the four Maile sisters

While our generations are far removed from the time of the *kapu* and *kānāwai* (restrictions and laws) of the *akua*, restrictions which were released, or "put to sleep," by the *po'e kahiko* (ancient people), it is important to remember the severity of these rules in old Hawai'i and the strictness with which the were practiced. The repercussions of breaking the rules of the gods, whether in the forests or in other areas of Hawaiian life, were extremely serious and potentially lethal. Here is an example, provided by Mary Kawena Puku'i:

> Kapo established a school for the *hula*, ritual dance-drama. Her nature was dual...This Kapo was a goddess whose temper was violent and vengeful. But when worshipped by dancers and chanters, this same person was the gentle Laka, the spirit of the wild wood. Yet when the *kapu* of seclusion was disregarded by a student or teacher during the period of devotion to *hula* training in the *halau,* the loving Laka quickly

...Ke lele la ka wai o Kawaikapu

E iho mai i na pali

E iho mai e Lau-ka-'ie'ie

Lau-ka-palai, pili me Lau-i-o-uka e

E iho mai

E hooulu ia!

...The water leaps from Kāwaikapu

It descends from the cliffs

Descend O Leaf-of-the-*'ie'ie*

Leaf-of-the-*palai*, who are related to the

Leaf-of-the-upland-ti-plants

Descend!

Inspire!

(translated by Mary Kawena Puku'i; chant in the collection of K. Maly)

Noho ana ke akua i ka nahelehele.

I alai ia e ke kiohuohu, e ka ua koko,

O na kino malu i ka lani,

Malu e hoe.

E hooulu aku ana ia ulu kupu,

Ia ulu noho, ia ulu kini o e akua,

Ulu i ke kapa kanaka.

Kahea ke akua kiai pali,

E wikiwiki, e holoholo, e na kaa loa,

Maile, ki ke 'kua ke ano mai.

E ulu, e ulu, i ko kahu

Ia ka hookapuhi noa.

The gods dwell in the woodlands,

Hidden away in the mist, in the low-hanging rainbow,

O beings sheltered by the heavens,

Clear our path of all hindrance.

We call to [the gods of] growth to inspire us,

To the [woodland] dwellers for inspiration, to the hosts of gods for inspiration,

To be given to the dwelling place of [us] human beings.

The guardian god of the hills calls

To hasten to hurry, to speed along the way,

The *maile* and *ki* thickets are the dwelling places of these revered ones.

Inspire us, inspire and dwell on your altar,

Give us the lithe freedom of an eel.

(Puku'i 1936 in Barrere et al. 1980)

changed into vengeful Kapo and smote the culprit. So was the *hula* respected in the olden times; it was beneficent when rules were kept, yet deadly when they were not.

The forests, as the home of the *akua*, were seen as awesome and profoundly spiritual places. One did not enter them, or take from them, without first asking permission, and respectful behavior was always shown to all of the beings that lived there. The prayer (*pule*) at left is an excellent example of the awe and reverence felt by the Hawaiians for their forests. It is called a *pule pale* (protection prayer), for protecting the way to the forest from evil of every kind.

What offering can one leave in such revered places? To the Hawaiian mind, the greatest offering one could make was that of voice. This is because the spoken word was "considered to be the highest form of cultural expression in old Hawai'i." But *'oli* were more than something that one "gave." They were a link—a spiritual connection—to the place and the dieties that lived there. In the words of the renowned *kumu hula* Winona Beamer, "The chants were so haunting, they seemed to flow like clear streams of consciousness from the deep green heart of the forest primeval."

Because of our emphasis here on plants for making *lei*, our examples of how the Hawaiians accorded love and respect to natural places are centered on Hawai'i's forests. Of course, other natural places were also accorded the same love and respect as that seen in the *'oli* on the next page. And, in any of these special places, a *lei* might be fashioned to allow the wearer to carry a bit of that beloved place with them for a while. This is demonstrated in the *'oli* describing the wind-blown lowlands of Ka'ū and speaking of a woman who gathers flowers to make into a *lei* (p. 190, right column).

Ke aloha 'āina, the love of the land, that is so apparent in these *'oli*, permeated Hawaiian experience, and this love compelled the Hawaiians to continually deepen their knowledge of the land and its many non-human inhabitants. Hawaiians called themselves *kama'āina*, literally "children of the land," a word that not only means "native born" but is also used to describe one that is intimately familiar with something or someone.

This Hawaiian knowledge of their homeland, this intimate familiarity, was also deeply emotional. Just as we become aware of and responsive to the emotions of our closest loved ones, so Hawaiians felt for their loved ones. The difference is that Hawaiians extended this love to many of the non-human inhabitants of their universe, for the Hawaiians and their emotions were one with the world around them.

The following *'oli* offers us a glimpse into the way the old Hawaiians felt for their environment. It is said to have been composed at the time that *hula* originated on the island of Moloka'i. It was offered before the chanter took a small piece of the *lehua* tree (*Metrosideros* species) to place upon the *hula* altar. In it, the chanter likens her love for the *lehua* tree to the type of affectionate love a woman might feel for her husband.

> *Ku'u ipo mau no me he kane la,*
> *He ipo na'u ka lehua iluna, lehua ilalo,*
> *Pupu weuweu e Laka e.*

> My loved one, dear as a husband,
> A sweetheart to me are the lehuas above and below,
> In the leafy bower of Laka.

> (Manu 1899, in Barrere et al. 1980, translated by Mary Kawena Puku'i)

With this insight, we can better appreciate the deep affection that is expressed in the following song written by Princess Likelike. Here the composer shares her family's affection for their estate at 'Āinahau, in Waikīkī, O'ahu.

> *Nā ka makani aheahe i pā mai makai*
> *I lawe mai i ke onaona līpoa*
> *E ho'oipo ho'onipo me ke 'ala ku'u home,*
> *Ku'u home, ku'u home i ka 'iu'iu.*

> Wind blowing gently from the sea
> Brings the fragrance of *līpoa* seaweed,
> Love and delight and perfume for my home,
> My home, my home in paradise.

> (from Elbert and Mahoe 1970: 30)

As we try to comprehend the many dimensions of the Hawaiian relationship to nature and the way they were simultaneously integrated into every aspect of Hawaiian life, we can find reassurance in the following words from Mary Kawena Puku'i, for they acknowledge that it is indeed a very difficult task. Still, we believe it is worth the effort, as the insights gained by exploring the Hawaiian relationship with nature can guide us to attitudes and practices that are much healthier for humans and the environment in Hawai'i today.

> It is hard for the modern intellectually [rigid] and extroverted mind to sense the subjective relationship of genuine Hawaiians to Nature, visible and invisible. But...without some comprehension of this quality of spontaneous being-one-with-natural-phenomena which are persons, not things, it is impossible for an alien (be he foreigner or city-hardened native) to understand a true country-Hawaiian's sense of dependence and obligation, his "values," his discrimination of the real, the good, the beautiful and the true, his feeling of organic and spiritual identification with the 'aina (home-land) and 'ohana (kin). (Handy and Puku'i 1972)

Kiekie Kau hanohano i ka makani

He ipu kai Pohina na ka Aeloa

He umauma i pa ia e ka Maaa

Ea ka Unulau o Maaounulau

Inu aku no i Nunuweuweu

Ka wahine kaili pua o Paiahaa

Alualu pua hala kai o

Kamilopaekanaka . . .

Majestic Ka'ū, glorious in the winds

Pōhina is like a dish that catches the A'eloa breeze

Its chest is struck by the Ma'a'a Wind

The Unulau wind rises up, it is the Ma'aounulau

Drinking at Nunuweuweu

The woman who gathers the flowers at Paiaha'a

Has gone to gather the *hala* clusters at Kamilopaekanaka . . .

(Taken from *Ka Hoku o Hawai'i*, December 17, 1911; translated by K. Maly)

Hawaiian practices and ethics that affected natural resources

The deep emotional ties between Hawaiians and the natural world did not prevent them from altering their environment, for the Hawaiian relationship to nature was based as much upon practicality as it was on intellectual and spiritual insight.

Hawaiians' alterations of native plant communities

Virtually anything in the Hawaiian environment could be taken or moved, if the cause was *pono* (right, appropriate) and the right prayers and offerings were made. For example, as we have already seen, the taro plant was believed to be genealogically superior to its human "cousins." It was also a *kinolau* of the Kāne, a deity that has been described as "the leading god among the great gods." Even so, taro was pulled up, cooked, and mashed almost every day in old Hawai'i.

What distinguishes the ancient Hawaiians from the people who live in Hawai'i today is not that they did not alter native ecosystems or remove native species, it is the *manner* in which they did these things. In Hawaiian society prior to 1778, large-scale environmental disturbance was generally limited to that needed for survival. Gathering and other smaller-scale removals of native plants and animals was strictly controlled.

The Hawaiian people removed large areas of lowland native vegetation to build the structures and cultivate the plants they needed for survival. Had they not done so, they would almost certainly have perished or been restricted to small populations. Among the thousands of plant and animals species native to Hawai'i, there are few that could support a human population for very long.

The Hawaiians also cleared some lowland areas with fire to encourage the growth of certain useful plant species such as *pili* grass (*Heteropogon contortus*), which was favored in many areas for thatching houses. The lower reaches of the inland forests (*wao*) were modified both by harvesting and by planting. Native plants and animals were removed when Hawaiians gathered and harvested in order to make such things as *lei*, medicine, and canoes. Native plants were displaced when Hawaiians planted species important to their way of life—introduced species like *kukui*, *'awa*, and wild yams were commonly planted in suitable areas, as was the native *'olonā* (*Touchardia latifolia*), an endemic plant used to make cordage. It has been estimated that only areas above about 2500 ft elevation were left relatively undisturbed by the early Hawaiians.

Limitations on gathering in ancient Hawai'i

Gathering was not always the "free-for-all" that many people today seem to believe it is or should be. In old Hawai'i, gathering was strictly controlled by three main factors: the values and beliefs of the Hawaiian people; their strict, often specialized, gathering protocols; and their system of land use, which limited the area from which people could collect.

Gathering ethics and beliefs

The Hawaiian people followed protocols when they gathered and harvested from native ecosystems. These required that the gatherers prepare themselves spiritually before setting out and that they maintain an appropriate mental attitude before,

What distinguishes the ancient Hawaiians from the people who live in Hawai'i today is not that they did not alter native ecosystems or remove native species, it is manner *in which they did these things.*

during, and after collecting the desired materials. The physical process of gathering always involved going about one's business quietly, asking permission, giving thanks, and treating the plants or animals to be collected—and everything else in their environment—with respect.

Every aspect of the gathering process, whether mental or physical, spiritual or practical, was reflected in a single guiding principle: "treat all of nature's embodiments with respect." The overall effect of this attitude was to minimize the impact of gathering on native ecosystems.

"Entry chants" were offered to ask permission of the forest or other plant community for entry and to protect the collector from misfortune. The chants were an expression of the gatherer's respect for and good intentions toward all of the beings that lived there, including the *akua*, plants, animals, rocks, streams, etc. Similarly, chants were offered before any plant was collected, out of respect for the plants themselves and for the *akua* to whom those plants were dedicated.

A quiet demeanor not only displayed the appropriate attitude of respect, but it allowed the collector to be alert to signs that were "bad omens." For example, some signs might indicate that a particular plant should not be picked for medicinal purposes, as it might make the medicine bad. Other signs might indicate that this was not the right time for collecting anything at all, and that the collector should turn around and go home.

Plants and plant parts were removed carefully, and one never took more than was needed. Ferns were broken carefully at the base of the frond, taking care not to uproot the plant. Besides showing appropriate respect for the plant, this conservation ensured that the plant would survive and remain healthy, so that it could produce more fronds later. Similarly, other plant parts were removed in ways that minimized the impact to the plant.

According to a *kupuna* (Hawaiian elder) we interviewed, these kinds of respectful procedures were still taught by the "oldsters" of her homeland when she was young. Raised in a Hawaiian-speaking family on Hawai'i in the 1920s and '30s, she was told frequently that "when you go into the mountains to pick the *liko* of the *lehua* tree…remember, the tree has feelings, too." She was told to pick "gently," and to remove only a few *liko* (young leaves) from each tree, so that the tree was left "looking beautiful and healthy." She added that "you would never denude or harm the tree, as you see people doing today!"

Gathering typically was spaced out in some way, taking a little here and a little there, as expressed just above. According to several other *kupuna*, the reasoning behind this practice was that it prevented the other plants of the type being collected from becoming *lili* (jealous) and squabbling among themselves. Ecologically, of course, this practice helped to ensure that no area was completely stripped of a certain plant species and that harvesting could be sustained.

Most people would agree that these gathering principles embody appropriate treatment of those we love and respect. For example, when we enter the home of a friend today, we usually ask permission; we try not to impose on their hospitality or damage their home. So it was that Hawaiians approached gathering from native ecosystems—good manners and plain common sense guided their behavior.

The physical process of gathering always involved going about one's business quietly, asking permission, giving thanks, and treating the plants or animals to be collected—and everything else in their environment— with respect.

Gathering protocols and specialization

Every member of Hawaiian society was trained to gather correctly, according to well established protocols. Compliance was not optional—it was mandatory! Wanton disregard for the established procedures, or mistakes made while carrying them out, could bring misfortune to the collector as well as to the person who received the product made from the gathered materials. An improper (negative or unclean) mental attitude could also have bad consequences. With certain protocols, even death could result if they were not followed correctly. Thus great care was always taken to strictly follow the protocols one had been taught.

Certain important activities required special knowledge and were carried out only by specialists. The most highly trained of these were the *kahuna* (experts), who served in roughly the same capacity as the professional specialists of contemporary society, such as medical doctors and certified arborists, for example. The *kahuna* received extensive training and learned to master very elaborate technical and religious protocols.

When gathering materials for such important purposes as carving a new canoe or making powerful medicine, choosing the right plant was vitally important. Not only did it need to have the right physical characteristics, but its spiritual characteristics were important as well, and the gatherer had to be specially trained or gifted to perceive these qualities in the plant. Thus specialists had to collect the plant materials needed for important purposes, because complex, specialized protocols had to be carried out correctly, and special sensitivity was required to select plants with the right qualities.

For example, only the *kahuna kalai wa'a* (canoe carving expert) could select and harvest the tree needed for a new canoe, only the *kahuna lā'au lapa'au* (literally "curing-plant expert") had the expertise to gather plants to prepare certain medicines, and only a *kahuna* expert in religion could gather the plants required for certain very important religious offerings.

Many other activities were considered important enough to warrant "specialized collectors," but they did not require a *kahuna*. For example, when religious offerings were needed for the altar of the *hālau hula*, one or a few well trained individuals were sent to the uplands to collect the appropriate plant materials.

The practice of having specialists collect materials for certain uses continued into the first half of the 20th century. One *kumu hula* (*hula* teacher) told us that when she was being trained as a dancer in the 1930s, her *hālau* had one person whose job it was to make *lei* for the entire group: "It was the *lei* maker's job to go to the forest and collect materials for *lei*. Our job was to learn the dances and the chants—nothing more. We weren't expected to do everything, like some of these young people are today."

Gathering boundaries

Hawaiians of old could not gather wherever they pleased. Their system of land management required that they gather only within the boundaries of their own *ahupua'a*—the land division in which they resided.

When their boundaries are drawn on a map, *ahupua'a* are usually somewhat wedge-shaped, because the boundaries extend from the uplands to the sea, "thus including fishing rights, cultivable lands, upland timber and planting zones, and areas of valuable bird-catching privileges in the higher mountains." Each *ahupua'a* had a specific name and fixed boundaries. Those who lived in it were generally allowed access to all of its various natural resources, and gathering outside the boundaries of one's *ahupua'a* was, with certain exceptions, not permitted. According to the testimonies of Hawaiians who lived under the *ahupua'a* system during the reign of King Kamehameha the Great (who died in 1819), *ahupua'a* boundaries were taken very seriously. Outsiders found gathering beyond the boundaries of their own *ahupua'a* without permission might be chased, punished, perhaps even killed by the rightful residents.

Hawaiians carefully monitored the quantity and condition of the natural resources in their *ahupua'a*. Where resources were plentiful, they were judiciously harvested. Where plants were not sufficiently abundant, harvesting might be restricted and the plants left to increase on their own, or additional plants might be cultivated. Important species, such as *kalo* (taro) and *'olonā* (used for cordage), were carefully tended.

Political structures also served to protect *ahupua'a* resources. Each *ahupua'a* was placed under the control of a *konohiki* (headman), who was in charge of the land and fishing rights and was responsible for maintaining the resources of the *ahupua'a*. The *konohiki* answered to an *ali'i 'ai ahupua'a* (chief who controlled the *ahupua'a* resources), who answered, in turn, to an *ali'i 'ai moku* (chief who claimed the abundance of the entire district).

However, Hawaiian *mo'olelo* (stories) tell us that not all *ali'i* were ethical or competent when it came to taking care of the people and resources in their *ahupua'a*. Some *ali'i* did not remain in position for very long, as political control often changed. And, some areas were less strictly controlled than others. Thus the ultimate responsibility for taking care of the natural resources of an *ahupua'a* rested with the families that lived there, generation after generation.

Part 3
Introduced organisms and cultural change since 1778

Soon after Captain James Cook arrived in the Hawaiian Islands in 1778, Hawai'i became known throughout the world. It was not long before people from many distant lands arrived and settled in the islands. Each cultural group brought with them new species of organisms and different ideas about how to treat the land and its resources. All of these "new additions" profoundly affected both nature and culture in the islands.

Changes in nature: introduced species

Since 1778, newcomers have brought thousands of plant and animal species to Hawai'i. We use the term "introduced" to refer to these species, whether they were brought deliberately or accidentally. These species are also referred to elsewhere as "alien," "exotic," "adventive," or "non-native." The first introduced plant species to reach Hawai'i were brought by the Polynesian ancestors of the native Hawaiian people. We call these "Polynesian introductions"; they are sometimes also called "canoe plants." We call the species introduced after 1778 "post-Cook introductions."

Ultimate responsibility for taking care of the natural resources of an ahupua'a rested with the families that lived there, generation after generation.

Many of the plant species introduced during the post-Cook period were immediately adopted into the *lei*-making culture, which welcomed the new fragrances, colors, shapes, and textures that the new plants brought to their craft. However, other introduced plants (and animals too) are now a threat to the existence of the native plants traditionally used in the Hawaiian arts of *hula* and *lei* making. We can help save these plants and the ecosystems where they grow if we understand why and how they are being threatened.

Polynesian introductions

About 33 species of plants were brought to Hawai'i by the ancient Polynesian people. These plants coexisted with the Hawaiian people throughout their history in the islands and were an integral part of their culture and everyday life. The most well known of these species are listed here. Plants used primarily for food and medicine are listed in the left column. The common Hawaiian name is given first, followed by the common English name and, in parentheses, the scientific name.

Some well known Polynesian introductions

'ape	elephant's-ear plant (*Alocasia macrorrhiza*)	*'auhuhu*	no English name (*Tephrosia purpurea*)
'awa	kava (*Piper methysticum*)	*'awapuhi kuahiwi*	shampoo ginger (*Zingiber zerumbet*)
kalo	taro (*Colocasia esculenta*)	*ipu*	bottle gourd (*Lagenaria siceraria*)
kō	sugarcane (*Saccharum officinarum*)	*kamani*	Alexandrian laurel (*Calophyllum inophyllum*)
mai'a	banana (*Musa* x *paradisiaca*)	*kī*	ti (*Cordyline fruticosa*)
noni	Indian mulberry (*Morinda citrifolia*)	*kou**	no English name (*Cordia subcordata*)
'ōlena	turmeric (*Curcuma longa*)	*kukui*	candlenut tree (*Aleurites moluccana*)
pia	Polynesian arrowroot (*Tacca leontopetaloides*)	*milo**	portia tree (*Thespesia populnea*)
'uala	sweetpotato (*Ipomoea batatas*)	*niu**	coconut (*Cocos nucifera*)
uhi	edible yam (*Dioscorea alata*)	*'ohe*	bamboo (*Schizostachyum glaucifolium*)
'ulu	breadfruit (*Artocarpus altilis*)	*wauke*	paper mulberry (*Broussonetia papyrifera*)

*These species may have existed naturally in Hawai'i before humans arrived.

Post-Cook introductions

Approximately 9000 new species of flowering plants were introduced to Hawai'i from all over the world during the 216-year period between 1778 and 1994. Some, including plumeria, carnation, ginger, *pīkake, pakalana, pua kenikeni*, and *pua male* (*Stephanotis*), quickly became favorites of island residents and staples of the *lei* industry. Many were also embraced by native Hawaiians, who incorporated them into their culture. The song, *Moloka'i Nui a Hina*, on the next page, provides an example of this adoption of post-Cook introductions into Hawaiian culture. Here, the author speaks of his love for his sweetheart and his homeland, Moloka'i. The flowers of two introduced plant species, the *kukui* (*Aleurites moluccana,* a Polynesian introduction) and the crown flower (*Calotropis gigantea*, a post-Cook introduction), are romantically linked to the singer.

Effects of introduced plants and animals on native ecosystems

Unfortunately, not all of Hawai'i's introduced plant species have had a positive influence on life in the islands. Many have had very negative effects on native ecosystems; fortunately, most species popular with *lei* makers are not threats to native ecosystems.

The word *ecosystem* refers to a plant community, together with all of the other organisms that live there and all elements of the physical environment, including rocks, soil, minerals, water, etc. It comes from the Latin word *oeco,* meaning "household." Thus, an ecosystem can be thought of as a house (which is provided by the plants) and everybody in it. Technically, ecosystems can be of almost any size (e.g., the world ecosystem, or the ecosystem on a leaf), but we will be talking about classes of ecosystems like forests, shrub lands, and grasslands.

Of the 9000 plant species that humans introduced to Hawai'i, 861 (about 10 percent), have become naturalized, meaning that they established themselves in our natural areas and are reproducing successfully without any help from humans. Some populations are not spreading, but most continue to increase in size. Of the 861, 29 are Polynesian introductions and 832 are post-Cook introductions.

Today, almost half (47 percent) of the flowering plant species found in nature here are naturalized introductions. In contrast, before 1778 only about 3 percent of the flowering plant species that occurred in nature were not native. (Hawaiian ecosystems are currently home to 956 native and 861 introduced plant species. Before 1778 there were about 1060 native species and 29 naturalized introduced species.)

Ten percent of Hawai'i's naturalized plant species are considered "serious pests of native ecosystems," and all of these approximately 86 pest species are post-Cook introductions. This number will only increase with time, because some species already present will become pests after they have had a few decades to spread, and other introduced plant species continue to pour into the state.

While many of the serious pest plants only invade native plant communities that have been disturbed, about a third (28) of the 86 are capable of invading native ecosystems that are "intact" (undisturbed). These few species, if left alone, can cause irreparable damage. One particularly dangerous introduction is *Miconia calvescens* (the velvet tree), a species that now covers about 70 percent of the vegetated area on the island of Tahiti. Without intervention by concerned humans, it could do the same thing here in Hawai'i.

The serious plant pests that require some kind of disturbance in order to become established in a native ecosystem have two advantages over native species. Most of the pest species are naturally suited to colonizing disturbed areas, while most native forest species are not well suited to responding to disturbance, because they evolved in environments where disturbances (like the falling of a dead tree) were relatively rare. Also, many more forces disturb native ecosystems today than before 1778. These forces include more frequent—and more destructive—visits by human beings, and by another formidable group of pests: terrestrial, plant-eating mammals.

Ecological studies have demonstrated that when vegetation is removed from a native rain-forest, either by human collectors or by herbivorous animals, the amount of light that reaches the forest floor increases. One result of this change is that the native species (adapted to lower light levels) are often replaced by introduced plant species adapted to higher light levels. This can occur whether the vegetation that has been removed is from the upper forest story (the tree canopy), the middle, or the lower story of the forest. For example, when pigs eat *hāpu'u* tree fern (*Cibotium* species) in native forest, the fern fronds (leaves) are removed from the middle story of the forest. This allows more light to reach the understory, and certain weedy introduced plants are able to colonize the forest in these areas. Similarly, studies have shown that weedy plant species can invade openings created in the soil by herbivores or humans, but they do not invade adjacent areas without such openings.

Ua nani nā hono a Pi'i-lani, i ke kū kilakila i ka 'ōpua.

'O ku'u pua kukui, aia i Lani-kāula, 'o ka hene wai 'olu lana mālie.

Ua like nō a like la—me ku'u one hānau, ke po'okela i ka piko o nā kuahiwi,

me Moloka'i nui a Hina, 'āina i ka wehiwehi, e ho'i nō au e pili.

E ka makani ē, e pā mai me ke aheahe, 'auhea ku'u pua kalaunu.

How beautiful are the bays of Pi'i-lani, that stand majestically by the billowy clouds.

My *kukui* flower is at Lani-kāula, where water flows with cool and soothing rustle.

Alike—the sands of my birth, the tops of all mountains,

and Hina's great Moloka'i, festive land, may I return to stay.

O wind, blow gently, heed, my crown flower.

(Elbert and Mahoe 1970)

Many land-dwelling herbivores have been introduced to Hawai'i since 1778, and some of them have become feral (surviving and reproducing in the wild without any help from humans). Native ecosystems are seriously threatened by many of them, especially pigs, goats, cattle, domestic sheep, mouflon sheep, axis deer, and mule deer.

The hooved plant-eaters kill and damage native plants in three ways. They deliberately remove native plants for food and other purposes, such as making birthing beds for piglets. They remove native plants from the soil incidentally when doing things like creating wallows and digging for earthworms or roots to eat. They physically impact native plants by trampling them or girdling trees (removing bark, which weakens and often kills them).

These animal pests help to increase the abundance and distribution of certain introduced plant species. They do this directly by carrying seeds on their bodies or by feeding on weedy plant species, such as strawberry guava and banana poka, and spreading the seeds throughout the environment when they defecate. They do this indirectly when they make openings in the vegetation and the soil that provide the right kinds of disturbances that plant pests need to become established. This space taken up by the non-native invader plants is space lost to native plants. The cumulative effect of introduced plant and animal pests is a serious, continual decline in the abundance and distribution of our native plant species.

Changes in human culture that affect Hawai'i's native ecosystems

In the 1800s, Hawai'i became populated by people from many different cultures, and many of these immigrants attached little importance to the spiritual value of the land and its natural flora and fauna. Members of these cultural groups sought instead to maximize the economic yield that could be generated by Hawai'i's lands. This philosophical change, and a switch to a cash economy, led to changes in land use that reduced native ecosystems to a small fraction of their former extent. This, and a huge increase in the size of the human population, together with the abandonment of the "environmentally friendly" gathering practices employed in old Hawai'i and the emergence of a new attitude of "unbridled entitlement," brought widespread devastation to Hawai'i's native ecosystems.

Changes in land use

We have mentioned how the Hawaiians had removed native vegetation from large areas in the lowlands and modified the lower forests by planting and harvesting there. After 1778, many additional factors greatly accelerated loss of Hawai'i's native ecosystems.

Cattle, goats, sheep, and European pigs were introduced, and their populations were deliberately allowed to increase. This alone caused the loss of extensive areas of native vegetation on all islands. Other new activities included exploitation of sandalwood (*Santalum freycinetianum*, for trade) and firewood (for whaling ships), cultivation and production of sugarcane and pineapple, logging of *koa* (*Acacia koa*) and *lehua* (*Metrosideros* species), ranching, real estate development, and planting of forests with introduced tree species.

Many land-dwelling herbivores have been introduced to Hawai'i since 1778.

By the early 1900s, virtually all of the native vegetation of the Hawaiian Islands that had existed at lower and middle elevations was gone—in chilling fulfillment of a prophecy uttered by Kalaunuiohua (a chief of Hawaiʻi island who tried to conquer all of the Hawaiian Islands many generations before the birth of Kamehameha the Great, but who was defeated in his attempt to take Kauaʻi):

> *O ka lāʻau o ke kula e noho ana i ka ʻāina, o ka lāʻau o ka ʻāina e nalowale aku ana.*

> The trees of the plains will dwell on the land; the trees of the native land will vanish.

Today, cattle pastures occupy about 50 percent of Hawaiʻi's total land area, while plantations and urban areas occupy another 30 percent. The remaining 20 percent is occupied by native and non-native plant communities, but only about a third of this land, roughly 6 percent of Hawaiʻi's total land area, is still covered by relatively undisturbed native forest. And, as our native ecosystems have continued to shrink, our human population has more than quadrupled since 1778.

Changes in population density

In old Hawaiʻi, simple technology provided all the needs of a completely self-sufficient economy. Today, the islands are very much dependent on food imported from other places. This dependency, combined with modern technology, makes it possible for the islands to support a much larger human population.

Estimates of the number of native Hawaiians living in the islands at the time of Captain Cook's arrival vary, but most modern authorities estimate that there were between 200,000 and 300,000 people in Hawaiʻi at that time, compared to a population of over 1,210,000 people in the state in 2000.

Changes in gathering practices

After the Hawaiian religion ceased to be widely practiced, the ancestors having chosen to "let the old gods sleep," subsequent generations of Hawaiians often did not experience or learn the gestures of respect that were part of the old belief system. Chanting and other gathering protocols that treated the elements of the natural world as living, spiritual forces were not passed on in many families.

As the accessible forests were replaced with buildings, pastures, farming systems, and trees imported from other countries, not only were native ecosystems lost, but those that remained became more remote and difficult to access. Thus elders were often unable to accompany young people into native plant areas to teach them how to gather properly.

With the demise of the *ahupuaʻa* system of land and resource management, and with the emigration of many Hawaiian families away from their ancestral lands, few remained to monitor and care for the land's natural resources, and many resources were lost due to neglect. Many people began to gather edible or useful plant materials wherever they pleased, usually in the areas that were easiest to get to. Because many collectors did not leave anything behind for future use, some resources were completely and permanently exhausted in certain areas.

Irresponsible gathering is, unfortunately, still a common practice these days. Over the years, both of this section's authors have witnessed forest damage by individuals and groups who were gathering *lei* materials. We have seen *palaʻa* and

With the demise of the ahupuaʻa *system of land and resource management, and with the emigration of many Hawaiian families away from their ancestral lands, few remained to monitor and care for the land's natural resources, and many resources were lost due to neglect.*

palapalai ferns that were ripped from hillsides and forest floors—roots and all—exposing bare soil. We have seen branches brutally torn from *lehua* trees, merely to acquire a few *liko* (young leaves), *'o-pu'u* (buds), or *pua* (flowers), and then discarded carelessly along the trail.

In alarming numbers, people are collecting far more than they need, walking down the trails with plastic grocery bags, even large garbage bags, stuffed with plant materials. The cumulative effect of such non-traditional methods of collection of *lei* materials is irreversible.

In the pre-Cook period, no one would have dared to *hana 'ino i ka nahelehele* (desecrate the wild growth) in this way, because of the Hawaiian belief that if they did so the spirits would punish them and misfortune would befall both the gatherer of the *lei* materials and the person to whom the *lei* was given.

"Modern" changes in attitude

One of the sad aspects of our modern society is that so many of its members now seem to possess an attitude of "entitlement" that is virtually unbridled and usually unearned. One outgrowth of this attitude that affects Hawai'i's ecosystems is the belief that we humans "have a right" to collect from nature. Those who espouse this view attribute their "entitlement" to several causes, including such ideas as "because I'm a native Hawaiian," "because native Hawaiians do it," "because I've lived here for so-many years," "because I pay my taxes," and "if *I* don't gather them, someone else will."

While the authors sympathize with the desire to hold fast to cultural tradition, and we have personally experienced the Hawaiian loss of property and privilege and culture to outside influences, we believe that the rationalizations just expressed are inappropriate for two reasons. First, the activities they justify can only bring about greater damage to our native ecosystems and the plant species that we wish to preserve for judicious, sustained gathering. Second, these attitudes are completely incompatible with Hawaiian ethics and values regarding the use of scarce or cherished resources. In the following paragraphs, these reasons are considered more fully.

Hawaiians believed that one must work for the privilege of taking

A fundamental tenet of Hawaiian belief was the ethical conviction that one must work for the privilege of taking. Hawaiian children were brought up with many *'o-lelo no'eau* (wise sayings) that conveyed the same message as the following one:

> *Aia no ka pono—o ka ho'ohuli i ka lima i lalo,*
> *'a'ole o ka ho'ohuli i luna.*

> That is what it should be—to turn the hands palms down [and work for what you need], not palms up [expecting to be given what you need].

In the case of resource management, the right to use or collect resources was predicated by the responsibility taken in caring for it. An excellent example of this principle is the Hawaiian rules used to determine water rights, where the amount of water allowed to flow into a farmer's fields was proportional to the amount of time he and his family spent building and maintaining the dams and ditches that provided the water. Put simply, "no work, no water."

Hawaiians were fiercely protective of scarce resources and fervently believed that those who had not worked to take care of a resource had no right to use it. In dryland areas without irrigation systems, for example, planters were so protective of their precious water resources that anyone who tried to steal water risked being killed.

Hawaiians considered themselves *kahu* (caregivers) to native ecosystems

The early Hawaiians considered themselves as caregivers of their land and its natural resources and of the gods and spirit entities that lived there. In modern terms, a *kahu* is roughly equivalent to a "steward," a person who actively protects and manages an area with the intention of keeping it as healthy and productive as possible for as long as possible—maintaining it as a sustainable resource. In Hawaiian religion, however, the word *kahu* implies an intimate and confidential relationship between the god and the guardian or keeper. Thus *kahu* were "honored attendants" who considered it a great privilege to serve the native plant communities that they loved and with whom they maintained a deeply personal, spiritual relationship.

The chant at right provides a glimpse into the relationship between *kahu* and their native ecosystems. It is a *pule pale* (protection prayer) used to protect the chanter from evil when travelling through the forest. In it, the chanters reaffirm that it is their duty to serve as *kahu* (caregivers).

Part 4
Hawai'i's natural and cultural future

Each of us can help reverse the damage done by recent generations of "less enlightened" gatherers by implementing the following three recommendations, each of which is based solidly on both Hawaiian ethics and our scientific understanding of the environmental circumstances of these times.

How to preserve our native ecosystems

1. *Grow* what you need, instead of gathering from nature, and substitute introduced plants for native plants.

An obviously effective way to maintain native ecosystems is by *not* gathering from them! The native plants we need can be grown, and introduced plant species can be substituted for natives we cannot grow in sufficient quantity.

A wonderful modern example of this idea was provided by *kumu hula* Auntie Mā'iki Aiu Lake, who gathered the young, supple branches of banyan trees and made them into *lei* of what she called "*hālau maile*" (maile for the hula troop). She used these *lei* for performances in which she considered the real *maile* unnecessary. This innovation is welcome, because populations of the native *maile* vine (*Alyxia oliviformis*) have been dangerously depleted by over-picking. (However, since banyan is a serious pest tree in Hawai'i, we strongly advise against planting any more; please gather only from the many existing trees, as Auntie Mā'iki did.)

E noho ana ke akua i ka nāhelehele

I ālai 'ia e ke kī'ohu'ohu, e ka uakoko

E nā kino malu i ka lani

Malu e hō e

E ho'oulu mai ana 'o Laka i kona mau kahu

'o mākou nō, 'o mākou nō, 'o mākou nō

The gods dwell in the woodlands

Hidden away by the mist in the low-hanging, blood-red rainbow

O beings sheltered by the heavens

Confer upon us your protection

Laka inspires her *kahu*

It is us! It is us! It is us!

(Source: oral tradition; translated in part by Puku'i (in Tatar 1989) and in part by the authors; similar published versions can be found.)

This idea was practiced by the ancient Hawaiians too. For example, when they discovered that the *'olonā* plant (*Touchardia latifolia*) growing in their forests made very strong cordage, they decided to cultivate it in lower forests to ensure an ample supply. The ethic underlying this practice is reflected in the old Hawaiian *'o-lelo no'eau*:

E kanu mea 'ai o nānā keiki i ka hai.

Plant edible food plants lest your children look with longing at someone else's.

(Puku'i 1983)

It has been said that the Hawaiian scholar Mary Kawena Puku'i lived her life in keeping with this advice. Instead of plants, she "cultivated and gathered" books and other materials that provide us with an abundant supply of information regarding the Hawaiian culture. We hope that the words of this *'o-lelo no'eau* can inspire modern Hawai'i's inhabitants to plant native Hawaiian plants, so that our children do not "look with longing at someone else's." This phrase can be interpreted in two ways. It could mean that our children will "look with longing at someone else's native Hawaiian plants or cultural knowledge" because they do not have any of their own. More ominously, it could mean that they will "look with longing at someone else's non-Hawaiian plants and culture" because native plants or culture no longer exist. Of course, there is nothing wrong with adopting things that are not Hawaiian. What is unacceptable is not having a choice.

In planting native species, however, care should be taken to obtain plants from growers who acquire their plants ethically and without harming native ecosystems. Also, certain native plants should not be planted in certain areas, for eco-genetic reasons, and knowledgeable nurseries provide appropriate instructions and precautions on their plants' labels. Much knowledge on native plant propagation, ecology, and cultivation has been collected recently due to the revival of interest in the subject, and a subset of the "green" industry (landscapers and plant nurseries) is devoted to encouraging the use of Hawaiian native species.

2. Support efforts to preserve our native ecosystems.
Those who use native plants should help care for the native ecosystems that are the plants' natural home. One way to do this is by supporting or joining the efforts of agencies and organizations that are working to eradicate harmful plant and animal species from native ecosystems.

3. *E nihi ka hele…* Go carefully, giving thought to what is *pono* (right).
Most people who love native plants are eventually drawn to "visit them in their homes." As we hope to have shown, it is more important now than ever to cause as little disturbance as possible to native ecosystems when we travel through them. In so acting, we are not only following the recommendations of modern ecologists, but we also heed advice that has been part of Hawaiian culture for centuries, as Hawaiians urged their loved ones to travel cautiously and respectfully in the forests with the words, "*e nihi ka hele*." This simple phrase means that one should "travel quietly and unobtrusively, with careful observances of taboos [prohibitions]." Hawaiians complied readily with this advice, in part because of the ethics of their cultural

upbringing, and in part because of their belief that misfortune would befall one who behaved otherwise. Here, for example, is an excerpt from a verse found in an old Hawaiian dictionary:

E hoopono ka hele i ka uka o Puna,
E nihi ka hele, mai hoolawehala,
Mai noho a ako i ka pua o hewa,
O inaina ke akua, paa ke alanui,
Aole ou ala e hiki aku ai.

Behave correctly while traveling in the uplands of Puna;
Walk with caution, do not cause offense;
Do not tarry and pick the flowers incorrectly,
Lest the gods become angry and conceal the path,
And you have no way out.

(In a dictionary by Andrews, cited by N. B. Emerson and translated by the authors.)

Similar advice was offered by Hiʻiaka (the sister of Pele, powerful goddess of Hawaiʻi's volcanoes) to her traveling companions in ancient times, and by loving supporters of Queen Kapiʻolani when she embarked on a journey to the then unknown and mysterious lands of California and England in 1887.

Today, our environmental "taboos" are self-imposed, arising from our Earth-husbandry conscience, from our knowledge of what is necessary and right and of the precious resources that are at risk if we fail in our stewardship of Hawaiʻi's unique ecological heritage.

How to gain a fuller appreciation of Hawaiian culture

Growing plants for *lei* not only helps to preserve native forests (by reducing the amount of gathering that takes place there) but it also allows the growers to participate in many more aspects of Hawaiian culture than can be experienced simply by making *lei*.

Hawaiians loved to grow things, and they loved the things they grew

When we grow plants for *lei*, we are participating in the activity that was at the very heart of Hawaiian culture. A well known *ʻo-lelo noʻeau* describes the way Hawaiians felt about the plants in their care with these words:

He keiki aloha na mea kanu.

Beloved children are the plants.

(Pukuʻi 1983)

Today, our environmental "taboos" are self-imposed, arising from our Earth-husbandry conscience, from our knowledge of what is necessary and right and of the precious resources that are at risk if we fail in our stewardship of Hawaiʻi's unique ecological heritage.

It has been stated that the practice of tending plants—especially the cultivation of *kalo* (taro)—was at the very core of Hawaiian culture and identity. We agree with this idea, and with the following characterization of the Hawaiian lifestyle:

> "The Hawaiians, more than any other Polynesians, were a people whose means of livelihood, whose work and interests, were centered in the cultivation of the soil. The planter and his life furnish us with the key to his culture." (Handy et al. 1972)

The practice of tending plants—especially the cultivation of kalo (taro)—was at the very core of Hawaiian culture and identity.

Cultivating *lei p*lants brings these sources of inspiration closer to us

Another very important reason to grow *lei* materials is that it brings these sources of beauty and inspiration closer to us. While this clearly is not exclusively a Hawaiian idea, it undeniably was a fundamental part of Hawaiian thinking. As we have seen, Hawaiians valued plants for the inspiration that these "fellow beings" could impart.

When the *lei* plants being grown are native species, this idea gains additional significance, because native plants were once considered body forms (*kinolau*) of the Hawaiian gods. Thus, by growing native plants we respectfully recall and are inspired by the depth of the relationship that once existed among these plants, the *akua*, and our Hawaiian ancestors or, genealogy aside, our Hawaiian predecessors in stewardship of these islands.

We function as *kahu* to native ecosystems

When we grow plants for *lei* instead of simply harvesting materials from our native forests, we become a vital part of the solution to—rather than remain a part of—the problem of native ecosystem degradation and loss. Those who choose to assist in the conservation of native ecosystems in this way are taking an important step toward fulfilling the role of *kahu*, or "honored attendant." In addition, in so doing we practice the fundamental Hawaiian belief that one must work for the privilege of taking.

Native species conservation for the future of Hawaiian culture

One perspective often shared with us by many of our Hawaiian *kūpuna* has been the belief that each native species that becomes extinct diminishes the Hawaiians as a people, because a part of their family has been lost to them forever. For this reason, many Hawaiian elders have been caring for endangered and rare Hawaiian plants in their homelands for decades, since long before the passage of the first Federal Endangered Species Act in 1973.

It is not just *native species* that are important to Hawaiians, however. *Intact native ecosystems* are critically important to Hawaiian culture, for just as these lands are the natural home of native Hawaiian species, they also made up the natural environment in which native Hawaiian culture grew. The Hawaiian culture evolved in the context of an intimate relationship among the people, the earth, and the other inhabitants of the islands' ecosystems. Anyone who wishes to "understand" Hawaiian culture or "truly know" what it is to be Hawaiian must also become familiar with the natural environments that were the nurseries of Hawaiian culture.

"No one can comprehend the so-called "lore" and "beliefs" relating to [Hawaiian religion] without knowing a great deal about the aspects and features of the locale and natural environment with which [their gods and deities] are identified. Equally, persons and *ohana* [family] in their human relationships can be comprehended only in the context of natural setting and "lore" *in terms of the psychic relations subsisting between Nature and its phenomena, ancestral and nature spirits, and native mankind in old [Hawai'i]."* [Italics as in original text.] (Handy, Handy, and Puku'i 1972)

The type of "understanding" described here is the type of spiritual, visceral in-sight that can only be acquired by forming emotional ties to a natural phenomenon, such as a native plant community. Many years spent teaching about and working in Hawai'i's natural ecosystems have led the authors to the conclusion that there is a vital spiritual power emanating from a native Hawaiian ecosystem that is much less felt in a predominantly non-native counterpart ecosystem.

If our native ecosystems become extinct, Hawaiian culture will be irrevocably damaged, for young people will no longer be able to experience the feelings that emanate from truly native Hawaiian places. A mutual dependency thus exists today between Hawaiian ecosystems and Hawaiian culture. By working to save native eco-systems, Hawaiians help to preserve their culture.

Native Hawaiian species conservation for humanity

The Polynesian ancestors of the Hawaiians brought various religious beliefs with them to Hawai'i centuries ago. However, nature played a very important role in shap-ing the religion that ultimately developed. Hawaiian *kumu hula* Winona Beamer stated that "[her family's beliefs were] based on the beauty of nature, the power of nature, the complexity, the puzzlement, the moods. All the love and the truth and the beauty— those three words go hand in hand. That was our religion."

Many conservation ecologists have admitted similar feelings, stating that native ecosystems are their religion; that is, that these places form the spiritual center of their personal religious culture. Feelings such as these are what has motivated many con-servationists to devote their lives to the study of native ecosystems and to choose to investigate the kinds of questions that they hope will provide the answers they need to better preserve native ecosystems and maintain the associated native cultures.

Our ability to appreciate and cherish native ecosystems is determined mostly by two factors: having been taught to respect them, and having been able to spend time in them. It has little to do with ethnicity or career, except that some cultures and professions are more likely than others to teach people respect for nature and to provide them with experience in native plant communities. The vitality and power of native ecosystems is evidenced by their ability to touch human souls throughout human history. This power transcends culture and can linger to nurture humans for a lifetime, as suggested by this excerpt from a song about native Hawaiian rainforests:

Our ability to appreciate and cherish native ecosystems is determined mostly by two factors: having been taught to respect them, and having been able to spend time in them.

I laila ho'i no ko'u pu'uwai.
Ua maluhia ho'i au i ke'āpona mai.
A i ko'u mau ala hele loa,
'Oia mau nō ke akahai pū me ia'u.

It is there that my heart belongs.
I am safe in the warmth of that embrace.
No matter where I may roam,
I carry that gentleness with me.

(by P. Anderson-Fung and K. Maly)

Hawaiians believe that the spirits of those who lived before are still present on the land, and that the spirits of their *akua* live in the forests and other natural areas. Thus, preserving native ecosystems not only provides a continuity of experience for humans from one generation to the next—by providing them the opportunity to experience the same feelings for nature—it also provides a place for people to go to feel the presence of their ancestors.

Hawai'i's native ecosystems can be symbolized by an intricately crafted quilt that has been tattered by the actions of human beings. Adopting the spirit of the Hawaiian relationship to nature, we leave you with this suggestion:

E hono pū kākou i ko kākou kapa moe welu
i'olu'olu ka hiamoe 'ana o nā pua i ka poli o nā kūpuna

Let us all together mend our tattered quilt,
so that our children too may sleep in the embrace of our ancestors.

(P. Anderson-Fung and K. Lopes)

Hawaiians believe that the spirits of those who lived before are still present on the land, and that the spirits of their akua live in the forests and other natural areas.

Section 3

Using the best production practices ensures that the greatest quantity of highest quality plant materials is produced. Good quality builds your reputation and sets your business apart from its competitors.

Best Production Practices for Lei Material Plants

Choosing which plants to grow, how to grow them, and when to plant them involves a complex mixture of considerations. The market situation is the first major factor involved—what demand there is for your product, who will buy it, how much volume is needed and how often, and how much your customer is willing to pay. Your production capability is equally important—how much land, time, labor, and capital are available. Whatever the production situation you want to create for yourself, you need to acquire horticultural knowledge as a basis for developing the production skills you need to be successful. Using the best production practices ensures that the greatest quantity of highest quality plant materials is produced. Good quality builds your reputation and sets your business apart from its competitors.

This book does not attempt to present the complete range of horticultural information you need to be a successful grower. Instead, it concentrates on key areas that are critical to getting started: propagating the plants, applying fertilizers, coping with pest problems, and pruning to control growth and harvest lei materials. Many other good sources of horticultural information are available in books and on the Internet, including many publications focusing on Hawai'i's plants and climatic conditions. For example, CTAHR's *Plant Nutrient Management in Hawaii's Soils: Approaches for Tropical and Subtropical Agriculture,* containing a distillation of decades of University of Hawai'i research on soils and fertilizers, can provide much useful information for the serious agriculturist.

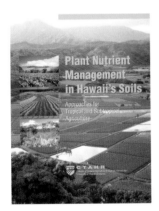

CTAHR's Plant Nutrient Management in Hawaii's Soils: Approaches for Tropical and Subtropical Agriculture *provides detailed advice on soil characteristics and improvement.*

General horticulture

Potting media
Some plants grown for lei material can be grown in containers, and others that are best grown in the ground are often started in containers and later replanted. The media used in these containers are often made up without soil, which (unless sterilized) can introduce weed seeds and plant pests and diseases. A good medium for potted plants has a balance between aeration and moisture retention. Adequate aeration allows water to move through it fairly rapidly; excessive moisture caused by lack of drainage leads to waterlogging, which is bad for root growth and invites diseases. Commercial media are mixtures that may include peat moss, perlite, silica sand (not beach sand), volcanic cinder, compost, and fir bark. A popular medium in the nursery industry is a combination of peat moss and perlite. These media generally do not provide much of the nutrients needed for plant growth, so supplemental fertilizers are usually required, and the pH of the medium may need to be adjusted to meet specific plant needs by adding lime.

Soil

Like potting media, the ideal soil has good aeration, and water drains freely beyond the root zone. If soil drainage is imperfect, a slight slope to the site can help drain excess water away, avoiding ponding. Excessive stoniness is bad for root growth and makes cultivation difficult. Soil pH, like the pH of potting media, should be slightly acid, around pH 6.0–6.5, which is ideal for most plants. Soil with an adequate organic matter content usually has good tilth, providing for ease of cultivation. Organic matter contributes to good soil structure, promoting aeration and drainage, and to the soil's capacity to retain water and plant nutrients.

Amending the soil is best done before planting, because most soil amendments should be thoroughly mixed into the surface 6–10 inches. A soil analysis will usually indicate the need for additions of phosphorus, calcium, or magnesium. Examples of soil amendments are

- compost to add organic matter
- phosphorus fertilizer to correct deficiency
- agricultural lime to raise soil pH to a desired level and add calcium
- dolomite to raise pH and to add magnesium as well as calcium
- sulfur to reduce soil pH and to add sulfur as a nutrient
- gypsum to improve structure of certain problem soils.

Organic mulches applied to the soil surface help improve soil properties. Mulch can reduce the evaporation of water from soils and reduce runoff by preventing the soil surface from being sealed by raindrop impact. Mulches can significantly reduce soil erosion. Organic mulches add to the soil organic matter when they break down to smaller particles and eventually to humus. This improves the soil's physical and chemical properties and enhances the conditions for beneficial soil microorganisms. In the initial stages of organic matter decomposition, soil nitrogen may be depleted when it is used by the decomposer microorganisms; therefore, supplemental fertilizer nitrogen may be helpful when organic mulch is applied.

Irrigation

In most locations in Hawai'i, plants need irrigation water to supplement rainfall during at least part of the year. Depending on your production situation, the options for delivering water to your plants are many and varied. Look for methods that reduce water use and the amount of your time needed to irrigate the crop. Choose a delivery system that minimizes spread of diseases and pests. Excessive moisture on the plants for too much time promotes plant diseases. Water running onto or between production areas can carry weed seeds, disease pathogens, and insects. Some diseases can be spread from plant to plant by splashing droplets resulting from rainfall or overhead irrigation, and plants sensitive to these diseases are often grown under a solid roof and with an irrigation system that wets only the medium.

Roots

A healthy root system is the key to plant productivity. Root injury can occur from excessive amounts of salts in applied fertilizer, manure, or irrigation water. Soil waterlogging and feeding by insects and nematodes can damage roots and make them susceptible to soil-borne plant diseases. With potted plants, root systems can and should be examined periodically to look for disorders. For plants in the ground, the

Organic matter contributes to good soil structure, promoting aeration and drainage, and to the soil's capacity to retain water and plant nutrients.

Keep plants appropriately moist with drip or overhead irrigation.

best approach is to create soil conditions that promote root health before planting. Avoid compacting the soil with unnecessary traffic over the root zone. Avoid water-logging by promoting drainage and eliminating ponding. Test new fertilizers or mulch materials on a small area and observe the results for a couple weeks before making large-scale applications. In some situations, soil fumigants or drenches can be applied before planting to rid the soil of pathogens within the root zone. When root health problems are suspected after planting, soil and root samples can be taken to be examined for the presence of nematode and fungal infection by a plant disease laboratory such as the CTAHR Agricultural Diagnostic Service Center.

Propagation techniques for lei plants

Each plant description in this book includes mention of the best ways to propagate it. Plants are propagated from seeds, cuttings, or divisions, and by air layering, and this section outlines these common propagation techniques. It should be noted that information is limited about the best techniques for propagating some of the native Hawaiian plants used in lei making.

Propagating from seeds

Propagating plants from seeds requires little special equipment. Two advantages of this method are that plants can be propagated without removing growing parts of the parent plant, and seeds often can be stored. However, many tropical plants' seeds cannot be stored for long, in which case they should be sown as soon as possible after collection.

Hybridized plants, such as marigolds, as well as plants that are not self-pollinating, produce offspring that may not have the same characteristics as the parent plant; that is, the seeds do not produce plants that are "true to type." Characteristics such as the color, size, or quantity of flowers may change for the better or the worse. Also, many hybridized annuals are sterile and never produce offspring.

Perennials—including trees and shrubs—grown from seeds may take several years before flowers are borne or before the plants have reached the size when they will produce significant numbers of flowers.

Collecting seeds

For optimum germination, collect seeds that are mature. Fruit ripeness usually is an indication that the seeds within are mature. Ripe fruits are identified by a color change in the case of fleshy fruits and by drying and turning brown in the case of seed pods. If seeds are gathered before the embryo is sufficiently developed, they will not germinate. Seeds that are thin, light in weight, or shriveled are likely to be immature and either nonviable, poor in quality, or short-lived.

Collect sufficient fruits to yield the quantity of seed needed. If collecting "from the wild," leave some fruits unharvested to maintain the native population. Label your collections with the plant name, date, quantity collected, and location. These can be important records later.

Cleaning seeds

Fruits that are dry when mature

(e.g., *‘a‘ali‘i, ‘ilima, kulu‘ī, ‘ōhi‘a lehua*)

1. Dry the fruiting body at room temperature. Do not expose the fruits or seeds to high temperature (>85°F) or place them on a dark surface in full sunlight, because high temperature may kill the seeds.
2. Set a strainer or piece of screen with holes slightly larger than the seed size over a container.
3. Break up the fruits to separate the seeds, which will fall into the container; discard the debris left behind.

Fruits that are fleshy or pulpy when mature

(e.g., *maile, ‘ūlei, ‘ākia, pōhinahina, pa‘iniu*)

1. If the fruit is not fully ripened, it can be kept in a plastic bag until soft (the seeds are easier to clean when the pulp is softened).
2. Once ripened, remove the flesh to prevent spoilage. It is wise to wear latex gloves while handling the fruits to prevent skin irritation; some fleshy fruits contain skin-irritating chemicals.
   a. One way to remove the fruit flesh is to put the fruits in a colander or strainer under running water and rub them to separate the seeds from the pulp (this works well with larger seeds).
   b. Another method is to put the seeds in a large bowl of water and massage them by hand to separate the seeds from the pulp. With many plants' seeds, the good ones will sink to the bottom, while the pulp and empty seeds will float to the top and can be poured off. (Note: this doesn't work with some plants that have seeds meant to float to aid natural dispersal.)
3. Wash the seeds thoroughly. Be sure that all the fleshy pulp has been removed, because fungus diseases can attack the pulp and spread to a germinating seedling.
4. Air-dry the seeds on a paper towel as further prevention of fungal infection.

Other types of fruits—manual cleaning

(e.g., *wiliwili, ma‘o, māmane*)

Seeds that are contained in hard fruiting bodies such as nuts, pods, or capsules can be manually removed by opening the fruit and removing the seeds. The hard shell must be removed to speed up the germination process. Various tools can be used to break or cut the fruit, but they must be used with care to avoid injury to the user and damage to the seeds.

Growing from seeds

For successful germination, seeds must be *viable*—they must have a live embryo. Cut open a few seeds to see if they are filled with a living embryo. Germination also requires the right amount of moisture, the proper temperature, a supply of oxygen, and in some cases exposure to light. Seeds usually should be germinated soon after harvest, because they begin to lose viability when they are dried and stored, and seeds of some plants die if dried and stored. Some plants' seeds lose viability rapidly after harvest, while those of others can be stored for years under the right conditions. Seeds that are discolored or desiccated should not be used, because they probably will not germinate. Weak seedlings developed from poor seeds are more susceptible to disease than vigorous ones and may become a reservoir of invasive pathogenic microorganisms.

Some seeds have a mechanism called *dormancy* that delays germination. The most common type of dormancy is seedcoat dormancy, in which the seedcoat is impermeable to water, and the seed cannot germinate until this barrier is broken down. Depending on the plant, a seed treatment is often required to overcome dormancy.

Get to know the seeds you are trying to grow by experimenting with seed treatments. For best results, be sure that dormancy has been broken *and* that the seeds are viable *before* planting them.

Seed treatments

Soaking
(e.g., *maile, ʻaʻaliʻi, ʻūlei, ʻilima, pōhinahina, ʻākia, maʻo, māmane*)
Soaking seeds in water before planting can overcome seedcoat dormancy. As the seed absorbs water it swells, and the seed coat breaks open. The soaking time required to start germination can vary from a few minutes to several days, depending on the seedcoat permeability. If cold water does not cause seeds to swell after soaking overnight, the use of heated water (hot to the touch, i.e., 120–135°F) sometimes helps. When using hot water, allow the water to cool with the seeds in it rather than maintaining heat on a stove. Excessive soaking can cause some seeds to rot. After an initial bath in water, placing seeds on (or between layers of) moistened paper or cloth towel is often preferable to continuous immersion.

With many seeds, viable ones sink and damaged or abortive ones float, which provides a convenient way to do an initial screening for viability. However, some seeds, such as those of *naupaka* and *maʻo*, are meant to float.

Absorbing water and swelling is not a guarantee of seed viability—dead seeds do this too. The first sign of growth after the seed swells is usually the emergence of the young root (called the radicle). With small quantities of seeds, it can be useful to germinate them on moist paper or cloth before planting them. By delaying planting until the radicle starts to grow, you can be sure you are planting a viable seed. When the radicle has emerged, move the seed to the planting medium, handling it carefully to avoid breaking the radicle.

Physical scarification
(e.g., *kukui, wiliwili, māmane, maunaloa*)
Disrupting the seedcoat surface by cutting or scratching it can also allow water to penetrate it and overcome seedcoat dormancy. Hard seedcoats can be physically scarified by scratching with sandpaper or a file, nicking with nail-clippers, or cracking with a hammer. These methods are useful for treating small amounts of seeds, and they are most convenient with seeds that are large enough to hold. Very small seeds can be carefully rubbed between two pieces of sandpaper. Do not scarify the seedcoat all the way through to the seed, because the injury may prevent germination by damaging the radicle or providing entrance to microorganisms that cause rot and death of the seed.

Seeds that do not require treatment
Seeds from wet habitats (e.g., *ʻōhiʻa lehua*) generally do not require pretreatment. The fruit pulp should be completely removed from the seed to avoid rot.

Some of these plants produce extremely tiny seeds within a fleshy fruit. Handle these fleshy fruits as described above under *Cleaning seeds*. The more the fruits

Some seeds have a mechanism called dormancy that delays germination.

Sometimes seeds need to soak before they will germinate.

ripen, the better. When ripening fruits in a plastic bag, a fungicide can be made into a solution and poured over the seeds. After 1–3 days, squeeze the bag gently to break up the pulp, pour it into a glass jar, mix with water, and let the seeds settle to the bottom. A fungicide mixed with the water can reduce the possibility of seed loss from disease. Remove as much of the floating pulp as possible, and rinse the seeds in clear water.

One way to sow tiny seeds is to put them in water, agitate it to disperse the seeds into a slurry, and pour it over the medium. Start these seeds either on moist sphagnum moss or a well drained medium (1 part peat moss or 1 part potting mix to ½ part perlite). Pour the slurry containing the seeds onto the planting medium and put the containers under protected conditions, such as a mist box.

Plants from wet habitats may need to be started in covered containers, creating a terrarium-like effect. Another way to accomplish this is to place the pot in a plastic bag and place it in a shady place. This helps to provide the damp growing environment that these plants need to germinate.

Sowing seeds

Surface-sow tiny seeds by dusting them onto the surface of the medium. Larger (but still small) seeds should be covered lightly with a layer of planting medium about as deep as the diameter of the seed. Even larger seeds may be planted at a depth two or three times their diameter. Place seed flats in a covered, shaded area (50% of full sunlight) protected from wind, and water them regularly to keep the medium moist.

Small-seeded plants such as *paʻiniu* and others from wet forest areas should be surface-sown on sphagnum moss and put under a closed mist system (mist every hour for 15 seconds from 6 a.m. to 6 p.m.).

Transplanting seedlings

When the seedlings have one or two true leaves, they are ready for transplanting. To avoid injury to the stem, gently hold the plant by a leaf when transferring it to a new container. Transplanting should be done early—sooner rather than later—because root systems can be damaged when crowded seedlings are separated, and smaller seedlings are less subject to root tangling. If there are only a few seedlings in a pot, they can be allowed to get bigger before transplanting.

Choose a pot according to the size of the root system. Don't "over-pot" seedlings by putting a small seedling into a pot many sizes larger than its root system.

Carefully planted seeds can turn into a tray of healthy seedlings ready to be transplanted.

To move the seedling, insert a fork, spoon, or pot label well under the seedling and carefully lift the seedling, keeping as much medium as possible with the roots.

Partially fill the pot with medium, add the seedling, then add more medium to cover the roots. Do not plant a seedling any deeper into the new medium than it was in the original medium. Tap the container gently to stabilize the plant and settle the medium. Water-in seedlings soon after transplanting.

It is important that the medium is well drained. To test this, make sure that water does not sit on top of the medium when it is watered. Keep the transplant in a sheltered area for 2–3 weeks. If the container can be placed on wet sand or watered from below in a saucer, the medium surface will be drier and less hospitable to damping-off disease. But do not allow the container to sit too long in water, because the roots will suffocate.

Seeds to be stored for any period of time should be removed from their pods, cleaned, have all the pulp removed, and then dried.

Many plants, like the plumeria shown, can easily be rooted from cuttings in the appropriate medium.

Storing seeds

Not all seeds can be stored; some, including *maile* and *kuluʻī*, lose their viability very rapidly after maturity.

Seeds to be stored for any period of time should be removed from their pods, cleaned, have all the pulp removed, and then dried. Inspect the seeds to be sure there are no insects among them and no holes indicating that insects may be inside them. Discard any seeds that are discolored or deformed.

The most important condition to retain seed viability during storage is low moisture content. Do not soak or scarify seeds that are to be stored. A light dusting of a fungicide will help prevent mold from growing.

Store dried seeds in airtight containers and keep them in a cool, dry place. Silica gel or other desiccants can be placed in the storage container to absorb moisture. Refrigeration (no colder than 45°F, 7°C) prolongs the storage life of most seeds. Tropical seeds should not be held at temperature below 50°F (10°C). A suitable temperature range is 55–65°F (13–18°C).

Identify the seeds on a label placed in the container that includes the plant name, quantity of seed, date, and source.

Propagating from cuttings

Plants produced from cuttings exhibit the same characteristics as the source plant. They sometimes can produce flowers more quickly than when the same species is grown from seed and has to pass through a juvenile stage before bearing.

Cuttings cannot be stored for more than a few days and may require a misting system to keep them from drying out. Cuttings are parts of live plants, which limits the number of them that can be taken without destroying the donor plant. When harvesting materials from plants growing in natural conditions, such as the forest, leave enough healthy plant stems behind so that the population can persist.

Cuttings are taken from the vegetative portions of the plant including stems, modified stems (tubers, rhizomes, etc.), leaves, and roots. The type of cutting to use depends on the plant. Most often, the cutting used is from a recently matured stem, with or without the tip but with leaves. A common size of stem cutting is 4–6 inches long with several (2–5) leaves. The cutting should be taken from a healthy, vigorous plant to ensure that the stem contains an ample supply of stored food to nourish the developing roots and leaves until the new plant becomes self-sustaining. A good time to harvest cuttings is in the morning. Use air-tight plastic bags to store the cuttings and keep them moist during transport to the nursery. Do not let the cutting material dry out at any time. A moist paper towel in the plastic bag helps to maintain humidity.

Remove the foliage from the portion of the cutting that will be inserted into the medium. Wash the cutting to remove any insects or fungus. If a mist system is not used, reduce the foliage on the cutting either by removing some of the larger leaves or trimming large leaves to just their basal halves. Rooting compounds containing growth-inducing plant hormones can be applied to the basal portion of the cutting. These compounds usually hasten rooting, particularly of semihardwood or hardwood cutting materials. A product that also contains a fungicide can be helpful.

Following treatment of the cutting, insert it into a clean, moist medium such as vermiculite, perlite, or a combination of these that allows good drainage but will remain moist during the rooting process. Only the basal third of the cutting needs to be in the medium. Arrange multiple cuttings so their leaves do not overlap and create an "umbrella" over each other. Maintain humid conditions for rooting success. Tenting the cuttings with a plastic bag promotes rooting by keeping humidity high.

Look for new leaf and root growth anywhere from several weeks to several months later. Pot the rooted cuttings carefully, as you would a seedling, to avoid damaging the roots. Keep the potted cuttings in a covered, shaded area for 2–3 weeks until established in the pot.

Propagating by air layering

Air layering (marcottage) causes adventitious roots to form on a stem or branch while it is still attached to the parent plant. It is especially useful for plants that are difficult or impossible to propagate by other methods or are of sufficient value to justify the cost (for example, *'ōhi'a lehua*). Air layering is not a rapid propagation method, and it is not useful for large-scale propagation unless many stock plants are available. It can, however, produce large plants in a relatively short time, although transplanting increases in difficulty with the size of the air-layered plant.

In the most common form of air layering, the stem is "girdled" by removing a section of bark and the cambium layer beneath it. The girdled section is usually ½–1 inch long and goes completely around the stem. Some woody plants, particularly dracaena and ti, do not require such a large, completely girdled section but will root when girdled by an upward slit made two-thirds of the way through the stem.

When air layering trees, the spring wood of the previous year's growth is used; wood older than a year is harder to root. Remove a section of bark ½–1 inch long. Scrape the surface of the wood beneath the bark to remove the thin, white layer of cambium. Apply a rooting hormone to the edge of the cut toward the growing tip. Apply a moist rooting medium such as sphagnum moss over the cut area and several inches of the branch above the girdle. Wrap the ball of sphagnum moss with plastic film or two layers of aluminum foil to prevent drying. Seal the wrap and support the branch, if necessary, with a bamboo stake tied like a splint above and below the girdled area. Roots generally form within 2–3 months. When roots are observed in the sphagnum moss, the branch can be removed and transplanted into pots containing medium of the same type used for seedling transplants. Maintain the containers in shaded and humid conditions until the roots have grown enough to support the plant. Staking is often necessary.

Air layering requires that the medium be covered so that it does not dry out.

Propagating from divisions

When an entire plant is cut into sections or pieces, these are referred to as divisions. This is often done with plants having fleshy roots, bulbs, and stems, such as ginger, *moa*, orchids, and many ferns. The cuts can be treated with fungicide and dried a little to prevent infection by fungi and bacteria. The divisions are placed for rooting in a well drained medium similar to that used for cuttings.

Suggested media formulations

Seed-sowing media (soilless mixes)

Using a medium free of soil reduces the risk of damping-off and other soil-borne diseases, as well as contamination with weed seeds or residual pesticides. The germination medium must retain moisture yet provide good drainage and aeration and maintain an open surface, without crusting. Different combinations of commercial potting mixtures, perlite, and volcanic cinder are used. Following are some examples.

2 or 3 parts perlite + 1 part potting mix (e.g., Sunshine Mix® #4)

Using a medium free of soil reduces the risk of damping-off and other soil-borne diseases, as well as contamination with weed seeds or residual pesticides.

1 or 2 parts fine cinder + 1 part potting mix (used for *'ōhi'a lehua*) or fine sphagnum moss

Media for potting-up transplants

4 parts potting mix + 2 parts compost + 4 parts perlite (#2 or #3 perlite) or medium-size cinder

Do not add vermiculite to the potting mix, because it will hold too much water.

Media for propagating cuttings

(e.g., ferns, *'a'ali'i, kulu'ī, 'ōhi'a lehua, wiliwili, pōhinhina, ma'o, 'ūlei*)
The cutting medium has three functions:

Several different media should be on hand for different propagation and potting purposes.

- to hold or support the cutting in place during the rooting period
- to provide moisture for the cutting
- to permit aeration to the base of the cutting.

Use a well drained medium such as 2–3 parts potting mix + 2 parts perlite, or 1 part potting mix + 1 part fine cinder (⅛–¼ inch).

Media for cuttings are made up of various combinations of perlite, vermiculite, and potting mix, such as

2–3 parts perlite + 1 part vermiculite, or
2–3 parts perlite + 1 part potting mix.

Also, Oasis® rooting cubes or similar products can be used.

Media for fern spores

Place mature fronds with sori in a paper bag for 3–5 days. With hot water, sterilize a clear plastic box and Oasis® cubes or sphagnum moss. Let the box and medium cool, then surface-sow spores on top of the medium in the box, cover it, and keep the medium moist. Germination can begin in 7–10 days, but development into a plantlet may take 6 months or more, depending on the species. Transplant into sphagnum moss or 3 parts potting mix + 1 part perlite, and put the container under a mist system for 1–3 months. When the developing plantlets are are 1–2 inches high, move the container out of the mist into a shaded area.

Fertilizers and propagation media

A potting machine is helpful for producing container plants in commercial quantities.

Fertilizers are not normally used in propagation media, because there is either no root system or only a very small root system to take up nutrients. Transplanting and growing-on media can be amended with fertilizer to support development of the root system and aerial part of the plant. The amount of fertilizer that is used depends either on the volume of medium (for containers) or the area to be fertilized. Add fertilizer preferably when mixing the medium rather than to the surface after potting. Fertilizer recommendations for media are expressed either as weight per cubic foot of media or weight per square foot of media. For example, 2 oz per ft^3, 1 lb per 1000 ft^2.

Suggested fertilizer programs for lei material production

Plant species naturally differ in the amounts of nutrients needed for growth, and growers often refer to different species as "light feeders" or "heavy feeders." In addition to their inherited characteristics, a plant grown in a production situation often has greater nutritional needs than when growing under natural conditions. When plants are frequently pruned, regrowth is encouraged, and the need for nutrients increases. Plants also differ in their tolerance of fertilizers—some are sensitive to salts in the soil and can be "burned" when too much fertilizer is applied, while others are not so easily damaged. Some native Hawaiian plants are considered sensitive to fertilizers, and therefore these plants as a group may be regarded as having "light" nutrient requirements.

Also, plants' demand for nutrients generally increases as they mature and grow larger. Plants need very little fertilizer during propagation. Cuttings at first don't have roots to take up nutrients; they usually need no fertilizer in the rooting medium, and at most they may occasionally require a highly diluted liquid fertilizer sprayed on the leaves or used as a drench once roots begin to emerge. Seed-propagated plants initially use nutrients that are stored in the seed endosperm. Because seedling roots are delicate, application of fertilizer is usually best delayed until the seedling approaches a transplanting size, and again, a diluted, liquid fertilizer is best.

The suggested fertilizer programs given on the next page are for plants that have become established. Use applications lighter than these before the plants are established and growing vigorously. For most of the plants described in this book, little or no research has been done to determine the optimum levels of nutrients, either in nature or in production situations. The amounts are suggested for use as a starting point in experimenting to find the best nutrient management program for healthy, productive plants. You will need to experiment to find the best application amounts for the plants you are growing.

The general types of fertilizers mentioned here are defined in the table below. In addition to the routine fertilizer applications suggested here, occasional foliar applications of liquid fertilizer solutions can be used to help correct micronutrient deficiencies, should they appear. Also, plant species grown for foliage rather than flowers are likely to benefit from supplemental nitrate nitrogen.

Some native Hawaiian plants are considered sensitive to fertilizers, and therefore these plants as a group may be regarded as having "light" nutrient requirements.

General types of fertilizer

Fertilizer type	Form in which applied	Typical application frequency	Examples
Granular	Dry	Four times a year for plants in the ground* Monthly for plants in containers	Gaviota® 16-16-16
Soluble	Dissolved in water	Weekly	Miracle-Gro®, Peters®
Liquid	Diluted in water	Weekly	Dyna Grow®, fish emulsion
Controlled-release	Dry	Variable release periods	Nutricote®, Osmocote®

*Note: Because soluble, liquid, and controlled-release fertilizers are expensive, they are seldom used on field-grown plants in production situations.

Fertilizers for plants grown in the ground

The amount and formulation of fertilizer applied should be based on a soil test to determine the amounts of nutrients already present in the soil and the soil's pH. Soil nutrient deficiencies and pH adjustment indicated by a soil analysis should be corrected before planting. Nutrients of particular concern for preplanting applications are phosphorus and calcium. Adequate levels of available calcium improve plant postharvest quality and resistance to disease.

Plants in the ground are usually given granular fertilizers in production situations, because this type of fertilizer is the most economical. For most field-grown plants, the fertilizer amounts given can be applied four times a year. Scheduling these applications for March, June, August, and November takes into consideration that plants grow more in the summer and have a lower nutrient requirement during the cooler, shorter days of winter. The suggestions in the boxes on this page use a balanced NPK ratio of 1:1:1. Applications of 1:2:1 ratio fertilizers often build up unnecessarily high soil P levels over time, because P applied to the soil surface does not readily move down into many of Hawai'i's soils. It is best to correct a soil P deficiency before planting. A 10-10-10 formulation is suggested, and a fertilizer with a different NPK analysis should be adjusted proportionally; for example, 1½ lb of 10-10-10 is roughly 1 lb of 16-16-16 (calculation: 10 ÷ 16 = 0.625, and 0.625 x 1.5 lb = 0.94 lb).

Suggested fertilizer program for plants in the ground

Nutrient-need category	Amount of 10-10-10 granular fertilizer in each of four applications per year (pounds per 100 sq ft of growing area)
Light	½–¾
Medium	¾–1
Heavy	1–1½

Note: Some fertilizer product containers give recommended application rates; follow the product recommendations if they differ from the generalized application rates suggested here.

Plants in containers

Plants grown in containers can be fertilized with granular fertilizers, but often other types of fertilizer are preferred. The first suggestion given for each plant type is based on a controlled-release formulation, 16-16-16 plus micronutrients, with a three-month release period, applied four times per year in March, June, August, and November. Adjust the application schedule for different release periods, and adjust the amount proportionally for different NPK analysis levels. If a granular chemical fertilizer is used, apply one-third of the amount of controlled-release fertilizer suggested, and apply that amount monthly.

The second suggestion given is for a soluble or liquid type of fertilizer, applied weekly as a drench. Apply only enough of the solution as is needed to wet the entire root zone, but not so much that it runs out of the pot.

Fertilizer basics

A fertilizer's nutrient content is indicated by a series of three numbers found on the fertilizer package. The numbers are the percentages of three major plant nutrients: nitrogen (N), phosphorus (P, as P_2O_5), and potassium (K, as K_2O), in that order. In general, most plants require these important nutrients in about equal amounts. A "balanced" fertilizer that has an NPK rating of 16-16-16 has twice as

Suggested fertilizer program for plants in containers

Nutrient-need category	Controlled-release fertilizer 16-16-16 + micronutrients, 3-month release, tbsp/gal
Light	½–¾
Medium	¾–1
Heavy	1–1½

Nutrient-need category	Soluble or liquid fertilizer 7-7-7 + micronutrients, tsp/gal water
Light	½
Medium	1
Heavy	2

Note: Some fertilizer product containers give recommended application rates; follow the product recommendations if they differ from the generalized application rates suggested here.

much of each of these nutrients as one rated 8-8-8. Other secondary nutrients often present in fertilizer formulations are calcium (Ca), magnesium (Mg), and sulfur (S).

Plants also require other nutrients than these main ones, but in such small quantities that they are called "micronutrients." These include iron (Fe), zinc (Zn), copper (Cu), manganese (Mn), boron (B), and molybdenum (Mo). Some fertilizers are formulated to include micronutrients in addition to the major nutrients. These "all-purpose" formulations contain most or all of the nutrients required for plant growth, and they are used for plants grown in containers, and particularly for plants grown in soilless media in containers.

Fertilizers that contain only the major nutrients are designed for plants grown in the ground, where they usually get enough of the secondary and micronutrients from the soil. Some soils are deficient in certain minor nutrients, or the nutrients may be present but are unavailable to plants because of the soil's pH. In such cases, these growth-limiting nutrients need to be applied as fertilizer, or the soil pH needs to be adjusted to favor their availability. For information on routine soil analysis, see CTAHR's brief publication *Testing Your Soil: Why and How to Take a Soil-Test Sample.* For more detailed information, see CTAHR's *Plant Nutrient Management in Hawaii's Soils: Approaches for Tropical and Subtropical Agriculture.*

Some growers prefer the slow-release characteristic of most organic nutrient sources. Organic fertilizers typically have a low nutrient content and release their nutrients slowly compared to the more concentrated, readily soluble inorganic fertilizers. Organic fertilizers usually contain a complete range of nutrients, in contrast to soluble fertilizers, which often contain only the major nutrients. And, the high organic-matter content of some organic fertilizers contributes to improving soil tilth (ease of cultivation), moisture absorption and retention, and the conditions favoring soil organisms. Because of their low nutrient content, organic fertilizers usually must be applied in large amounts to keep up with the needs of rapidly growing plants. Also, the nutrient content is often less well defined for commercial organic fertilizers than for inorganic ones.

Be careful when applying fertilizer, because more is not always better. When in doubt, use less. In an unfamiliar situation, such as with a new plant species, soil, potting medium, or fertilizer formulation, apply only to a small area or a few plants and observe the effects over a two-week period before doing broad-scale applications.

Pruning is done to "train" or direct the plant's growth in a particular way.

Pruning plants grown for lei material production

Appropriate pruning is important when growing plants for lei materials. The objective of pruning plants that are regularly harvested for flowers and foliage may be different from that of pruning plants in landscapes, which is usually to maintain a neat and attractive plant shape and appearance. Pruning is done to "train" or direct the plant's growth in a particular way. This may be intended either to establish a desired plant structure or to encourage development of certain plant parts, such as more leaves or flowers. For lei-material plants, pruning for structure is usually done to make the harvest more convenient (e.g., to keep branches within reach), and pruning to encourage growth is done to maximize development of the part harvested. Also, each harvest taken is a mini-pruning that needs to be done in a way most favorable to continued harvesting. With both types of pruning—to train and to harvest—the primary goal should be to maintain the plant in as healthy a condition as possible.

It is important to have a clear idea of what you want to accomplish before you start pruning. As you get to know the plant you are growing, you will gain the necessary understanding of how it responds to pruning. You will learn which seasons are best for pruning, and which are bad times to prune. You will learn whether to cut new or old wood, and how to favor production of the part you want to harvest.

Pruning is a skill that is best learned in the doing, and success is proved only over time. Proceed thoughtfully, experiment with various strategies, and keep notes of the dates of prunings, which plants were pruned, and the methods used. Observe the effects and compare treatments. Note how the plants grow and respond to pruning during different seasons of the year. It is said that the most important ingredient in successful crop production is the grower's shadow. Be present and patient, prune carefully and consciously, and observe how your actions manage the plant's growth, health, and productivity.

Pruning strategies

Heading back removes the end of a branch or stem. The cut is made above a node, toward the branch tip. Nodes are the places on a branch or stem where leaves or other branches originate. Nodes contain buds, and heading back the terminal growing point causes these buds to grow and produce new shoots at the node (or nodes) below the cut. Forcing this growth from nodes closer to the main stem of the plant increases the density of the foliage and makes the plant sturdier.

Pinching is a lighter type of heading back. It is beneficial for most herbaceous plants grown for lei materials, especially when the flowers are borne at the branch tips. Some lei materials are harvested by pinching. Using the nails of your thumb and forefinger, pinch back soft growth throughout the growing season. This redirects growth back to lower nodes and increases the density of the foliage. Pinching is also useful for debudding flowers and thinning fruits.

Thinning removes entire branches back to a main branch or the trunk. Thinning is done to remove broken, diseased, crossing, or tangled branches, and it can be done at any time. In landscapes, thinning gives the plant a more open appearance, but this may not be important in managing plants for lei material production. Thinning shrubs to remove about a third of the older branches at their base near ground level will open the canopy, allowing new shoots to grow and rejuvenating the plant.

When to prune

Trees and shrubs may be *lightly* pruned year-round in Hawai‘i. Remove dead, broken, or diseased branches whenever they appear. Plants grown for foliage may be pruned at any time, because flowering is not important for these plants. With plants grown for their flowers or fruits, timing of pruning affects future flower development, and pruning should be timed to maximize blossoming.

The right time to prune depends on the plant, its condition, and the results desired. For rapid shoot development and the greatest overall growth, plants should be pruned just before the buds begin to swell. Pruning after each flush of growth, when the new leaves are fully expanded, tends to retard growth. If a species flushes several times a year, pruning in late summer may encourage an additional flush of shoot growth.

Plants flower from either current growth (the ends of twigs and branches), or older wood (further back on branches).

Plants that flower on current growth (new shoots and stems) usually blossom and form fruits several times a year, sometimes almost continually, in Hawai'i. Prune them periodically throughout the year after a blooming flush to encourage new shoot development. Take care to prune lightly. Continuously heading-back this type of plant (for example, a hibiscus hedge), results in dense foliage, fewer flowers, and a flattened plane of branch stubs on the hedge surface.

Plants that flower on older wood generally flower and fruit at a distinct time once each year. To maximize flowering on plants that flower on older wood, prune immediately at the end of their blooming cycle. Pruning or pinching shoots at this time encourages more lateral branches and many more flowers. Pruning later in the season removes flower buds and reduces the next flowering and fruiting. Plants of this type include some azaleas and hydrangeas, camellias, magnolias, Indian hawthorn, crape myrtle, royal poinciana, jacaranda, cassia, and bottlebrush.

Deciduous plants, which drop leaves before a growth flush, are best pruned late in the dormant (bare) cycle. Plants that do not lose their leaves are best pruned several weeks after a growth flush. At this time, wounds caused by pruning rapidly develop callus and close, which discourages insects, disease, and decay from entering the plant. Undesirable sprouting may result from pruning at other times. When trees produce excessive sprouts, they are easily damaged when pruned during active shoot elongation. The worst time to prune is when leaves are forming. Do not prune plants when they are under stress, such as drought stress.

Annual plants vary in the extent to which their production of flowers can be managed by pruning. Some annuals' growth cannot be prolonged by harvesting or pinching back, and the plants just have to be replaced regularly to maintain production of lei material.

Pruning tools

Choose the right tool for the job, and keep it sharp and clean. Hand pruners are the most frequently used tool for pruning branches up to ½ inch diameter, and loppers are used for larger branches. Anvil-style pruners work best for small or soft stems. By-pass pruners cut like scissors and are generally preferred to anvil types because they cut cleanly without crushing the tissue. Hedge trimmers are for landscape maintenance and may not be useful for managing plants for harvest of lei materials. Pole pruners are useful for harvesting flowers, seeds, and foliage from tall plants; their use is preferable to climbing trees, the hazards of which are not worth the risk. Machetes and "cane knives" are not pruning tools, do not leave a clean cut, and should not be used to prune plants managed for lei materials.

Pruning tools work best when they are well maintained. Keep the blades sharp, and replace worn anvils. Oil the metal parts to prevent rust and lubricate the movement, but wipe the oil from the blades before using them to prune.

People maintaining plants for production of lei materials or harvesting from the wild should be aware that pruning and harvesting tools can spread plant diseases. In many commercial situations where this is a significant hazard, tools are cleaned by dipping the blades in alcohol or flaming them before moving from one plant to the next. Also, well maintained tools produce cleaner cuts that heal rapidly, reducing the opportunity for disease organisms to enter.

Choose the right tool for the job, and keep it sharp and clean.

Pruning plants in the wild

Plants growing in natural conditions are not usually pruned except in the act of harvesting. In harvesting lei materials from these plants, we should have the same regard for their health and use the same care in pruning technique as though we were managing plants cultivated on our farm or in our yard for the same purpose. Harvest lightly—don't take too much from any one plant, and leave enough leaves and strong shoots to nourish it and provide for continued, new growth to support a future harvest.

Other pruning tips

- Prune hedge plants narrower at the top to allow sunlight to reach the bottom foliage. (Not all plants respond well to being managed as a hedge.)

- When pruning light branches, hold the branch below where the cut is to be made. Cut at a slight slant in the direction you want the new branch to grow.

- When thinning, remove the branch in such a way as to leave the shortest possible stub. But, never cut a branch flush to the trunk; begin it just outside any bark ridge in the crotch, and angle it slightly away from the trunk (see upper drawing, cut 3).

- When removing heavy limbs, use a 3-cut technique to avoid damage to a tree by splitting:
  - Cut 1 under the limb prevents the bark from tearing as the limb is removed.
  - Cut 2, above Cut 1 but further out, removes the limb.
  - Cut 3 removes the stub.
  Heavy limbs should be supported with a rope.

- Prune branches carefully in relation to the buds that will form new growth. Make cuts about ¼ inch above an out-facing bud or lateral branch.

- Choose the direction of new growth by selecting the bud to leave in place. When pruning plants with buds opposite each other on the branch, rub off the interior bud, or angle the cut to damage or remove the bud.

This information on pruning is adapted from CTAHR publication L-8, *Pruning Trees and Shrubs*, by Ginny Meade and David Hensley, with illustrations based on drawings by Cameron Rees, and from *Basic Pruning*, by Joe Freeman, chief horticulturist, Cypress Gardens, Florida, published by Ames Lawn and Garden Tools, Parkersberg WV (copyright 1999, Florida Cypress Gardens, Inc., used with permission).

Three steps to pruning a large branch.

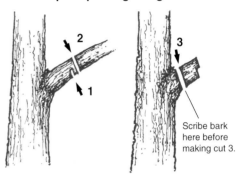

Scribe bark here before making cut 3.

Prune branches carefully in relation to the buds that will form new growth.

too close   too far   just right

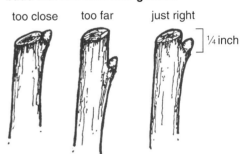

¼ inch

Choose the direction of new growth by selecting the bud to leave in place.

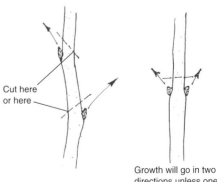

Cut here or here

Growth will go in two directions unless one bud is removed; preferably, the one toward the interior of the plant is removed.

Control of plant pests and diseases

The presence of pests (including weeds, insects, plant disease organisms, and animals) can reduce plant numbers, growth, yield, and quality. The current approach to control of plant pests involves much more than merely applying a pesticide when a problem occurs. There are numerous social, economic, and ecological reasons for minimizing the use of herbicides, fungicides, insecticides, and even fertilizers.

The approach to pest control called "integrated pest management," or IPM, attempts to be environmentally sound and avoid routine dependence on pesticides. The goal of an IPM program is to maintain pests below an economically damaging level in a way that is safest for the environment. IPM includes selection, when possible, of crops resistant to pests; regular observation of the crop's condition and monitoring of pests in the crop environment; and a suite of control alternatives including mechanical controls (e.g., pest-avoidance measures), biological controls (beneficial organisms), and, when necessary, judicious and timely use of chemical pest control materials. When selecting a pesticide, it is preferable to choose a "biorational" pesticide, which controls pests but does not harm beneficial organisms and does not accumulate in the environment. An example of a useful biological control for some situations is Chinese geese; if they are not attracted to your crop plant and can be contained, a dozen or so per acre can provide excellent control of weeds, mollusks, ants, beetles, and many other pests. The following paragraphs describe some key aspects of the IPM approach.

Keeping pests such as insects under control is important for healthy plant growth.

Monitor the crop and keep a log

Study your plants closely. Watch for any changes in their appearance. Look for leaf spots, yellowing, wilting, tip burning, and mushy or discolored roots—all symptoms of disease. Look for insects, mites, slugs, and other pests; for leaf or flower damage (including holes, bronzing, curling, yellowing, browning, mold); and for insect evidence (cast skins, fecal material, slime trails). IPM experts can suggest specific monitoring techniques to keep track of pest populations in a particular crop; an example is the use of yellow sticky cards. Observations at night with a flashlight may reveal the presence of mollusks, rose beetles, roaches, mice, and other vermin. Systematic observations and recordkeeping can allow comparison of pest populations with damage observed, enabling the grower to decide if and when a pesticide control is needed and, after application of a control measure, to determine whether it was effective. These observations can also be tuned to look at levels of beneficial organisms.

Good recordkeeping will aid in making sound production and business decisions.

Use of a logbook to keep records and record observations is a sign of a serious grower. It is impossible to remember all the details of even one crop over a period of months or years. Written notes can start from the day you purchase the first plants or seeds, and they should continue on a regular basis. Include all relevant information, such as when and where the plant was purchased and how much was paid, when it was planted, which medium was used, which fertilizer was applied (how much and how often), and the weather conditions. When monitoring the crop, record plant appearance, symptoms, type and number of pests found, control measures taken, fertilizers and pesticides (which, how much, when and how applied, and by whom). If you have people helping you, train them to make observations of the plants and keep records of their activities.

Prevent pest introductions by using clean propagation stock, media, and pots.

Monitoring plants closely and often will help keep them free of pests and diseases.

Start clean and stay clean

It is best to avoid plant diseases, weeds, and insects by trying to exclude them from your growing environment. Prevent pest introductions by using clean propagation stock, media, and pots. Practice sanitation by keeping hands, tools, equipment, and footwear clean and disinfested. Remove piles of debris, especially diseased plant materials, from the growing area, and sanitize the area before bringing in a new, clean plant to grow in these spots again. Control weeds, because they compete with the crop and can be hosts for insects and disease organisms affecting the crop. Treat the soil before planting if it is known to be infested with nematodes or diseases your crop is susceptible to. Set up a quarantine area for introductions to avoid placing new plant materials within or near your established plantings.

Know the crop and its pests

Learn as much as possible about the crops you plan to grow. Learn which diseases, insects, and other pests are problems and watch for signs and symptoms. Learn about a pest's life cycle, its alternate hosts, the environmental conditions that favor it, and the various biological, cultural, mechanical, and chemical control measures that might help reduce or eliminate it. Learn what level of the pest population is indicative that economic damage to the crop is soon to result.

Take action in a timely manner

Deciding how to control pests and when to apply pest control measures takes some trial-and-error practice. By keeping detailed records, you can improve your methods from year to year and respond faster because you have a point of reference—your notes. When a pest's population reaches an economic threshold, use an effective control measure. Do not procrastinate—under some conditions pest populations can skyrocket in a matter of days. For example, a small population of 100 immature, nonreproductive spurge, fern, or grass weeds left unchecked can result in over 100,000 weeds in less than a month under favorable conditions.

Tips on avoiding plant diseases

- Select plants that are disease resistant and adapted to your growing conditions.
- Use cuttings selected from disease-free mother plants, and plant them in a clean, soilless medium.
- Obtain certified seeds, or give seeds a preplanting treatment to avoid disease.
- Some microorganisms on the surface of seeds and cuttings can be eliminated by a hot-water soak at 118–120°F for 10–15 minutes (to avoid damage to your propagating material, test this method on a few seeds or plants before treating large numbers).
- Rotate plantings, when possible, with species that do not have the same pest problems.
- Control the environment to control diseases (for example, use drip irrigation to keep the foliage dry, and space or prune plants to provide for air movement through the crop).
- Apply overhead irrigation early in the day so that the leaves dry rapidly; this helps prevent spread of fungal and bacterial diseases and foliar nematodes.
- Immediately remove diseased plants, leaves, flowers, and other plant parts that have disease symptoms. Burn them, or discard them in plastic bags.
- Keep hands, footwear, clothing, tires, tools, and working surfaces clean.

Tips on controlling weeds

Weeds compete with crop plants for water, nutrients, space, and light. Weeds can be hosts of pests and diseases that can harm your crop. If weeds are not managed in a timely manner, their control can significantly add to the cost of production. Large weeds are harder to eliminate than small ones, and when weeds are not controlled before they have produced seeds, you will have another generation to contend with.

Mechanical methods of weed control include tilling, hoeing, and burning (long-handled torches are available for weed control). Also, some weed infestations can be avoided by eliminating the sources of their seeds. Chemical weed control methods include preemergence herbicides, which can be applied to the soil to prevent weed seeds from germinating, and postemergence herbicides, which are applied to the growing weeds (emerged weeds usually are easiest to control when they are small). A particular herbicide may only control particular types of weeds.

Mulches are useful for controlling weeds. Mulches work well in suppressing annual weeds but generally will not suppress perennials as effectively. Mulches can be classified as organic (bark, wood chips, compost, leaves), inorganic (crushed rock, crushed coral, gravel), and synthetic (black plastic, woven polyethylene fabric). Mulches limit light and physically block seedling growth.

As organic mulches break down into finer particles, the mulch layer becomes a good growing medium for weeds. Inorganic and synthetic mulches therefore usually provide better weed control than organic mulches. Although natural inorganic mulches such as gravel or stone are generally more expensive than organic mulches, they are stable over time and allow good water drainage and air flow.

Coarse-textured organic mulches such as wood chips can be applied up to 4 inches deep and provide long-term weed control. Fine-textured mulches pack more tightly and should be limited to a depth of 2 inches. They degrade more quickly and consequently provide weed suppression for a shorter period of time. The optimum mulch is relatively coarse-textured with a low water-holding capacity.

Perennial weeds often have sufficient root reserves to penetrate even thick mulch layers. Some annual weeds can grow through mulches or germinate on top of a mulch as it decomposes. Weeds with wind-borne seeds are most likely to become established in a mulch.

Pulling weeds and using woven weed cloth will help create a cleaner and healthier production environment.

Tips on managing insects

Like weeds, insect pests need to be eliminated before they can damage plants and salable products. Here are some tips:

- Look on the undersides of the leaves for insects and mites, their eggs, or signs of their feeding.
- Monitor pest populations using techniques such as surveys to count insects on certain plant parts, or insect traps.
- If you see no improvement after taking a control measure, try something different—a different type of control or a different pesticide or application method.
- Regularly till the soil to interrupt insect life stages that occur underground.
- Avoid seedling pests such as slugs by using transplants.
- Destroy heavily infested plants before the problem spreads.
- Get advice from IPM experts on strategies for maximizing the effects of biological controls.
- Investigate the availability and utility of cultural control methods such as resistant cultivars, pruning, crop rotation, trap crops, and field sanitation, and apply them when appropriate.

Yellow sticky cards are useful to monitor pest populations; at lower pest population levels, the cards can help keep certain pests under control.

- Use mechanical controls such as barriers and structures to exclude insects, suction devices, hosing down with water, pest traps, and hand destruction.
- Find out the best time of day or stage of the pest's growth cycle to apply treatments.
- Avoid repeated use of pesticides of the same chemical classification to maximize efficacy and avoid causing the pest to develop resistance.

Safe and effective use of pesticides

Use pesticides with care and respect for their toxicity. Make sure that the intended use is allowed by the pesticide label. Follow all the label directions, and observe all the precautions mentioned on it. Check with the Hawai'i Department of Agriculture, the CTAHR Cooperative Extension Service, or agrichemical suppliers for up-to-date information about suitable pesticides for the purpose required. Choose pesticides that have a minimal impact on beneficial insects and organisms and the environment.

Some pesticides require special training and licensing to purchase and apply them. Training programs for pesticide applicators are available through the Hawai'i Department of Agriculture and the Cooperative Extension Service. Even if you are not going to be applying restricted-use pesticides requiring certification, you should consider taking a training program if you will regularly apply pesticides. These programs will inform you about the health and environmental hazards you should be aware of to handle pesticides safely and responsibly. You will learn about the safety gear you should have, what to do in event of a spill, and how to store pesticides and dispose of their containers properly.

Anyone using a pesticide, even the "reduced risk" ones, should heed the following advice (not necessarily listed in the order of importance):
- Positively identify the pest to be controlled.
- Read the pesticide label and follow the directions.
- Purchase the smallest amount of pesticide that fills your immediate need, thus avoiding problems with storage or disposal of excess material.
- If you have leftover pesticides, store them in their original container in a secure, vented area where children, pets, and persons not familiar with pesticides cannot reach them.
- Never store pesticides near food or food preparation equipment.
- Do not mix or apply pesticides around children.
- Do not apply pesticides during hot or windy weather.
- Always wear protective clothing and any other safety equipment specified on the pesticide label.
- Shower and shampoo your hair after using pesticides.
- Wash work clothing separately from family laundry after applying pesticides.
- Do not smoke or eat while mixing or applying pesticides.
- Prepare pesticide solutions outside or in a well ventilated area.
- Keep written records of pesticide use in your grower's log.
- Use the application rate given on the label to ensure the desired effect while minimizing the possibility that pests will survive and develop resistance.
- Rotate pesticides and use chemicals from different chemical classes.
- Match the chemical and application timing with the most susceptible life stages of the pests.
- Use separate sprayers for herbicides and other pesticides, and clean the equipment as soon as you finish applications.
- Never apply pesticides if it is raining or rain is expected.

Use pesticides with care and respect for their toxicity.

Keeping agricultural chemicals in a labeled, locked, waterproof area is important to worksite safety.

Harvesting and postharvest handling of lei materials

Production of quality lei materials requires that great care be taken in the harvesting and postharvest stages of storage, packing, and transport of the product. The best time of day for harvesting varies among plant species. Often the best time to harvest is in the morning when the plants are still fully hydrated but surface moisture on the plant has dried. The plant part to be harvested should be at the right stage of maturity for the intended use. Damaged, diseased, or dying material should be separated from the harvested product and discarded.

The harvested material should be moved to and stored in the appropriate temperature and humidity conditions as soon as possible. It should not be left where it will be heated in the sun or dried in the wind. A storage temperature of 42–45°F is suitable for most tropical lei materials, while cooler conditions, down to 33°F, are best for temperate species, such as carnation, gypsophylla, and rose.

Beware of packing mixtures of foliage, flowers, and fruits together. Some plant materials give off ethylene gas, which causes accelerated maturation of plant materials and can lead to premature spoilage and reduction of the useful life of the product.

Production of quality lei materials requires that great care be taken in their harvesting and handling.

Ideas on establishing a community or school lei flower garden can be found in the National Tropical Botanical Garden's, Growing an Education Garden at Your School. *It provides case studies on successful school gardens and advice on how to plan, plant, and maintain one.*

Section 4

One of the first steps in making the transition into small-business ownership is to make an honest assessment of yourself.

The Business of Lei Plant and Materials Production

One of the reasons for this book is to encourage alternatives to forest gathering of lei materials, because overharvesting can create long-term negative impacts on natural plant stocks and the environment. Small-scale, backyard growing of lei plants for personal use can be part of the solution, but this contribution is limited. A larger source of lei materials can be from commercial horticultural businesses—nurseries and farms—engaged in propagating lei plants and growing and harvesting lei flowers and greenery. This section is for this group of grower-entrepreneurs.

If you start a small commercial business to produce lei plant materials, you will need to know how to grow plant materials. Your interest and skill in growing plants may be exactly why you think such a business is suited to you. But a successful hobby does not always become a successful business. A business exists to serve customers, not to serve the owner. Small-business owners often feel that the business controls them, instead of them controlling the business.

One of the first steps in making the transition into small-business ownership is to make an honest assessment of yourself. Going into business for yourself can be fun and scary, rewarding or unsatisfying, profitable or unprofitable, exhilarating and exhausting. The effort that starting a small business requires is not for everyone. Before you jump into anything, take a look at yourself and your life. Depending on the size of operation, you may need to fit in 12–16-hour workdays and face constant demands for "cash in." You will also have to do your business planning homework, put your customers first, strive to innovate at all times, and be ready for the unexpected.

Deciding if the lei materials production business is right for you

The following questions can help you decide if you are ready to commit to your dream of being a small-business owner:
- Do you have clear business goals?
- Have you had any experience running a business?
- Have you had any experience running a *plant production* business?
- Are you willing to gamble your savings on this venture?
- Do you have the full backing of your significant other?
- Do you have a secondary source of income in your household?
- Do you have a strong desire to make money?

- Do you know how to set up and operate a record-keeping system?
- Do you have an understanding of legal matters such as
  - joint and several guarantees
  - personal guarantees
  - city ordinances and zoning restrictions
  - sole proprietorship, partnership, and incorporation
  - contracts and legal obligations
  - tax calculation, withholding, and filing?
- Do you like dealing with people?
- Do you understand what it takes to make people satisfied with their purchases?
- Can you stand up to adversity and keep smiling?
- Are you a life-long learner?
- Can you quickly adapt to changing conditions in the marketplace?

(adapted from Frederick Rice's *Starting a Home-Based Business*)

If your answers to these questions seem to indicate that starting a plant materials business would be a little challenging for you, don't be discouraged. You can learn new skills and get more experience. You could find a partner or employees who have skills to complement yours. Or, maybe it is time to set your sights to another vision of the future. Remember that having a successful life is most important. If having a business in your life will not make it more successful, then look elsewhere for success.

Matching your vision to reality

Now, turn your attention to your vision for your business. It is probably safe to assume that people will continue wanting to buy plant materials. Think about what type of goods or services your business could provide to meet people's needs and make a profit over a period of 20–30 years. Orient your thinking toward your current and potential customers to ensure that you can stay ahead of the competition. Remember that your customers may change over time, and you will want to change with them because your competition will. This clarity of purpose is needed to keep you on track.

By breaking down this vision into a set of five-year goals or milestones, you can begin to see what the near future holds in store for your business. Each five-year goal can then be broken down into one-year objectives that serve as the basis for your yearly plans of action. Your vision and your goals help you re-focus your efforts should you ever get away from your core purpose. Remember, the key components that should appear in your vision, goals, and objectives are satisfying the customer, staying ahead of your competition, and staying profitable. Your activities as you strive to meet each milestone will include

- researching consumer tastes and preferences, researching products and services, and determining target markets in which customers' needs can be met with the products available
- researching and implementing ways to keep costs down
- juggling several activities at once
- managing and leading employees
- selling products and pleasing customers
- controlling the financial affairs of the business and production operations.

By breaking down your vision into a set of five-year goals or milestones, you can begin to see what the near future holds in store for your business.

These may seem like a lot to manage, but without them most businesses fail. The predictable reasons for business failure include

- lack of a management system
- lack of vision and purpose by the owners
- lack of financial planning and review
- over-dependence on specific individuals in the business
- poor market segmentation and strategy
- failure to establish and repeatedly communicate company goals
- unaffordability of your product
- competition, or lack of market knowledge
- inadequate capitalization
- absence of a standardized quality-control program
- owners concentrating on technical rather than strategic tasks.

(modified from Gerber Business Development Corporation, 1994)

According to the U.S. Small Business Administration, four out of five small businesses fail within five years because of poor management and lack of knowledge about the product or service. Risk is greater in the nursery business than in many others because plants are alive and are subject to a large list of potential problems. One disease outbreak or storm can wipe out an entire operation. Plant materials damaged during transportation will cost you money and could cause you to lose a good customer.

Starting a business and making it a success require a multitude of business management skills. If you've decided that you have what it takes, congratulations on making the commitment! You are now ready to start putting your business together.

Risk is greater in the nursery business than in many others because plants are alive and are subject to a large list of potential problems.

Starting out

One way of starting a new business is to buy someone else's "old" business. The advantages of this option include having a complete production/marketing system with permits, equipment, buildings and plant stock, suppliers, and an existing customer base. The downside of purchasing someone else's business is that you are taking over someone's project and you may be taking over challenges that you know nothing about. You may also be taking over headaches that are not revealed before the sale.

Lacking an opportunity to buy an existing business, you will need to build your business from the ground up. This takes a lot of effort, but you can have more control over the outcome, and it may be more rewarding in the long run. For a look at these alternatives in greater detail, read the appendix, *Buying or Building?*, at the end of this section.

Making your business plan a roadmap to success

Success comes from planning...and a lot of hard work; no escape from these essentials is possible. Writing a business plan is jokingly referred to as "worse than going to the dentist," but it does provide you with a general outline for your business. Like going to the dentist, you will live through it and be better for the experience. Your business plan does not need to be fancy, but it does need to be written down. The physical process of writing helps you better conceptualize your plans and allows you to get past the "thinking about it" stage. It also forces you to "test drive" your dreams and ideas before you begin spending money. For instance, will you be growing and selling just lei flowers or sewing lei as well? Even if you are hiring someone to help you with the plan, get actively engaged in the writing so that you "own" the plan. Ultimately, regardless of who writes the plan, you are the one that needs to put it into action and take full responsibility for its success or failure.

The important questions to ask

A thorough analysis of your market is needed *before* you seriously begin producing crops or stocking a retail inventory. Thinking the project out in advance is less expensive than spending the money and learning the hard way from experience. Be sure to consider the following questions when thinking about going into business, and take the time to write out your answers.

- Who will buy the plants or plant materials, and exactly what will they buy? Think of potential consumers: lei makers and lei shops, home gardeners, visitor-greeters and tour companies, *hula hālau*, retail florists, garden center operators, landscapers, interior decorators, supermarkets, institutions, municipalities, and others.
- What are the costs of producing each plant you plan to raise?
- Will you be selling retail, wholesale, or both?
- Will you sell only what you grow, or do you plan to purchase additional products for resale?
- Are there existing businesses available to buy, or must you start from scratch?
- If you are buying an existing business, what market share does it have now, who are the customers, how many are you likely to keep as the new owner, and are they the customers you want?
- If starting from scratch, what are the possible sites for your business? What is the potential market area?
- How many customers do you think you can generate, and how will you do it?
- How many customers do you want, and will you be able to fill all their requirements for your products?
- What do your potential customers *really* want? Have you asked them directly?
- How are you going to let your customers know (advertise) what you have?
- What services, in addition to products, should you provide to your customers?
- Who is your competition, and what do you think you can do better than they? Be specific. Count your competitors and describe them; consider their successes and their weaknesses in detail.
- What restrictions do you face, such as zoning and sign ordinances, taxes, costs of doing business, and limits on resources such as water, soil quality, drainage, and parking space?
- How is the transportation infrastructure, and are markets easily accessible?
- Is there a prevailing local community atmosphere or attitude that might support

Success comes from planning...and a lot of hard work; no escape from these essentials is possible.

the development of your type of business? Is it wanted? Is it needed? Is it encouraged?

- Do the capital requirements for your business match your cash resources? You will probably need at least 50 percent of the start-up costs as personal equity, maybe more. The rest can be borrowed in certain categories when the lender is sure you are a good risk: namely, you have experience, you have collateral, and you have done your homework in terms of what dollar amount you need, what it will cost you to produce each product, and what you expect your revenue stream to be.
- What sorts of regulations must you follow, such as licensing, collection of sales tax, pest control, etc.?
- How much business must you generate to properly support your household? (This is where business, personal, and family goals interconnect.)
- What does it take to grow the plants you are going to sell? Or, what cultural systems and technology do you plan to employ in your operation?
- Who will supply you with the materials and equipment you need to operate?
- Who will provide the labor, and how much do you need? What is the labor pool like in the market area? What is the wage and benefit scale in the area? What sort of training do you have to provide to get workers operating at peak efficiency?

These are tough questions, and they should be thoughtfully considered and answered before you make a big investment. The more "facts" you have, the more informed you can be when you make your decision about going into the plant production business. The answers to these questions are the foundation of a business plan. For more complete guidance on business plans, we recommend that you consult CTAHR's *This Hawaii Product Went to Market*. Its Chapter 6 has a more thorough discussion of business plans and recommends additional books and software to help you get started on the right foot.

For more complete guidance on business plans, consult CTAHR's This Hawaii Product Went to Market.

Finding people who will purchase your lei materials

Satisfying the client's wants and needs is what business is all about. If people do not want or need your lei materials, or if they cannot afford them, then you will not succeed. You prove this everyday with your purchasing practices!

To be successful, you need to identify the particular plants a segment of the population wants to buy and learn how much they are willing to pay for them. If they are willing to pay more than it costs you to produce and deliver, then you can start to think about the possibility of entering the business. Cost is not the only factor when people decide how much they will pay. For example, it may cost you 50¢ to grow a lei plant that buyers will buy only at 35¢; at the bloom level, if it costs you 4¢ to grow a blossom and your buyer is willing to pay only 3¢, then there is a mismatch in supply and demand. At this point you can either lose money, convince people to pay more, grow another more profitable plant, find a way to lower your production cost, or choose another business to pursue.

How Hawai'i plant materials go to market

A commercial plant product can take many paths from the farm, shadehouse, greenhouse, or home to the consumer, as illustrated here. Certainly, gathering in the "wild" is a source of product, but we are encouraging those who desire plant materials to "grow their own" or buy from other sources that are harvesting from renewable stocks, such as a commercial nursery. You have many options to take, but the longer the marketing chain, the lower the price you can typically expect to receive, because a long chain means that your product has to pass through many hands. All who help get the lei materials into the consumer's hands need to be paid for their efforts.

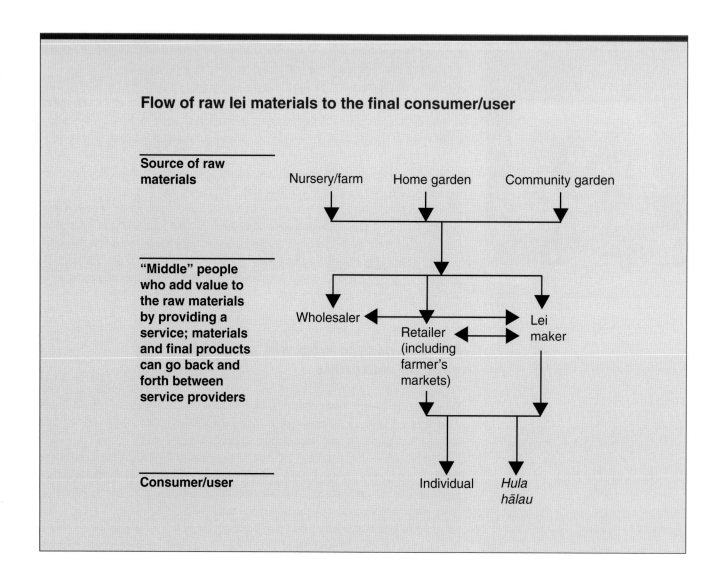

Flow of raw lei materials to the final consumer/user

Source of raw materials: Nursery/farm, Home garden, Community garden

"Middle" people who add value to the raw materials by providing a service; materials and final products can go back and forth between service providers: Wholesaler, Retailer (including farmer's markets), Lei maker

Consumer/user: Individual, *Hula hālau*

The key to a successful business is to meet ongoing demand and generate additional demand in between.

The final market for lei materials can take many forms.

The market for lei drives the demand for raw materials

The most recognized occasions for giving lei include (in generally descending order from the most popular giving days):

Occasion	Day or month (on or about)
Graduations	May, June, December
May Day	May 1
St. Valentine's Day	February 14
State-wide celebrations, such as Aloha Week	Late August–late October
Merry Monarch Festival	April
King Kamehameha Hula Competition	June
Mother's Day	Mid-May
Secretary's Day/Week	Late April
Boss' Day/Week	Mid-October
Sweetest Day	Mid-October
Father's Day	Mid-June
Memorial Day	Late May
Veterans Day	November
Easter	March/April
Christmas	December 25
New Years	January 1

In Hawai'i, most any day is a good day to give or receive a lei. The key to a successful business is to meet this ongoing demand and generate additional demand in between. Other occasions for giving include

- birthdays
- anniversaries
- weddings
- welcoming visitors
- going-away, farewell
- retirements
- conventions
- competitions (marathons, canoe races)
- cultural events (theatre, concerts, performances)
- speakers at meetings.

Whatever the occasion, plant materials are required unless a lei that is not plant-based is given. Non-plant materials include candy, silk, paper, paper money, ribbons, plastic mesh, and so forth.

Each of the Hawaiian Islands has a lei they call their own. These theme lei are not generally the most popular lei sold on a particular island, but they are often used in big events and ceremonies, such as the Aloha Festivals, to indicate the origin of a group of participants.

Official lei materials of the islands of Hawai'i

Island	Lei or plant color	Plant
Hawai'i	red	*lehua*
Kaho'olawe	silver gray	*hinahina*
Kaua'i	violet	*mokihana*
Lāna'i	orange	*kauna'oa*
Maui	pink	*lokelani*
Moloka'i	silver green	*kukui*
Ni'ihau	white	*pūpū* Ni'ihau (sea shells, not a plant)
O'ahu	yellow	*'ilima*

The demand for lei and lei materials

A state-wide study of the demand for the plants, plant materials, or finished lei types described in this book has never been done. An article in *Pacific Business News* (July 6, 2001) provided a general overview of the marketplace on Oahu (see table, page 235). The authors of the article sent out hundreds of surveys to lei vendors and sellers, and the table illustrates their findings.

More comprehensive information on both lei sales and the production of plant materials for lei is desirable but is likely to remain unavailable because the market for the seven reported lei flowers or flower groups was only $3,680,000 in 2000 (see table, page 237). This makes it a relatively small agricultural product line with only a few dozen growers reporting sales. Helping further to create a data shortfall, many lei material sales go unreported because the growers or harvesters are not considered "commercial" by the national and Hawai'i agricultural statistics services. To be considered commercial, a grower must generate more than $10,000 in total sales per year. Also, some growers simply do not report sales. Thus there is no solid set of public data from which to make well informed business decisions. As an entrepreneur, you will need to survey potential clients and build relationships to decide if this is a sound business opportunity for you.

A variety of materials makes a lei burst with color and excitement.

Potential markets

In Hawai'i there are several different markets for lei materials, lei plants, and finished, strung lei. Each of these "products" can have different buyers. The buying differences can be due to location (Mainland vs. Asia vs. Hawai'i), type of customer (plant wholesalers vs. retail florists) or needs (*hula hālau* vs. funeral homes). Following are some of the markets found in Hawai'i and their distinguishing characteristics.

Wholesale florists

Wholesale florists provide a valuable service to many small producers. They find a customer for you so you can concentrate on production. They often re-pack your product, store it, and provide transportation. This service is not free. The cost of these services to you is the difference between what a retail florist or final consumer would pay you and what the wholesaler pays you. Wholesale and retail florists may not to pay you the day you deliver. Often, you must extend them credit as a business courtesy.

In Hawai'i there are several different markets for lei materials, lei plants, and finished, strung lei.

Flower lei sold in the Oʻahu market, 2001 (Ranked by units sold annually)

Rank	Name of flower	Most popular use	Retail price range ($) Low	High	Prominent feature	Availability
1	Dendrobium, single	Special occasions	3.00	10.00	Life	All year
2	Micronesian ginger	Holidays, greetings	7.50	30.00	Fragrance	May–Oct.
3	Pīkake, strand	Weddings, greetings, graduations	2.00	7.50	Fragrance	Feb.–Oct.
4	Tuberose, single	Weddings, greetings, departures	3.00	8.00	Fragrance	All year
5	Maile	Weddings, graduations	18.00	35.00	Tradition	All year*
6	Orchid, specialty	Special occasions	15.00	35.00	Appearance	All year
7	Ginger, single	Special occasions	3.00	10.00	Fragrance	May–Oct.
8	Cigar	Holidays, festivals	15.00	22.50	Appearance	Feb.–Oct.
9	Pakalana, strand	Weddings, popular for any occasion	3.00	7.00	Fragrance	April–July
10	Tuberose, double	Weddings, greetings, departures	10.00	25.00	Fragrance	All year
11	Pua kenikeni, strand	Greetings	6.00	15.50	Fragrance	April–July
12	Kukui nut	Fashion accessory, festivals	9.00	23.00	Life	All year
13	Plumeria	School programs, greetings, departures	3.00	10.00	Price	Feb.–Oct.
14	Ti / heʻe	Weddings	4.00	10.00	Life	Summer
15	Carnation, single	Weddings, greetings, political rallies	4.00	8.00	Color	All year
16	Crown flower, strand	Weddings	3.00	5.00	Price	Feb.–Oct.
17	Dendrobium, double	Special occasions	10.00	15.00	Life	All year
18	Pīkake, rope	Weddings	15.00	30.00	Fragrance	Feb.–Oct.
19	Ginger, double	Special occasions	8.00	17.00	Fragrance	May–Oct.
20	Haku	Weddings, greetings, graduations, luau	15.00	25.00	Appearance	All year
21	ʻOhai aliʻi	Weddings	8.00	12.50	Appearance	June–Aug.
22	Orchid / carnation	Special occasions	5.00	10.00	Color	All year
23	Tuberose / carnation	Special occasions	5.00	10.00	Price	All year
24	Carnation mix	Special occasions	3.50	7.00	Price	All year
25	ʻIlima, strand	Weddings, greetings, departures	8.00	15.00	Color	March–July
26	Plumeria mix	Greetings, departures	5.00	10.00	Price	Feb.–Oct.
27	Tuberose / orchid	Special occasions	5.00	15.00	Fragrance	All year

Source: Natalie Watanabe and Brian Fujita, "Know your lei: Florists turn occasions into good business." *Pacific Business News*, July 6, 2001, pp. 21–22; modified slightly; used with permission.
*Subject to weather.

Retail florists

Many producers choose to market a greater share of their products to retail florists. You should receive a higher price when going retail, rather than wholesale, but expect to have higher costs as well. Most retail florists will not buy all of your production, so you must find additional clients, and that can take time. In addition, most retail florists do not have the capacity to store much product, so you may need to deliver more frequently. This is just one example of the higher costs you may incur. However, if you are an effective and efficient marketer, retail florists may be a viable and profitable outlet for your lei materials.

Hula hālau

Hula groups have very special needs compared to other market outlets. Because of the cultural and historical significance of the *hula, hula hālau* demand greater quantities and a greater variety of "native" plants. On the other hand, the demand for nursery products and flowers by other market outlets is primarily for plants that are not "native" to Hawaii, if the HASS data on page 237 are any indication.

In addition to different plants, a *hālau* may also demand a more finished product, such as a head lei (*lei po'o*). Many *hālau* will also require lei and other arrangements that meet their specific needs. Their seasonal demand for products is also different. Most wholesale and retail florists have their greatest demand during holidays and special occasions—Valentine's Day, for example. With a *hālau*, the demand is more centered around a particular performance, such as during the annual Merry Monarch Festival held in Hilo in April or the King Kamehameha Hula Competition held in June in Honolulu.

Hula groups have very special needs compared to other market outlets.

Direct to the final consumer

Selling directly to consumers is made possible by operating your own retail outlet or by selling with a toll-free number or over the Internet. Some of the advantages of selling your plants from your own retail operation include

- supplying the highest quality products direct to customers—you have greater control over the quality of products supplied to the customer
- making cash sales (including credit card purchases) with immediate payment rather than the delayed payments typical in wholesale or florist markets
- interacting with your customers and gaining valuable feedback on how to improve your business
- having more control over prices within the limits of what the market will bear
- selling additional non-plant products, such as food and gift items.

Many buyers prefer smaller plants.

With the advent of overnight mail deliveries and marketing via toll-free numbers or over the Internet, producers of all sorts of products are marketing direct to the final consumer. In such a case, you would be providing all of the marketing functions. And, as is always the case, the more marketing functions you perform, the higher your cost of production will be. The development and maintenance of a Web site, or the ability to take payment by credit card number over the Internet or phone, are typical, additional marketing costs. You need to get a price for your lei or lei materials that covers these as well as your other costs.

Marketing statistics on sales of lei flowers (by major sellers*), state of Hawai'i, 1996–2000

Flower	Year	Farms having sales**	Quantity sold	$ Value of sales	$ Value per unit	$ Value per 100-unit bag
Carnation	1996	11	10,000,000	538,000	0.054	5.38
(blooms)	1997	7	7,500,000	410,000	0.055	5.47
	1998	9	6,800,000	448,000	0.066	6.59
	1999	7	5,600,000	397,000	0.071	7.09
	2000	6	5,300,000	372,000	0.070	7.02
Dendrobium	1996	33	24,700,000	740,000	0.030	3.00
(blooms)	1997	35	24,800,000	725,000	0.029	2.92
	1998	28	28,900,000	855,000	0.030	2.96
	1999	27	21,700,000	673,000	0.031	3.10
	2000	26	19,800,000	596,000	0.030	3.01
Pīkake	1996	4	21,700	86,000	3.96	
(strands)	1997	***	***	***	***	
	1998	5	55,600	128,000	2.30	
	1999	7	82,500	222,000	2.69	
	2000	8	77,800	270,000	3.47	
Plumeria	1996	12	29,900,000	717,000	0.024	2.40
(blooms)	1997	11	31,800,000	833,000	0.026	2.62
	1998	9	23,800,000	601,000	0.025	2.53
	1999	10	45,000,000	931,000	0.021	2.07
	2000	12	25,700,000	627,000	0.024	2.44
Tuberose	1996	7	***	***		
(blooms)	1997	4	***	***		
	1998	6	19,500,000	912,000	0.047	4.68
	1999	6	20,400,000	959,000	0.047	4.70
	2000	7	22,100,000	987,000	0.045	4.47
Vanda,	1996	12	22,200,000	627,000	0.028	2.82
Miss Joaquim	1997	9	22,300,000	657,000	0.029	2.95
(blooms)	1998	9	10,900,000	292,000	0.027	2.68
	1999	7	11,300,000	396,000	0.035	3.50
	2000	7	13,900,000	503,000	0.036	3.62
Other	1996	NA	NA	1,235,000	NA	
	1997	NA	NA	1,188,000	NA	
	1998	NA	NA	249,000	NA	
	1999	NA	NA	473,000	NA	
	2000	NA	NA	325,000	NA	

Source: Hawai'i Agricultural Statistics Service
NA = Not available
*   Includes only producers having total sales of $10,000 or more.
** Number for each individual flower item is the count of those farms having sales of that item during each year.
*** Included with "Other" to avoid disclosure of individual operations.

A final word about marketing to your potential customers

Many producers of agricultural products make the mistake of thinking they can do their own marketing and make more money. However, most new businesses lack the marketing savvy to market their products efficiently. Also, most people greatly underestimate the time and money required to market and transport a product to a buyer. This cost may be greater than the cost of producing the product itself unless you have a large operation or resell the products of numerous small-scale growers. On average, for every dollar spent on food in the USA approximately 80 cents goes to cover marketing and distribution costs.

Overall, new growers are likely to do better by starting with high-quality products sold to florists and garden centers, rather than trying to sell to low-margin outlets or chain stores. As your business skills and production capacity grow, you are more likely to be able to keep your costs low enough to make a profit in the low-margin markets.

Making your first sale

Once you have identified your customers and your competition, you need a strategy for ensuring the customers buy from you and not from your competitors. A professional attitude is very important when making a first sale to a customer. Customers need to be convinced that you, as a new supplier, are worth taking a risk on, because they likely already have numerous sources of supply. Some tips on establishing your professional image and business's credibility include the following.

Business cards and Rolodex® cards

Everyone is busy. A business card implies that you are professional and gives them something to remember you by. Some growers have also developed low-cost brochures with pictures of their nursery and their product. These can be very cost-effective. In addition, Rolodex cards can provide the buyer with a conveniently accessible tool for quickly contacting you.

Fax and answering machines

Telephone answering and fax machines will ensure that you don't miss an order. If you are the one trying to make a sale, no one should have to call you back. You should call them.

Web site and e-mail

More and more these days, if your business does not have a Web presence then you are missing out on sales opportunities. Similarly, if you don't have e-mail, you are missing a chance to communicate with customers cheaply and efficiently. Like phone calls, return e-mails promptly.

Professional invoices

Professionally designed invoice forms are more convenient for both you and your customers and are preferred to loose slips of paper. Invoices will also simplify your bookkeeping tasks and be useful at tax time. Computer software is available to ease and enhance the use of invoices.

A professional attitude is very important when making a first sale to a customer.

Samples

Examples of your materials will help customers check quality. You may enhance their first impression of you by bringing nicely packaged samples with you to your first meeting.

Production records and schedules

Many customers like to know the quantity and types of plant materials you will be producing throughout the year. Typically these will correspond to holiday schedules. For a new grower, meeting these schedules may be difficult. Coping with these demands is aided by keeping accurate records of production from the inception of your business.

Flexibility

Not all customers will be a perfect match for you with respect to the types of materials needed, delivery schedules, ability to pay in a timely manner, and the like. However, you should demonstrate a willingness to work with a buyer and consider their suggestions and business conditions. You should look for this flexibility in buyers as well.

Costing and pricing your production

Many producers are less interested in costing than in production.

Developing cost-of-production information for each type of plant covered in this book would require much time and research and, therefore, is beyond our scope. Also, data used in a cost-of-production analysis vary because production practices differ from grower to grower. The process of "costing" is similar for most producers, but some are more experienced and interested in the process than others.

Many producers are less interested in costing than in production. However, you must be able to estimate your cost of production so you can predict profits. If you do not make a profit, you will not have a business for long. Your cost of production tells you the lowest price at which you can sell your product and pay all your expenses, including paying yourself for the time and money you put into the business.

Starting a lei material business can require a medium to large up-front investment in equipment, buildings, vehicles, and so forth. It can take three to five years or more to pay off the cost of the initial investments. This means you may not be making any profit for years and perhaps not even be able to pay yourself what you are worth. This situation is evident in the following examples. We have purposely chosen examples that have reasonably large investments to illustrate this point. You do not have to invest so much in your operation, but you should realize the financial burden involved if you do. How your operation is organized from the very beginning will affect how soon you will be able to pay down the cost of business investments and how soon you will be able to generate profits. Thus, you typically will need to have at least five years of capital available to you to even consider any type of medium to large investment.

Know your cost types

Production costs can generally be broken down into four categories.

Cash or variable or out-of-pocket costs
The direct costs for production are called variable costs. Pots, media, fertilizer, seeds, plants, and labor to grow the plants are examples. These costs change as the amount you produce changes, and if you produce nothing, these costs are zero.

Fixed or overhead costs
The costs that stay the same, no matter how much you produce, are called fixed or overhead costs. They include rent or mortgage payments, insurance, loans, a percentage of equipment costs, and utility connections. Your management labor is also included here. Even if you produce nothing, you will still have to pay these costs, including paying yourself something to cover your living costs.

Depreciation
The cost of structures, furnishings, and machinery that wear out over a period of time is called depreciation. These are non-cash costs, because you have already paid for the shadehouse, benches, or vehicle. But wear and tear on these assets should still be accounted for in determining the actual cost of production. The passage of time will also affect the value of these items. For example, buildings need repair as time passes, and if you don't use and maintain them they might wear out even faster.

A shadehouse is a necessity for certain plants to provide protection from the sun.

Losses
This is the amount or percentage of the crop that for some reason or another cannot be sold. Losses may occur any time during the production or marketing process. You may also have losses from customers who buy on credit and then do not pay you. Therefore, especially in the following annual crop scenario, you need to account for some level of loss in your cost-of-production calculation.

More on costs
Some types of costs will increase as you produce more (variable costs), while others, such as overhead or fixed costs, are pegged to the passage of time. Even if a cost is not related to time, if you cannot immediately pay the whole cost with revenues, then you will have to borrow money or use your personal funds until sufficient revenues are available. The longer you use borrowed money or your own funds, the more interest you will owe to the bank or to yourself. This means the cost is now related to time. If you have to wait for more than one year before you can pay the bank or yourself back, then cost of production usually accounts for the cost of waiting through interest payments.

Understanding how to calculate cost of production: two examples

This book includes annual and perennial plants. The production process differs for these two types of plants, and the costing process must reflect these differences. For example, the production of an annual would take several weeks, and then it lives only weeks or months after that. A perennial tree for lei flower production, in contrast, can take three or more years to reach full production and will remain in full production for many years. In both cases, you will need to

- calculate costs of production for each product (or service) before you start a new business or add a new product to your line; gather information from observation, by reading trade publications and production manuals, by talking to public and private agricultural advisors, and by making phone calls or visits to input suppliers
- account for all the time and resources invested in a plant (or service), whether it took only a few weeks or many years; if you do not account accurately and completely for all costs, your selling price will be too low and you will not make enough money to stay in business.

In the following two examples of calculating cost of production, one (an annual) is for growth and sales within one year, and the other (a perennial) is for growth—and eventually sales—taking more than one year. *These examples are strictly illustrations of the costing process and do not necessarily represent an actual farm, accurate input costs, optimal use amounts, realistic farmgate prices, or the best plants to grow for lei.* The cost, revenue, and yield numbers are close approximations given a set of circumstances, but you should use only your own numbers and cost categories when doing cost estimations. To illustrate the wide variability in how a business is established and capitalized, the first example has more and higher fixed costs than the second. Again, your operational costs may vary.

Example 1. Cost of production for an annual plant

Annual plants, those that live a year or less, have a different cost structure than do perennials, those that live longer than a year. In this book, lei plants such as carnation, baby's breath, dusty miller, pansy, aster, joy weed, kalanchoe, corn flower, marigold, and others would be treated similarly, but not identically, when it came to calculating cost of production. Nonetheless, the example provided below illustrates the concepts behind "costing out" an annual plant. Note that in Hawai'i some annuals can live longer than a year, but usually they would not be in a nursery production situation that long.

Angel's Annuals and Other Pleasant Plants is a new nursery business on 5 acres of land (5 x 43,560 sq ft = 217,800 sq ft). To start her business, Angel uses $100,000 of her own money and takes out a 15-year loan for $275,000 to finance equipment, buildings, benches, irrigation, weed mat, and many production supplies for her multicrop operation. Fortunately, Angel has assets that can be used as collateral for the substantial loan. Angel estimates that she will do much of the work on the farm herself and desires an annual salary (and some profit) of $65,000. She may realize that in the first few years, but this goal may not be reached fully. Note that about $9,000 of the anticipated $65,000 is what Angel is paying herself for the loan of her $100,000 at 9 percent interest.

Angel plans to plant many flower species, and she also has buildings and roadways on her property that are needed for business but do not generate revenues directly. Angel is aware that a commercial plant nursery requires land to be set aside for both non-production uses as well as for production uses. Non-production space includes land allocated for buildings (storage, processing, cooling, etc.) and parking. There is no set formula for this allocation, but the cost of this land allocation and the infrastructure on the land must be covered by plant sales in the fixed cost factor.

Potting media is just one of the costs to be factored into a cost-of-production analysis.

Within the actual plant production area, only about 65 percent is available for plant production, because roads, paths, and walkways require about 35 percent of the area.

Angel does a cost of production study so that she can compare what annual plant buyers are willing to pay for a particular species (wholesale or retail price) to what it might cost her to produce them (farmgate price or cost). Some of her buyers will immediately pick all the flowers off the plant for use in a lei, and others will plant the annual in a garden and pick what they need from the plant over a short period of time. She does this calculation, hopefully, on her business plan *before* she gets her bank loan or even begins planting. That way, if it costs her more to grow the flower than she can sell them for, she will have time to make some alternative plans about flower and input choice. *Again, while the costs used in this example are considered somewhat realistic for a typical annual, they should not be taken as exact, because a number of production assumptions have been made. Therefore, you will need to do your own cost research that reflects your location and your exact production situation.*

To calculate the farmgate price for the annual under study, Angel starts by gathering all the facts about the operation, along with projected costs for inputs and utilities. (If she is doing this study after a production cycle, so that she can learn what she can do better to optimize her operation and drive down her costs, she would use numbers from her receipts for purchased inputs and invoices for sales in the calculations.) Here is what she has found out about her operation, including some details about overhead and variable costs that are not covered in the spreadsheet on page 245.

- the entire operation including buildings, roadways, and production areas is 5 acres, or 217,800 sq ft.

Overhead or fixed details for entire property
- annual land lease or mortgage including property taxes: $320/acre/month or $19,200/year for 5 acres
- loan: $270,000, 9 percent interest for 15 years (monthly payment of $2,789)
- equipment (new and used): $65,000; includes light truck ($20,000), 200-gallon sprayer ($15,000), delivery van ($15,000), potting and soil mixing machine ($15,000), and straight-line deprecation for 10 years
- buildings: $100,000; includes small new office, garage, parking and storage, and a straight-line deprecation for 20 years
- benches, irrigation, and weed mat: $114,000, with a straight-line deprecation for 10 years.

Variable details
- annual grown from plugs grown out in 4-inch pots in 12 weeks on 10,000 sq ft of benches above mat-covered ground
- marketing and delivery costs have materials, transportation, and labor included.

A covered delivery truck can protect lei plants and materials during transport.

Angel knows that this particular annual takes about 12 weeks to grow from a plug to a salable product, although the time could be shortened on her end (and her costs, and perhaps profits, lessened as a result) if customers wanted to grow out the plants themselves. The costs and relevant calculations are presented in the table. A competitor might have more or less costs or cost categories. Generally, the table addresses overhead or fixed costs, those that do not change with a change in output, and variable costs, those that go up or down depending on how many plants are grown.

In Step 1, all annual overhead or fixed costs for the entire farm are collected, and then that sum is divided by the sq ft of the operation, 217,800, and then again by the number of weeks in a year, 52, to arrive at an overhead or fixed cost per sq ft per week. This sq ft cost must be covered by revenues from the operation, sales of flowers or other products, for Angel to be successful.

In Step 2, Angel isolates the input or variable costs for the 10,000 sq ft of annual production. In doing so, she may have to make some guesses about exactly how much utility, water, or other costs are attributable to this flower crop, since she is growing other plants, but educated guesses, based on legwork, are better than not putting any cost into the calculation. After summing all costs and dividing the sum by the actual amount of space she is using for this plant, 10,000 sq ft, she arrives at a total variable cost per sq ft. All variable costs must also be covered by revenues from plant sales. Ultimately, if Angel cannot pay her suppliers for inputs such as media, fuel, etc., she will go out of business.

In Step 3, Angel accounts for the cost of the walkways and cartways that allow for easy access to the 10,000 sq ft of plants. Since she is not applying any variable inputs such as potting media or pots to the walkways, she knows that in this situation she must work with an overhead or fixed cost rather than a variable cost. Generally, 35 percent of the overhead cost is used as a guideline for the additional space needed beyond the actual production area. Thus overhead is multiplied by 35 percent, and then that figure is added again to the overhead to arrive at a total overhead amount.

In Step 4, now that the total overhead and total variable costs per square foot are known, total overhead is multiplied by the number of weeks in production, 12, and added to the total variable cost. That number is then divided by the number of flower pots in a square foot, in this case 9, to arrive at a total overhead and variable cost per plant.

Finally, in Step 5 Angel needs to account for the fact that not all of the 90,000 plants that she planted and spent money on growing were salable when they were harvested at the end of 12 weeks. Similarly, some plants were originally salable when delivered to a buyer, but later got returned, for whatever reason, and Angel needed to absorb the cost of the non-resalable return. Generally, there is about a 15 percent loss factor assigned to commercial production of annual plants. By multiplying the cost per plant by 15 percent, and then adding that value back again to the cost per plant, a final farmgate cost or price for the annual is calculated. This farmgate cost or price also includes the owner's desired salary and profit as factored into the overhead costs.

The farmgate cost or price in this imaginary scenario is $0.34. Are the buyers of this particular annual willing and able to pay this much? If so, for how long? How profitable are all the other plants grown in the nursery—do they completely cover their individual costs? These questions are important to ask because the biggest danger in this particular operation is the $270,000 loan that needs to be repaid regardless of sales difficulties. Some businesses can pay a loan like this with little difficulty, and others go into bankruptcy because of it. Of course, since your costs may vary, your farmgate cost or price can be very different from this imaginary scenario. In order to keep your costs as low as possible, and thus increase your chances of providing a product that people can afford, look for ways to reduce input costs with buying in bulk or using machinery, where appropriate, to reduce the amount of labor for a certain task.

Example 2. Cost of production for a perennial plant

Some lei material plants, like the perennials plumeria, 'ohai ali'i, and pua kenikeni, require more than a year before the plant comes into maturity and produces a significant amount of marketable product. Because there can be large recurring costs for businesses growing perennials, it is important to understand how to account for and pay for those costs. These costs many not be all that different from those in Example 1, but in this case revenues are not expected within the first year as they are in Example 1. Thus costs are accumulated, and that can create a large financial burden on the business owner.

The following imaginary description of an operation growing a perennial species illustrates how to conceptualize the costing process and generally how to set up a cost-of-production analysis for a plant that is not salable within the first year of its production. The numbers used here are very general, and a change in production location (thus potentially affecting land cost and production volume), or labor cost, or sales price, or any of a number of factors, can have a significant impact on the potential profitability of an operation. *As in Example 1, use this example as a learning tool, rather than taking the numbers as being an absolute representation of a functioning business.*

Pat's Perennials is a new business on a 5-acre site, and Pat has just planted a 4-acre grove of a perennial plant that will not produce marketable flowers until Year 3. In his business plan, he has budgeted that he will be doing most of the work himself, but he also has part-time hired labor for a number of tasks. In his business plan he has estimated a revenue stream based on historical price data and the costs on price reconnaissance work. He feels confident that he has both the production and business knowledge to create a successful business.

Unlike Angel's operation in Example 1, Pat does not have a lot of new equipment or buildings for which he needs to take out a large loan, but he does use a combination of his own money and a small bank loan to finance his operation. In both cases, he needs to pay something back as interest. All the initial planting and yearly maintenance costs, up until the first sale, and for every year thereafter, need to be included in the cost of production. Pat knows that to count only the production costs of the year when sales occur would ignore the significant cost from earlier years' investments and thus is not accurate accounting (see the spreadsheet on page 247). Here are further details of his operation:

- the entire operation is 5 acres, but only 4 acres are generating revenues; the other acre contains roads, buffer areas, parking areas, a home, and so forth
- 190 trees per acre are planted on 15-foot centers
- average annual yield for each tree in Year 3 is 4500 flowers, or 855,000 flowers for the 190 trees on 1 acre or 3,420,000 flowers for the 4 acres of trees; and in Years 4 and 5, 5000 flowers per tree, or 950,000 per acre, or 3,800,000 for 4 acres
- farmgate price for this flower: $0.025 each
- labor cost: $7.00 per hour for part-time labor
- annual land lease: $250/acre/year or $1,250/year for 5 acres
- equipment (used): $20,000; light work-truck ($10,000), 200-gallon spray rig ($5,000), refrigerator ($5,000) purchased in Year 3, costs depreciated over 10 years
- buildings: it is assumed that the grower will be using existing structures and that $300/year will be allocated for maintenance of these structures

Cost of production for an annual lei material plant*
Example: 10,000 sq ft of production on a 5-acre facility

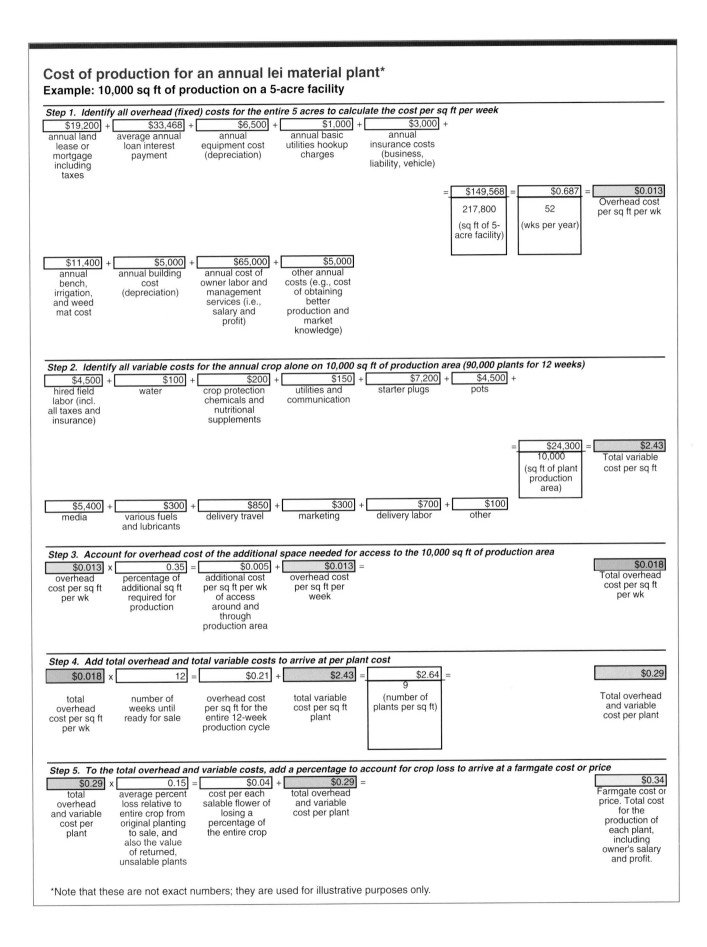

*Note that these are not exact numbers; they are used for illustrative purposes only.

- loan interest cost or opportunity cost of using Pat's own capital: the first three years incur $72,050 in costs, and if all those funds need to be borrowed, then there would be an interest charge of at least $7,205 at 10% interest, but that figure is higher, because debt is carried over from Year 1 to Year 2, and Year 2 to Year 3, so there are interest-compounding charges that boost the cost of borrowing funds to $13,351 when all costs are added.

Pat plans to plant his trees in Year 1 and tend them throughout that year and the next two until a significant harvest is ready in Year 3. Variable costs such as water, weeding, and fertilizer trend various directions, because his grove needs different amounts of each over time. Pat has been watching the market and knows what the price of the perennial flowers will be; he feels it sufficient in amount and stability over the long run to eventually bring his business into profitability—this was projected in his business plan. But, Pat knows that he must cover the lease, production, and upkeep costs on the entire 5-acre parcel with the revenues generated only on 4 production acres, and that can be tough. Adding to this requirement, he also knows that he will not be generating any revenues until Year 3 and so must either use his savings or borrow money, with interest, from the bank to fund his fixed and variable costs, perhaps including his personal expenses. In this fictitious scenario, Pat will have spent $85,401 in Years 1, 2, and 3, including compound interest charges, before he makes his first dollar. These "carry over" costs will finally start to be offset with the $85,500 in revenues at the end of Year 3. In order for Pat to be as profitable as possible as soon as possible, he will need to do everything in his power to keep his costs low. Equally important will be his relationship with buyers—3,800,000 flowers is a lot of flowers to sell year after year!

Getting your finances in order

Calculating your cost of production shows that production and marketing do not occur at the same time; this is especially true with a perennial that may take years before the first sale is made. Many business owners wait until taxes are due before they figure out how well they have done in production and marketing. You may pay production costs for labor, supplies, and other inputs for weeks, months, or even years before you sell anything. Waiting until tax time is too late to begin your cost-of-production analysis and monitoring. Following are tips on developing a system for collecting and analyzing your business's financial information.

First, use your cost-of-production information and marketing plan to create a monthly cash-flow budget for your business for the next five years. Be sure to write down all the information and estimates that you made as you put the budget together. Use this budget to determine if your business is meeting its financial goals. Plan to check back weekly or monthly to see if you are on track with your estimates and make adjustments to your operation if warranted. Many people use computers for these tasks because a computer can easily and quickly add and subtract numbers. A software program such as Intuit's QuickBooks™ or the less powerful Quicken™ is all most small businesses will need. These programs can help you put together a cash flow budget and track your progress. Software written specifically for nursery businesses is also advertised in most industry trade magazines.

Cost of production for a perennial lei material plant*
Example: 4 acres of production on a 5-acre facility with 190 plants per acre

COST TYPE	Year 1 (start-up)	Year 2	Year 3 (first revenues generated)	Year 4	Year 5
REVENUES on 4 acres in production					
Value of products sold (4,500 flowers / tree / year @ $0.025 / flower)			$85,500		
(5,000 flowers / tree / year @ $0.025 / flower)				$95,000	$95,000
AVERAGE ANNUAL OVERHEAD COSTS **					
Land lease or mortgage (including property taxes)	-1,250	-1,250	-1,250	-1,250	-1,250
Equipment and vehicles	-1,500	-1,500	-2,000	-2,000	-2,000
Utilities: basic service charges	-250	-250	-250	-250	-250
Insurance (business, liability, vehicle)	-1,000	-1,000	-1,000	-1,000	-1,000
Buildings (use existing storage, office, and garage)	-300	-300	-300	-300	-300
Cost of owner labor and management services ("salary")	0	0	-6,500	-40,000	-40,000
Other annual costs (e.g., financial services)	-500	-500	-500	-500	-500
Total annual overhead cost	-$4,800	-$4,800	-$11,800	-$45,300	-$45,300
AVERAGE ANNUAL VARIABLE COSTS ***					
Hired field and harvest labor	-2,000	-2,000	-21,000	-23,000	-23,000
Land preparation	-1,500	0	0	0	0
Planting materials (plants @ $10)	-7,600	0	0	0	0
Water	-200	-300	-400	-500	-500
Irrigation equipment/supplies	-2,400	0	0	-200	-200
Fertilizer and lime	-400	-300	-250	-200	-200
Insect control	-300	-400	-500	-600	-600
Fungus control	-200	-200	-200	-200	-200
Field maintenance (pruning, disposal)	0	0	0	-700	-700
Weeding (herbicide)	-400	-400	-300	-200	-200
Fuels and lubrication on farm	-300	-300	-500	-500	-500
Communications (phone, land and cell; fax; e-mail)	-600	-600	-600	-600	-600
Delivery and marketing labor	0	0	-1,000	-2,000	-2,000
Delivery costs (fuel and lubrication)	0	0	-500	-500	-500
Packing and shipping supplies	0	0	-1,500	-2,000	-2,000
Equipment repair and maintenance	0	0	-500	-500	-500
Other costs	-1,000	-1,000	-1,000	-1,000	-1,000
Total annual variable cost	-$16,900	-$5,500	-$28,250	-$32,700	-$32,700
Total overhead and variable cost	-21,700	-10,300	-40,050	-78,000	-78,000
Carry-over (accumulated costs in previous year)	0	-23,870	-37,587		
Interest expense (cost of borrowing or using your own money (rate=10%) to	-2,170	-3,417	-7,764		
Accumulated costs (Current assets + expenses + carry-over)	-23,870	-37,587	-85,401	-78,000	-78,000
Net Profit (above owner "salary") = Revenues minus Overhead and Variable Cost minus Interest Cost	-$23,870	-$37,587	$99	$17,000	$17,000

* Note that these are not exact numbers; they are used for illustrative purposes only.

** Overhead or fixed costs are costs that do not vary with different levels of production.

*** Variable costs are costs that vary with different levels of production.

Another tool that might help you get a handle on your costs is CTAHR's *Easy Profit Estimator* poster. This 42 x 36-inch poster allows you to quickly calculate costs without using a calculator or computer. Another publication you might consider reading is *You and Your Money: Financial Reflections for a Lifetime*. This straightforward book on personal finances is a good primer on money management in general (see *Selected Bibliography*).

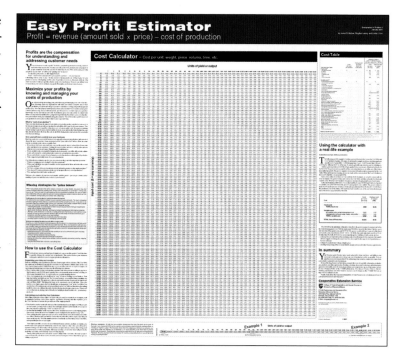

In addition to cost and income information, you need to know your financial goals. At first your goal may be simply to pay the bills. As your business grows, you need to develop specific, measurable, written financial goals and regularly monitor your progress toward them. For example, you need to put a dollar amount on your hourly wage for working in your business. You should also determine how much you want to make on the money you have invested in the business. After all, no one works for free or lets you use their money for free! Your financial management system tracks your financial information and helps you determine if you are meeting your goals. Our book *This Hawaii Product Went to Market* covers this topic in more depth.

Pricing your plants and materials— a basic understanding

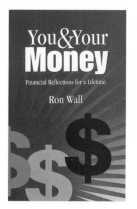

The market for lei materials has many buyers and sellers. Often one supplier like yourself can do little to convince buyers that your product is worth considerably more money than your competitors' "identical" product. You are then a "price-taker," because you have to sell at the price the market is willing to pay. A supplier who has some control over price because of providing larger-than-average volume or a unique product is called a "price-setter" or "price-maker." Whatever situation you find yourself in, your estimated or actual cost-of-production analysis will tell you whether or not a price is high enough to cover your overhead and variable costs, including paying for your salary, the money you invested, and your management talent (this is where profit is attributed). Ask potential buyers how much they are willing to pay for your material, and compare that to your cost of production. If you find that you are not getting a price that is paying for all your costs and providing you with the living that you desire, you have three options:

- try to lower your cost of production through efficiencies and less costly inputs
- look into alternative plants or products that have a higher sale price relative to their cost of production
- choose another profession.

About banks and other lending institutions

Many businesspeople feel uncomfortable about borrowing money. You may not like to "owe" anyone, you may be uncomfortable about banks, or you may not be as prepared as you would like when you go in for a loan. Bankers are good people to have on your business team. You have a lot in common with your banker—you both have a product to sell (or loan) and in return you expect to be reasonably compensated. Learning a bit about the language of banking can help you make your banker a member of your team. Robert Woods, chairman of a company that helps businesses obtain loans, talked about how to overcome many obstacles to successful loan acquisition in *Greenhouse Business* (June 1996, pages 32–34).

Woods said that when you come in for a loan, bankers usually have few questions about your skills as a grower; what they are worried about are your financial skills, your ability to manage their money so that it can be paid back on time, along with the interest. Woods' suggestions for a successful loan application include the following points.

Get your banker excited about you and your business

The person you speak to about your loan does not usually make the final decision on the loan. If you can demonstrate to the loan officer, via your business plan, that your company is credit-worthy, the loan officer can become your advocate within the lending institution. Sell yourself, your product or service, and your plan to your bankers by getting them excited about lending you money. Practice your presentation on a friend to get comfortable with it. Encourage your friend to ask you tough questions, and practice your responses until they feel natural; this will help you create a more professional presentation.

Develop "pro formas" for your business

Pro forma statements, literally the Latin words for "according to form," are standard written statements that show the bank, in their language, that you are a good credit risk. Your pro forma statement should include an income statement, balance sheet, and cash flow budget to tell the story about your expected business success. If you have your five-year cash flow budget, the other two statements can easily be assembled. You also need to provide an analysis of these statements using the ratios discussed in *This Hawaii Product Went To Market* so that you are speaking the same language as the lending institution. Watch out for forecasting too rosy a financial picture, as lenders are armed with Robert Morris Associates' *Annual Statement Studies*, an annual publication that has expected average earnings for just about every type of business and is one of the bank's yardsticks for evaluating the soundness of your lending proposal.

Conquer loan-rejection dejection

Remember the first time you got turned down from a job you wanted? You lived through it, right? Likewise, rejection by a lending institution is not the end of the world, and many loan applications for businesses that eventually were highly successful were rejected on the first try. The most prevalent reason for rejection is that the loan applicant did not do the two things just discussed: sell the plan, and speak in banker's language. If you have carefully and realistically prepared your application and business plan, your chances of success are higher. If your application is rejected, politely ask a lot of follow-up questions of the reviewer, and use this information to revise your plan and bolster your case for the next lender. A list of potential lending agencies in Hawai'i is included in the chapter "Acquiring Business Funding" in *This Hawaii Product Went to Market*. Or, look for a list of funding sources on the Web at Hawai'i's Agricultural Gateway, <www.hawaiiag.org>.

Developing your business team and keeping it together

Labor is one of the largest expenses of your business, typically *the* largest. You, members of your family, and your friends are likely to be your primary source of labor in the beginning. When you can afford to hire an employee, you are likely to find that the wages you can afford to pay are generally not large enough to attract the most highly motivated and skilled people. Thus, if you think in advance about the challenges associated with this type of workforce, you can be prepared to make the most of your labor resources. One key to success with workers of any caliber is knowing exactly what you want them to do, how you want them to do it, and what a successful activity looks like at the end. Learning to write down all these characteristics for every job and task will save you a lot of discomfort when dealing with employees, especially if they are family. It will also be a great time-saver when new employees are added to your payroll. Here's how to get going on this task.

As you work out your cost of production, look at the types of activities that need to be done. Make a list of every step in the production process, including an estimate of the time needed to complete the task, along with the materials and equipment to be used. For evaluation purposes, be sure to write down how you know a job is done well. Describe any clean-up activities and spare-time chores, along with maintenance work that is needed on a regular basis. You might want to make a production calendar as a guide to daily activities. *This Hawaii Product Went to Market* has such a calendar in its chapter "The Business of Production Agriculture." While this effort of identifying what your employees will need to do for your business will never truly be done, as you will no doubt evolve your business over time, the work descriptions will become your employee manual. You can add general policies and procedures as you need them.

Writing down tasks for your employees is critical, but doing the same for yourself or other management personnel can also be of great value. The areas of production, marketing, and finance are the usual starting places. Write down the management activities needed in your business in terms of the steps to be taken and the time, materials, and equipment needed in these areas. Quality at the management level may be more difficult to assess, but evaluation criteria set before a person is hired will help keep your business focused on projected results.

In the area of production, for example, considering new types of plants and technologies to keep you ahead of the competition will require time and good observational techniques. On-farm research may be needed. In marketing, you will need a system, typically a computer system, for keeping up with existing customers, and you will need marketing materials to attract new customers. Finance involves keeping up with books and checking that the business is on budget. You may also need activities aimed at educating your workforce, such as training programs on various subjects, including on-farm safety.

One key to success with workers is knowing exactly what you want them to do and what a successful activity looks like at the end.

Once you have all the necessary activities listed for labor and management, you can assemble them into specific jobs by grouping similar activities. The list of activities for one person becomes the job description. Then look at what skills and abilities are needed to complete each job. Try to match people with jobs that are suited to their skills, abilities, and attitude. This may be tough if you are using family labor. Family members may want to do jobs that are not well suited to them, or they may not perform all activities equally well. Thus you will need to work hard to keep family and business desires appropriately balanced and your labor force totally focused on business goals. Keeping people well led and well informed is a key component in your business's success.

In leading and managing your workforce, remember that each person has personal goals and values, in addition to the ones that are "imposed" by the business. You have goals for your business that need to be shared with everyone who is expected to help achieve these goals. Most people seeking employment will understand that any business needs to serve customers and make a profit. In turn, listen to the personal goals of your workforce. You might be able to grow an employee into a dedicated partner if you help them realize their goals. Think of times when you have worked for a boss who you felt did not care about you. The attitude of the boss sets the tone for the business, and an unhappy worker could do a hundred things to get back at the boss that also will hurt the business. But, if you feel a boss listens to you and cares about you, you are likely to do a hundred things to help the boss and make the business more successful! *This Hawaii Product Went to Market* has an entire section on employee relations, along with some helpful suggestions for further reading on this topic.

Navigating to success

The world changes quickly these days. The global nature of the marketplace has accelerated change to such as pace that is seems like you will never catch up. Consumers can get just about anything they want with a phone call or e-mail and a credit card. While this may be difficult for many older businesses to adjust to, it is reality. Meeting the needs of a changing world will require you to be innovative and take risks. Staying involved with your industry associations, reading trade publications, and attending industry trade shows will do a lot to reduce your uncertainty and thus your level of risk. Use your own creativity and curiosity to develop your business. Explore new plants and test their adaptability to being used as lei material. Try using "old standards" in new ways. Producers who always have a few new ideas up their sleeve are a step ahead of the rest. Don't worry about others "stealing" your ideas—consider it a compliment. Your customers will appreciate being the first ones to provide a lei with a different plant, flower, or twist in the making of it. They will also thank you for your innovative thinking and look forward to seeing you and your latest ideas. The best way to predict the future of your company is to purposely invent it!

You will need to work hard to keep family and business desires appropriately balanced and your labor force totally focused on business goals.

Appendix—Buying or Building?

Buying an existing business
Asking the right questions of the seller will give you more information about the challenges you may face. You need to ask,

- "Why are you selling your business?"
- "Can I inspect your maintenance records for equipment and buildings?"
- "Are there any liens on this property and its contents?"
- "What is the age and condition of your stock?"
- "What is the history of pesticide use on the property?"
- "What do your customers say about your products?"

And you should think of many other questions. Also, learn as much as you can about the financial status and market stability of the business you wish to buy. Three to five years' financial statements are needed to spot trends and potential problems. If the business has been declining, determine why. You should also consult an attorney about the correct purchase documentation. Don't be afraid to ask questions about the business's operations, sales, marketing, customers, and costs. If you're buying an existing business, you have the right to ask. Also, write down all questions and answers for your records. Do not rely on your memory.

Once you have complete information about the business you might buy, you need to decide how to fit the business into your own goals as a grower-operator. Your profit expectations, the plants you would like to grow and sell, and the possibilities of loss require you to do some soul-searching and research. Consider the business in relation to the market(s) you wish to serve. Analyze the market area to determine its stability, dynamics of change, potential growth, and consumer buying behavior. The market area could be as narrow as a neighborhood or as big as the world. Avoid locating in a shrinking market or one that is moving away from the products sold by the business you wish to buy. Also, look carefully at the company's "hard" assets— structures, equipment, fixtures, and supplies. If structures require major renovation, equipment must be replaced, hazardous chemicals need to be dug up and removed, or fixtures are out of date, you may gain little from buying the business, unless the location is superb for serving "your" customers.

A publication called *How to Buy or Sell a Business*, produced by the U.S. Small Business Administration (SBA), details the decision-making process for you. This guide, and many other business publications, are available through local SBA offices and from the Superintendent of Documents, Washington, D.C., and on their Web site at <www.sba.gov>. In general, the closer the existing business is to the goals you have, the better the chance you will have of being successful.

Building a new business from scratch
When starting a business "from the ground up," you will first need to find suitable land that you are able to buy or lease on a long-term lease. Next, you will need to work with a licensed architect to design your physical operation structures. You will also need to get permits and be prepared to deal with the associated regulations and requirements. Then, you need to decide what is to go inside the new structures. Following are some pointers in this general area. For a more comprehensive discussion, consult *The Greenhouse and Nursery Handbook: A Complete Guide to Growing and Selling Ornamental Plants*, by F. Jozwik (see *Selected Bibliography*).

There are many ways to construct growing structures, other nursery facilities, and retail stores to grow and sell nursery products.

Location

Three types of considerations on locale that you will need to make are (1) what is the best location relative to your customers, (2) what is the best location relative to where you want to live, and (3) what is the best location for the products you want to grow. The third criterion is probably the most important, because it is usually difficult to overcome the disadvantages of an unsuitable growing environment. To make good decisions about location, you will need to investigate the nursery and floral industry and learn where existing production facilities are located, how they market their products, and where potentials for new sales exist (see above for more information on particular markets). The Hawai'i Agricultural Statistics Service's annual summary and updates on floriculture and nursery products may be helpful. While they do not pinpoint the location of every nursery business, they provide useful production and sales data. Hawai'i's Agricultural Gateway at <www.hawaiiag.org>, under the Hawai'i Department of Agriculture's site, has many of these reports available on-line, and they can also be obtained through public libraries.

Construction

There are many ways to construct growing structures (shadehouses and greenhouses), other nursery facilities, and retail stores to grow and sell nursery products. Many materials may be used for covering growing structures, and the considerations related to support buildings and plant culture systems are complex. *Greenhouse Engineering,* by the Northeast Regional Agricultural Engineering Service (NRAES) at Cornell University (<www.NRAES.org>) thoroughly covers the subject of growing structure planning and development. The book contains worksheets and much of the data necessary to plan virtually all shadehouse-greenhouse systems. Existing structures on a property that might need to be updated can also be evaluated using this guide. A new manual called *Greenhouse Systems—Automation, Culture, and Environment* is also available from NRAES. It is the proceedings of an International Conference on greenhouse systems and automation held at Rutgers University in July 1994. It is an excellent companion volume to *Greenhouse Engineering,* with good coverage of automation and resource management in greenhouse systems. Of course, there may be suggestions in these books that are not applicable to or need to be modified for Hawai'i conditions. *The Greenhouse and Nursery Handbook: A Complete Guide To Growing and Selling Ornamental Plants,* mentioned above, also covers shadehouse and greenhouse construction.

In addition, the trade publication *Greenhouse Business* (<www.greenhousebiz. com>) can provide information on the latest growing structure construction trends as well as what is happening in the shadehouse-greenhouse and nursery industry. Finally, some construction firms specializing in growing structures can be found in local Yellow Pages.

Selected Bibliography

Section 2: Growing plants for *lei* helps to preserve Hawai'i's natural and cultural heritage

Principal sources and further reading

Barrere, D.B., M.K. Puku'i, and M. Kelly. 1980. *Hula: Historical Perspectives*. Pacific Anthropological Records no. 30. Dept. of Anthropology, Bernice P. Bishop Museum, Honolulu.

Carlquist, S. 1970. *Hawaii: A Natural History*. Pacific Tropical Botanical Garden, Lawai, Kaua'i, Hawai'i.

Charlot, J. 1983. *Chanting the Universe: Hawaiian Religious Culture*. Emphasis International, Honolulu.

Cuddihy, L.W., and C.P. Stone. 1990. *Alteration of Native Hawaiian Vegetation: Effects of Humans, Their Activities and Introductions*. University of Hawai'i Cooperative National Park Resources Studies Unit, Honolulu.

Elbert, S.H., and N. Mahoe. 1970. *Nā Mele o Hawai'i Nei: 101 Hawaiian Songs*. University of Hawai'i Press, Honolulu.

Gagne, W.C. 1988. *Conservation Priorities in Hawaiian Natural Systems*. BioScience 38(4): 264–271.

Gagne, W.C., and L.W. Cuddihy. 1990. *Vegetation*. In: W.L. Wagner, D.R. Herbst, and S.H. Sohmer, *Manual of the Flowering Plants of Hawai'i*. Bishop Museum Special Publication no. 83. Bishop Museum Press, Honolulu. pp. 45–114.

Handy, E.S.C., E.G. Handy, and M.K. Puku'i. 1972. *Native Planters in Old Hawaii: Their Life, Lore, and Environment*. Bernice P. Bishop Museum Bulletin 233, Bishop Museum Press, Honolulu.

Handy, E.S.C., and M.K. Puku'i. 1972. *The Polynesian Family System in Kā'u, Hawai'i*. Charles E. Tuttle Co., Rutland, Vermont.

Hunt, T.L., and R.M. Holsen. 1991. *An Early Radiocarbon Chronology for the Hawaiian Islands: A Preliminary Analysis*. Asian Perspectives 30(1): 147–161.

Kirch, P.V. 1982. *The Impact of the Prehistoric Polynesians on the Hawaiian Ecosystem*. Pacific Science 36(1): 1–14.

Malo, D. 1951. *Hawaiian Antiquities (Moolelo Hawaii)*. Bernice P. Bishop Museum Special Publication no. 2. Bishop Museum Press, Honolulu.

Nagata, K.M. 1985. *Early Plant Introductions in Hawai'i*. The Hawaiian Journal of History 19: 35–61.

Nixon, W. 1997. *How Nature Shapes Childhood: Personality, Play, and a Sense of Place*. The Amicus Journal, The National Resources Defense Council.

Patterson, R. 1955. *Phylogenetic Analysis of Hawaiian and Other Pacific Species of Scaevola (Goodeniaceae)*. In: W.L. Wagner and V.A. Funk (eds.), *Hawaiian Biogeography: Evolution on a Hot Spot Archipelago*. Smithsonian Institution Press, Washington, D.C. pp. 363–378.

Puku'i, M.K. 1983. *'Ōlelo No'eau: Hawaiian Proverbs and Poetical Sayings.* Bernice P. Bishop Museum Special Publication no. 71. Bishop Museum Press, Honolulu.

Puku'i, M.K., and S.H. Elbert. 1986. Hawaiian Dictionary. University of Hawai'i Press, Honolulu.

Spriggs, M., and A. Anderson. 1993. *Late Colonization of East Polynesia.* Antiquity 67(255): 200–217.

Section 3: Best production practices for growing lei material plants

Carroll, C. 1998. *Growing an Educational Garden at Your School.* National Tropical Botanical Garden, Lawa'i, Kaua'i, Hawai'i. 102 pp.

Silva, J.A., and R.S. Uchida (eds.). 2000. *Plant Nutrient Management in Hawaii's Soils: Approaches for Tropical and Subtropical Agriculture.* College of Tropical Agriculture and Human Resources, University of Hawai'i at Mānoa, Honolulu. 158 pp.

Free publications from the Web site of the UH College of Tropical Agriculture and Human Resources, <www.ctahr.hawaii.edu/freepubs>.

Section 4: The business of lei plant and materials production

References and further reading

Aldrich, R., and J. Bartok. 1994. *Greenhouse Engineering.* NRAES-33, Northeast Regional Agricultural Engineering Service. Cooperative Extension, 152 Riley-Robb Hall, Ithaca, NY. 212 pp. <www.nraes.org>.

Ball Publishing. GrowerTalks Bookshelf. <www.growertalks.com>. Ball Publishing, Batavia, IL.

Barton, S.S., J.J. Haydu, R.A. Hinson, R.E. McNeil, T.D. Phillips, R. Powell, and F. Stegglin. 1993. *Establishing and Operating a Garden Center: Requirements and Costs.* Garden Centers of America. Washington D.C. 50 pp.

Gerber, M. 1994. "Why a Large Number of Small Businesses Fail." Home Office Computing, May, 1994, p. 16.

Giacomelli, G., and K.C. Ting (eds.). 1994. *Greenhouse Systems: Automation, Culture, and Environment.* NRAES-72, Northeast Regional Agricultural Engineering Service. Cooperative Extension, 152 Riley-Robb Hall, Ithaca, NY. 300 pp. <www.nraes.org>.

Greenhouse Business [trade magazine]. <www.greenhousebiz.com>.

Grudens Schuck, N., W. Knoblauch, J. Green, and M. Saylor. 1988. *Farming Alternatives; A Guide To Evaluating the Feasibility of New Farm-Based Enterprises.* NRAES-32, Northeast Regional Agricultural Engineering Service. Cooperative Extension, 152 Riley-Robb Hall, Ithaca, NY. <www.nraes.org>.

Hawaii's Agricultural Gateway. <www.hawaiiag.org>.

Hollyer, J., J. Sullivan, and L. Cox (eds.). 1996. *This Hawaii Product Went To Market: The Basics Of Produce, Floral, Seafood, Livestock, and Processed-Product Businesses in Hawaii.* College of Tropical Agriculture and Human Resources, University of Hawai'i at Mānoa, Honolulu. 168 pp.

Hollyer, J., PS. Leung, and L. Cox. 2001. *Easy Profit Estimator.* College of Tropical Agriculture and Human Resources, University of Hawai'i at Mānoa, Honolulu. 1 p. poster.

Horticultural Research Institute. 2002. 2001 Landscape operating cost report. Washington, DC. <www.anla.org>.

Jozwik, F. 2000. *The Greenhouse and Nursery Handbook: A Complete Guide To Growing and Selling Ornamental Plants.* Andmar Press, Mills, WY. 806 pp.

Rathbone, E., and A.T. Whitman. 1993. *Business Planning for Growth and Profit.* Floraculture International. November 1993. Ball Publishing, Batavia, IL. pp. 28–31.

Rice, F. 1990. *Starting a Home Based Business.* Kansas Rural Enterprise Institute. Manhattan, KS. 99 pp.

Robert Morris Associates (The Risk Management Association). 2002. Annual Statement Studies. Philadelphia. <www.rmahq.org>.

Small Business Administration. 1991. *How To Buy or Sell a Business.* Small Business Administration, Washington, DC. MP 16, 32 pp. <www.sba.gov>.

Stanley, J. 2002. *The Complete Guide To Garden Center Management.* Ball Publishing, Batavia, IL. 400 pages. < www.ballbookshelf.com>.

Wall, R. 2001. *You and Your Money: Financial Reflections for a Lifetime.* College of Tropical Agriculture and Human Resources, University of Hawai'i at Mānoa, Honolulu. 191 pp.

Watanabe, N., and B. Fujita. 2001. "Know Your Lei: Florists Turn Occasions into Good Business." July 6, 2001. *Pacific Business News.* Honolulu. pp. 21–22.

Woods, R. 1996. "Bank Loans: Stacking the Odds in Your Favor." *Greenhouse Business.* June 1996. pp. 32–34.

Plant Name Index

Main entries are indicated in **bold** type.

A

'a'ali'i, **6–7**
    as companion plant, 8
    in lei, 9, 23, 35, 49
    propagation, 210, 211, 215
'a'ali'i kū ma kua. See 'a'ali'i
'a'ali'i kū makani. See 'a'ali'i
Abutilon
    pictum. See lantern *'ilima*
    grandiflorum. See royal *'ilima*
Acacia koa, 185
African lily. *See* agapanthus
African marigold. *See* marigold
agapanthus, **52–53**
    in lei, 83, 149, 159
Agapanthus africanus. See agapanthus
ageratum, **148–149**
    in lei, 81, 87, 89, 151
Ageratum houstonianum. See ageratum
ajisai. *See* hydrangea
'ākia, **8–9**
    as companion plant, 6, 10, 12, 14, 18,
      22,
    in lei, 49, 87, 163
    propagation, 210, 211
akulikuli (*Lampranthus*). *See akulikuli-lei*
'ākulikuli (Sesuvium), 185
akulikuli-lei, **54–55**
Aleurites moluccana. See kukui
Alternanthera tenella. See joyweed
alyssum, **150–151**
Alyxia oliviformis. See maile
American marigold. *See* marigold
anthurium, 55
aralia, fern leaf. *See* panax
Argyranthemum frutescens. See marguerite
    daisy
Argyroxiphium sandwicense, 185
Asparagus
    densiflorus var. *sprengeri. See*
      asparagus fern
    densiflorus var. *myersii. See* asparagus
      fern

    setaceus var. *plumosus. See* asparagus
      fern
asparagus fern, **56–57**
    in lei, 101, 151, 157, 169, 173, 175
Astelia. See pa'iniu
aster, **58–59**
    in lei, 87, 91, 119, 143
Aster ericoides. See aster
    novi-belgii. See aster
Australian violet. *See* violet
'awapuhi ke'oke'o. See ginger (white and
    yellow)
'awapuhi melemele. See ginger (white and
    yellow)
'awikiwiki, 178
azalea, 88
azucena. *See* tuberose

B

baby orchid. *See* epidendrum
baby's breath, **60–61**, 226
    as companion plant, 80
    in lei, 75, 81, 89, 93, 139, 147, 157,
      173
bachelor's button. *See* cornflower
    See also globe amaranth
beach heliotrope. See *hinahina*
    See also tree heliotrope
beach *naupaka. See naupaka kahakai*
beach vitex. *See pōhinahina*
begonia, 94
bird of paradise, 97
bleeding heart, **62–63**
    in lei, 59, 61, 87, 163
blue jade vine, **64–65**
blue lily. *See* agapanthus
blue sage. *See* salvia
bluewings. *See* torenia
bougainvillea, **66–67**
    in lei, 33, 43, 51, 57, 59, 61, 83, 87,
      91, 135, 139, 165, 175
bozu. *See* globe amaranth
butterfly orchid. *See* epidendrum
buttonhole orchid. *See* epidendrum

C

Caesalpinia pulcherrima. See ʻohai aliʻi
Calotropis
　　gigantea. See crown flower
　　procera, 72
Canavalia cathartica. See maunaloa
candlenut tree. *See kukui*
Carnation, **68–69**, 226, 235, 237
Cassytha filiformis. See kaunaʻoa
celosia, **152–153**
Celosia argentea var. *cristata. See* celosia
　　argentea var. *plumosa. See* celosia
Centaurea
　　cineraria. See dusty miller
　　cyanus. See cornflower
Chinaman's hat. *See* cup-and-saucer plant
Chinese violet. *See pakalana*
Chrysanthemum, **154–155**
　　in lei, 61, 81, 89
Cibotium, 185
cigar flower, **70–71**, 235
Clerodendrum
　　thomsoniae. See bleeding heart
　　x *speciosum. See* bleeding heart
clover. *See* globe amaranth
cockscomb. *See* celosia
Colocasia esculenta. See kalo
coral tree. *See wiliwili*
Cordia
　　subcordata. See kou
　　sebestana, 18
Cordyline fruticosa. See ti
cornflower, **156–157**
cotton, Hawaiian. *See maʻo*
crown flower, **72–73**, 235
　　in chant, 195, 196
　　in lei, 45, 93, 161, 163
cup-and-saucer plant, **74–75**
　　in lei, 23, 107, 133, 169
Cuphea ignea. See cigar flower
Cuscuta
　　campestris. See kaunaʻoa
　　sandwichiana. See kaunaʻoa
cymbidium, 55, **106–107**

D

daisy
　　marguerite. *See* marguerite daisy
　　michaelmas. *See* aster
Davallia. See shinobu
dendrobium, **108–109**, 125, 235, 237
Dianthus, **158–159**

Dianthus barbadus, 60
　　caryophyllus. See carnation
dodder. *See kaunaʻoa*
Dodonaea viscosa. See ʻaʻaliʻi
Dole's beard. *See* Spanish moss
Dracaena marginata var. *tricolor. See*
　　dracaena tricolor
dracaena tricolor, **76–77**, 105
Dubautia, 185
dusty miller, **78–79**
　　in lei, 33, 45, 75, 77, 101, 151, 167,
　　　169
dwarf poinciana. *See ʻohai aliʻi*

E

Egyptian starflower. *See* pentas
epidendrum, 91, **110–111**, 161, 165
epis. *See* epidendrum
Erythrina
　　Hawaiian. *See wiliwili*
　　sandwicensis. See wiliwili
everlasting. *See* strawflower

F

Fagraea berterana. See pua kenikeni
fern
　　asparagus. *See* asparagus fern
　　lace. *See palaʻā*
　　leatherleaf, 147
　　maile-scented. *See lauaʻe*
　　rabbit's foot. *See shinobu*
　　sword. *See kupukupu*
　　whisk. *See moa*
fern leaf aralia. *See* panax
feverfew, 75, **80–81**, 89
　　See also *Chrysanthemum*
floradora. *See* stephanotis
florist mum. *See Chrysanthemum*
floss flower. *See* ageratum
frangipani. *See* plumeria
French marigold. *See* marigold
Freycinetia arborea. See ʻieʻie

G

galphimia, 75
garden mum. *See Chrysanthemum*
gardenia, **82–83**
Gardenia augusta. See gardenia
　　brighamii, 82
　　mannii, 82
　　remyi, 82

geiger tree, 18
Geraldton waxflower, 47, 61
German statice, 147
giant milkweed. *See* crown flower
ginger (white and yellow), **84–85**, 214, 235
globe amaranth, **160–161**
　　as companion plant, 118
　　in lei, 51, 57, 59, 61, 75, 87, 153
glorybower. *See* bleeding heart
goldenrod, 127, 147
Gomphrena globosa. See globe amaranth
Gossypium tomentosum. See maʻo
green jade vine. *See* blue jade vine
Grevillea wilsonii, 123
Gypsophila paniculata. See baby's breath

H

hala, **10–11**
　　in chant, 186, 190
　　as companion plant, 12, 18
halapēpē, 188
hāpuʻu, 32, 36, 185
Hawaiian cotton. *See maʻo*
Hawaiian erythrina. *See wiliwili*
Hawaiian sunflower. *See* pincushion protea
Hedychium
　　coronarium. See ginger (white and
　　　yellow)
　　flavescens. See ginger (white and
　　　yellow)
Helichrysum bracteatum. See strawflower
heliconia, 131
heliotrope
　　beach. *See* Hinahina
　　beach. *See also* tree heliotrope
　　tree. *See* tree heliotrope
Heliotropium anomalum var. *argenteum.*
　　See *hinahina*
Heteropogon contortus. See pili grass
hinahina, **12–13**, 234
　　as companion plant, 14, 18, 42
　　See also Spanish moss
hinahina kūkahakai. See hinahina
hōʻehapuʻuwai. See bleeding heart
Holmskioldia
　　sanguinea. See cup-and-saucer plant
　　tettensis. See cup-and-saucer plant
honey plant. *See* hoya
hop bush. *See ʻaʻaliʻi*
hopseed bush. *See ʻaʻaliʻi*
hortensia. *See* hydrangea
hoya, **86–87**
huluhulu. See *maʻo*

hydrangea, **88–89**
    in lei, 81, 139, 149, 157
Hydrangea macrophylla. See hydrangea

I

ice plant. *See akulikuli-lei*
'ie'ie, 188
ilie'e, 6, 8
'ilima, **14–15**, 234, 235
    as companion plant, 6, 8, 10, 12, 18,
       26
    lantern. *See* lantern *'ilima*
    propagation, 210, 211
    royal. *See* royal *'ilima*
    triple. *See* royal *'ilima*
'ilima papa. See 'ilima
'ilima-koli-kukui. See 'ilima
'ilima-ku-kahakai. See 'ilima
'ilima-ku-kula. See 'ilima
'ilima-lei. See 'ilima
ixora, **90–91**
Ixora casei. See ixora
    chinensis. See ixora
    coccinea. See ixora

J

jade vine. *See* blue jade vine
jasmine. *See pīkake*
    Madagascar. *See* stephanotis
    single-flowered star. *See pīkake*
Jasminum sambac. See pīkake
Joseph's coat. *See* joyweed
joyweed, 61, **92–93**
Justicia
    betonica. See shrimp plant (white and
       yellow)
    brandegeana. See shrimp plant (white
       and yellow)

K

kalanchoe, **94–95**, 107
Kalanchoe blossfeldiana. See kalanchoe
kalo, 187, 191, 194, 203
kaluaha. See pa'iniu
kangaroo paw, 107
kauhi. See 'ākia
kauna'oa, **16–17**, 18, 234
kauna'oa kahakai. See kauna'oa
kauna'oa lei. See kauna'oa
kauna'oa-pehu. See kauna'oa

kepalo. See bougainvillea
ki. See ti
kiele. See gardenia
kīkānia, **96–97**, 155
koa, 24, 185
kolokolo kahakai. See pōhinahina
koniaka. See aster
kou, **18–19**, 178
kukui, **20–21**, 234, 235
    in lei, 29
    in chant, 195, 196
    propagation, 211
kulu'ī, **22–23**
    as companion plant, 6, 8, 26
    in lei, 25, 39
    propagation, 210, 215
kūmakani. See 'a'ali'i
kupaloke. See tuberose
kupukupu, 6, 8, 18, **24–25**

L

lace fern. *See pala'ā*
la'i. See ti
Lambertia inermis, 123
Lampranthus. See akulikuli-lei
lantern *'ilima,* 83, **98–99**
laua'e, **100–101**
laua'e iki, 100
lauwa'e. See laua'e
lavender, sea. *See* statice
leatherleaf fern, 147
lehua. See 'ōhi'a lehua
lehua-pepe. See globe amaranth
lei-hua. See globe amaranth
lei-pīkake. See pīkake
lepe-a-moa. See celosia
Leucospermum
    bolusii. See pincushion protea
    erubescens. See pincushion protea
    muirii. See pincushion protea
    mundii. See pincushion protea
    oleifolium. See pincushion protea
    parile. See pincushion protea
    rodolentum. See pincushion protea
    saxosum. See pincushion protea
Lily
    African. *See* agapanthus
    Blue. *See* agapanthus
    Peruvian, 107, 111, 159
Lily of the Nile. *See* agapanthus
Limonium
    latifolium. See statice
    sinuatum. See statice

liriope, 93
Lobularia maritima. See alyssum
loke. See rose
lokelani. See rose
loke-lau. See rose
loulu, 10

M

Madagascar jasmine. *See* stephanotis
maiele. See pūkiawe
maile, **28–29**, 200, 235
    in chant, 189
    as companion plant, 20
    in Hawaiian culture, 188
    in lei, 17, 34
    propagation, 210, 211
maile-hohono. See ageratum
maile-scented fern. *See laua'e*
make-man. See plumeria
mokihana, 234
māmane, **30–31**, 210, 211
mamani. See māmane
mangrove, 97
ma'o, **26–27**
    as companion plant, 10, 12, 14, 22, 42
    propagation, 210, 211, 214
    See also lantern *'ilima*
marguerite daisy, **162–163**
marigold, **164–165**, 209
    African. *See* marigold
    American. *See* marigold
    French. *See* marigold
Marsdenia floribunda. See stephanotis
maunaloa, **102–103**, 211
mealycup sage. *See* salvia
melia. See plumeria
messerschmidia. See tree heliotrope
Metrosideros
    excelsus. See pohutukawa
    macropus, 34
    polymorpha. See 'ōhi'a lehua
    rugosa, 34
    tremaloides, 34
Mexican creeper, 105, 163
michaelmas daisy. *See* aster
Microlepia strigosa. See palapalai
Microsorum scolopendria. See laua'e
mil flores. *See* hydrangea
milkweed, giant. *See* crown flower
Miss Joaquim. *See* vanda
moa, **32–33**
    in lei, 35, 91, 93, 155, 159, 163, 175
    propagation, 214

mock orange, 67
Moloka'i osmanthus. *See 'ākia*
money tree. *See* dracaena tricolor
moss, Spanish. *See* Spanish moss
mountain *naupaka*. See *naupaka kuahiwi*
mum
    florist. *See Chrysanthemum*
    garden. *See Chrysanthemum*

N

na'ena'e, 185
Nama sandwicensis, 185
nardo. *See* tuberose
naupaka kahakai
    as companion plant, 10, 12, 18
    in Hawaiian culture, 182–183
naupaka kuahiwi, 182–183
nehe, 12
Nephrolepis cordifolia. *See kupukupu*
New York aster. *See* aster
New Zealand Christmas tree. *See*
pohutukawa
ni'ani'au. See *kupukupu*
noni, 16
noon flower. *See akulikuli-lei*
Nototrichium sandwicense. See *kulu'ī*

O

'ohai ali'i, **104–105**, 235
ohe naupaka, 182–183
'ōhi'a. See *'ōhi'a lehua*
'ōhi'a lehua, **34–35**, 185, 199, 234
    in chant, 186, 190
    as companion plant, 10, 24
    in Hawaiian culture, 188, 190, 192
    in lei, 9, 23, 37, 39, 49, 51, 79, 107, 131, 151, 159, 175
    propagation, 210, 211, 214, 215
'okika. See marguerite daisy
    See also orchid
'ōkole-'oi'oi. *See* marigold
'ōkupukupu. See *kupukupu*
ōla'a beauty. *See* torenia
'olonā, 191, 194, 201
oncidium, 111
orchid
    baby. *See* epidendrum
    cymbidium, 55, **106–107**
    dendrobium, **108–109**, 125, 235, 237
    epidendrum, 91, **110–111**, 161, 165
    oncidium, 111

reed. *See* epidendrum
    vanda, **112–113**, 237
Osteomeles anthyllidifolia. See *'ūlei*

P

pa'iniu, **36–37**
    in lei, 79, 153, 157
    propagation, 210, 212
pakalana, 57, **114–115**, 235
pala'ā, 23, **38–39**, 198
palae. See *pala'ā*
palai. See *palapalai*
palapala'ā. See *pala'ā*
palapalai, **40–41**, 199
    in chant, 188
    as companion plant, 20, 34
    in Hawaiian culture, 188
    in lei, 9, 33, 37, 43, 79, 163
palewāwae. See joyweed
panax, **116–117**
    in lei, 91, 95, 119, 139
pāneki. See pansy
pandanus. *See* hala
Pandanus tectorius. See *hala*
pansy, **166–167**
parsley panax. *See* panax
pentas, 93, **118–119**
Pentas lanceolata. See pentas
Peruvian lily, 107, 111, 159
Phymatosorus grossus. See *laua'e*
pīkake, **120–121**, 235, 237
pili grass, 191
pincushion protea, **122–123**
pink. *See* carnation
Pleomele. See *halapēpē*
plumeria, 57, **124–125**, 235, 237
pōhinahina, **42–43**
    as companion plant, 6, 8, 12, 14
    propagation, 210, 211, 215
pohutukawa, **126–127**
poinciana, dwarf. *See 'ohai ali'i*
Polianthes tuberosa. *See* tuberose
Polyscias. See panax
ponimō'i. *See* carnation
ponimō'i-li'ili'i. *See* dianthus
po'o-kanaka. See pansy
pōpōhau. See hydrangea
pōpōlehua. See ixora
pride of Barbados. *See 'ohai ali'i*
protea, 31
    pincushion. *See* pincushion protea
Psilotum nudum. See *moa*
pū hala. See *hala*

pua kalaunu. *See* crown flower
pua kenikeni, **128–129**, 137, 235
pua kika. *See* cigar flower
pua male. *See* stephanotis
pua melia. *See* plumeria
pua pākē. See *Chrysanthemum*
pua-hōku-hihi. See hoya
pua-pepa. *See* strawflower
pua-pihi. *See* Zinnia
pukanawila. *See* bougainvillea
pūkiawe, **44–45**
    in lei, 9, 35, 37, 49

R

rabbit's foot fern. *See* shinobu
reed orchid. *See* epidendrum
rondeletia, 155
Rosa. *See* rose
rose, **130–131**, 226, 234
    in lei, 79, 81, 89, 143, 153, 159
roselani. *See* rose
royal *'ilima*, **98–99**

S

sage
    blue. *See* salvia
    mealycup. *See* salvia
    scarlet. *See* salvia
salvia, **168–169**
Salvia farinacea. *See* salvia
    splendens. *See* salvia
sampaguita. *See pīkake*
Scaevola chamissoniana, 182
    coriacea, 182
    gaudichaudiana, 182
    gaudichaudii, 182
    glabra, 182–183
    kilaueae, 182
    mollis, 182
    taccada, 182–193
scarlet sage. *See* salvia
screw pine. *See* hala
sea grape, 29
sea lavender. *See* statice
Senecio cineraria. *See* dusty miller
Sesuvium portulacastrum, 185
shinobu, **132–133**
    in lei, 63, 95, 145, 159, 173
shrimp plant (white and yellow), **134–135**
Sida fallax. See *'ilima*
silversword, 185

single-flowered star jasmine. *See pīkake*
Solanum capsicoides. See kīkānia
Sophora chrysophylla. See māmane
Spanish moss, 57, **136**
Sphenomeris chinensis. See pala'ā
squirrel's tail. *See* shrimp plant (white and yellow)
star flower. *See* hoya
star jasmine, single-flowered. *See pīkake*
starflower, Egyptian. *See* pentas
statice, **138–139**
as companion plant, 60
German, 147
in lei, 81, 89, 133, 147, 159, 175
stephanotis, **140–141**
strawflower, 153, **170–171**
Strongylodon macrobotrys. See blue jade vine
Styphelia tameiameiae. See pūkiawe
sunburst. *See* pincushion protea
sunflower, Hawaiian. *See* pincushion protea
sweet alison. *See* alyssum
sweet alyssum. *See* alyssum
sweet violet. *See* violet
sweet william. See dianthus
sword fern. *See kupukupu*

T

Tagetes
erecta. See marigold
patula. See marigold
tahinu. See tree heliotrope
Tanacetum parthenium. See feverfew
taro. See *kalo*
Telosma cordata. See *pakalana*
temple tree. *See* plumeria
ten-cent flower. *See pua kenikeni*
thumbelina. *See Zinnia*
ti, **46–47**, 235
in chant, 188, 189
in lei, 13, 15, 91, 119, 171
Tillandsia usneoides. See Spanish moss
torenia, **172–173**
Torenia fournieri. See torenia
Touchardia latifolia. See 'olonā
Tournefortia argentea. See tree heliotrope
tree heliotrope, **142–143**
triple *'ilima. See* royal *'ilima*
tuberose, 65, **144–145**, 235, 237

U

'ūlei, **48–49**
as companion plant, 6, 8, 10, 42
in lei, 143
propagation, 210, 211, 215
'umi'umi-o-Dole. See Spanish moss
u'ūlei. See *'ulei*

V

vanda, **112–113**
Viola
hederacea. See violet
odorata. See violet
x *Wittrockiana. See* pansy
violet, **146–147**
Australian. *See* violet
Chinese. *See pakalana*
Sweet. *See* violet
Vitex rotundifolia. See *pōhinahina*

W

waioleka. See violet
walking fences. *See hala*
wāwae'iole, 35, 37, 39
waxflower. *See* stephanotis
Geraldton, 47, 61
wax plant. *See* hoya
western field dodder. *See kauna'oa*
whisk fern. *See moa*
white ginger. *See* ginger (white and yellow)
white shrimp plant. *See* shrimp plant (white and yellow)
Wikstroemia uva-ursi. See *'ākia*
wiliwili, **50–51**, 178
as companion plant, 24
propagation, 210, 211, 215
wishbone flower. *See* torenia

Y

yarrow, 31
yellow ginger. *See* ginger (white and yellow)
yellow shrimp plant. *See* shrimp plant (white and yellow)

Z

zinnia, **174–175**
Zinnia angustifolia. See zinnia
elegans. See zinnia

Notes

Notes

Notes